Kudos for the first edition of *Reel Justice*

"Juxtaposing so many law-related films makes a telling point: how many great films, like *The Caine Mutiny* and *To Kill a Mockingbird,* have used the trial process to indict injustice, and how many celluloid clunkers have settled for rehashing clichés such as unidentifiable corpses, surprise witnesses, extralegal justice, and forbidden love affairs between lawyers and clients or lawyers and jurors."

—ALLEN D. BOYER, *New York Times*

"Why do lawyers in movies do what they do? Films are described thoroughly in cogent prose, analyzed for their handling of the legalities, and rated from one gavel to four for their lawyerly perspicacity.... So weigh the evidence and go rent the videos."

—PETER M. NICHOLS, *New York Times*

"In this informative, entertaining, and unique book, the authors, two UCLA law professors, dissect a broad cross section of courtroom films with wit, humor, and professional expertise but without any stilted legal jargon."

—*Library Journal*

"A worthwhile and handy companion at the video store, *Reel Justice* means you'll never be forced to settle for renting *Adam's Rib* again"

—JONATHAN S. SHAPIRO, *American Lawyer*

"[The] non-lawyer filmgoer has no way of knowing that the legal system depicted in the film may be as far from reality as the Death Star in *Star Wars*. Unless, that is, she has *Reel Justice: The Courtroom Goes to the Movies* by Professors Michael Asimow and Paul Bergman of the UCLA School of Law."

—PROFESSOR THOMAS D. GRIFFITH, *Entertainment Law Journal*

Reel Justice

The Courtroom Goes to the Movies

Paul Bergman
and
Michael Asimow

**Andrews McMeel
Publishing, LLC**

Kansas City • Sydney • London

Andrews McMeel Publishing, LLC
an Andrews McMeel Universal company
1130 Walnut Street, Kansas City, Missouri 64106

Library of Congress Cataloging-in-Publication Data

Bergman, Paul, 1943–
    Reel justice : the courtroom goes to the movies / Paul Bergman
    and Michael Asimow.
        p. cm.
    Includes biographical references.
    ISBN: 978-0-7407-5460-9 (pbk.)
        1. Justice, Administration of, in motion pictures. 2. Jury in motion
pictures. I. Asimow, Michael. II. Title.

PN1995.9.J8B47 2006
91.43'6554–dc27
                                                                    2005058911

www.andrewsmcmeel.com

Design by Pete Lippincott

ATTENTION: SCHOOLS AND BUSINESSES

Andrews McMeel books are available at quantity discounts with bulk purchase for educational, business, or sales promotional use. For information, please e-mail the Andrews McMeel Publishing Special Sales Department: specialsales@amuniversal.com

To Andi and Bobbi,
with love and appreciation.

For Harold and
Jeanne,
With best
wishes,

Paul Bergman

Contents

6. It's Just a Bunch of Circumstantial Evidence

7. Uncivil Actions

Acknowledgments

For their encouragement and many helpful suggestions, we want especially to thank our agent Angela Rinaldi; Rich Stim of Nolo Press; UCLA law student researcher Matthew Meyer; Lane Butler and Chris Schillig of Andrews McMeel Publishing; copyeditor Peggy Hoover; Photofest, for its great work with the photos; and Andrea Sossin-Bergman, Richard Johnson, and Eileen Sossin-Johnson, relatives who had no choice but to say yes when asked to read parts of the manuscript.

Foreword

by Judge Alex Kozinski

Scratch almost any lawyer and you'll find a movie buff. That's no coincidence, for the moviemaker's art is not all that different from the lawyer's—especially the courtroom advocate's. Both must capture, in a very short space, a slice of human existence and make the audience see a story from their particular perspective. Both have to know which facts to include and which ones to leave out; when to appeal to emotion and when to reason; what to spoon-feed the audience and what to make them work out for themselves; when to do the expected and when to do the unexpected; when to script and when to improvise.

It's not surprising, then, that lawyers and trials are a perennial subject of moviemaking. Trials, by their nature, concentrate human conflict; they force a head-on clash of opposing forces. Any trial has the potential (especially in the movies) to raise difficult questions about the cornerstones of society—law, justice, morality—and the conventions that hold us together. Trials also raise one of the most fundamental doubts of human existence: whether, and to what extent, we can achieve an objective, true account of past events. Fair trials present the tantalizing possibility that the little guy can take on the big guy and win, because brains, wit, and justice count far more than money, power, and influence. Unfair trials make excellent tragedies: The outrage of justice betrayed, coupled with often pitiful consequences, can stir the blood with empathy.

It was while contemplating such matters that I first got the notion of becoming a lawyer. I remember exactly when it happened: It was 1963 or 1964 and I was living in Baltimore. We had come to the United States only a year or so earlier, and I was in the process of absorbing American culture (and language) by plugging myself into the endless stream of black-and-white images that materialized in our living room through an ancient, round-tube TV set. I found much of what I saw interesting, if strange, and some of it funny but not much of it very memorable.

One exception I still remember vividly: The scene was a small room filled with a bunch of guys sitting around a conference table arguing about the fate of someone who wasn't there to stand up for himself. I almost changed channels when the vote was 11 to 1 to convict, but there was something in the quiet determination of the lone dissenter that kept me from turning the knob. (For those too young to remember, channels in those days were changed by clicking large knobs on the front of the TV set, rather than by pushing buttons on a remote control.) He wasn't sure the defendant was innocent, the holdout told the others; he wanted to talk about it.

No reader has failed to recognize that I was watching *12 Angry Men,* or that the dissenting juror was Henry Fonda. As I sat there watching, struggling a bit with the language, trying to figure out the jury's function in American law (Why, I wondered, didn't they just convict by a vote of eleven to one and go home?), my whole adolescent conception of certainty, of knowledge itself, was shaken. The case against the defendant sounded so airtight; the reasons offered by the eleven sounded so irrefutable. I couldn't imagine how (or why) anyone could reach a different conclusion. Then, as one reason after another started to come apart, as inconsistencies crept into the picture, as jurors began changing their votes, I came to understand that truth does not spring into the courtroom full-blown, like Athena from the head of Zeus. Rather, facts have to be examined carefully and skeptically, moved around and twisted like pieces of a puzzle, before they will yield a complete picture. Could it, might it be, that I had the talent for this type of work?

Further research was clearly necessary before I could sort out the realities of law practice. Were real trials, real jury deliberations, anything like what I was seeing? As my interest in law grew, and along with it my interest in law-related movies and TV shows, I came up with more unanswered questions: Was the Scopes monkey trial anything like it was portrayed in *Inherit the Wind?* Did the War Crimes Tribunal bear any resemblance to *Judgment at Nuremberg?* I eventually went to law school, passed the bar, and became a judge, but questions of this sort persisted. What *was* the true story behind *Breaker Morant?* Was Sir Thomas More's defense as it was portrayed in *A Man for All Seasons?* To be sure, the answers could be found out there somewhere, given enough time and effort. But human nature being what it is, I put it off.

And a good thing too. When Michael Asimow (who taught me most of what I know about tax law) told me about the book that he and Paul Bergman were writing, I immediately realized they were on to something that could be quite useful. Selected background material would supply the real story (if there was one) and the historical context of the action. Carefully researched legal analysis would help you figure out what might have happened (or did happen) in a real trial. No longer would inquiring minds have to wonder whether the trial judge's outrageous actions in *The Verdict* were at all plausible, or whether the procedures in *Whose Life Is It Anyway?* or *Nuts* bore any resemblance to reality. I wondered why no one had thought of writing a book like this before.

The book is, of course, more than a disconnected series of answers to questions one might have in watching law-related movies. It is a thoughtful collection of some of the best—and a few of the worst—movies having to do with the legal process. And law-movie buffs desperately need such a guide. The advent of home videos and DVDs as staples of entertainment in most American households has opened up the possibility of seeing great movies of the past—including movies concerning the law. Videos and DVDs have emancipated our movie-viewing from the whims of local TV station program managers. (It took me almost twenty-five years before I saw *12 Angry Men* again.) But freedom can be treacherous without some compass to guide your steps. Stroll into your vast neighborhood movie rental store with no plan and several friends or family members of divergent tastes, and you're likely to emerge three hours later with a made-for-TV comedy about Albanian werewolves. In these challenging times, *Reel Justice* gives you an edge in the movie-selection game. By giving just enough information up front to help you know whether a particular movie is likely to be of interest, it allows you to select a movie you haven't yet seen (or vaguely remember), to cajole your friends and family into concurring, and, later, to fully understand and enjoy the film.

A dog-eared copy of *Reel Justice* will find a place in the living room of most thoughtful movie-watchers. Its only defect, alas, is that it is too short: Where do you get the skinny on *First Monday in October, The Story of Qiu Ju, The Return of Martin Guerre,* and *Hang 'Em High*? I, for one, have already put in my order for the next edition of *Reel Justice.*

Alex Kozinski
United States Circuit Judge

Introduction

Reel Justice is an analysis of and a tribute to courtroom movies. The book illuminates a world of fascinating legal films. It will help you select films to buy, rent, or choose while channel-surfing.

One way to use the book is first to watch a film, then read our legal analysis and trial briefs to answer your questions about what you've just seen. We suggest that you consult the "Index by Number of Gavels" at the end of the book to help you decide what to watch.

This book is intended to be much more than a handy guide to courtroom movies. We hope our discussions enhance your understanding of our legal system while helping you think through the messages about law, lawyers, and the legal system that the films convey. After all, courtroom films (along with television shows and novels about legal subjects) are more than great entertainment. Popular culture is the raw material out of which people extract information and construct opinions about how the law works and what lawyers do. Courtroom movies should be taken seriously because they reflect what people already believe (or at least what filmmakers think they believe). Even more important, these films reinforce and have the potential to change those beliefs. For all these reasons, it's well worth reflecting on the messages that courtroom movies send to viewers.

From the silent-film era to the present, the courtroom genre has proved to be endlessly fascinating for filmmakers. There are always plenty of conflicts between lawyers, lawyers and witnesses, lawyers and clients, or lawyers and judges. There is almost always suspense: Did the defendant really do it? Will the jury send the defendant to the electric chair or to freedom? And the trial setting offers filmmakers a chance to dramatize and personalize divisive issues, such as racial tensions or the teaching of evolution, along with values that underlie our culture, such as fairness and justice. Of course, it may also be that filmmakers like courtroom films because they typically don't rely on expensive special effects or exotic settings.

The boundaries of the courtroom genre are debatable. In this book, the genre consists of feature films in which events important to the narrative happen in the course of a trial or an appeal that takes place in a state-operated courtroom. However, we sometimes push the envelope a bit. For example, most observers would identify the great film *12 Angry*

Men as a courtroom film, and it is one of our "full-length features." Yet the crucial events occur in the jury room rather than the courtroom. Our genre definition eliminates such films as *Stairway to Heaven* and *The Devil and Daniel Webster* (celestial trials), *M* and *The Ox-Bow Incident* (vigilante-style trials), and such documentaries as *The Thin Blue Line*. Because of space limitations, we do not include many fine courtroom films made for television (such as *The Penalty Phase* or *Indictment*) or courtroom-centered television series (*Perry Mason, Law & Order, L.A. Law*).

To enhance the book's value as a film guide, we've assigned a gavel rating to each film. The ratings reflect our judgment about the entertainment value of the courtroom scenes, not their legal accuracy or the aesthetic value of a movie as a whole. A four-gavel rating means the courtroom scenes in the film are classic, three gavels means good, two gavels means just okay, and one gavel means ask for a new trial.

Of course, many more courtroom films have been made than we could watch or include in a publishable book. We think we've included all the classics, as well as a fair sampling of really good films. We have also included a few of the genre's potboilers whose stars or themes may interest readers. If the coverage is necessarily less than encyclopedic, we expect that our chapter headings at least identify the full scope of topics covered by courtroom films. Most courtroom movies, after all, are about "something else"—that is, filmmakers use the courtroom process to create suspense, critique lawyers, examine military justice, make audiences laugh, dramatize a true story, score political points, or depict injustice. We've tried to capture the full range of "something elses" that courtroom films are about.

Here are some of the overarching themes of the genre that we've identified:

• The formal justice system rarely works as it's supposed to. Even when correct legal procedures are followed, the actual result is highly unjust, either because the law itself does not fit our conceptions of justice or because the judge or jury gets it all wrong. Sometimes, as in films like *The Verdict* or *Suspect,* the system blunders its way to justice, but only because of good luck or because lawyers ignored the rules. Justice, it turns out, has almost nothing to do with formal legal rituals.

• In older films, lawyers are usually fine human beings and competent professionals. In newer movies (say from 1980 onward), lawyers are usually greedy, unethical, or incompetent. Corporate law firms are nests of thieves.

• Women are tough and aggressive lawyers, but they are inclined to be overemotional, have bad personal lives, or exercise poor judgment as a result of becoming romantically involved with their clients.

• Victory belongs to the lawyer who is more charismatic, tricky, or just plain lucky, rather than to the lawyer who prepares harder or has the better case.

• Judges are often biased, crooked, or incompetent, juries are unpredictable, prosecutors are ambitious to win higher office at all costs, defense lawyers are devious, and clients can never be trusted.

As this is a second and we hope improved edition, we should mention ways in which this book differs from the first edition. Most notably, we have more than doubled the number of films we discuss by following the "full-length features" that consider the most important films in each chapter with "Short Subjects" devoted to other (often equally entertaining) films featuring the same theme. The Short Subjects highlight the films' most notable legal images while providing readers with at least some sense of their stories. We've also developed chapter headings that more accurately capture the films' central legal themes.

The legal analyses that "set the record straight" are not meant to criticize filmmakers (whose job is to entertain, not instruct), but rather to enhance readers' enjoyment of courtroom films while providing information about the legal system. We also try to explain unfamiliar legal jargon or procedures: circumstantial evidence (and whether there is anything wrong with it), the hearsay rule, the exclusionary rule, and spousal privilege, to name a few. And we've tried to do a better job of recognizing that the broader cultural messages embedded in narratives may be more important and more interesting to viewers than narrow legal disputes that arise in the course of a trial.

We've tried in a variety of ways to bring readers closer to the underlying legal messages in the films we discuss. For example, we often quote particularly memorable law-related dialogue. Most of our reviews include a paragraph called "Picturing Justice," where we try to identify a scene or a bit of dialogue that illuminates an issue of justice or ethics. We've also expanded the number of analyses in which we discuss the real situations that gave rise to the dramatized stories.

Subheads. Finally, our analyses include reader-friendly subheads that target the topics of discussion. Like this one.

We do not pretend that our prose is equally as entertaining as the films, but we've tried to write a book that captures the enchantment of movies while providing insights about law and lawyers and the' cultural background in which they operate.

The opportunity to prepare a second edition has deepened our appreciation and enjoyment of courtroom films. We hope that this book does the same for readers.

The Gavel Rating System

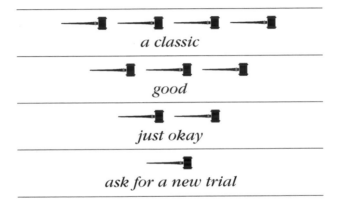

a classic

good

just okay

ask for a new trial

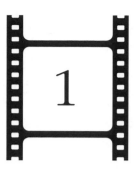

Courtroom Heroes

Every myth needs a hero, and the movies are the primary mythmakers of our society. A hero is someone (often an ordinary mortal in extraordinary circumstances) who courageously sacrifices for a noble cause. The act of courage may be financial, physical, professional, social, or even emotional in nature. In addition, heroes must act sacrificially, meaning that they do not expect to be compensated for the risks and losses they may suffer. This chapter celebrates the many courtroom films that center on heroic lawyers, judges, clients, or even jurors. Like the great heroes of mythology, these stories about legal heroes often stick in our minds long after we've left the theater or turned off the television.

Though lawyers are rarely action heroes, they can display great physical courage by facing down mobs, as they do in *Young Mr. Lincoln* and *To Kill a Mockingbird*. But heroism can also consist of standing up for what you believe, even if everyone around you disagrees, as exemplified in *12 Angry Men, To Kill a Mockingbird, Inherit the Wind, Judgment at Nuremberg,* and *The Accused*.

The halcyon days of heroic cine-lawyers were the late 1950s and early 1960s, perhaps the golden years of courtroom drama. Mythic heroes in the mold of Abraham Lincoln or Atticus Finch are rare in modern courtroom films. Such exalted characters don't satisfy our postmodern tastes, and there are probably more antiheroes (such as Frank Galvin in *The Verdict* or Arthur Kirkland in *And Justice for All*) than true heroes in current movies.

Although the lawyer-hero may need the protection of the Endangered Species Act, a few specimens of the breed still remain. In *The Accused*, Kathryn Murphy vindicates the rights of a rape victim against the opposition of her boss, while in *Ghosts of Mississippi* Bobby DeLaughter fights the entire community to convict the killers of civil rights leader

Medgar Evers. Alan Isaacman stands beside a despised pornographer and fights for freedom of speech in *The People vs. Larry Flynt,* while Judge Herb Stern resists heavy pressures from the State Department in order to give accused airline hijackers a fair trial in *Judgment in Berlin.* In *Snow Falling on Cedars,* the aged Nels Gudmundsson overcomes local prejudice against Japanese with his staunch murder defense. In *Veer-Zaara,* a courageous young Pakistani lawyer frees an Indian pilot who had been imprisoned for twenty-two years.

There are still plenty of heroes in real courtrooms as well. All over America, thousands of lawyers work hard for their clients and in the public interest, often in circumstances where they are despised by the community and paid only a modest salary or nothing at all for their efforts. Government lawyers, public defenders, prosecutors, legal-aid lawyers, and countless other lawyers working *pro bono* carry on the spirit of Atticus Finch in twenty-first-century courtrooms.

The Accused

Synopsis: A tenacious prosecutor tries the men who cheered on a gang rape.

Paramount, 1988. Color. Running time: 110 minutes.

Screenplay: Tom Topor. Director: Jonathan Kaplan.

Starring: Jodie Foster (Sarah Tobias), Kelly McGillis (Kathryn Murphy).

Academy Award: Best Actress (Jodie Foster).

Rating: ——■ ——■

The Story

After fighting with her boyfriend, Sarah Tobias heads for The Mill, a working-class bar. She is dressed provocatively, gets drunk, smokes grass, and performs sensuous maneuvers not usually taught at dance studios. Suddenly she is shoved onto a pinball machine and brutally raped by three men. The rapists are cheered on by a boisterous crowd. After the rapists' arrests, Tobias finds herself being ground up by another type of mill—the criminal justice system.

Worried that the rapists' lawyers might raise a reasonable doubt based on a claim that Tobias consented to intercourse, Prosecutor Kathryn Murphy negotiates a plea bargain in which the three rapists

The Accused: Prosecutor Kathryn Murphy (Kelly McGillis) argues to the jury that the men who cheered on the rapists are themselves criminals.

plead guilty to "reckless endangerment" and receive a light sentence. Tobias accuses Murphy of selling her out without giving her a chance to testify. Stung by Tobias' attack, Murphy charges the barflies who cheered on the rapists with "criminal solicitation," meaning that they persuaded or encouraged the actual rapists to commit a felony. Murphy's boss, D.A. Paul Rudolph, orders her to abandon the case because it's a waste of time and a loser to boot. Murphy refuses to back down, promising Tobias that she will make no deals this time.

Ken Joyce, who witnessed the rape, is Murphy's key witness. Much of Joyce's testimony unfolds through a flashback that depicts for the first time the brutal gang rape and the cheering crowd. The flashback supports Murphy's decision to prosecute the barflies, because the second and third rapes would probably not have occurred without the crowd goading the men into it. The jury convicts the three cheerleaders.

Legal Analysis

The Accused graphically depicts the horror of violent rape, the trauma that frequently follows it, and the cold impersonality of the criminal justice system. The film undoubtedly brought home to millions of viewers the brutal reality of rape and may have facilitated the passage of laws that make it easier to convict rapists. For example, Federal Rule of Evidence 413, enacted about five years after the film's release, allows judges in sexual assault cases to admit evidence of defendants' previous sex crimes.

The film also portrays the difficulty of successfully prosecuting rape cases, especially when victims are less than saintly. Many rape victims aren't willing to endure all the procedural hurdles and to relive the nightmare by testifying in court and being cross-examined. Instead, they don't bother to report the crime (some estimates say that more than 60 percent of rapes are never reported to the police). Even with modern-day rape shield laws, the victim is often the one who feels like "the accused." Tobias is the courageous exception. She is anxious to testify to get even with the men who attacked her.

Plea bargains. The vast majority of criminal cases, probably well over 90 percent, end with plea bargains. Even clearly guilty defendants have leverage, because prosecutors can't possibly try all or even most of the criminal cases that arrive on their desks. Murphy is quite realistic about the weakness of her case against the three rapists. Everyone except Tobias will testify that she consented. Add in the provocative outfit, plus the dope, booze, and sexy dancing, and you have a typical TV soap opera and a very shaky rape case. While Tobias understandably feels betrayed, Tobias is not Murphy's client, and Murphy does not need her consent to dispose of the case before trial.

Disclosure of exculpatory evidence. Before the rape, Tobias told her friend Sally Fraser that she was interested in having sex with Bob, one of the rapists. Tobias' statement is exculpatory evidence, and Murphy properly discloses it to the defense pursuant to the rule of *Brady v. Maryland* (1963).

"You quit? You're fired!" When Murphy's boss, Rudolph, orders her to drop the case against the barflies, she threatens to quit and sue everybody in sight, but this is nonsense. The D.A.'s office cannot be sued based on refusal to prosecute. No court can review an act of prosecutorial discretion. Rudolph could properly have fired Murphy for insubordination.

Criminal solicitation. Solicitation is the crime of inciting or otherwise encouraging another person to commit a crime. Indeed, one can be prosecuted for solicitation even if no crime was actually committed. Perhaps that's why Murphy chose to prosecute for solicitation. She wouldn't have to prove that a rape occurred, only that the barflies tried to make it occur. In most states, solicitation carries a lower potential penalty than does the crime that was solicited. If Murphy had prosecuted the cheerleaders for the more serious crime of aiding and abetting the rapes, they could have received the same punishment as if they had actually committed the rapes themselves.

Picturing justice. Unlike many portrayals of female lawyers, Kathryn Murphy is ethical, committed, and competent and appears to have a normal personal life. She develops a caring and supportive relationship with Tobias. Yet Murphy has a tantrum when Rudolph tries to kill the case against the barflies. In that respect the film may reinforce the stereotype that female lawyers are driven by emotion rather than by intellect.

Trial Brief

The Accused is based on a notorious gang rape that occurred in New Bedford, Massachusetts, in 1983. The victim, a twenty-two-year-old mother of two, was raped by three men on a pool table in Big Dan's Bar as several other men cheered them on. The trial was one of the first covered by live television and was a national sensation.

The victim testified that she visited the bar to buy cigarettes, had a drink, and was attacked by the men. The defense witnesses, including the bartender, said she had three drinks and was flirting with the men. One of the accused rapists claimed that she agreed to "fool around" with him but that he was physically unable to have sex with everybody watching.

The local Portuguese American community rallied around the defendants, but to no avail. The three rapists were convicted and sentenced to nine to twelve years; a fourth man, who had tickled the victim during the rapes, got six to eight years. The two cheering onlookers were acquitted. The convictions were affirmed by the Massachusetts Supreme Judicial Court. The victim moved to Florida and was killed in an auto accident several years later, orphaning her two children.

Ghosts of Mississippi

Synopsis: A Mississippi D.A. prosecutes a racist for a thirty-year-old murder.

Castle Rock, 1996. Color. Running time: 130 minutes.

Screenplay: Lewis Colick. Book: Maryanne Vollers. Director: Rob Reiner.

Ghosts of Mississippi: Bobby DeLaughter (Alec Baldwin) tries to persuade the jury to convict Byron De La Beckwith of the murder of Medgar Evers.

Starring: Alec Baldwin (Bobby DeLaughter), James Woods (Byron De La Beckwith), Whoopi Goldberg (Myrlie Evers).

Academy Award Nominations: Best Supporting Actor (James Woods), Best Makeup.

Rating:

The Story

In June 1963 in Jackson, Mississippi, Byron De La Beckwith shot and killed Medgar Evers. Evers was the NAACP's Mississippi field secretary and a prominent black civil rights leader. Two trials of Beckwith before all-white, all-male juries resulted in hung juries. Evers' wife, Myrlie, continued to pursue the case but to no avail, until in 1990 journalists uncovered information showing that a state agency had improperly helped Beckwith by screening potential jurors in the second trial. Bobby DeLaughter, an assistant district attorney, then decided over his boss' opposition to reopen the case.

Missing the physical evidence, many of the witnesses, and the transcripts from the earlier trials, DeLaughter and his investigator Charlie

Crisco have to climb an uphill road. DeLaughter finds the murder weapon with Beckwith's fingerprint on it in the gun collection of DeLaughter's deceased father-in-law, Judge Russell Moore. Some witnesses are still alive and willing to testify. Crisco finds a new witness, Delamar Dennis, an FBI informant who infiltrated the KKK and heard Beckwith brag about the killing. Finally, Myrlie Evers produces the critical missing piece: a certified transcript from the first 1964 trial.

Beckwith's 1994 trial jury includes both blacks and women. The transcript allows DeLaughter to read into the record the testimony of deceased witnesses. Other witnesses place Beckwith's car in a fast-food parking lot only a few hundred yards from the murder scene. Dennis testifies to Beckwith's statements that he had killed Evers. The defense presents only a single witness, a cop who claimed he had seen Beckwith in a town ninety miles from Jackson at the time the killing occurred. DeLaughter destroys this witness on cross by pointing out that, although he was a friend of Beckwith, he didn't come forward with this alibi until eight months after Beckwith had been initially charged with the crime. The jury quickly convicts Beckwith, who is sentenced to life imprisonment.

Legal Analysis

Disregarding opposition and distrust from all sides, DeLaughter embarks on what seems a hopeless quest: reopening a thirty-year-old case in which all the evidence has disappeared. There is nothing in it for DeLaughter except a desire to see justice done. His wife divorces him, white society shuns him, and he and his children are in physical danger. The film is an inspiring testament to a heroic lawyer.

Speedy trial. The Mississippi Supreme Court twice ruled on the legality of Beckwith's 1994 trial, first refusing to prevent it and afterward affirming the conviction, each time by a single-vote majority. Even though there is no statute of limitations for murder cases, the thirty-year gap between the crime and the third trial arguably violated the "speedy trial" guarantee of the Sixth Amendment and the "due process of law" guarantee of the Fourteenth Amendment. Technically, the Sixth Amendment applied to the period between Beckwith's arrest in 1963 and the D.A.'s dismissal of the case in 1969. The Fourteenth Amendment applied to the gap between 1969 and 1994, when the third trial began.

Under both amendments, courts must balance a number of factors in deciding whether a delay is excessive. The most important factor is the extent to which a delay prejudices a defendant's ability to present a defense, and Beckwith had a realistic argument that the thirty-year gap prevented him from presenting a defense. Much of the evidence was missing, such as the bullet that killed Evers and the spent cartridge. Beckwith's attorney could not cross-examine the witnesses who had died and whose prior testimony was read to the jury from the transcripts. The memory of live witnesses, including Beckwith himself, had surely dimmed over time. And Beckwith was more than seventy years old and in poor health.

The reason for delay is also a factor in Beckwith's favor. The state could have prosecuted him again at any time during the thirty-year period. The long delay occurred simply because the climate for convicting racist killers in Mississippi had radically changed between the 1960s and the 1990s and because a prosecutor came along with the gumption to retry the case. By comparison, the only factor that favors the state is that Beckwith never protested the delay or requested a third trial; obviously he just wanted the whole thing to go away.

Mississippi—then and now. The two 1964 trials of Byron De La Beckwith were exceptional because the prosecutors made a sincere effort to convict him. At that time, most prosecutors refused to bring such cases, because all-white juries consistently refused to convict whites who killed blacks or white civil rights workers. This was the time of the civil rights movement, and white society felt deeply threatened by the fundamental legal, political, and social changes that were sweeping the South. Whites still clung to control of the justice system, and the results in murder cases reflected that control.

Modern-day Mississippi is very different. Blacks vote and run for office, and politicians have to pay attention to the needs of the black community. Juries are racially mixed, and many whites find the history of segregation and racism deeply repugnant. Yet, as the film showed, white society of the 1990s was deeply threatened by reopening the Beckwith case and by raking up the old muck associated with it.

Truth and reconciliation? The Beckwith case raises the question of whether retrying ancient cases is the best method of promoting racial reconciliation. After all, the Beckwith case consumed enormous prosecutorial resources, and the conviction came perilously close to being thrown out on appeal. By contrast, South Africa also confronted a horrible history of apartheid (a system of mandatory segregation imposed by law) and racial slaughter. When black majority rule finally arrived in

1994, the new constitution created a "Truth and Reconciliation Commission." The commission's staff investigated human rights abuses during the apartheid era. Victims of racial violence put their stories on the record. Whites who had perpetrated the violence were immune from criminal prosecution if they came forward and confessed. Victims of apartheid received monetary compensation. Perhaps this is a better model of justice than retrying thirty-year-old cases.

Picturing justice. DeLaughter's closing argument to the jury (and to the film's viewers) is an eloquent plea for racial justice. He summarizes the key evidence quickly: "His gun, his scope, his fingerprint, his car, and lastly but certainly not least, his mouth." He goes on to say, "When that kind of murder happens, no matter who the victim, no matter what his race, there is a gaping wound laid open on society as a whole. Justice has sometimes been referred to as the soothing balm to be applied to the wounds inflicted on society. Where there is no justice, those wounds can never be cleansed, those wounds can never be healed." He concludes: "Is it ever too late to do the right thing? For the sake of justice, and for the hope of us as a civilized society, I sincerely pray that it is not."

Trial Briefs

1. Beckwith died in prison in 2001. In addition to assassinating Evers, Beckwith, who hated Jews even more than blacks, was caught transporting a bomb intended to blow up the home of a Jewish activist in New Orleans; he served several years in jail for this crime. DeLaughter's deceased father-in-law, Judge Russell Moore, was a notorious racist. As in the film, Judge Moore kept the murder weapon as a souvenir; however, he did not preside over either of Beckwith's 1964 trials.

2. DeLaughter's closing argument is considered a classic and has been reprinted in trial-practice handbooks. The screenwriters were able to use only brief portions of the argument, but these included the language about justice serving as a "soothing balm" on society's "gaping wound."

Judgment in Berlin

Synopsis: An American judge presides over the West German trial of East German hijackers.

20th Century Fox, 1988. Color. Running time: 92 minutes.

Screenplay: Leo Penn and Joshua Sinclair. Director: Leo Penn. Book: Herbert Stern.

Starring: Martin Sheen (Judge Herbert Stern), Sean Penn (Guenther).

Rating: ——◼ ——◼

The Story

In 1978, East Germans Sigrid Radke and Helmut Thiele escape from East Germany by hijacking a Polish airliner and forcing the pilot to land in West Berlin. Thiele and Radke are heroes to the West Berliners, but hijacking is a "wurst" case scenario for all the governments concerned. The West Germans don't want to touch this political hot potato, so they get the Americans to prosecute. The Germans build a courtroom at an American base in West Berlin to conduct the trial. Luckily, the architects left enough room for a jury box, because Herbert Stern (a federal judge from New Jersey) rules that the defendants are entitled to trial by jury.

Radke's case is dismissed after Stern decides that her confession is not admissible in evidence. As for Thiele, the aircraft's crew testifies that he brandished a gun and threatened them. However, the intimidating presence of a Polish government prosecutor undermines the credibility of the crew's testimony. Moreover, Radke and other passengers testify that the gun was only a toy, that the crew knew it, and that the pilot willingly dropped off Thiele in the West. Guenther, another East German who took advantage of the hijacking to stay in the West, testified that everyone was having a good time smoking and looking at photos of Thiele's children before the plane landed. Luckily for Thiele, smoking was still permitted on airplanes or he might have been charged with another crime.

The jury compromises by acquitting Thiele of hijacking and convicting him of taking a hostage. The *cause célèbre* ends with a whimper: Thiele is sentenced to time served and walks free.

Legal Analysis

Judge Stern is under pressure to convict Thiele and end an embarrassing trial quickly. With all countries bound by treaties to either prosecute

Judgment in Berlin: Judge Herbert Stern (Martin Sheen) withstands pressure to convict the hijackers as quickly as possible.

hijackers or return them to their country of origin for prosecution, everyone on both sides of the Iron Curtain wants to avoid a precedent that hijackers can get away with it. Stern has a reputation as a no-nonsense judge with a strong prosecutorial background. The State Department figures it can count on him to deliver a conviction quickly. Stern also has his eye on a Supreme Court appointment, so he has an incentive to play ball.

But Stern sees his role differently. As a Jew, he is acutely conscious that Nazi judges lost their independence, and he is not about to take directions from the prosecution or the State Department. (The film *Judgment at Nuremberg* depicts a trial of German judges who rolled over for the Nazis.) As a result, Stern courageously rules that the criminal procedure protections in the U.S. Bill of Rights apply to Radke and Thiele. Stern also follows the jury's lead by sentencing Thiele to time already served. Stern thus ends up with a better chance of being elected mayor of West Berlin than being appointed to the U.S. Supreme Court.

The "choice of evils" defense. Under U.S. law, Thiele would be guilty of hijacking the plane regardless of why he did it or whether the pilot cooperated. However, West German law allowed a "choice of evils" defense, which permits a court to acquit Thiele if the reasons for the hijacking outweighed the harm it caused. Thiele desperately wanted to flee to the West to be with his children. Furthermore, West Germany did not recognize the Communist government's laws that made it illegal to leave East Germany. Finally, no harm was done to the crew or the passengers. In short, the jury verdict in Thiele's favor was a reasonable application of German law.

A German jury. In Germany and most other continental European countries, decisions in criminal cases are made by a panel of professional judges and lay assessors. The lay assessors are nonlawyers who sit with the judges for a period of several months and hear numerous cases. The assessors are carefully selected for their judgment and educational background and are nothing like American jurors, who are randomly selected from voter lists and have a wide variety of backgrounds. Most Germans are familiar with juries from watching American pop culture, but the jury in the Thiele case was the first and the last U.S.-type jury in modern German history.

Judge Stern and due process. In 1955, the U.S. High Commission established a U.S. Court for Berlin that was empowered to take over the trial of criminal cases arising out of offenses committed in West Berlin. However, that court had never heard a case until it was ordered to do so in the case of Thiele and Radke, and it never heard another one.

U.S. Supreme Court cases provided little precedent for Judge Stern on the question of whether American procedural rights apply to criminal trials conducted by an American court in Berlin. Judge Stern observed that the Americans could not ignore the U.S. Constitution by imposing slavery, punishing free speech, or imposing the death penalty without trial. Instead, he declared, the West Berliners live in freedom and should have the benefit of the U.S. Constitution. Of course, it didn't hurt that by appointing a jury Judge Stern got the monkey off of his own back. He didn't have to decide whether Thiele was a hero or a pirate.

Trial Brief

Judgment in Berlin is an accurate depiction of the trial of East Germans Hans Tiede and Ingrid Ruske that occurred in West Berlin in 1979. As in the film, Judge Stern ruled that both defendants were entitled to a jury trial. The character of Guenther, however, didn't exist in the real trial. Perhaps writer and director Leo Penn created Guenther to give his son Sean Penn a role in the film.

The People vs. Larry Flynt

Synopsis: A pornographer battles the authorities and his inner demons all the way to the U.S. Supreme Court.

Columbia Pictures, 1996. Color. Running time: 129 minutes.

Screenplay: Scott Alexander and Larry Karaszewski. Director: Milos Forman.

Starring: Woody Harrelson (Larry Flynt), Courtney Love (Althea Leasure), Edward Norton (Alan Isaacman).

Academy Award nominations: Best Actor (Woody Harrelson), Best Director.

Rating: ——▌ ——▌ ——▌

The Story

Larry Flynt, publisher of the pornographic *Hustler* magazine and a notorious troublemaker, is regularly charged with distributing obscene material. With the help of lawyer Alan Isaacman, Flynt generally manages to stay out of jail. However, during one trial a sniper shoots them both. Isaacman's injuries are minor, but Flynt is paralyzed from the waist down.

Flynt's most significant legal skirmish begins when *Hustler* publishes a fake Campari liqueur ad. The ad claims that televangelist Jerry Falwell's "first time" sexual experience consisted of committing incest with his mother in an outhouse. Falwell doesn't get the joke, so he sues Flynt for libel and intentional infliction of emotional distress. Coming straight out of the psycho ward, Flynt is totally out of control at the trial. The jury rejects the libel claim but awards $200,000 to Falwell on the emotional distress claim. The federal court of appeals affirms this decision.

The U.S. Supreme Court grants a hearing. Isaacman wisely concedes that the ad is in bad taste and focuses instead on the importance of the right to parody public figures. The Court rules unanimously in Flynt's favor, holding that free speech trumps the emotional-distress claim.

Columbia Pictures/Photofest.

The People vs. Larry Flynt: Alan Isaacman (Edward Norton) has nothing but trouble keeping client Larry Flynt (Woody Harrelson) under control.

Legal Analysis

This film illustrates that law is part of culture and that culture is part of law. Perhaps more than any other person, Flynt contributed to the coarsening of American culture during the 1970s and 1980s through the publication of *Hustler*, which thrived on unabashed hard-core pornography and misogyny. Every step in Flynt's legal odyssey was a skirmish in America's culture wars. Sometimes trying to make a buck, sometimes fighting for free speech, sometimes just being wild and crazy, Flynt usually came away victorious and in the process made some significant First Amendment law. Yet Flynt and his wife, Althea, paid a terrible personal price. Flynt was crippled for life, he and Althea became hooked on drugs (Flynt eventually kicked the habit), and Althea died of AIDS.

Obscenity and pornography. Obscenity is not protected by the First Amendment. Publishing obscene materials is a crime, but pornography is protected speech. The line between the two is extremely vague. Indeed, U.S. Supreme Court Justice Potter Stewart once famously observed that he could do no better than say that when it came to obscenity, "I know it when I see it."

In many localities it is politically popular to go after pornographers. As a result, local prosecutors often attempt obscenity prosecutions. Because of the dangers to free speech from politically motivated obscenity prosecutions, appellate courts have a duty to independently determine whether the material is protected, regardless of what a jury has found.

Under a 1973 U.S. Supreme Court decision, *Miller v. California,* a film or book is legally obscene if (a) the average person would believe that the work, taken as a whole, appeals to a "prurient interest" in sex (meaning that it excites lustful thoughts); (b) the work describes or depicts, in a patently offensive way, "hard-core" sexual conduct specifically defined by state law; and (c) the work, taken as a whole, lacks serious literary, artistic, political, or scientific value.

Under this three-part test, obscenity cases often boil down to a determination of whether, based on local standards, particular material appeals to a prurient interest and is patently offensive. For example, people in big cities and rural areas have different ideas about what is patently offensive. Thus publishers like Flynt, who distribute material all across the country, are constantly at risk of being prosecuted for obscenity in any locality where the material is sold.

The Falwell case. The Falwell case is a First Amendment landmark. To be found liable for libel (sometimes lawyers use the same word but spell it two different ways), a defendant must have made a false and damaging statement about the plaintiff. In the case of a public figure like Falwell, the libel must be intentional. However, there is a special rule for parody. If nobody would believe the statements, they aren't libelous. Isaacman readily established that no one would believe that Falwell would get drunk on Campari or have sex with his mother in an outhouse or anyplace else. As a result, the jury correctly concluded that the parody was not libelous.

Falwell's claim for intentional infliction of emotional distress required proof that Flynt intentionally (or at least recklessly) caused severe emotional distress by means of extreme and outrageous conduct. This claim seemed more viable, because Flynt gleefully admitted at trial that he intended to cause Falwell (a longtime antagonist) emotional distress. However, as Isaacman argued to the Supreme Court, this claim runs head-on into the First Amendment. Unfair criticism or cruel parodies of public figures probably cause them distress, but such claims would be subjective and impossible to verify. More significant, allowing such claims would inhibit public debate as well as political satire, which has existed since the days of the founding fathers.

Chief Justice Rehnquist's opinion said: "At the heart of the First Amendment is the recognition of the fundamental importance of the free flow of ideas and opinions on matters of public interest and concern. The freedom to speak one's mind is not only an aspect of individual liberty—and thus a good unto itself—but also is essential to the common quest for truth and the vitality of society as a whole."

Trial Briefs

1. The Isaacman character in the movie is a composite of several different lawyers who represented Flynt over the years. One of them, Gene Reeves, was shot during a Georgia obscenity trial. Flynt hired Isaacman when he moved to Los Angeles after being shot. Alan Isaacman no longer represents Larry Flynt. Isaacman is a successful Los Angeles litigator who still specializes in First Amendment and privacy cases, such as those growing out of pornographic Internet sites.

2. Jerry Falwell made a million copies of the parody and mailed them to his contributors in fund-raising letters. Thus he probably made more money out of the parody than *Hustler* did. Flynt sued for infringement of his copyright. However, the courts dismissed the claim on the ground that Falwell's use of the parody came under the "fair use" defense to copyright infringement.

3. Falwell was represented by Norman Roy Grutman, who had been a longtime nemesis of Flynt's. Grutman was played by Burt Neuborne, a First Amendment scholar whose real views are the exact opposite of those he speaks in his role as Grutman. In another unusual casting decision, Larry Flynt himself played Judge Morrissey, the hostile judge in the Cincinnati trial.

4. Feminist leaders, particularly Gloria Steinem, were sharply critical of the film because they believed it portrayed Flynt too favorably. In particular, they believed that the film whitewashed *Hustler*'s apparent endorsement of violence against women. One famous cover, which appears briefly in the movie, shows a woman being fed into a meat grinder. These attacks generated publicity that undoubtedly hurt the film at the box office and at Academy Award time. The ironic effect was that a movie that denounces censorship was itself the victim of censorship.

To Kill a Mockingbird

Synopsis: Atticus Finch defends an innocent black man in a hopeless rape case.

Universal International, 1962. Black and white. Running time: 129 minutes.

Screenplay: Horton Foote. Book: Harper Lee. Director: Robert Mulligan.

Starring: Gregory Peck (Atticus Finch), Brock Peters (Tom Robinson), Mary Badham (Scout), Robert Duvall (Boo Radley), Phillip Alford (Jem).

Academy Awards: Best Actor (Gregory Peck), Best Screenplay.

Academy Award nominations: Best Picture, Best Director, Best Cinematography, Best Musical Score, Best Supporting Actress (Mary Badham), Best Art Direction.

Rating: ——🔨 ——🔨 ——🔨 ——🔨

The Story

In a languid summer during the early 1930s, Atticus Finch ekes out a living as a lawyer in Maycomb, Alabama. His son, Jem, his daughter, Scout, and their friend Dill are terrified by their unseen next-door neighbor, a mysterious recluse they refer to as Boo Radley.

At Judge Taylor's request, Finch agrees to represent Tom Robinson. Robinson, a black farm laborer, is accused of raping Mayella Ewell, a poor and ignorant white woman. A lynch mob tries to snatch Robinson, but Finch (aided by his children) stays outside the jail and faces down the mob.

The courtroom is packed, whites downstairs and blacks upstairs. The jury is all male and all white. Mayella (who seems to avoid touching the Bible when she takes the oath) can't keep her story straight and is reduced to screaming that Robinson took advantage of her and that the jury has to protect her honor. Her father, Bob Ewell, an alcoholic racist, lies through his gums. He claims that he saw Robinson attacking Mayella. Finch's questions show that Ewell is left-handed, which is important because the sheriff has testified that a left-handed person beat Mayella. Moreover, by quickly tossing a glass at Robinson, Finch demonstrates that Robinson's left arm is paralyzed.

Robinson denies harming Mayella. He went into her house because she'd asked for his help. He had helped her often because he felt sorry for her. This time she suddenly grabbed and kissed him. Robinson ran

To Kill a Mockingbird: Atticus Finch (Gregory Peck) and Tom Robinson (Brock Peters) get the bad news from the jury.

away after hearing Mayella's father scream that he was going to kill her, and Robinson doesn't know how she was injured.

Finch's closing argument is eloquent. He pities Mayella, a product of "cruel poverty and ignorance." She lied to rid herself of guilt for breaking a time-honored code by kissing a black man. He tells the jurors, "The courts are the great leveler. In our courts, all men are created equal." He concludes by asking the jurors to do their duty and find Robinson not guilty. However, the result is inevitable: Robinson is convicted and shortly thereafter is dead, shot by a deputy sheriff supposedly while trying to escape from custody.

It's left to Boo Radley to deliver justice. When Bob Ewell attacks Jem and Scout, Boo saves their lives by stabbing him to death. The sheriff decides to close the matter by reporting that Ewell accidentally fell on his own knife. To involve Boo in the legal system would be like killing a mockingbird.

Legal Analysis

Atticus Finch is an iconic lawyer hero. He had nothing to gain and everything to lose by assaulting the entrenched social order. A caring father, Finch explains to Scout that if he had refused to defend Robinson he could never hold his head up in the town or advise her on how to live.

Finch's trial strategies. Tom Robinson's defense is probably doomed from the start. Yet lawyers often represent unpopular clients (such as banks or insurance companies) and must employ trial strategies that will give them a fair shot at justice. Here are a few strategies Finch might have considered.

First, he should have sought a change of venue to a far-off Alabama city. In tiny Maycomb, everybody knew everybody, and the jurors would have been pariahs had they acquitted Robinson. Likewise, Judge Taylor would have been kicked out of office had he set aside the jury verdict as illogical.

Second, knowing the jury was stacked against him, Finch should have tried to work out a plea bargain. Perhaps the prosecutor would have accepted a guilty plea to assault and battery. Robinson might have gone to jail, but rape carried the death penalty at the time. If the plea-bargain strategy didn't work, Finch might have asked the judge to include assault as a lesser included offense. That would have given the jury a middle ground between finding Robinson guilty of rape or not guilty of anything.

Third, Finch should have urged Robinson not to testify. If the jurors were going to believe Mayella's and Ewell's testimony, nothing Robinson said would make a difference. Moreover, Robinson ends up severely damaging his own cause when he testifies that he felt sorry for Mayella. Placing himself in a superior position to a white woman could only have inflamed the jury's hostility.

Fourth, Finch should have taken his closing argument down several notches. His language was probably a lot more impressive to film audiences of the 1960s than to the poor Maycomb jurors in the 1930s. The jurors probably didn't use words like "unmitigated temerity" very often. They were not receptive to a head-on challenge to the myth of virtuous white womanhood or to the idea that a black man could be believed over two white people. They did not want to hear that the law was a great leveler, because they would never want to be leveled down to the blacks.

Finally, Finch might have tried to use the jurors' likely anti-Yankee sentiment to his advantage, by arguing that the case was an opportunity to show northerners that southerners truly were fair and impartial.

The all-white jury. About fifty years before Robinson's trial took place, the U.S. Supreme Court outlawed state laws that barred black men from serving on juries (*Strauder v. West Virginia*, 1879). Nevertheless, Alabama jurors of the 1930s were virtually all white and male. Women were considered unsuited by their feminine nature to be able to serve on juries. As for race, jurors were drawn from voter lists, and blacks in general were not allowed to register to vote. If a few blacks did manage to register, the jury commissioner would remove their names from the jury pool. And if one or two blacks somehow were initially seated as jurors, the prosecutor would have used peremptory challenges to kick them off. Not until the *Batson* case in 1986 did the U.S. Supreme Court rule that lawyers could not challenge jurors based on race.

Picturing justice. Harper Lee's book was written and the film of *To Kill a Mockingbird* was made during the civil rights era, a turbulent time of racial violence and resistance by southern states to court decisions that invalidated school segregation and Jim Crow laws. Lee undoubtedly intended to soften the message of her book and make it more acceptable to white southerners by setting it during the early 1930s.

Trial Briefs

1. Harper Lee, the author of the book on which the film is based, attended law school at the University of Alabama but did not graduate. The Tom Robinson case is apparently fictional, though Ms. Lee's father, A. C. Lee, was an Alabama lawyer who once represented two black men who killed a merchant and were hanged while in jail. The character of Scout is undoubtedly the author herself, while Dill is based on author Truman Capote, a childhood friend of Harper Lee. The Maycomb courtroom in the film is an almost perfect copy of one in Monroeville, Alabama, where Harper Lee grew up. Harper Lee is a key character in the film *Capote* (2005). She helps Truman Capote investigate the murders he wrote about in his book *In Cold Blood*.

2. Harper Lee's book was heavily influenced by the 1931 case of the Scottsboro Boys. The Scottsboro Boys were a group of eight young

black men who were riding the rails in hopes of finding a job. They found themselves alone in a freight car with two white women, who accused them of committing gang rape. A lynching was narrowly averted when the governor of Alabama called in the national guard. The defendants were almost certainly innocent of this charge because the women were not credible and there was no physical evidence of rape. Still, the defendants were not provided with lawyers and were hastily convicted and sentenced to death.

The U.S. Supreme Court reversed the convictions because the denial of legal counsel deprived the defendants of due process (*Powell v. Alabama*, 1932). The Scottsboro Boys were tried again, and this time out-of-town attorneys provided them with an aggressive legal defense. One of the complaining women changed her story and denied that she had ever been raped. The defense lawyer ripped the other woman to shreds on the stand, but the strategy backfired. The white jurors felt sorry for her and again convicted the defendants. Another U.S. Supreme Court decision set aside these convictions because blacks had been excluded from the jury (*Norris v. Alabama*, 1935). The parallels between the trials of Tom Robinson and the Scottsboro Boys are obvious.

12 Angry Men

Synopsis: One juror holds out against conviction of a poor youth charged with murdering his father.

United Artists, 1957. Black and white. Running time: 96 minutes.

Screenplay and teleplay: Reginald Rose. Director: Sidney Lumet.

Starring: Henry Fonda (Juror No. 8), Lee J. Cobb (Juror No. 3), Jack Klugman (Juror No. 5), Ed Begley (Juror No. 10), Jack Warden (Juror No. 7), E. G. Marshall (Juror No. 4).

Academy Award nominations: Best Picture, Best Director, Best Screenplay.

Rating:

The Story

The judge's instructions send the jurors off to deliberate the fate of an eighteen-year-old Puerto Rican slum-dweller charged with stabbing his

12 Angry Men: The jury debates the fate of a young defendant.

father to death. All but Juror No. 8 vote immediately to convict. No. 8 admits that the defendant may well be guilty. However, he thinks that the jury ought to talk about the case before sentencing him to death: "He's had a pretty miserable eighteen years. I think we just owe him a few words, that's all."

With unanimity required to convict, No. 8's obstinacy causes many of the jurors to go rapidly from 0 to 60 on the fury scale. The prosecution's evidence emerges as they try to bully No. 8 into changing his vote:

• Around midnight, an older man who lived in the apartment directly below the victim's heard a loud fight, heard the defendant scream "I'm going to kill you" and saw the defendant run out of the apartment house.

• The defendant testified that he was alone at the movies when the murder occurred, but when he was arrested a few hours later he couldn't remember what films he had seen. (Apparently they weren't memorable courtroom films.)

• A woman who lived across the tracks saw the murder through the empty windows of a passing elevated train and identifies the defendant as the killer.

• The father punched the defendant a few hours before the killing.

• After his father hit him, the defendant bought a knife with an unusual design that was identical to the murder weapon found by the police. When he was arrested, the defendant claimed to have lost the knife.

• The defendant had a criminal record and had been involved in knife fights.

No. 8 responds that the defense attorney was court-appointed and inept. He argues that being punched was hardly a motive for murder because the father beat the defendant regularly. The murder weapon was not unusual; No. 8 displays a nearly identical knife that he purchased just the night before in a pawn shop. The noise made by the passing elevated train would have prevented the downstairs neighbor from being sure that it was the defendant who screamed "I'll kill you."

The discussion becomes more tense as, one by one, the jurors find gaps in the prosecution's case and switch their votes to not guilty. The downstairs neighbor walks with a limp and probably couldn't have gotten to his front door in time to see the defendant run past. If the defendant had killed his father, why did he return to the apartment a few hours later? And the eyewitness who saw the stabbing through the train windows while lying in bed was probably not wearing her glasses, creating doubt about the accuracy of her identification. When the last holdouts collapse, the jurors file back into the courtroom to report the not guilty verdict.

Legal Analysis

Twelve Angry Men is undoubtedly the movies' most fervent defense of the jury system, and it is by far the best account of jury deliberations A few hotheads aside, the jurors are decent and open-minded people trying their best to arrive at truth and achieve justice. They take the concept of reasonable doubt seriously, and in the end reason triumphs over passion and bigotry. A foreign-born juror makes the larger point that trial by jury is a central American value: "We are not here to fight. We have a responsibility. This is a remarkable thing about democracy. . . . We come down to this place to decide on the guilt or innocence of a man we have never heard of before. . . . This is one of the reasons why we are strong. We should not make it a personal thing."

The right to trial by jury. As interpreted by the U.S. Supreme Court, the Sixth Amendment of the U.S. Constitution guarantees the right to trial by jury in criminal cases whenever a defendant may be incarcerated for longer than six months. As a practical matter, juries are generally available for even petty criminal cases. Most Americans defend juries as an important bulwark that protects individuals from arbitrary government power. Indeed, in a recent survey, 78 percent of respondents agreed that the jury system is the fairest way to determine whether a person is guilty of a crime. To officials in many other democracies, however, it is lunacy to leave important questions of guilt and innocence to people more or less plucked off the street. Most countries do not use juries at all, and those that do (such as Great Britain) use them in far fewer cases.

Unanimous verdicts. Most states require unanimous verdicts in criminal cases. Split decisions are acceptable only in civil trials and boxing matches. However, the U.S. Constitution does not mandate unanimous verdicts, and some states allow for nonunanimous verdicts in less-serious types of criminal cases.

Studies of actual juries reveal that lone holdouts rarely turn around entire juries. When one juror insists on holding out, the result is almost always a hung jury. Occasionally, a judge may remove a lone holdout from a jury and substitute an alternate juror. This can happen if other jurors complain and the judge concludes that the holdout is "refusing to deliberate" or otherwise violating the jurors' oath. However, judges are reluctant to remove holdouts from juries, because doing so can deny the defendant the right to be tried by the twelve jurors who were initially seated in the box. (As in *12 Angry Men,* a lone holdout typically favors a criminal defendant.)

Why do jurors come by the dozen? No one is quite sure, though some states authorize juries with as few as six people even in criminal cases. The film indicates why there may be value in numbers. More jurors tends to ensure more diversity on the panel, which could be beneficial to a criminal defendant from a minority group. Even so, the jurors in the film were all white and all male, a somewhat unlikely scenario for a big-city jury in 1957.

In addition, only one juror observed that the eyewitness who saw the stabbing through the train windows had small marks on either side of her nose, which suggested that she wasn't wearing her glasses when she saw the stabbing while lying in bed. As the film implies, multiple sets of eyes and ears provide some assurance that important evidence will be observed and remembered.

"I know from personal experience . . ." Most of us evaluate information in accordance with our own personal experiences. That's certainly true in the film. One juror, who had worked next to elevated train lines, assures the others that the noise would have deafened the downstairs neighbor. Another juror, who like the neighbor is an older man, explains that the neighbor might have fudged his testimony so he could feel important for once in his life. Yet another juror, a father who is estranged from his own son, subconsciously takes his anger out on the defendant. Lawyers use the *voir dire* process to question prospective jurors about their personal experience, because that background is critical in how they react to evidence.

Bigotry. Juror No. 10 is an all-purpose racist. Fed up with the turn toward a defense verdict, he argues: "You're not going to tell me you believe that phony story about losing the knife and being at the movies? You know how these people lie. It's born in them. . . . They don't need any real big reason to kill someone either. . . . No one's blaming them for it, that's the way they are. . . . Human life don't mean as much to them as it does to us. . . . There's some good things about them too. I'm the first one to say that. I've known a couple of them who are okay. This kid is a liar. I know it. I know all about them." Had No. 10 expressed these opinions during *voir dire*, the judge would certainly have prevented him from serving on the jury. However, once No. 10 was impaneled as a juror, his bigoted attitude would not disqualify him from continuing to serve. Jury deliberations are sacrosanct, a bastion of democracy in which jurors can express opinions free of outside controls. As in the film, we must trust other jurors to counter biased and inflammatory arguments.

No more "Mr. Knife Guy." One of the film's most dramatic moments occurs when Juror No. 8 responds to the argument that the murder weapon was unique by displaying an identical knife that he had just bought. (No. 8 thrusts the sharp point of the knife into the jury table, perhaps explaining why the furniture in jury rooms is often so dilapidated.) However, jurors are not allowed to conduct their own investigations. If the other jurors had complained to the judge, No. 8 might well have been kicked off the jury and replaced with an alternate who probably would have been much less sympathetic to the defendant.

Did the jurors get it right? The film creates a sense of reasonable doubt through the trick of focusing on each piece of prosecution evidence separately. As suggested by an old legal saying, "A brick is not a wall," any individual item of circumstantial evidence can be consistent with guilt or innocence. But the totality of the prosecution's evidence (particularly the evidence about the knife), together with the lack of any other suspect and the reality that most murders are committed by family members, means that almost certainly the defendant killed his father.

Picturing justice: (1) The film opens with shots of the exterior and interior of a majestic classical courthouse. The image is quickly mocked by the attitude of the judge, who delivers the jury instructions in a bored, weary monotone. (2) The film persuades the audience of the correctness of the final verdict by having the angriest, most narrow-minded jurors hold out the longest for guilt.

Trial Brief

Twelve Angry Men began life as a live television drama presented in 1954 on *Studio One*. A Showtime TV remake in 1997 had an all-male but ethnically diverse jury. To achieve gender balance, the story is sometimes presented as a stage play titled "12 Angry Persons."

The Winslow Boy

Synopsis: A boy's expulsion from a naval college becomes a test of British democracy.

British Lion Films, 1948. Black and white. Running time: 117 minutes.

Screenplay: Terrence Rattigan and Anatole de Grunwald. Original play: Terrence Rattigan. Director: Anthony Asquith.

Starring: Robert Donat (Sir Robert Morton), Cedric Hardwicke (Arthur Winslow).

Rating: ———■ ———■ ———■

The Story

Twelve-year-old Ronnie Winslow enters the prestigious Royal Naval College. But before Ronnie can see the sea, or even a second term, he's expelled for stealing a five-shilling postal order from a gym locker. When Ronnie insists he didn't do it, his father, Arthur, tries to overturn the decision. Arthur succeeds only in drawing unwanted national attention to his family and seriously disrupting their lives. Sir Robert

British Lion Films/Photofest

The Winslow Boy: Sir Robert Morton (Robert Donat) and Ronnie Winslow (Neil North) celebrate victory.

Morton, a member of Parliament and one of England's greatest barristers, agrees to represent the family after Ronnie withstands a withering mock cross-examination and convinces Morton of his innocence. Morton even turns down an appointment as Lord Chief Justice in order to stay on the case. Morton wants to defend every citizen's right to a fair hearing, though the fact that Ronnie has an attractive older sister doesn't hurt.

Private citizens need permission to sue the king, forcing Morton to petition Parliament for the right to go to court. The writ hits the fan with Morton's emotional speech in the House of Commons, when he attacks "the monstrous assumption . . . that the king can do no wrong. . . . Let them not rest until the attorney general has endorsed Mr. Winslow's petition with the time-honored phrase. . . . 'Let right be done.'" Parliament grants the Petition of Right, giving the Winslows their day in court.

The attorney general attacks Ronnie's denial that he stole the postal order by showing that Ronnie was alone in the locker room and therefore had a good opportunity to steal it. Another problem for Ronnie is the conflicting estimates he has given as to how long he was alone. Trying to support Ronnie's testimony that he was in the locker room for only ten minutes, Morton has Ronnie admit that he went there to smoke a cigarette. However, Morton worries that his tactic has given the attorney general an opening to argue that "a boy who is capable of breaking one of the strictest college rules by smoking is more likely than not to have broken another by stealing five shillings."

Morton effectively embarrasses the naval college's witnesses. An official testifies that the college conducted a formal inquiry before expelling Ronnie, but he admits that Ronnie did not have representation and that the official would not want his own status determined by the kind of hearing that Ronnie got.

During a recess, the attorney general concedes that Ronnie is innocent, and the case is settled. Morton later tells the Winslow family, "Right has been done. Not justice, it's easy to do justice, but very hard to do right."

Legal Analysis

Cine-lawyers typically become heroes by defending unpopular clients facing serious charges. By contrast, Morton is a hero because he fights on behalf of a principle and sacrifices his appointment to become Lord Chief Justice, the most powerful legal position in England. Merely a private citizen, Arthur Winslow is powerless against an entrenched bureaucracy. He needs a great barrister's political skills and power of oratory to "let right be done."

Sovereign immunity. Morton needed Parliament's permission to sue because of a basic tenet of British law that "the king can do no wrong." The doctrine of sovereign immunity is still applied in the United States, and in general the government cannot be sued unless it has given permission. For example, Congress cannot authorize people to sue states for violating federal law unless the state has consented to the suit (*Seminole Tribe of Florida v. Florida,* 1996). In *The Winslow Boy,* permission to sue the government had to be obtained on a case-by-case basis. In the United States, by contrast, the federal government and all state governments have enacted laws forfeiting their right to claim sovereign immunity in broad categories of cases involving matters such as breach of contract or personal injuries or in cases of judicial review of administrative action.

Justice is easy, right is hard. Morton's profound comment that it's very easy to do justice but very hard to do right highlights the difference between procedural justice and substantive justice. In the U.S. and U.K. adversary systems, the promise of "justice to all" generally means the former. In other words, litigants have a fair chance to present evidence and arguments to impartial judges and jurors, but there's no guarantee of substantive justice, meaning that their decisions will be correct. Morton's excellent advocacy produces both types of justice. Ronnie at long last gets a fair hearing, and acquittal on the theft charge is the correct outcome.

Attorney's fees. Under U.S. law, each side generally pays its own attorney's fees, but under British law the losing party usually pays the winner's fees. As a result, the government must pay Morton's substantial fee for representing Ronnie. The British rule can be a great equalizer, allowing people like the Winslows to take on the government. However, it can also deter litigation: If the Winslows had lost, as they very well might have if the government had not conceded, they would be responsible for paying the government's counsel fees.

Picturing justice. (1) Cross-examining Ronnie in the Winslows' parlor, Morton is hostile and confrontational. The moment he ends the questioning, Morton reverts back to his normally laconic demeanor. The rapid change is a reminder that no matter how sincerely and forcefully stated, lawyers' arguments do not necessarily reflect their personal beliefs. (2) Pressed by Ronnie's sister Catherine to explain his lack of emotion, Morton replies: "In my profession I must necessarily distrust it. Cold, clear logic, and buckets of it, should be the lawyer's only equipment."

Trial Briefs

1. An excellent 1999 remake of the film written and directed by David Mamet omits the courtroom scenes entirely. Morton's powerful parlor-room cross-examination of Ronnie remains, however.

2. In the actual case, George Archer-Shee was expelled in 1908, and the trial took place in 1910. Many students were suspected of stealing the postal order, and a popular theory is that Archer-Shee was selected for expulsion because he was a Catholic. As in the film, the government accepted that Archer-Shee was innocent four days into the trial. Archer-Shee truly won the battle but lost the war: He died in combat in 1914 in World War I. He was represented by a famous barrister, Edward Carson, who had prosecuted Oscar Wilde in 1895.

3. The pound-shilling-pence monetary system that Britain used until the early 1970s had twenty shillings to a pound. Thus Ronnie was

accused of stealing one-quarter of a pound, or twenty-five pence in current decimal terms (less than fifty U.S. cents). Even in 1908, it could have been hardly enough for a clotted-cream tea.

Young Mr. Lincoln

Synopsis: Skilled at precedent before becoming president, Abe Lincoln defends two brothers accused of murder.

20th Century Fox, 1939. Black and white. Running time: 100 minutes.

Screenplay: Lamar Trotti. Director: John Ford.

Starring: Henry Fonda (Abraham Lincoln).

Academy Award nomination: Best Screenplay.

Rating: ——🔨 ——🔨 ——🔨 ——🔨

The Story

In the 1830s, Abe Lincoln is a lawyer in dusty Springfield, Illinois. He's popular with the locals, maybe because he judges a pie-tasting contest without submitting a bill. The Clays are humble farmers passing through Springfield. At night, brothers Adam and Matt Clay get into a fight with a local ne'er-do-well, Scrub White. As they struggle, White's pal J. Palmer Cass runs onto the scene, bends over to check on White, and holds up a bloody knife. Adam and Matt each tell the sheriff that he was the one who stabbed White. Their mother, Abigail, saw the fight, but she refuses to say anything. Both Adam and Matt are charged with White's murder.

The townfolk form the World's Quickest Lynch Mob, no doubt figuring that breaking into the jail should be easy because it's made entirely of Clay. Lincoln confronts the mob at the jailhouse door and disperses it with humor and wisdom: "I'm just a new lawyer trying to get ahead, but some of you boys seem like you're trying to do me out of my first clients. . . . Maybe these boys do deserve to hang. But with me handling their case, don't look like you'll have much to worry about on that score. All I'm asking is to have it done with some legal pomp. . . . Trouble is, when men start taking the law into their own hands they're just as apt in all the confusion and fun to start hanging someone who's not a murderer as someone who is. . . . We do things together that we'd be mighty ashamed to do by ourselves."

Young Mr. Lincoln: Abe Lincoln (Henry Fonda) tries to save the lives of the Clay brothers (Richard Cromwell and Eddie Quillan).

Prosecutor Felder offers Abigail a chance to save the life of one of her sons by testifying to which one stabbed White. Though Felder browbeats her repeatedly, Abigail refuses to answer. Lincoln intervenes with an impassioned speech about Abigail's decency and values, and ends by saying that he'd "rather see you, Mrs. Clay, lose both your boys than to see you break your heart trying to save one at the expense of the other. Don't tell them." Felder defuses the situation by excusing Abigail as a witness.

The key witness is Cass, who testifies that Matt was the killer. It was dark, and he was about one hundred yards distant, but Cass could see what happened because it was "moon bright."

* * *

SPOILER ALERT: You may not want to read further if you plan to see the film.

* * *

As Cass walks off the witness stand, Lincoln suddenly accuses Cass of being the killer. Cass protests, but Lincoln hands him an almanac showing that the moon had set almost an hour before White was killed. Caught in a lie and badgered by a now relentless Lincoln, Cass falls apart. He admits that he killed White, with whom he'd quarreled earlier in the evening.

As Lincoln says good-bye to the grateful Clays, Abigail hands him the few coins she can afford to pay. Presumably none was a Lincoln penny. Lincoln then strides off into the future, the soaring "Battle Hymn of the Republic" playing majestically in the background.

Legal Analysis

Young Mr. Lincoln provides an inspiring portrait of a resourceful and caring lawyer. Lincoln is skilled in court, compassionate toward the Clays, and courageous when facing down a mob. Though on the surface Lincoln seems to be a simple country bumpkin, the film portrays him as having the qualities and values that enable him to overcome adversity and achieve justice, whether as a lawyer or a statesman.

Moonstruck. Cass trips himself up by lying about a seemingly small detail. Nevertheless, Lincoln deserves credit for recognizing the false note and confronting Cass with indisputable proof of his lie. Just as in Lincoln's time, an almanac provides conclusive proof of the time that the moon set. In the words of Federal Evidence Rule 201, an almanac is a source of information "whose accuracy cannot reasonably be questioned."

Playing dial-a-defendant. Though Felder offers to drop the charges against the nonstabber, both Adam and Matt could have been convicted of murder. If Cass is believed, Adam and Matt set upon White and knocked him to the ground before one of them stabbed him. Thus, the jurors could reasonably conclude that Adam and Matt were accomplices who acted in concert, making both legally responsible for White's death regardless of which one stabbed him.

Abigail's choice. Abigail has no legal right to refuse to answer Felder's question about which of her sons killed Scrub White. Nevertheless, Felder's strategy is awful. Undoubtedly the jurors would empathize with a mother's refusal to call a child a murderer. Even if Felder had been able to prove that one of the brothers killed Scrub White, some of the jurors might well have voted for acquittal because of their distaste for Felder's tactics.

Taking the Fifth. Today, Lincoln's accusation that Cass murdered White would require a judge to advise Cass of his rights under the Fifth Amendment. (At the time of the events depicted in the film, the provisions of the Bill of Rights did not apply to the states.) The hard-drinking

Cass would probably have interpreted a suggestion that he "take the Fifth" as an invitation to take a few more swigs from his jug. However, a judge would explain to him that he has a right not to say anything that might expose him to criminal prosecution, and a right to consult an attorney before answering any more questions. Any attorney would have advised Cass to shut up. Of course, this would deprive Adam and Matt of their own right to cross-examine Cass. The upshot would be that the judge would strike Cass' testimony in its entirety and instruct the jurors to disregard it. As Felder had no other evidence that either Adam or Matt killed White, they would have to be set free.

Picturing justice. Studying a dusty copy of the historic British legal treatise known as *Blackstone's Commentaries,* Lincoln reads aloud: "The right to life, reputation, and liberty. Rights to acquire and hold property. Wrongs are violations of those rights." He then adds, "By jing, that's all there is to it—right and wrong. Maybe I ought to begin to take this up serious." The scene seems subtly critical of lawyers, chiding them for complicating a simple moral principle. The film returns to this theme when Felder demands that Abigail identify which of her sons stabbed Scrub White. When Felder asserts that Lincoln should know that the law entitles him to an answer, Lincoln responds: "I may not know so much of the law, Mr. Felder, but I know what's right and wrong, and what you're asking is wrong."

The film takes viewers back to the more freewheeling days of frontier justice. Judge Bell dozes off and snores loudly during prosecutor Felder's flowery opening statement. When Judge Bell wakes up, he tells the crowd to quiet down because "we have to give these boys a fair trial before we hang 'em."

Trial Briefs

1. Abraham Lincoln was generally regarded as one of the finest lawyers of his day, devoting much of his law practice to complex railroad cases. Before becoming president, Lincoln handled about five thousand cases. Less than 10 percent of them involved criminal charges.

2. The murder trial featured in the film is a composite of two actual trials. One was an 1857 trial in which Lincoln represented a defendant named Armstrong. In that trial, Lincoln used an almanac to undermine the believability of a prosecution witness who testified to seeing a crime take place by the light of the silvery moon. The second took

place in Georgia in the early part of the twentieth century and resulted in the hanging of two brothers for a murder to which their mother was the only witness.

3. In his first great film, Henry Fonda looks more like Lincoln than Lincoln did himself. Originally Fonda was too intimidated to even consider playing Abe Lincoln, but John Ford persuaded him to take the role. In many later roles, Fonda projected qualities similar to those he displayed in *Young Mr. Lincoln*: integrity, resourcefulness, simplicity, and physical courage. For example, in *12 Angry Men* he was the lone juror who held out against all the others. In *The Ox-Bow Incident,* he unsuccessfully held out against a lynch mob. Fonda was Tom Joad in *The Grapes of Wrath,* the beaten-down farm worker who becomes a union organizer. Each of these films and many others helped establish a unique Fonda persona that lent great authenticity to each new role he played.

4. John Ford, whom some regard as America's greatest director, made numerous historical pictures, usually focused on the American frontier. These landmark films include *Stagecoach, The Grapes of Wrath, My Darling Clementine, Rio Grande,* and *The Man Who Shot Liberty Valance*. Ford had a wonderful knack for capturing the ambience of a remote time and place, like the captivating frontier trial in *Young Mr. Lincoln*. As in many of his movies, Ford tells a great story about common people and demonstrates strong concern for social justice. As always, the heroes are mythic and there's plenty of sentimentality.

Short Subjects

Boomerang!, 1947. Dana Andrews, Arthur Kennedy. Directed by Elia Kazan. ——◼ ——◼ ——◼

In a dramatization of a true story, valiant prosecutor Henry Harvey chooses justice over political ambition. John Waldron is charged with murdering a town's beloved minister. Eyewitnesses identify him as the killer, and a brutal police interrogation produces a confession. But in a court hearing, Harvey justifies his decision not to prosecute Waldron to a hostile judge and community. Harvey discredits his own witnesses' identifications and proves that Waldron's gun could not have fired the fatal bullet. *Courtroom highlight*: After the judge loads the alleged murder weapon, Harvey has an aide point it at Harvey's head and pull the trigger; it fails to fire. *Picturing justice*: "America the Beautiful" plays in the background as Harvey walks out of the courthouse, signaling that fair play and justice are American values.

Count the Hours, 1953. Teresa Wright, Macdonald Carey.
—■ —■

Doug Madison loses his clients and his fiancée because of the time and money he invests in trying to prove that migrant worker George Braden is innocent of murder. Braden is convicted, partly because of a confession he gave in an effort to halt the overbearing police interrogation of his pregnant wife, Ellen. Hours before Braden is to hang, Madison finds the real murderer. *Courtroom highlight*: Madison calls an expert witness in a fruitless effort to prove that Braden's gun could not have fired the fatal bullets. *Picturing justice*: (1) Shortly after he's arrested, Braden tells Ellen, "We didn't kill those two. Maybe they'll believe us if we keep on telling them." (2) The angry townspeople threaten to lynch Braden and murder Ellen. *Trial brief*: Director Don Siegel went on to direct such classic films as *Invasion of the Body Snatchers* and *Dirty Harry*.

Criminal Lawyer, 1937. Lee Tracy, Eduardo Ciannelli. —■ —■
Mobster Gene Larkin installs his mouthpiece Barry Brandon as D.A. Instead of making life easier for Larkin, Brandon closes down his gambling operations and charges him with murder. Larkin's death threats force Brandon's girlfriend, Madge, to testify that Larkin shot in self-defense. Brandon is reluctant to cross-examine Madge, but when Larkin gloats, Brandon tears apart her story and she admits that Larkin shot an unarmed man. Brandon then confesses to his past misdeeds in open court, resigns as D.A., and walks happily out of the courtroom with Madge. *Courtroom highlight*: As D.A., Brandon goads a wife into confessing that she murdered her husband by confronting her with the bed where the bloody deed was done. *Picturing justice*. After extracting a courtroom confession from the wife, Brandon tells Madge: "I won because I was a better actor than she was."

Eye Witness (also titled **Your Witness**), 1950. Robert Montgomery.
—■ —■

Adam Heywood, a busy New York lawyer, travels to England to help Sam Baxter, who saved Heywood's life during the war but is charged with murder. Heywood finds the crucial eyewitness who establishes that Baxter shot in self-defense. *Courtroom highlight*: Heywood has to overcome legal and grammatical obstacles when testifying to Baxter's good character.

Lawyer Man, 1933. William Powell, Joan Blondell. ———∎ ———∎

Anton Adam and his wisecracking secretary operate a legal-aid clinic on Manhattan's teeming Lower East Side. When Adam moves his practice uptown, the city's political insiders make him rich and powerful. However, after realizing that the insiders are "so crooked they can hide behind a circular staircase," he returns to his clinic to serve as "a big brother to a lot of poor trampled slobs who can't hold their own against party bosses." *Picturing justice*: Adam's big cigar suggestively rises in his mouth when the bosses introduce him to a starlet. The sexual imagery suggests that wealthy clients can easily manipulate lawyers' values.

On Trial, 1939. John Litel. Story: Elmer Rice. ———∎ ———∎ ———∎

In an unusual portrayal of jury nullification, defendant Robert Strickland is charged with murdering Gerald Trask. The jury acquits Strickland after deciding that Trask was trying to pressure Strickland's wife into having an affair. *Courtroom highlight*: The jurors interrupt their deliberations, return to the courtroom, and question the defendant, Strickland. Lawyers might find the film threatening because the jurors ask such darned-good questions. *The Amazing Dr. Clitterhouse* is another film in which jurors break off deliberations in order to question a defendant.

The People Against O'Hara, 1951. Spencer Tracy, James Arness. ———∎ ———∎

Film noir characters with colorful names like Charlie the Sleep complicate James Curtayne's defense of Johnny O'Hara. O'Hara is charged with killing mobster Bill Sheffield and, despite lots of evidence to the contrary, Curtayne is convinced that O'Hara is innocent. Curtayne is ineffective at trial, and O'Hara is convicted. Afterward, Curtayne finds a witness who convinces the police and the prosecutor that O'Hara is innocent. They set a trap for the killer that requires Curtayne to secretly record the real killer's confession. The plan succeeds, though Curtayne is killed in a shootout. *Picturing justice*: (1) Prosecutor Barra is compassionate and committed to justice. Barra is hesitant to report that Curtayne attempted to bribe a witness, and when Barra realizes that O'Hara is innocent, he works hard to clear him. (2) Curtayne's death is as much tragic as heroic. Alcoholism has greatly eroded his trial skills, so, feeling he has little to live for, Curtayne risks almost certain death to prove O'Hara's innocence.

State's Attorney, 1932. John Barrymore. ───■ ──■ ──■

Like *Criminal Lawyer*, the film depicts lawyers as independent and committed to justice. Mobster Vanny Powers arranges for Tom Cardigan, his alcoholic mouthpiece, to become D.A. The idea is that Cardigan will go easy on the mob and will eventually be the governor. Cardigan takes his job seriously and prosecutes Powers for murder. Frightened by Powers' death threat, an eyewitness testifies falsely that Powers is innocent, but Cardigan's aggressive cross-examination reveals the truth. The eyewitness cries out, "You tricked me," to which Cardigan replies, "The truth tricked you." Cardigan then dramatically resigns as D.A., ruining his chances of becoming governor. Cardigan promises to return to "the defense of those unfortunates who like myself were reared in the gutter." *Courtroom highlight:* In a separate case, a wife is charged with murdering her husband by beating him with an iron weight. Cardigan rattles the wife into admitting guilt by banging the iron weight on the deathbed

The Talk of the Town, 1942. Cary Grant. ───■ ──■ ──■

During the dark days of World War II, this film reassured audiences that the U.S. legal system was worth fighting for and dying for. Radical factory worker Leopold Dilg is framed and wrongly convicted of murder. Dilg escapes from prison and hides out in a remote cabin owned by childhood sweetheart Nora Shelley. Dilg and Shelley have to keep his status a secret from Michael Lightcap, a no-nonsense law professor who has rented the cabin so he can finish writing a legal treatise while awaiting his appointment to the U.S. Supreme Court. *Courtroom highlight:* Dilg is rearrested and Lightcap realizes that Dilg is innocent. Lightcap disperses the frightening lynch mob that has broken into the courtroom by asking, "What are you doing in a court of law with weapons and ropes? . . . This is your law and your finest possession, and it makes you free men in a free country. . . . Think of a world crying for this very law. . . . We can't even exist unless we're willing to go down into the dust and blood and fight a battle every day of our lives to preserve it." *Picturing justice:* The film suggests that Supreme Court justices are chosen for their intellectual ability, not their political views, and that they spend the time before they are confirmed doing research rather than lobbying senators.

Veer-Zaara, 2004. Shahrukh Khan, Rani Mukherjee.

———■ ——■ ——■

Bollywood goes to the courtroom in this Indian story of forbidden love. Veer Singh, an Indian pilot, falls madly in love with Zaara Khan, a young Pakistani beauty who, unfortunately, is engaged to someone else. Singh is framed for spying and spends twenty-two silent years in a Pakistani jail. Ultimately, a courageous Pakistani lawyer, Saamiya Siddiqui, takes up Singh's case. She does an outstanding bit of detective work and in her first trial wins a smashing victory. The court frees Singh with apologies for the wrongful imprisonment. *Picturing justice*: (1) The thunderous applause from everyone in the courtroom following Singh's poetic plea for reconciliation between India and Pakistan underlines the film's political message. (2) Competent and ethical female attorneys are in short supply in American films, but Siddiqui is a true hero: she is dedicated to winning what seems like a hopeless case against a skilled adversary, and she does her job with great skill and compassion.

Injustice for All

A high-quality legal system should produce justice, both by convicting the guilty and by acquitting the innocent with reasonable speed and economy. In the real world, of course, law and justice are not always equivalent. The films in this chapter (many of which dramatize actual events) focus on the law-justice dichotomy and are sobering reminders that thorough and fair processes do not necessarily guarantee correct outcomes.

The courtroom film genre teaches that the most frequent cause of injustice is a state's need to set an example by picking on particular defendants to achieve a political objective. For example, in completely different eras and locales, the South African government's desire to maintain apartheid, and King Henry VIII's desire to legitimate a divorce, produce tragically unjust verdicts in *A Dry White Season* and *A Man for All Seasons*. Police sometimes resort to intimidation or lies to convince the populace that they have crime under control, as they do in *Let Him Have It* and *In the Name of the Father*. Prejudice and racism may infect the jury process, as happens in *To Kill a Mockingbird, A Cry in the Dark,* and *They Won't Forget*.

Even more disturbing is the message of other films that occasional injustice is an inevitable by-product of any legal system. If eyewitnesses are honest but mistaken (*The Wrong Man*) or circumstantial evidence simply points in the wrong direction (*A Cry in the Dark, 10 Rillington Place, Stranger on the Third Floor*), the results can be catastrophic for the individuals involved.

While many of the films in this chapter concern disturbing true-life examples of injustice, filmmakers don't hesitate to alter historic facts to make stories more entertaining or compelling, as occurred in *Evelyn* or *In the Name of the Father*. Though injustice usually consists of wrongful convictions, wrongful acquittals, like the ones in *Ghosts of Mississippi, Chicago, Witness for the Prosecution, The Letter,* and *Unashamed,* are equally possible. Whether a story involves an erroneous conviction or an acquittal, courtroom films serve to remind viewers that our justice system is fallible.

A Dry White Season

Synopsis: An inquest exposes the brutal injustices of South African apartheid.

MGM, 1989. Color. Running time: 97 minutes.

Screenplay: Colin Welland and Euzhan Palcy. Novel: Andre Brink. Director: Euzhan Palcy.

Starring: Donald Sutherland (Ben du Toit), Marlon Brando (Ian McKenzie).

Academy Award nomination: Best Supporting Actor (Marlon Brando).

Rating:

The Story

Ben du Toit is considerate and fair-minded, but as a privileged white South African he is unaware of the terrible impact of apartheid on blacks. Rioting breaks out in Soweto and other poverty-stricken black townships in 1976. The police torture and kill du Toit's black gardener, Ngubene, and Ngubene's son Jonathan. Ngubene's widow, Emily, demands an inquest so she can contest the official story that Ngubene committed suicide. At du Toit's request, experienced civil rights lawyer Ian McKenzie agrees to represent Emily, "if only to make it abundantly clear how justice in South Africa is misapplied when it comes to the question of race."

The inquest is a complete sham. Captain Stolz of "Special Branch" testifies that Ngubene was arrested because he had "incriminating documents," one of which turns out to be a newspaper that McKenzie also subscribes to. Stolz's story is that Ngubene hung himself in his jail cell and that the gruesome scars on Ngubene's body resulted from his repeatedly throwing himself against the bars and window of his cell. Wisely, Stolz refuses McKenzie's invitation to demonstrate how the scars or burns to Ngubene's genitals could possibly have been caused that way. Stolz has a different explanation for the scars covering the back of Ngubene's friend Archibald Mabaso: They were inflicted by "terrorists and Communists." The judge refuses to consider a post-mortem report on the condition of Ngubene's body prepared by Dr. Hassiem, because Hassiem has been arrested for treason and is in solitary confinement.

The judge rules that "all the available evidence clearly and indisputably proves that the death of Gordon Ngubene cannot be attributed to the security forces of South Africa." If Stolz had so testified, the judge no doubt would also have concluded that gravity is a communist myth.

The inquest's illogical result radicalizes du Toit, who secretly gathers affidavits documenting abuse by the Special Branch. As a result, most of du Toit's family despises and deserts him, he loses his job, and finally Stolz kills him. But before he dies, du Toit passes along his documents to reporter Melanie Bruwer. The next day, stories and photos detailing torture and killings are all over her newspaper's front page.

Legal Analysis

During the years between the 1976 Soweto uprisings and the film's release more than a decade later, the South African government's physical and economic abuse of its black population was well documented in the popular media. *A Dry White Season* uses an inquest to expose a particular example of brutality and injustice and provoke viewers' anger. Du Toit was initially content to turn a blind eye to abuse because it happened far away, in the black townships. But when du Toit, and by extension the film's viewers, personally experienced the legal system's cruelty and immorality, he was roused to action.

The courtroom setting adds power to the film's message by transforming a huge political problem into a concrete story of horror and injustice. Ngubene was not a public figure, nor was the way he died unusual. Thus, the suggestion that what happened to Ngubene could happen to any black South African adds to the viewer's sense of outrage. Moreover, the courtroom format means that Stolz has to respond to McKenzie's sarcastic questions. The absurdity of his answers suggests that the government cannot defend the regime of apartheid and doesn't believe that it has to.

Inquests. Inquests are held to determine whether a criminal act caused a suspicious death. The advantage of an inquest over a routine police investigation is that the magistrate has the power to subpoena witnesses to appear and they have to testify under oath. As in the film, South Africa's rules allowed a victim's family to retain an attorney to participate in the questioning of witnesses. The magistrate's conclusion that Ngubene took his own life ended the investigation into Stolz's potential criminal responsibility.

Trappings of justice. Even under the evil regime of apartheid, the South African government tried to demonstrate legitimacy by providing the outward trappings of a system of justice. For example, Emily's request for an inquest is granted, and before searching du Toit's house for treasonous antigovernment affidavits, Stolz takes the trouble to obtain a search warrant. These are recognizable features of due process, but procedures are meaningless without the will to apply them fairly.

Picturing justice: (1) The shabby, dusty streets of Soweto contrast with the neatly manicured lawns of du Toit's home. (2) McKenzie tells du Toit that "justice and law can be described as distant cousins, and here in South Africa they're simply not on speaking terms at all."

Trial Brief

The National Party began putting apartheid in place when it came to power in 1948. Apartheid separated the white and black populations while allowing whites to exploit blacks for cheap labor. Urban blacks lived in ghettos ("townships"), such as Soweto. They were allowed into white areas to work but had to return home each night. Black South Africans had to carry passes, were subject to curfews, and could not change residences without permission. Black children received only a basic education designed to do little more than equip them to perform manual labor. Even a person like du Toit, a kind and generous man who paid school fees for Ngubene's son Jonathan, might have been unaware of the appalling conditions in which blacks lived.

Only whites voted for members of Parliament, and as the uprisings among the black populace grew, Parliament enacted laws conferring vast discretion on the president and the police to maintain order and repress dissent. Around the time the film came out, South Africa was becoming an international pariah where few governments or outside investors would put their money. Eventually the country abandoned apartheid during the presidency of F. W. de Klerk. Nelson Mandela, the leader of the African National Congress, was freed, and he and de Klerk cooperated in a peaceful transfer of power and free elections. The harsh abuses of apartheid are now in the rear-view mirror, but its social and economic effects will take generations to overcome.

In the Name of the Father

Synopsis: Police misconduct sends the Guildford 4 to prison for a pub bombing they didn't commit.

Universal Pictures, 1993. Color. Running time: 127 minutes.

Screenplay: Terry George and Jim Sheridan. Book: Gerry Conlon. Director: Jim Sheridan.

Starring: Daniel Day-Lewis (Gerald Conlon), Emma Thompson (Gareth Peirce).

Academy Award nominations: Best Picture, Best Director, Best Adapted Screenplay, Best Editing, Best Actor (Daniel Day-Lewis), Best Supporting Actor (Pete Postlethwaite), Best Supporting Actress (Emma Thompson).

Rating:

The Story

Gerry Conlon and Paul Hill are arrested for carrying out an IRA bombing that killed five people in a Guildford pub in 1974. Conlon and Hill were in a London park far from Guildford on the night of the bombing, but the only witness who can substantiate this alibi is Charlie Burke, a homeless drunk who cannot be found. Conlon and Hill also burglarized a London hooker's apartment that night, but no record of the crime exists.

The police torture Conlon and Hill into confessing. To enable the defendants to go down in history as the "Guildford 4," the police also charge Paddy Armstrong and Carole Richardson with the pub bombing. Conlon's father, Giuseppe, his aunt Annie Maguire, and her family (the "Maguire 7") are charged with supporting the Guildford 4's activities.

The police officers deny resorting to torture and swear that they searched for Charlie Burke but couldn't find him. They probably wouldn't have been able to find Big Ben from Westminster Bridge

In the Name of the Father: The Guildford 4 (Mark Sheppard, Beatie Edney, John Lynch, Daniel Day-Lewis) in the dock.

either. Hill and Conlon deny that they had anything to do with the bombing, but as admitted thieves and drug users they lack credibility. The jury convicts all the defendants, and they receive lengthy prison sentences.

Fifteen years later, civil rights lawyer Gareth Peirce is still trying to prove the Guildford 4 innocent. A government clerk mistakenly hands her a secret police file containing a document showing that the police had interviewed Charlie Burke before trial and that he had confirmed Hill's and Conlon's alibi. Peirce presents the startling information to a furious judge, who dismisses the charges and releases the prisoners. Conlon had earlier told Peirce, "Justice, mercy, clemency, I literally don't understand the language." Conlon wasn't alone; neither did the police.

Legal Analysis

In times of terror, legal protections are often sacrificed in the name of security. In response to continued IRA bombings, the British Parliament enacted the Prevention of Terrorism Act. The act authorized the police to detain suspected terrorists for a week without bringing them to court or giving them access to a lawyer. The police sometimes used torture when suspects refused to confess and the police were certain they had the right people. As in the film, the police often had to cover up their illegal behavior by lying in court, even if they realized they were mistaken. Without plain evidence of abuse, judges and jurors almost always accepted the stories of police heroes over those of the "outsiders" in the dock.

The September 11, 2001, World Trade Center disaster in the United States provoked a similar example. Congress authorized a broad range of new investigatory powers in the USA Patriot Act. During the Iraq and Afghanistan wars, soldiers tortured prisoners, especially at Abu Ghraib prison. The United States also imprisoned suspected foreign terrorists in Guantanamo Bay without hearing or trial, until the U.S. Supreme Court ordered the government to provide them with hearings before military tribunals. England lacks a written constitution, which partly explains why British courts did not overturn any provisions of the Prevention of Terrorism Act.

Miranda warnings. In the United States, the *Miranda* rule (*Miranda v. Arizona*, 1966) is an important protection against the sort of police abuse depicted in the film. The police must warn suspects when they take them into custody that they have a right to remain silent and to request a lawyer. If they cannot afford to pay for a lawyer, one will be appointed for them. And once suspects request a lawyer, the police must stop questioning them. None of these precautions was employed in the police investigation of the Guildford 4 case.

The Supreme Court reaffirmed the *Miranda* rule in the case of *Dickerson v. United States* (2000), stating that *Miranda* warnings had become "part of our national culture." The Court was certainly right. Starting in the 1960s with the famous TV show *Dragnet*, the public has heard thousands of *Miranda* warnings on television. *Dickerson* is a good example of how law and popular culture can influence each other.

A heroic lawyer. Gareth Peirce is one of the few heroic female cine-lawyers. She believes in her clients' innocence and persists in the search for exculpatory evidence. Acting as a surrogate for the film's viewers, Peirce loses her cool while questioning Inspector Dixon about Charlie Burke: "Some people ordered that these people be used as scapegoats by a nation that was baying for blood . . . in return for innocent blood spilled on the streets of Guildford. . . . And by God, you got your blood, Mr. Dixon! . . . You got fifteen years of blood and sweat and pain from my client, . . . whose only crime was that he was bloody well Irish." As a lawyer, of course, Peirce is supposed to be more restrained.

Picturing justice. After Peirce brings forth her devastating evidence, the government barrister frantically tries to contain the damage to the police and the government. He approaches the bench without Peirce and offers a "mercy deal," dismissing the case against the Guildford 4 in return for an immediate halt to the hearing.

Trial Briefs

1. The Guildford 4 were released from prison in 1989 after it was revealed that the police failed to disclose evidence in their possession that Charlie Burke had been with Conlon and Hill in London on the night of the bombings, and also that they failed to follow up on information from the IRA that the Guildford 4 were innocent. The Maguire 7 were also convicted on the basis of false or at least highly dubious forensic evidence. Their convictions were reversed in 1989, but all had already finished serving their sentences. Giuseppe Conlon died after five years in prison.

However, the film embellishes a number of facts. For example, the burglary of the hooker's apartment occurred ten days after the bombing and thus was not part of Conlon's alibi. Hill and Conlon were not together on the night of the bombing. Charlie Burke was a grocer who lived in the same hostel with Conlon. Conlon and Giuseppe did not spend their prison years in the same cell.

Solicitor Gareth Peirce, a well-known fighter for wrongfully accused prisoners, was involved in the case only at the end. She did not argue the case in court, and her fiery courtroom speech never occurred. In fact, the government prosecutors disclosed to the Court of Appeal all the sorry facts about the coerced confessions and the suppression of evidence.

The truly heroic lawyer was Alastair Logan, a humble family lawyer who fought for the Guildford-Maguire defendants for the whole fifteen years of their imprisonment (mostly without compensation) and continued fighting to clear their names after the charges were dismissed. Logan interviewed the real IRA bombers (the Balcombe Street defendants) while they were in prison pending trial in 1976. They said that they were responsible for the Guildford bombings and would never have allowed untrustworthy drug abusers like Conlon or Hill into an IRA active service unit. Logan was airbrushed out of the film, along with many others.

2. In 1993, Paul Hill married Courtney Kennedy, daughter of Robert and Ethel Kennedy. At the time of the marriage, Hill was appealing a

separate conviction for murdering a British soldier in Belfast. The conviction was overturned in April 1995.

Let Him Have It

Synopsis: A mentally retarded youth is executed after his crime partner kills a police officer.

Canal Plus, 1991. Color. Running time: 115 minutes.

Screenplay: Neal Purvis and Robert Wade. Director: Peter Medak.

Starring: Chris Eccleston (Derek Bentley), Paul Reynolds (Chris Craig).

Rating: ———■ ——■ ——■

The Story

Derek Bentley, age nineteen and living in a working-class section of London, is mentally retarded and virtually illiterate. His only friend is sixteen-year-old Chris Craig, a gun-happy thug. To impress Craig, Bentley joins him in his attempt to burgle a warehouse. Police officers quickly trap Bentley and Craig on the warehouse roof and demand that they surrender. Bentley does so at once. Craig pulls out a gun and points it at Sergeant Fairfax. According to Fairfax, Bentley then shouts to Craig, "Let him have it, Chris." Craig goes on a shooting spree, wounding Fairfax and killing Officer Miles.

Bentley and Craig are both convicted of murder. Because he was under age eighteen at the time of the killing, Craig cannot be executed and is sentenced to an indefinite term in prison. Though the jury recommends mercy for Bentley, the judge, Lord Goddard, sentences him to hang. Bentley's parents and sister spearhead national protests calling for government officials to overturn the death sentence. The protests reach Parliament, where many members call for inquiries into the verdict. However, Bentley is executed about a month after his conviction.

Legal Analysis

The film focuses on the injustice of executing the mentally limited Bentley but leaves it to viewers to decide what led to the miscarriage

Let Him Have It: Chris Craig (Paul Reynolds) and Derek Bentley (Chris Eccleston) stand trial for murder.

of justice. One factor may have been that Lord Goddard wanted to demonstrate to "young toughs" that lawbreaking would not be tolerated. Lord Goddard no doubt also wanted to exact revenge for the death of Officer Miles, who like almost all British police officers of that era was unarmed. Even if Bentley had been properly convicted of murder, his execution was wrong. Bentley's lawyer inexplicably failed to offer evidence of his client's limited mental functioning during the trial. Nevertheless, Lord Goddard and other officials in the Ministry of Justice were well aware of Bentley's mental limitations before his execution. Bentley's case illustrates the dangers of a "rush to judgment." Scarcely two months separated the botched burglary and the execution. Like a fine wine, justice often benefits from the passage of time.

Bentley's unfair conviction. The case against Bentley for murder was based in part on a theory of "unlawful joint enterprise," sometimes known as "accomplice liability." Under this theory, Bentley is responsible for killing Officer Miles if he could have reasonably anticipated that Craig would use violence either to carry out the crime or to escape capture. The evidence on this point was conflicting. Favoring the prosecution was the fact that Bentley himself was armed with brass knuckles and a knife. On the other hand, Bentley and Craig both testified that

Bentley did not know that Craig was armed or would resort to violence. On balance, disregarding Bentley's mental limitations, the jury could have reasonably concluded that Bentley was aware that Craig might resort to violence, a conclusion that would support the murder conviction.

The prosecutor argued also that Bentley should be convicted of murder because his shout of "Let him have it, Chris" incited Craig to start shooting. Again, the evidence on this point was in conflict, police officers swearing that Bentley did make this statement, and Bentley and Craig swearing that he did not. Even if the jurors believed the police officers, they might have accepted the argument of Bentley's defense attorney that Bentley was telling Craig to hand his gun to Sergeant Fairfax. However, the evidence before the jury was sufficient to support a conclusion that Bentley incited Craig to shoot and therefore was legally responsible for Officer Miles' death.

Nevertheless, Bentley's conviction was a miscarriage of justice. One reason is that the defense lawyer's failure to present evidence of Bentley's mental limitations prevented the jury from assessing what Bentley anticipated Craig might do. Moreover, Bentley meekly surrendered to Sergeant Fairfax well before Craig shot Officer Miles, and Bentley also warned other officers that Craig had a gun. Based on this evidence, Lord Goddard should have instructed the jurors that they could find Bentley not guilty of murder if they determine he had withdrawn from the joint criminal enterprise before Officer Miles was shot. Lord Goddard's failure to give this instruction was a crucial error.

Summing up. Lord Goddard's "summing up" also denied Bentley a fair trial. Before sending the jurors off to deliberate, Lord Goddard offers them his view of the case. U.S. judges rarely engage in this practice, and Goddard's one-sided description illustrates its dangers. Goddard suggested that a claim that the brave police officers committed perjury amounted to treason. Commenting on Bentley's credibility, Goddard asks the jurors, "Can you believe [that] Bentley did not know that Craig had the gun? You are not bound to believe Bentley if you think the inference and common sense of the matter is overwhelming that he must have known that he had it." Goddard's lecture was less a summing up and more a dressing down of the entire defense case.

Improperly opinionated. Sergeant Fairfax testifies that by shouting "Let him have it, Chris," Bentley was telling him to "start firing." Fairfax's opinion provided crucial support for the prosecution's incitement theory, but it was probably improper. Speculation as to what somebody meant by what he said or did is usually improper. Moreover, the jury was in as good a position to decide Bentley's meaning as Fairfax.

Picturing justice. (1) During Bentley's cross-examination, the camera closes in on his bruised face as the prosecutor and judge bombard him with questions he can barely comprehend. Bentley is depicted like a deer in headlights, incapable of saving himself. (2) Two poignant scenes magnify the sense of wrong by emphasizing Bentley's illiteracy. In one, Bentley listens as a jailer reads him a newspaper story about the wide public protests against his execution. In the second, the night before his execution, Bentley asks the jailer to write down his last wishes for his family.

Trial Briefs

1. Bentley's conviction was set aside, and he was pardoned by England's Supreme Court of Judicature in 1998. The court's opinion cites Lord Goddard's failure to instruct the jury properly and his biased comments to the jury, some of which are set out verbatim in the film. The opinion condemned the summation as a "highly rhetorical and strongly worded denunciation of both defendants. . . . The language used was not that of a judge but of an advocate." The court went on to say that Lord Goddard's summing up denied Bentley "that fair trial which is the birthright of every British citizen." While justice was certainly delayed, at least the 1998 opinion belatedly let Goddard have it.

2. Following the pardon, Bentley's family received compensation from the British government.

3. Christopher Craig was released from prison in 1963 and went on to become a law-abiding plumber and farmer.

4. Derek Bentley is the only person to have been executed in Britain after a jury's recommendation of mercy.

5. Bentley's and Craig's insistence that Bentley never said "Let him have it, Chris" is supported by the opinions of linguistic experts who as part of the process leading to the 1998 pardon examined Bentley's written confession. The experts' opinions, summarized in the Lord Chief Justice's opinion, were that the written confession was not consistent with Bentley's patterns of speech and that many of the phrases it contains are "redolent of police usage."

6. Bentley's execution became an important rallying point in the debate over the legitimacy of capital punishment, which Britain abolished in 1965.

A Man for All Seasons

Synopsis: In a contest between a lawyer with a conscience and a king with none, the king wins by a head.

Columbia Pictures, 1966. Color. Running time: 120 minutes.

Screenplay: Robert Bolt. Stage play: Robert Bolt. Director: Fred Zinnemann.

Starring: Paul Scofield (Sir Thomas More), Wendy Hiller (Alice More), Robert Shaw (Henry VIII).

Academy Awards: Best Picture, Best Screenplay, Best Director, Best Actor (Paul Scofield), Best Cinematography.

Academy Award nominations: Best Supporting Actress (Wendy Hiller), Best Supporting Actor (Robert Shaw).

Rating: ——▉ ——▉ ——▉

The Story

King Henry VIII is desperate to dump Catherine of Aragon and free himself to marry a wife who will bear a son. Henry has his eye on the vivacious and hopefully fertile Anne Boleyn. Alas, a papal dispensation had previously been secured to allow Henry to marry Catherine and the pope refused to invalidate that dispensation.

Henry elevates his trusted counselor Sir Thomas More, one of England's greatest lawyers and judges, to the post of Lord Chancellor. Henry assumes that More will support his request for an annulment, but More refuses to do so because he believes unshakably in the pope's supreme authority. More does everything possible to avoid a clash with Henry but ultimately is forced to resign.

Henry renounces papal authority and proclaims himself Supreme Head of the Church of England, whose doctrine conveniently allows divorce. Henry then pushes a law through Parliament requiring all subjects to take an Oath of Supremacy accepting Henry's actions. More refuses to take the oath but declines to explain his reasons, even after a year's imprisonment in the Tower. Finally, More goes on trial for high treason.

The notorious Richard Rich is the key witness against More. Rich went to More's jail cell to take away his books. According to Rich, More said that Parliament lacked the power to make the king head of the Church of England. In return for this helpful bit of perjury, Rich is made attorney general for Wales. The jurors, keenly interested in hanging on to

A Man for All Seasons: Sir Thomas More (Paul Scofield) pleads his hopeless case.

their own heads, immediately return a verdict of guilty. With nothing left to lose, More denounces the king's actions and affirms papal authority. So much for his chance for a successful appeal! Forgiving his executioner, More is beheaded in 1535. But what goes around comes around. Many of More's accusers are executed for treason themselves. Anne Boleyn is beheaded in 1536. Sir Richard Rich, however, dies peacefully in bed.

Legal Analysis

Though King Henry subverts the law to his own ends, the film powerfully affirms the rule of law. More's son-in-law William Roper argues that the devil should not receive due process of law. More responds, "This country is planted thick with laws from coast to coast—man's laws, not God's—and if you cut them down . . . do you really think you could stand upright in the winds that would blow then? . . . Yes, I'd give the devil benefit of law, for my own safety's sake." In the end, More is blown down by those very winds.

When client demands and personal convictions conflict.
Unable to reconcile Henry's demand with his own belief in papal

supremacy, More resigned. In more prosaic contexts, clients often ask lawyers to pursue goals with which the lawyers profoundly disagree. Sometimes a lawyer's duty is clear. For example, if a client demands that a lawyer present perjured testimony, the lawyer must withdraw from the case or take other action to prevent a fraud on the court. Similarly, a lawyer must never facilitate a client's plans to commit a crime or fraud.

In other situations, lawyers may have to choose between career and conviction. A prosecutor who personally opposes the death penalty may be assigned to seek a death sentence. An attorney opposed to abortion may be asked to represent a doctor who performs abortions. In such situations, attorneys often subordinate their personal beliefs to what they regard as professional duty and do their best to assist the client. Other times, lawyers resign out of deep personal conviction, and More's resignation as Lord Chancellor is an inspiring example of such a resignation.

The sound of silence. While refusing to take the oath, More uses every trick in the book to try to keep his head. He vouchsafes his views to nobody, not even his faithful and despairing wife, Alice. Silence, he argues at the trial, is ambiguous; it can't be considered treason and could even be considered assent to the king's actions. More also points out an obvious implausibility in Rich's testimony: Having refused to speak to anyone on the subject, why would he make the fatal concession to Rich, a man he never trusted? And Rich's sudden promotion to attorney general for Wales suggests that he had a motive to lie. But when King Henry is determined to take your head, such small details count for nothing.

Sham trials. Perhaps all countries have had their sham trials in which the forms of justice are followed but perverted to achieve a political end. This was certainly true of Nazi justice, as stirringly depicted in *Judgment at Nuremberg.* The court system in the Soviet Union once dispensed "telephone justice," meaning the judge would call the local Communist Party official before deciding what to do. France had its historic Dreyfus case, in which a trial was fixed to blame a spying incident on an innocent Jewish officer, as illustrated in *The Life of Emile Zola.* Military justice has often been a political charade, as so movingly explored in *Breaker Morant* or *Paths of Glory.* And in America the courts upheld the unjustified removal of Japanese citizens to internment camps early in World War II. So the trial of Sir Thomas More isn't historically unique, but it does serve as a reminder of the vulnerability of any justice system to political pressure.

Picturing justice. More's dignity emphasizes the images of injustice. He insists on the right to speak before sentence is pronounced. He declares he remains the king's true subject and says: "I do none harm. I say none harm. . . . And if this be not enough to keep a man alive, then in good faith I long not to live."

Trial Briefs

1. Sir Thomas More (1478–1535) was a Renaissance man who wrote scholarly books on a variety of subjects. (His *Utopia* leads some to regard him as the first socialist.) He was a wily lawyer, a loving family man, and a heroic defender of principle. He served in Parliament and in a variety of diplomatic, judicial, administrative, and educational posts. His friend, the Dutch philosopher Erasmus, originally called him "a man for all seasons," and so he still seems. More was unflinching and quite fanatical in his defense of the Catholic Church. Like many pious people of the time, he favored the burning of heretics, including Protestants.

2. More is said to have slept only two hours a night, a regimen made easier by the fact that he wore a hair shirt and slept on planks with a log for a pillow. He married Alice only a month after the death of his first wife, who had borne him four children. She also must not have gotten much sleep. More educated his daughters as well as his sons and always corresponded with them in Latin, which probably gave them a good excuse for not writing back. More's house in Chelsea had eighty-three servants, and he often fed one hundred people a day.

3. The new archbishop of Canterbury upheld the legality of Henry's marriage to Anne Boleyn and she was crowned queen in 1533. More did not attend the wedding, saving the cost of a gift but earning the hatred of Anne's family. A revered martyr, More was elevated to sainthood by Pope Pius XI in 1935. He is often considered the patron saint of lawyers, his tragic manner of death perhaps reflecting what society wishes would happen to lawyers more often.

4. Henry apparently ordered More's execution before the trial even started. More was not permitted to call witnesses in his own behalf. After fifteen minutes of deliberation the jury found More guilty and he was sentenced to die. His speech in open court was much as it was presented in the movie. He stated that the Act of Supremacy was repugnant to the laws of God and the Church. On the scaffold, as in the movie, he said that he "died the king's good servant, but God's first."

10 Rillington Place

Synopsis: A simpleton is executed for murders committed by a psychopath.

Columbia Pictures, 1971. Color. Running time: 111 minutes.

Screenplay: Clive Exton. Original book: Ludovic Kennedy. Director: Richard Fleischer.

Starring: Richard Attenborough (John Christie), John Hurt (Tim Evans).

Rating: ▬▬■ ▬▬■ ▬▬■

The Story

Creepy John Christie lures women to his shabby flat at 10 Rillington Place by offering to cure their minor ailments, then he kills them. Beryl and Tim Evans, a poor and uneducated couple, move into a flat above Christie's. When Beryl becomes pregnant with the couple's second child, Christie offers to perform an abortion. Christie kills Beryl instead. After Christie convinces the gullible Tim to help hide Beryl's body, Christie frightens him into leaving town before the police arrest him for murder. Christie promises to care for the Evans' infant daughter, Geraldine, but as soon as Tim leaves, Christie kills Geraldine too.

Tim eventually goes to the police and confesses that he and Christie disposed of Beryl's body after she died during an abortion procedure. After the police find Beryl's and Geraldine's bodies, a flustered Tim admits to strangling them both. At Tim's murder trial, Christie's testimony links Tim to their deaths. Moreover, the medical examination finds no sign that Beryl had an abortion. Tim's lawyer tries to pin the deaths on Christie, but beyond showing that Christie has a string of convictions he makes little headway. Tim denies the killings, but the prosecutor destroys his credibility with the varying accounts he gave to the police. Pathetically, Tim admits that he can't explain why Christie would have strangled Beryl or Geraldine. Tim is convicted and goes to the gallows repeating "Christie done it."

Christie murders his wife and moves out of his flat. New tenants discover the remains of multiple bodies concealed in the walls. The grisly discovery leads to Christie's conviction and execution. More than a decade after Tim's execution, the government pardons him. And Rillington Place joins Elm Street as two roads to avoid if you're thinking of moving.

10 Rillington Place: Murderer John Christie (Richard Attenborough) gives perjured testimony.

*2*Copyright © 1970 Genesis Productions, Ltd. All rights reserved. Courtesy of Columbia Pictures.

Legal Analysis

No matter how fair and elaborate the criminal justice system seems to be, its elaborate procedures cannot guarantee a correct outcome. As portrayed in *10 Rillington Place,* the police conduct themselves fairly, Tim has a fair trial, and he is represented by a competent lawyer. Nevertheless, he becomes another of Christie's victims. The film's message is that sometimes innocent people are convicted and even executed, which many people in the United States consider a strong argument for abolishing capital punishment.

False confessions. Most of us believe that people do not confess to crimes, especially murder, unless they are guilty. Thus, Tim's confession had to be a major factor in the jury's conclusion that he murdered Beryl and Geraldine. Yet various rules demonstrate skepticism toward confessions. For example, the *corpus delicti* rule provides that convictions cannot be based on confessions alone. The *Miranda* rule prohibits the police from seeking a confession after a suspect has asked for a lawyer. Finally, courts exclude confessions that result from coercion.

If not the jurors, at least the judge and prosecutor had ample reason to doubt the veracity of Tim's confession. Tim was illiterate and unlikely to use the legalistic language of the confession. He was overcome by guilt for failing to protect his family. He may well have been coerced by the police. Moreover, he gave confused and conflicting accounts of what happened, and some of them were implausible. Tim's attorney did well in hammering away at Christie, but he can be faulted for not attacking the credibility of Tim's confession.

Picturing justice. While testifying at Tim's trial, Christie mentions that he has severe back pain, and the solicitous judge allows him to sit while he testifies. The irony of the judge's concern for a killer's comfort magnifies the injustice done to Tim.

Trial Brief

The film is largely factual, though in actuality Tim Evans was tried for and convicted only of killing Geraldine. Evans was not charged with killing Beryl, apparently because the prosecution feared that their history of violent quarrels might lead the jury to conclude that he was provoked into killing her and thus guilty only of manslaughter. Tim had the mental ability of an eleven-year-old, with an IQ of around 70. He was hanged in 1950 and posthumously pardoned in 1966. England abolished the death penalty around the same time, in part because of the terrible miscarriage of justice in the Tim Evans case.

In the United States, the Supreme Court has ruled that retarded persons cannot be executed (*Atkins v Virginia*, 2002). The *Atkins* rule might well have spared Tim's life had it been in effect in England at the time of his trial.

John Christie was a sexual psychopath who admitted to murdering eight women, most of whom were prostitutes. He also admitted killing Beryl Evans. Christie was tried for murdering his own wife; the defense was insanity. Christie was convicted and executed in 1953, on the same gallows as Tim Evans.

The film's gritty feeling of authenticity results from the fact that it was shot in 6 Rillington Place, next door to the site of the killings. Undoubtedly to the consternation of London tour guides but to no one else, the entire street was demolished shortly after the film was made and replaced by a public housing scheme called Rushton Mews.

The Wrong Man

Synopsis: Eyewitnesses pick out an innocent man as an armed robber.

Warner Bros., 1956. Black and white. Running time: 105 minutes.

Screenplay: Maxwell Anderson and Angus MacPhail. Director: Alfred Hitchcock.

Starring: Henry Fonda (Manny Balestrero).

Rating: ——◼ ——◼ ——◼

The Story

Manny Balestrero is a family man who stops by his life insurance company's office to arrange for a small loan. The company's employees are convinced that he's the man who recently robbed them twice at gunpoint. When Balestrero leaves they call the police, who arrest him as he's about to enter his apartment, refusing to let him tell his wife, Rose, what happened.

The police repeatedly assure Balestrero that he has nothing to worry about if he's innocent, and they really seem to believe it. They read Balestrero the holdup note and ask him to write down what it says. When Balestrero's note has the same misspelled word as the actual holdup note, and the insurance company employees identify Balestrero at a lineup, the police lock him up.

Balestrero is taken to court, where he is formally charged with armed robbery. The hearing is over almost before it starts, leaving Balestrero anxious and puzzled about what was decided. Fortunately, Rose's relatives help Balestrero make bail. Lawyer Frank O'Connor takes the case even though he has little criminal experience. That's obvious from the fact that when Balestrero mentions "the money problem," O'Connor replies, "Let's not worry about that."

At trial, the D.A.'s witnesses describe the insurance office robbery and identify Balestrero as the perpetrator, while O'Connor tries to demonstrate that the lineup was unfair. One juror is so exasperated by O'Connor's picky questions about what the other people in the lineup looked like that he stands up and denounces O'Connor for wasting everyone's time. O'Connor has to ask for a mistrial, and Balestrero is disheartened when O'Connor tells him that they'll have to start the trial all over again.

The Wrong Man: Manny Balestrero (Henry Fonda) looks for someone who'll believe he didn't do it

Balestrero finally catches a break when a police officer who arrested Balestrero asks the insurance company employees to take a look at a man who was recently arrested for the robbery of a grocery store. Sure enough, they identify the new suspect as the man who robbed them. The charges against Balestrero are dropped. However, the ordeal has been too much for Rose. She falls into a deep depression and has to be institutionalized. When she's well enough to leave, the family moves to Florida. Balestrero resolves to stay out of life insurance offices, which in Florida is no mean feat.

Legal Analysis

Stories of inmates who have served years in prison based on eyewitness identifications only to be later cleared by DNA testing have become all too common. *The Wrong Man* demonstrates how terrifying it can be for an innocent person to be shoved through the criminal justice process even if no conviction occurs. The film depicts what it's like to be interrogated, booked, arraigned, isolated in a jail cell, transported in a police wagon, and put on trial. That the police as well as the eyewitnesses act in complete good faith only increases viewers' fears that what happened to Balestrero could happen to them.

Enhancing the accuracy of eyewitness identifications. The combined efforts of cognitive psychologists, police agencies, and judges have produced pretrial identification procedures calculated to lessen the risk of mistaken eyewitness identifications. The lineup at which the insurance company employees identified Balestrero would never pass muster today. Here are some of the features of modern pretrial identification procedures that offer better protection against misidentifications:

• A defense lawyer is often present to observe the lineup process, which helps ensure that correct procedures are followed.

• Lineups are photographed. A photo or videotape enables judges and jurors to evaluate how closely the other participants in the lineup resemble the suspect.

• In the film, the eyewitnesses make the lineup identifications in each other's immediate presence. To avoid the danger that the first identifier's opinion will influence others, eyewitnesses view lineups separately and cannot communicate with each other in advance.

• Many police agencies no longer use the familiar type of lineup depicted in the film, where five or six people stand next to each other. Instead, eyewitnesses view lineup participants one at a time and see a later participant only if they fail to identify an earlier one as the perpetrator. The purpose of this process is to prevent eyewitnesses from simply identifying the participant who most resembles the person they think committed a crime.

While complete protection against human error is impossible, procedures such as these can at least lessen the risk of future Balestreros.

Bailing out. Balestrero is thrilled to be bailed out of jail so he can rejoin his family. But just as important, statistics prove that the outcomes of criminal cases are much more favorable for people who make bail before trial. *The Wrong Man* illustrates one reason for this: After he's released, Balestrero looks for the witnesses who can provide him with an iron-clad alibi for one of the robberies. (However, he comes up empty; two of the witnesses have died and he can't find the third.)

Picturing justice. (1) When Balestrero is in jail, he leans with his back to the cell wall. The dark shadow of one of the cell's bars falls across his neck. The shadow seems to be a rope, suggesting that Balestrero has already been found guilty and executed even before he appears in court. (2) As the trial testimony unfolds, Balestrero is one of the few people in the courtroom who appear to pay attention. The prosecutor and his assistant doodle and chat, and police officers joke with one another. The image suggests that while the proceedings may be life-altering for Balestrero, for the "professionals" it's just another in a long line of routine, humdrum cases.

Trial Brief

Alone among Hitchcock's films, *The Wrong Man* closely tracks a real story. Manny Balestrero was wrongly charged with armed robbery in New York in 1953. Hitchcock was fascinated by the story because he had a lifelong fear of the police and jails. Balestrero's defense attorney, Frank O'Connor, later became the District Attorney for the borough of Queens. Balestrero's trial ended with a juror's mid-trial outburst, just as the film depicts. A week later, the man who actually robbed the insurance company office confessed and Balestrero was freed. The locations in the film, including the courtroom, are those where the real events took place.

Short Subjects

Unashamed, 1932. Helen Twelvetrees, Robert Young.

Hostility to female sexual freedom leads an all-male jury to acquit Dick Ogden of murder. Ogden shot the man who was after his sister Joan for her money. Joan initially contradicts Ogden's phony testimony that the gun fired accidentally, then saves his life at the cost of her reputation. Against Ogden's wishes, Joan testifies that he was protecting the family's honor after finding out that Joan and the victim spent the night together in a hotel room. *Courtroom highlights*: (1) The prosecutor's thunderous opening statement warns the jurors not to apply the "unwritten law" but concludes by acknowledging that he doesn't know whether Ogden will rely on that defense. (2) During the prosecutor's cross-examination, Ogden is unable to demonstrate how the gun fired accidentally. *Picturing justice*: Ogden's lawyer, Trask, suborns perjury from Ogden, Joan, and the family cook. Yet, Trask abides by Ogden's wishes to keep Joan out of the trial, which until Joan comes forward on her own prevents Trask from relying on an unwritten-law defense.

Vera Drake, 2004. Imelda Staunton. 2 gavels. ——■ ——■

In 1950s England, rich women can get safe and legal abortions, but poor women must resort to dangerous back-alley procedures. Vera Drake is a kindly housecleaner who performs abortions to help desperate women, but does not ask for money. Completely intimidated by the police and the criminal justice system, she confesses and pleads guilty at her trial. The judge imposes the maximum sentence as a deterrent to others. *Picturing justice*: As the judge pronounces the sentence, the camera closes in on the stunned and tear-stained faces of Drake and her family. *Trial brief*: The film was nominated for three Academy Awards.

Experts or Charlatans?

The explosion in scientific and technical knowledge has been matched (some may say exceeded) by the number of forensic experts willing to bestow their learning and experience on judges and jurors—for a price.

The legal system has long allowed properly qualified experts to testify on issues that judges and jurors can't resolve accurately by using their own knowledge and common sense. Of course, judges and jurors still have to fall back on their common sense to figure out which side's experts are more reliable. Thus, psychiatrists offer opinions on the sanity of killers (*Anatomy of a Murder, Primal Fear, The Amazing Dr. Clitterhouse, Compulsion, Final Analysis*) and of people who make socially questionable choices (*Nuts, Whose Life Is It Anyway? Miracle on 34th Street, Mr. Deeds Goes to Town*). Psychologists testify to living arrangements that would serve children's best interests (*Losing Isaiah, I Am Sam*). Doctors testify to the cause of death (*An Act of Murder*), to the reason that a patient fell into a coma (*The Verdict*), and to the cause of a patient's paralysis (*The People vs. Dr. Kildare*).

Films also suggest some of the more esoteric subjects that can properly be the subject of expert testimony. These include how to interpret tire marks (*My Cousin Vinny*), the habits and abilities of dingos (*A Cry in the Dark*), whether environmental poisons were the cause of disease (*A Civil Action, Erin Brockovich*), the source of sperm (*Presumed Innocent*), the odor of expensive scotch (*The Young Philadelphians*), and the interpretation of the Bible (*Inherit the Wind*).

While respecting experts' legitimate contributions, judges are wary of charlatans peddling "junk science." For example, should a judge allow the testimony of a person who claims expertise about the symptoms of possession by the devil (*The Exorcism of Emily Rose*)?

Traditionally, judges have required that technical or scientific principles be generally accepted by experts themselves before those principles could be testified to in court. Critics of this rule have pointed out that it would have prevented Galileo from testifying that the world was round, because that principle was not generally accepted in Galileo's day. The modern rule allows judges to accept testimony based on principles that the judge believes are reliable, regardless of whether a body of experts concurs. This rule may be more flexible, but it puts a heavier burden on judges to distinguish good science from junk science.

Ironically, the pressure on lawyers to produce expert testimony may emanate as much from popular culture as from attorneys' desire to win. Movies and television shows often glamorize forensic experts and depict them using sophisticated equipment to implicate and exonerate suspects. As a result, jurors may distrust claims that are not backed up by forensic evidence that may in reality be unavailable or too costly.

Anatomy of a Murder

Synopsis: A murder trial focuses on whether the victim raped the defendant's wife and on the defendant's mental condition at the time of the killing.

Columbia Films, 1959. Black and white. Running time: 161 minutes.

Screenplay: Wendell Mayes. Original book: Robert Traver. Director: Otto Preminger. Jazz Score: Duke Ellington.

Starring: James Stewart (Paul Biegler), Ben Gazzara (Lieutenant Frederick Manion), George C. Scott (Claude Dancer), Lee Remick (Laura Manion), Joseph N. Welch (Judge Weaver).

Academy Award nominations: Best Picture, Best Actor (James Stewart), Best Supporting Actor (Arthur O'Connell, George C. Scott), Best Screenplay, Best Cinematography, Best Editing.

Rating:

The Story

Army Lieutenant Frederick Manion is charged with murdering Barney Quill, who owned the Thunder Bay Inn. Manion's lawyer, Paul Biegler, tells Manion about the four types of defenses to murder and advises him that three don't apply to his case. Biegler's "lecture" helps Manion decide that he went crazy after his wife, Laura, told him that Quill had beaten and raped her. Biegler prefers fishing to practicing law, and it's lucky for him that the seductive Laura doesn't have gills, or he might get hooked for a serious ethical gaffe.

Icy prosecutor Claude Dancer's witnesses testify that Manion appeared calm and rational when he shot Quill. Dancer's evidence also suggests that Manion was a hothead who beat up Laura and shot Quill after finding out that they had been having an affair. An army psychiatrist supports the defense by testifying that Manion shot Quill in the grip of "irresistible impulse," a form of temporary insanity. However, Biegler's inability to produce Laura's panties, which Quill supposedly ripped off her, casts doubt on the rape story.

*　*　*

SPOILER ALERT: You may not want to read further if you plan to see the film.

*　*　*

Surprise defense witness Mary Pilant, who manages the Thunder Bay Inn, brings Laura's torn panties to court and testifies that she found them in the Inn's laundry chute the morning after Quill was killed. Dancer immediately accuses Pilant of lying. He insists that Pilant and Quill were lovers and that she is crucifying Quill's character because he'd cheated on her with Laura. When Pilant starts to explain, "Barney Quill was my—" Dancer shouts out the fatal one question too many: "Barney Quill was your *what,* Miss Pilant?" Pilant softly responds: "Barney Quill was my father." His theory shot to pieces, Dancer slinks back to the counsel table. The jury finds Manion not guilty by reason of insanity.

Biegler drives out to the Manions' trailer to collect his fee, but all he finds is a note informing him that they had an irresistible impulse to leave town quickly. Biegler had forgotten the part of the lecture that says that criminal-defense lawyers should always get paid in advance.

Legal Analysis

The film is perhaps the grittiest and most compelling trial movie ever made. Featuring eloquent attorneys, great acting, and sharp writing, the film depicts the courtroom as an arena filled with drama and suspense. The apparent miscarriage of justice might also lead viewers to question the deep-rooted American mythology that the best way for truth to emerge is through no-holds-barred courtroom combat.

Irresistible impulse. The widely used "M'Naghten Rule" defines insanity as the inability to distinguish right from wrong. Irresistible impulse, by contrast, regards insanity as mental disease that impairs the power to choose. Under the irresistible-impulse test, Manion was not guilty by reason of insanity if Quill's attack on Laura prevented Manion from controlling his conduct, even if he realized that killing Quill was wrong. However, many states do not allow the irresistible-impulse defense, in part because psychiatrists have no way to measure a person's capacity for self-control.

Dancer's questionable strategies. Dancer should have attacked Manion's irresistible-impulse defense head-on by calling a psychiatrist to testify that Manion (a war veteran) had plenty of time to control his impulses. And though he was surprised by Pilant's answer that Quill was her father, Dancer might have recognized that the answer undermined the rest of her story. If Pilant's father had just been brutally gunned down, would she be sorting clothes in the laundry the very next morning? Isn't it more likely that she found the panties a day or two later, giving someone, perhaps Laura, time to plant them there?

Biegler's questionable strategy. Biegler should realize that the lapse of time between the time Manion saw Laura and killed Quill substantially weakens his irresistible-impulse defense. Therefore, Biegler should have given the jurors a middle-ground alternative to finding him either not guilty or guilty of murder, a "heat of passion" defense. If the jurors concluded that Manion acted in the heat of passion, the result would be a conviction for manslaughter, a much less serious crime than murder.

The "lecture." Before asking Manion to tell him what happened, Biegler lectures him about the "letter of the law." It's fine for Biegler to tell Manion about the possible defenses to murder. After all, if lawyers couldn't inform clients of relevant legal principles, sophisticated clients would have an advantage over those without experience.

After concluding the lecture, however, Biegler doesn't ask Manion what happened, but rather asks Manion, "What's your excuse for killing Quill?"—suggesting that Manion must have one. When Manion asks whether he's getting warmer when he says he must have been crazy, Biegler surely should realize that his client is lying.

Yet Biegler doesn't respond with another lecture about the need for truth-telling. (He apparently kept that lecture locked away in a dusty file labeled "Myths I Learned in Law School.") Instead he tells Manion to think about how crazy he really was. While many criminal-defense and other lawyers defend Biegler's tactics, most legal ethicists believe that he slid over the line and suborned perjury.

Picturing justice. Judge Weaver subtly controls the lawyers by giving them leeway to pursue their theories while cutting off intemperate remarks and redundant or improper questions. Judge Weaver is courteous to the attorneys and witnesses alike, and his rulings are fair to both sides. His humanity shines through; he's reached an exalted social position, but he never flaunts it. Courtroom films and real courtrooms would benefit equally by the presence of more Judge Weavers.

Trial Briefs

1. Robert Traver, the author of the book on which the film is based, is a pseudonym for Justice John Voelker, who was an associate justice of the Michigan Supreme Court from 1956 to 1960. Voelker also wrote several books about trout fishing. The book and film are based on a 1952 murder trial in which Voelker appeared as defense counsel. He represented Lieutenant Peterson, who was charged with the fatal shooting of Maurice Chenoweth, a tavern owner. Peterson was found not guilty by reason of insanity. In 1960, Chenowith's widow, Hazel Wheeler, and Chenoweth's illegitimate daughter, Terry Ann Chenoweth, sued both the book publisher and Columbia Pictures for defamation and invasion of privacy. The court ruled that people who knew Hazel and Terry Ann would not confuse them with characters in the book or the film and dismissed the case.

2. Judge Weaver was played by Joseph N. Welch, a Boston lawyer who became a national figure as counsel for the army in the "Army-McCarthy hearings" in 1954. The hearings, one of the first nationwide events to be broadcast live on television, pitted Welch against "red baiter" Senator Joseph McCarthy at the height of the Cold War. At one point, McCarthy mentioned that a young associate of Welch's firm had once been a member of the National Lawyers Guild, which McCarthy identified as a Communist organization. Welch responded, "Let us not assassinate the character of this young lad further, Senator. You have done enough. Have you no sense of decency, sir? At long last, have you left no sense of decency?" Welch's words became the symbol of the hearings, depicting McCarthy as a reckless bully. Many historians mark Welch's response to McCarthy as the beginning of the end for McCarthyism. Welch's inclusion in the film effectively enhanced its

authenticity. The famous exchange appears in the films *Point of Order* (1964) and *Good Night and Good Luck* (2005).

3. *The Hays Code.* American movies made between 1934 and 1968 were subject to the Production Code, or the Hays Code, which required extreme discretion in the treatment of sexual matters and insisted that crime could never pay (see Sidebar: The Production Code). For its time, *Anatomy of a Murder* was extremely explicit about sex. For example, the characters make repeated references to Laura's panties, and Biegler holds them up for all to see. The film hints that Laura had an extramarital affair, yet she was not punished for it. Even more significant, Manion apparently got away with murder. Chicago's Board of Censors tried to prevent the film from being shown on the grounds of obscenity, but a federal district judge overturned the ban.

Anatomy of a Murder would never have survived in anything close to its final version had the Production Code been strictly enforced. However, by the late 1950s, code enforcement was breaking down. One important reason was that American filmmakers had begun to flout the code and get away with it. Among the most significant challengers was *Anatomy*'s director, Otto Preminger. Preminger despised censorship and had already released two successful films without code approval: *The Moon Is Blue* (1953), a racy comedy that created a sensation by using the word "virgin," and *The Man with the Golden Arm* (1955), a brutal drama about heroin addiction. The censors may have felt that they had to pass *Anatomy of a Murder* or Preminger would defy them again.

The Production Code

Movies have been engulfed in culture wars since the first silents flickered on the silver screen. People have always worried that films will corrupt the young, promote violence, or destroy social values. As a result, from the earliest times, both public and private systems of movie censorship emerged. In 1915, the U.S. Supreme Court held that the First Amendment did not apply to movies (*Mutual Film Corporation v. Ohio Industrial Commission*), so local governments could freely censor them—and many did. Many foreign governments also censored American films. In addition, the Catholic Church discouraged the faithful from attending movies that the Church thought were bad for them, and these recommendations had a major effect on box-office revenues of the banned films.

These censorship systems posed major problems for Hollywood studios. They decided to blunt the effect of censorship by adopting a system of self-regulation. In 1930, the studios adopted a code consisting of a set of principles that filmmakers were supposed to follow. The code (initially called the Hays Code after Will Hays, who was then head of the studios' trade association) was ineffective because it had no workable enforcement mechanism. As a result, the films of the early 1930s were quite lurid. Moreover, filmmakers ignored the code because the Depression radically reduced the number of people who could afford to buy tickets. Instead, people stayed home and listened to the radio. At the same time, the studios faced huge expenditures in converting from silent films to sound, so within a few years several studios were bankrupt. And the sexy and violent films that did come out in the early 1930s set off new waves of censorship.

The industry solved its censorship problem in 1934 by adopting an enforcement mechanism for the Hays Code. No picture could be exhibited in theaters without first being approved by the Production Office, headed by Joseph Breen. Literally every word of movie scripts, as well as every song lyric and costume, was scrutinized by Breen and his staff. The system came to be called "The Production Code." The code worked because the Catholic Church and the various local and foreign government censors trusted the Production Office to clean up the films.

The Production Code was quite effective for about twenty years, but for several reasons it began to break down in the 1950s. First, in 1952 the U.S. Supreme Court ruled that films were protected speech under the First Amendment (*Joseph Burstyn Inc. v. Wilson*). That knocked out the local censorship boards that had tormented filmmakers for decades. Second, the onset of television meant that filmmakers needed to put content on the screen that people couldn't see for free at home. Third, foreign films weren't subject to censorship, and they began to take an increasing share of the market. Fourth, Breen's successors were more flexible about applying the code. Fifth, some filmmakers, such as Otto Preminger, confronted the code by releasing unapproved pictures. (See Trial Brief for *Anatomy of a Murder*.) These filmmakers were able to find theaters willing to exhibit unapproved films, and the films did well at the box office. Ultimately, the code became a nuisance and an embarrassment to the industry and was abandoned in 1968. It was replaced by the ratings system that still exists today.

Of course, the Production Code couldn't remove sex, crime, and violence from movies, or there would have been nothing left to make films about. However, the code required that sex had to be treated with extreme discretion. Coarse language was never permitted. People could engage in brief closed-mouth kisses, but all the rest of the action had to be suggested rather than shown. Double entendres or off-color comments were ruthlessly pruned from scripts. Even married couples always slept in separate beds, and bathrooms never had toilets. If people engaged in sex outside of marriage, they had to be punished for it, either through disgrace or death (this especially applied to women). And some sexual themes could never be shown at all. These included homosexual relationships and abortion.

A second important requirement of the Production Code was that crime couldn't pay. Criminals never got away with their misdeeds and were always punished or killed by the end of the film. Related to the rules about crime were that law enforcement officials (such as prosecutors or judges) could never be held up to ridicule. Thus early-1930s pictures like *Night Court*, which involved a corrupt judge, could never be made under the code.

The Production Code was written by Catholics (a priest and a prominent Catholic layman were its authors) and administered by Catholics (Breen was well connected to the Church hierarchy). This made sense, because Hollywood was trying to give its self-regulatory system credibility with the Church. As a result, the Production Office interpreted vague language in the code about preserving family values as a prohibition on serious treatment of divorce. The theory, apparently, was that if people didn't see movies about divorce, they wouldn't get divorced. Thus for many years, divorce as it really existed simply didn't appear in the movies. Couples with troubled marriages always got back together (as in films like *Penny Serenade*). If couples got divorced, they remarried by the end of the film (as in *The Philadelphia Story* or *The Awful Truth*). In the rare cases in which a character was allowed to get and stay divorced (generally because the other spouse had committed adultery), the guilty spouse was punished by a life of misery and disgrace. Serious films about divorce reappeared only in the late 1970s (as in *Kramer vs. Kramer*) and are quite common today.

The Production Code deeply influenced every film made from 1934 to the mid-1950s and had at least some effect on films made from the mid-1950s to 1968. Even today, opinions differ about whether the code was a good or a bad thing. Of course, the code interfered with the creative process and prevented the industry from dealing realistically with important issues like sexuality, divorce, or crime. Yet, great films were made during the Production Code years, including many that dealt with mature themes, because filmmakers found ways to get around its restrictions. Since the code disappeared, movies have become much more coarse and extremely violent. As they did a century ago, culture wars continue to rage around the movies, and they probably always will.

A Cry in the Dark

Synopsis: A mother charged with killing her baby claims that a dingo did it.

Cannon International, 1988. Color. Running time: 122 minutes.

Screenplay: Robert Caswell and Fred Schepisi. Original book: John Bryson. Director: Fred Schepisi.

Starring: Meryl Streep (Lindy Chamberlain), Sam Neill (Michael Chamberlain).

Academy Award nomination: Best Actress (Meryl Streep).

Rating: ——▪ ——▪ ——▪

The Story

Michael and Lindy Chamberlain and their three children go camping near Ayers (now Uluru) Rock, one of Australia's prime tourist sites. When Lindy hears a cry coming from the tent and goes to check on their infant Azaria, she sees a dingo run out of the tent with Azaria in its mouth. Her anguished cry, "A dingo took my baby," leads to a massive search, but Azaria is never found.

Michael and Lindy, both Seventh-Day Adventists, seek comfort in their religious beliefs, while the Aussie media seek comfort in profits.

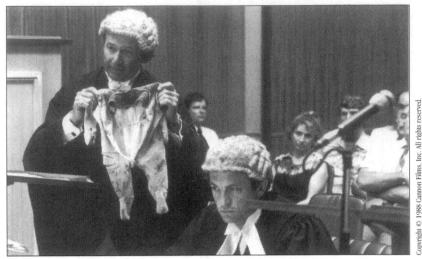

A Cry in the Dark: Prosecutor Baker (Bruce Myles) displays the bloody jumpsuit.

Journalists swoop down on the Chamberlains. Many of the resulting stories are sensationalist and inaccurate and emphasize the Chamberlains' unfamiliar religious beliefs. Soon many Aussies believe that Lindy sacrificed Azaria as part of a bizarre religious ritual and even gave her a name that means "sacrifice in the wilderness." The discovery of Azaria's bloody jumpsuit in the rugged countryside near Ayers Rock converts the whispers into a murder investigation. Lindy is charged with Azaria's murder, and Michael with being an accessory for helping her conceal the crime.

Prosecutor Barker's case relies entirely on forensic experts, but their testimony is conflicting, confusing, and boring to the jurors and the media. For example, traces of an infant's blood are found in the Chamberlains' car, but it might have come from vomit or nasal secretions and could even be rust residue rather than blood. Also in dispute is whether the holes in Azaria's jumpsuit were made by a dingo's teeth or by scissors. Similarly, experts disagree about the behavior of dingoes and about whether a dingo is capable of picking up an infant by her head, as Lindy claims it did. All that's clear is that a dingo is a poor choice for a household pet.

Michael's and Lindy's testimony goes badly. Lindy is hostile and aggressive, and Michael is weary and confused, at one point testifying that Lindy said she saw nothing in the dingo's mouth. Despite the judge summing up the evidence in a way that favors them, both Lindy and Michael are convicted. Lindy is sentenced to life imprisonment, and Michael receives a suspended sentence.

A few years later, the police find near Ayers Rock the jacket that Lindy testified Azaria wore over her jumpsuit. The jacket explains the absence of dingo saliva on the jumpsuit. Lindy is immediately freed, and the Northern Territory Court of Appeals unanimously exonerated the Chamberlains of all charges, eight years after Azaria disappeared.

Legal Analysis

Many people hope that science and technology will be more capable than eyewitness testimony of proving "what really happened." The most sobering aspect of *A Cry in the Dark* is that scientific evidence is no panacea. The experts who testified at the Chamberlain trial could not agree on how to interpret the evidence, and much of their testimony was technical and mystifying to the jurors.

Forensic experts. Advances in science and technology that enable experts to "say more and more about less and less" have made expert testimony increasingly common in both civil and criminal cases. This has led to concerns about the ability of lay jurors to pay attention to, comprehend, and evaluate their testimony. A big danger is that jurors will ignore the substance of experts' testimony in favor of their person ality traits, such as which expert seems more sincere or self-assured.

An additional problem is that criminal cases based on expert testimony are often stacked in favor of the government, which can afford to operate costly crime labs; defendants typically can't pay for their own analyses. Another concern about expert testimony is the risk that it's for sale. If the price is right, lawyers can often find an expert to testify to almost anything.

The judge sums up. Along with *Let Him Have It* (discussed in Chapter 2), *A Cry in the Dark* depicts the uniquely British tradition of the judge "summing up" before sending the jurors off to deliberate. In each film, the judge's summary not only includes a recapitulation of important evidence but also provides insight into the judge's own evaluation of the credibility and reliability of the testimony. The judge's summary in *A Cry in the Dark* was extremely favorable to the Chamberlains, but apparently it had little impact on the verdict.

Picturing justice. While the jurors deliberate, a copy of a tabloid headlining the Chamberlain case rests on a chair in the jury room. The image suggests that the media frenzy was responsible for the guilty verdicts.

Trial Briefs

1. The film accurately depicts some of the complex forensic evidence that occupied many of the seven weeks of trial. The film does not show the many defense witnesses who testified that Lindy was a loving mother to Azaria. Nor does it show two defense witnesses who testified that dingoes had attacked their children in the vicinity of Ayers Rock around the same time that Azaria disappeared.

2. Following Lindy's release, the Chamberlains petitioned for compensation. Lindy eventually received about $900,000, and Michael received about $400,000. The long ordeal severely strained the Chamberlains' relationship, and they divorced. Lindy remarried an American (also a Seventh-Day Adventist) and became Lindy Chamberlain-Creighton. The couple lived in Seattle for some time and later moved to Hunter Valley, Australia.

3. Fueled by lingering suspicions that Lindy might be guilty, many Australians remain interested in the case. The story was the subject of a four-hour TV mini-series in 2004.

Inherit the Wind

Synopsis: Science and religion clash in the famous Scopes Monkey Trial.

United Artists, 1960. Black and white. Running time: 127 minutes.

Screenplay: Nathan E. Douglas and Harold Jacob Smith. Original play: Jerome Lawrence and Robert E. Lee. Director: Stanley Kramer.

Starring: Spencer Tracy (Henry Drummond), Fredric March (Matthew Harrison Brady), Gene Kelly (E. K. Hornbeck).

Academy Award nominations: Best Actor (Spencer Tracy), Best Screenplay, Best Cinematography, Best Editing.

Rating: ———■ ——■ ——■ ——■

The Story

A 1925 Tennessee law forbids the teaching of "any theory that denies the story of the divine creation of man as taught in the Bible, and to teach instead that man has descended from a lower order of animals."

Inherit the Wind: Henry Drummond (Spencer Tracy) examines Matthew Harrison Brady (Fredric March) about nonliteral interpretation of the Bible.

The law was no doubt opposed by many lower orders of animals. Bert Cates is arrested for teaching evolution to a high school class, and hordes of true believers descend on the small town of "Heavenly Hillsboro" to watch the courtroom fireworks and brimstone.

Heading the prosecution team is former three-time presidential candidate and religious fundamentalist Matthew Harrison Brady. Famed atheist Henry Drummond represents Cates. Brady believes that Drummond's participation will magnify his triumph: "If Saint George had slain a dragonfly instead of a dragon, who would have noticed?" Coyly explaining to Brady why he twice campaigned for him but now opposes him, Drummond says, "That's evolution for you."

Drummond concedes that Cates taught evolution and seeks to call leading scientists and theologians to testify that evolution is consistent with the biblical story of creation. When the judge rules that their testimony is irrelevant, Drummond argues that the law makes a fair trial impossible: "You cannot administer a wicked law impartially. A wicked law destroys everybody, its upholders as well as its defiers. If you can make it a crime to teach about evolution in public schools, soon it'll be a crime to teach about it in the private schools. Then it'll be a crime to read about it. If you can do one you can do the other, because fanaticism and ignorance are forever hungry and need feeding. And soon, with banners flying and drums beating, we'll be marching backwards through the glorious ages of the sixteenth century when bigots burned the man who dared to bring enlightenment and intelligence to the human mind."

Drummond stuns Brady by calling him as an expert on the Bible. He confronts Brady with some of the Bible's seemingly implausible stories, such as Joshua stopping the sun in the sky, but Brady insists that everything in the Bible is literally true. Brady also testifies that the Creation began no more than a few thousand years ago. However, Brady admits that the first day may have been longer than twenty-four hours, because the sun was not created until the fourth day. The first day may even have been as long as *Ishtar*. The admission leaves open the possibility that creation went on for millions of years before man appeared, so that the Creation and evolution may indeed be compatible. Nevertheless, Cates is convicted, but the only punishment is a fine of one hundred dollars.

Legal Analysis

Inherit the Wind brilliantly dramatizes the Scopes Monkey Trial's historic clash between scientific theory and religious fundamentalism and between expert witnesses (including Brady) who differed on the validity of evolutionary theory and the compatibility of evolution with the biblical story of creation. Henry Drummond is one of film's most heroic lawyers. He remains humane in the face of the community's hostility. He is passionate, but his arguments appeal to reason, not to emotion and prejudice. As Drummond argues, "An idea is a greater monument than a cathedral."

The constitutionality of the Tennessee law. The judge improperly refused to consider the constitutionality of the Tennessee law. Every judge has the responsibility to decide constitutional issues that arise in the cases that come before them. Like most important constitutional controversies, the Tennessee law implicated two conflicting principles. On the one hand, a state has the right to decide what will be taught in its public schools. On the other hand, the law threatened to breach the separation of church and state. In 1925, the "establishment clause" in the First Amendment to the U.S. Constitution applied only to laws enacted by Congress, not to state laws. However, the judge should have considered whether the law violated similar provisions in the Tennessee constitution.

Over the next several decades, the U.S. Supreme Court applied most provisions of the Bill of Rights to the states, including the establishment clause. However, the Court did not resolve the conflict over whether a state can prohibit the teaching of evolution, until *Epperson v. Arkansas* (1968). That case decided that an Arkansas law almost identical to the Tennessee law was unconstitutional because it promoted the views of a particular religious group. Later, in *Edwards v. Aguillard* (1987), the Court invalidated a Louisiana law requiring that "creation science" be taught alongside evolution. Today, the issue of how evolution should be taught in the public schools remains as contentious as in 1925. School boards continue to fight over whether to teach evolution as scientific fact or as merely a theory, and whether to teach the theory of "intelligent design" alongside evolution.

Picturing justice. (1) The judge issues only a small fine after Hillsboro's mayor advises him that state politicians want the case to go away quietly. (2) As the film ends, Drummond walks out of the empty courtroom carrying a Bible and Darwin's book on evolution. The imagery suggests that the courtroom is not the place to resolve disputes about the validity of scientific theories or about the clash between religion and science.

Trial Briefs

1. For all its notoriety, the Scopes case was a setup. The American Civil Liberties Union was anxious to challenge the antievolution law, and the business leaders of the small Tennessee town of Dayton ("Hillsboro") wanted to host the trial to drum up business. The ACLU advertised for a teacher willing to violate the law, and John Scopes ("Bert Cates") volunteered. Scopes was a recent college graduate who was the football coach and a substitute biology teacher. He believed in the principles of evolution, but as a substitute he had not actually taught the subject. He agreed to be arrested so that the law could be tested in court, and after being arrested he went back to his tennis game. His students didn't want to get him in trouble, so Scopes had to persuade them to testify that he had taught them about evolution so the case could go to trial.

2. Fundamentalist preacher and lawyer William Jennings Bryan ("Brady") was not a trial attorney, but he participated so that he could deliver a stirring closing argument. Although Bryan lost three elections as

the Democratic candidate for president, he was secretary of state under President Woodrow Wilson. Bryan was known as "The Great Commoner" because of his belief in the wisdom of everyday people and his distrust of experts. He supported the right of people to bypass the legislature and enact laws through the initiative process and also supported women's suffrage, prohibition, and a national income tax.

Bryan was not a scientist and was unfamiliar with the scientific principles of evolution. His fight against the teaching of evolution was based on more than religious fundamentalism. It was inspired partly by his opposition to the theories of Herbert Spencer. Spencer argued that only the fittest humans deserved to survive and that the races of superior human beings had the obligation to rule over the inferior ones. Spencer's theory later became known as "social darwinism," although it has little in common with Charles Darwin's theory of evolutionary biology. The Great Commoner saw the fight against the teaching of Darwinian evolution as a way to stop the spread of the loathsome theory of social darwinism.

3. Clarence Darrow ("Drummond") was one of the most gifted orators ever to appear in American courtrooms. He devoted most of his career to representing socially marginalized clients. Several other well-known attorneys also defended Scopes, including Dudley Field Malone and Arthur Garfield Hays. All of them served without fee.

4. Many of the film's memorable lines are taken from the transcript of the Scopes case. For instance, Drummond's "marching backwards through the glorious ages" argument closely parallels one that Darrow made to the judge. As in the film, after Darrow showed him a rock full of fossils, Bryan testified: "I am more interested in the Rock of Ages than I am in the age of rocks."

5. Darrow's cross-examination of Bryan took place on a platform outside the courthouse in front of hundreds of spectators because the temperature inside the courtroom was unbearable. The jury was not present when Bryan testified. After Bryan testified for two hours, the judge ruled that his testimony was irrelevant because the only issue was whether Scopes had taught evolution and thus violated the law.

6. After the judge ruled that the testimony of the defense experts and Bryan was irrelevant, Darrow waived his final argument and asked the jury to convict Scopes to pave the way for an appeal. Darrow's tactic prevented Bryan from delivering the final argument he had worked on for months. It was published after his death.

7. The Tennessee Supreme Court upheld the antievolution law on the ground that the state had the power to decide what could be taught in public schools. It rejected the defense argument that the law

violated the portion of the Tennessee constitution providing that the state would "cherish science." The court also denied that the law established a religious preference. However, the court reversed Scopes' conviction on a technical but convenient ground: Tennessee law required that a fine in excess of fifty dollars must be imposed by the jury rather than the judge. The court informally advised the Dayton prosecutor to dismiss the case, because Scopes had already moved out of Tennessee. The outcome disappointed the ACLU because it prevented further appeals. The antievolution law remained on the books in Tennessee until 1967, but nobody other than Scopes was ever prosecuted.

8. The film depicts Bryan dying in mid-speech on the courthouse floor, just after the trial concludes, an account that is close to the truth. Bryan embarked on a round of speeches in defense of fundamentalism. He died of apoplexy while taking a nap after one of these speeches, five days after the trial concluded.

9. The announcement of the verdict was the first event to be nationally broadcast live on radio.

Nuts

Synopsis: A belligerent prostitute tries to prove that she's competent to stand trial.

Warner Bros., 1987. Color. Running time: 116 minutes.

Screenplay: Tom Topor, Darryl Ponicsan, and Alvin Sargent. Play: Tom Topor. Director: Martin Ritt.

Starring: Barbra Streisand (Claudia Draper), Richard Dreyfuss (Aaron Levinsky).

Rating:

The Story

Claudia Draper, a New York prostitute from an affluent background, killed a client after a fight. Draper is charged with manslaughter but has a plausible self-defense claim. Her behavior is hostile and erratic, and Dr. Morrison, the examining physician at Bellevue Hospital where Draper is confined, believes that she is not competent to stand trial. Her mother, Rose, her stepfather, Arthur, and the lawyer they've hired all agree.

In court for a competency hearing, Draper punches her lawyer in the nose, and the lawyer immediately withdraws from the case. The judge spots legal-aid lawyer Aaron Levinsky in the courtroom and orders him to represent Draper. Levinsky gets a postponement so he can meet with Draper and perhaps buy a nose guard. When the competency hearing resumes, Morrison testifies that Draper is paranoid, a danger to herself and others, and unable to understand the legal proceedings or assist in her own defense. Draper's outbursts constantly interrupt the hearing. Prosecutor MacMillan, who also thinks Draper needs treatment, offers testimony from Rose that Draper was a promiscuous drug abuser as a teenager. When stepfather Arthur testifies to his love for Draper, however, Levinsky forces him to admit that he also sexually molested her.

Draper testifies and demonstrates understanding both of the manslaughter charges and of the consequences of being found incompetent. Levinsky concedes, "My client is a real pain in the ass. . . . She is ill-mannered, and she is irritating, . . . but we shouldn't confuse her behavior with her capacity to stand trial." Judge Murdoch reluctantly concludes that Draper is competent to stand trial.

Legal Analysis

At the core of *Nuts* is the moral issue of society's right to force treatment on people who either do not want it or don't think they need it. Draper is belligerent and antisocial. Perhaps medications could lessen her hostility; perhaps therapy could persuade her to change careers. Yet Draper argues that her lifestyle is her own business. If she's guilty of manslaughter, she has a right to be *punished*, not *treated*, no matter what others think is best for her.

But the answer to the punishment versus treatment question is not so clear. If Draper truly is suffering from serious mental disease, she can't make decisions about her own treatment. The streets in big cities are full of homeless people who once would have been institutionalized but who have been turned loose to fend for themselves. Someone has to decide whether they are "nuts." Yet too broad a definition of mental illness poses a risk of characterizing antisocial behavior as mental illness. Doing so may result in the institutionalization of people who are competent and entitled to live as they see fit.

Competence to stand trial. For the criminal justice system to be fair and respectful of Draper's autonomy, she must be capable of comprehending what is happening at trial and of helping her lawyer prepare a defense. As a practical matter, many defendants who might be able to establish an insanity defense at trial are diverted into mental institutions because a pretrial hearing establishes that they are not competent to stand trial. In most cases, of course, the defendant's lawyer argues that the client is *not* competent, in order to get treatment for the client and keep her out of jail. *Nuts* is the rare case in which the defendant insists on being tried for a crime rather than be treated for mental illness.

The difficult client. *Nuts* illustrates the difficulties that lawyers (especially court-appointed lawyers like Levinsky) face when they have to represent uncommunicative or hostile clients like Draper. Unless Draper trusts Lewinsky enough to share embarrassing or even harmful information, a successful defense is unlikely. Levinsky, however, triumphs even though Draper discloses almost nothing to him, even her stepfather's sexual abuse. As a result, Levinsky unwittingly elicits damaging information, such as Dr. Morrison's disclosure that Draper punched another patient at Bellevue.

Picturing justice. (1) Morrison is paternalistic, and he confuses Draper's antisocial behavior with mental illness. Indeed, filmmakers often use the courtroom to portray government psychiatrists or social workers as pompous and meddlesome, as in *Losing Isaiah* and *I Am Sam*, discussed in this book. (For a similar attitude in a classic non-courtroom film, see *A Thousand Clowns*.) (2) Out on the street awaiting trial, Draper walks among people behaving bizarrely. The scene underlines the film's message about the uncertain dividing line between mental illness and eccentricity.

Presumed Innocent

Synopsis: A prosecutor is charged with committing a murder that he was investigating.

Warner Bros., 1990. Color. Running time: 127 minutes.

Screenplay: Frank Pierson and Alan J. Pakula. Original book: Scott Turow. Director: Alan J. Pakula.

Starring: Harrison Ford (Rusty Sabich), Raul Julia (Sandy Stern).

Rating: ⚖ ⚖ ⚖

The Story

Assistant prosecutor Carolyn Polhemus is brutally murdered. D.A. Raymond Horgan asks Rusty Sabich, his chief deputy, to oversee the investigation. Sabich works on the case with his cop buddy, Detective Lipranzer. Lipranzer tells Sabich that Polhemus was "bad news." Because both Horgan and Sabich had been sleeping with Polhemus, apparently they didn't think so.

The hunter becomes the hunted, and Sabich is charged with murdering Polhemus. Sabich's lawyer is his frequent courtroom adversary, Sandy Stern. At the trial, Horgan protects his rear by falsely testifying that Sabich insisted on taking charge of the Polhemus investigation in order to sabotage it. Lipranzer testifies honestly but reluctantly that Sabich neglected to have a bar glass found in Polhemus' apartment tested for fingerprints and had also asked Lipranzer to conceal the records of phone calls made from his house to Polhemus' apartment.

Forensic analysis provides the strongest evidence linking Sabich to Polhemus' death. Sabich was a likely source of semen found in Polhemus' vagina. The police found a strand of Polhemus' hair on Sabich's jacket, and fibers from a carpet in Sabich's house on Polhemus' bloody skirt. Finally, Sabich's fingerprints were on the bar glass. However, prosecutor Nicco Della Guardia admits that he has no idea what's become of the glass. Stern then annihilates the prosecutor's pathologist by showing that the semen he tested could not have come from Polhemus' vagina. The semen sample contained a spermicide. Yet Polhemus had had her fallopian tubes tied years earlier and would not have used a spermicide. Infuriated by the prosecution's bumbling, Judge Lyttle dismisses the charges.

* * *

SPOILER ALERT: You may not want to read further if you plan to see the film.

* * *

Sabich uses his freedom to do some work around the house and finds a bloody hammer in the bottom of his toolbox. His wife, Barbara, confesses to him that she used it to kill Polhemus. She framed Sabich by leaving one of their bar glasses in Polhemus' kitchen and planting Sabich's sperm in Polhemus' vagina. Barbara assures Sabich that she was "prepared to tell the truth" at some point. Whether she would have confessed had Sabich been convicted, and whether Della Guardia would have believed her, are questions left for viewers to ponder.

Presumed Innocent: Sandy Stern (Raul Julia) confers with Rusty Sabich (Harrison Ford) and his wife, Barbara (Bonnie Bedelia).

The film concludes with Sabich's voice-over message: "The murder of Carolyn Polhemus remains unsolved. It is a practical impossibility to try two people for the same crime. Even if it wasn't, I couldn't take his mother from my son."

Legal Analysis

Sabich assures his son, "This trial is going to give me a chance to clear myself." The irony of the film's title is that Sabich has no way to do that. Because Judge Lyttle dismisses the case before it gets to the jury, Sabich will no doubt continue to be "presumed guilty." Surely the public will interpret the dismissal as due to a technicality or as the system protecting one of its own.

For lawyers too the result is unsatisfying, because a just result was achieved though unjust means. Stern helped bring about the dismissal by committing extortion, advising Judge Lyttle that he knew a secret: Polhemus and the judge had once been involved in a bribery scheme. And Della Guardia couldn't produce the bar glass in court because

Lipranzer had unlawfully concealed it by hiding the glass in his desk drawer. Thus, the legal system produced the right result only because a defense lawyer and a cop were willing to break the law.

A viewer who, like a juror, is trying to figure out who killed Polhemus is likely to confine the possible suspects to Sabich, Horgan, and Judge Lyttle. Thus, the film's surprise ending works in part because of a second irony about the title. As a loving wife and mother, Barbara may be the only character who is truly "presumed innocent."

Wrongful dismissal. Even without the discredited forensic evidence indicating that Sabich and Polhemus had sex before she was murdered, Della Guardia had more than enough evidence to survive Stern's motion to dismiss the charge. The balance of the forensic evidence (involving hair and carpet fibers), Sabich's hiding of the phone-call records, and his failure to test the bar glass for fingerprints would have been sufficient to take the case to the jury. Yet there's no way for Della Guardia to appeal the dismissal. Once Judge Lyttle dismisses the case, the double-jeopardy rule protects Sabich from being tried again for the murder of Polhemus. Of course, Barbara could be charged with Polhemus' murder. The double-jeopardy clause protection is "one per customer" not "one per family." However, there is no evidence against Barbara, and Sabich couldn't testify to her confession even if he wanted to, because of the spousal privilege.

If Della Guardia had a hammer . . . he probably would have hammered out a guilty verdict, because the hammer was stained with Polhemus' blood and came from Sabich's toolbox. Barbara no doubt intended for the police to find the hammer when they searched the house. Of course, the surprise ending requires the police not to find the hammer. To make this appear plausible, Sabich explains that the police wouldn't have searched for a murder weapon because the jury might infer from their failure to find it that Sabich is not guilty. However, this explanation is silly. Della Guardia's inability to produce the murder weapon weakens his case whether the police searched for it or not.

Don't ask, don't tell. Before trial, Sabich insists to Stern that he's innocent. Stern stares at him silently. Sabich immediately regrets what he said, realizing that he sounds no different from all Stern's other clients, most of whom were undoubtedly guilty. Stern says nothing, because Sabich's claim of innocence is irrelevant. As a seasoned defense attorney, his main concern is what the state can prove.

Stereotypes about female lawyers. The portrayal of Carolyn Polhemus is viciously stereotypical. She moved up the ladder in the

D.A.'s office by sleeping with Sabich and Horgan. Female lawyers could do without the portrayal of another glamorous female cine-lawyer who gets ahead by selecting the right sex partners.

Picturing justice. The film begins and ends with the austere image of an empty courtroom. At the beginning, Sabich's voice-over solemnly explains that if a jury "cannot find the truth, what is our hope of justice?" With Judge Lyttle and Polhemus implicated in bribery, Stern in extortion, Horgan committing perjury, and Lipranzer concealing evidence, the film suggests that an empty courtroom may offer our best hope for justice.

Primal Fear

Synopsis: A defendant changes personalities while on trial for murder.

Paramount Pictures, 1996. Color. Running time: 129 minutes.

Screenplay: Steve Shagan and Ann Biderman. Original story: William Diehl. Director: Gregory Hoblit.

Starring: Richard Gere (Martin Vail), Laura Linney (Janet Venable), Edward Norton (Aaron Stampler).

Academy Award nomination: Best Supporting Actor (Edward Norton).

Rating:

The Story

Aaron Stampler, a former altar boy, is charged with the brutal murder of Archbishop Rushman. Recognizing a golden opportunity for publicity, hotshot Chicago lawyer Martin Vail represents Stampler for free. Stampler insists that he's innocent and that at the time of the murder he just happened to be at Rushman's house to return a book.

Prosecutor Janet Venable offers expert testimony that Rushman's blood was all over Stampler's clothes and that the pattern of bloody footprints makes it probable that only Stampler was in the room with Rushman when he was killed. When Vail finds a videotape depicting Rushman in the act of forcing Stampler and others to engage in sex, Vail gives it to Venable to show that others had a motive to kill Rushman. Because the videotape also shows that Stampler had a motive to kill Rushman, Venable offers it into evidence.

Paramount Pictures/Photofest.

Primal Fear: Martin Vail (Richard Gere) opposes prosecutor Janet Venable (Laura Linney).

During a strategy session with Vail, Stampler suddenly changes from a meek stutterer into a belligerent psychopath. "Aaron" becomes "Roy," and as Roy he mocks Aaron and is proud that he murdered Rushman. Dr. Arrington, Stampler's psychologist, wants to testify that Stampler suffers from multiple personality disorder, but the judge rules that Vail can't change the plea to insanity in mid-trial. But Vail has an alternate way of proving insanity. Vail calls Stampler as a witness, and as the meek "Aaron" he testifies that he didn't kill Rushman. Then, as Vail anticipated, Venable tears into Stampler during cross-examination. As Venable belittles him, Aaron suddenly turns back into Roy and leaps at Venable. The shaken judge dismisses the jury and finds Stampler not guilty by reason of insanity.

* * *

SPOILER ALERT: You may not want to read further if you plan to see the film.

* * *

Pleased by the success of his strategy, Vail gives Stampler the good news that he'll probably be quickly released from the state mental hospital. Stampler gloats that he's fooled everyone into thinking he has dual personalities. Stampler didn't change personalities, he was Roy all along. He killed Rushman and made up the meek Aaron persona to create a defense. Vail slinks off, probably thinking that in the future he'll need his own new personality, one that's a lot less arrogant.

Legal Analysis

Primal Fear is another courtroom film in which the formal legal system gets it all wrong. In this instance, an obviously guilty defendant games all the trial participants, including a psychologist, into concluding that he's not guilty by reason of insanity. Because the film inclines viewers to see the case from Vail's perspective, we too are likely to feel that we've been had.

Pleas be on time. Judge Sloat's ruling to the contrary, Illinois law allows for mid-trial changes of plea. Because Vail became aware of Stampler's seeming personality disorder only after the trial was in progress, Judge Sloat abused her discretion by forbidding Vail to change the plea to not guilty by reason of insanity. The insanity defense was crucial, and Vail acted diligently and in good faith. Assuming she had allowed the plea change, the judge could then order a continuance to give Venable's expert a chance to examine Stampler.

Was Stampler legally insane? Under the Illinois test of insanity, a person is not criminally responsible if "as a result of mental disease or mental defect, he lacks substantial capacity to appreciate the criminality of his conduct." Assuming that Stampler really had a multiple personality disorder, whether he would be legally insane under this definition is unclear. If the jury concluded that the meek Aaron personality was the primary or "host" personality and that he did not plan or participate in the offense, he could be found not guilty. And if the jury concluded that the Roy personality was in control, it might have concluded that Roy was insane because he could not appreciate the criminality of his conduct.

Illinois law offers an alternative that does not exist in most states and is not mentioned in the film. An Illinois jury can find a defendant "guilty but mentally ill" (GBMI). A defendant is GBMI if he suffers "from a substantial disorder of thought, mood, or behavior" that impaired his judgment. GBMI defendants are sentenced to prison, not confined in a mental institution, but the court can require psychiatric treatment in prison or recommend other sentencing alternatives. A GBMI finding also makes it unlikely that a defendant will receive the death penalty. In practice, GBMI may often be a compromise verdict when jurors can't decide between guilty and not guilty by reason of insanity.

Photo finished. Vail objects to Venable's plan to show the gruesome close-up photos of Rushman's bloody body to the jury. Judges are supposed to exclude evidence if its appeal to a juror's emotions outweighs its probative value. As one law scholar put it, judges should exclude evidence that is likely to make jurors vomit. Judge Sloat overrules the objection, and most judges probably would do so as well. The photos demonstrate the ferocity of the act and thus are probative of the killer's intent.

Back so soon? After Judge Sloat pronounces Stampler not guilty by reason of insanity, Venable protests that he'll probably be back out on the streets in thirty days. The judge responds, "Take it up with the legislature." This response helps to explain why jurors might be reluctant to find defendants not guilty by reason of insanity. In reality, Stampler would remain institutionalized until mental health professionals decided that he is no longer dangerous. Given the heinous nature of the crime, he'd probably be locked away for many years—perhaps even longer than if he'd been found guilty and sentenced to prison!

Picturing justice. A number carved into Rushman's body leads the police to an underlined passage in the book *The Scarlet Letter*. Read into the record at trial, the passage says: "No man . . . can wear one face to himself and another to the multitude without finally getting bewildered as to which may be the truth." The image of two faces underlies the entire film. Rushman is publicly a pious man, but privately he is a sexual monster. Stampler has at least two faces. Shaughnessy, Venable's boss, publicly enforces the law while privately trying to line his own pockets by manipulating real-estate developments. To the public, Vail is a brilliant criminal-defense lawyer and Chicago's most eligible bachelor. In private, Vail seems to have no personal life beyond work, materialism, and publicity-seeking. Ultimately, even the criminal justice system is two-faced. Outwardly it appears to be a powerful institution, but inwardly it is fooled by a murderer.

Short Subjects

An Act of Murder (aka ***Live Today for Tomorrow***), 1948. Fredric March, Edmond O'Brien. ——▌ ——▌ ——▌

Judge Calvin Cooke intentionally crashes his car and kills his wife to spare her from a painful impending death. As tough on himself as he is with criminal defendants, Cooke demands to be charged with murder, planning to represent himself and plead guilty. Defense attorney Dave Douglas, who has frequently clashed with Cooke, convinces Judge Ogden to appoint him as Cooke's attorney. Douglas dates Cooke's daughter, and Cooke would no doubt have preferred that Douglas be thrown in jail for contempt of courting. Douglas saves Cooke's life by showing that Cooke's wife knew that she was going to die and was already dead from an overdose at the time of the crash. The case is dismissed. *Courtroom highlight:* A reformed Cooke promises that, if he remains a judge, in his court "a man shall be judged not alone by the law, but by the heart as well." *Picturing justice:* A sympathetically portrayed police officer shoots a severely injured dog to put it out of its misery. The scene suggests that Judge Cooke's attempt to kill his wife is an equally legitimate act of euthanasia. *Trial brief:* Judge Cooke was not guilty even of attempted murder. One cannot be convicted of an attempt to commit a crime that was impossible to commit.

The Amazing Dr. Clitterhouse, 1938. Edward G. Robinson, Humphrey Bogart. ——■ ——■

To gather data for a book about the physiological effects of criminal activity on the perpetrators, Dr. Clitterhouse joins a gang of burglars and runs around measuring their vital signs as they carry out crimes. When Rocks Valentine, the gang's male CEO, tries to stop Clitterhouse from publishing his findings, Clitterhouse kills him and is tried for murder. *Courtroom highlights:* (1) A shrink's psychobabble so confuses the jurors that they interrupt their deliberations to question Clitterhouse. (2) Clitterhouse's testimony that he's sane convinces the jurors that he's insane. *Picturing justice:* Asked by Clitterhouse whether she thinks her gang activities are wrong, Jo, the gang's female CEO, connects with the film's Depression-era audience by talking about larger social injustices: "Would you ask that same question of a stock promoter who robs widows and orphans, or one of them society mugs who owns a lot of them firetrap tenement houses? . . . The way I look at it, me, you, all of us here are more on the level than those guys."

The Exorcism of Emily Rose, 2005. Tom Wilkinson, Laura Linney. ——■ ——■

This film is the first attempt to fuse the horror and courtroom genres, though admittedly some courtroom films have been horrible. Father Moore's trial for negligently allowing Emily Rose to die provides a platform for arguments about science versus religion. Rose was either psychotic or possessed, and defense attorney Erin Bruner argues that Moore did his best to save Rose's life by performing an exorcism. After weighing the testimony of experts in medicine and possession, the jury convicts Moore but asks that he be sentenced to time served. *Courtroom highlight*: Bruner tries to align herself with skeptical jurors (and viewers) by arguing that a not-guilty verdict is compatible with doubt about the reality of possession. *Picturing justice*: (1) The attorneys and the judge are competent and realistically combative. (2) Redeemed by the case, Bruner turns down a partnership with a greedy law firm and accepts tea instead of alcohol as her beverage of choice. *Trial brief*: The film is based on the case of Anneliese Michel, an epileptic German teenager. Michel died of starvation in 1976 after several exorcisms had taken place, leading to criminal charges against the two priests involved. The Church initially approved of the exorcism, but after the priests were convicted denied that Michel was possessed.

Final Analysis, 1992. Richard Gere, Kim Basinger, Uma Thurman.

The film trashes psychiatric experts and, like so many other films, suggests that justice has to be found somewhere other than inside a courtroom. In this film it's found in a fall from the top of a very tall lighthouse. *Courtroom highlight*: The defendant's claim that she was temporarily insane when she killed her husband with a barbell leads prosecution and defense psychiatrists to argue the existence of "pathological intoxication." Neither expert seems qualified to testify to the time of day. *Trial brief*: Very few jurisdictions recognize voluntary intoxication as mitigation for committing a crime.

Miracle on 34th Sreet, 1947. Edmund Gwenn, Natalie Wood.

A department store Santa Claus claims to be the real thing. He's a bit odd, and he punches another employee (substituting a K.O. for a HoHo). At a commitment hearing, the judge believes that "Santa" is bonkers but is afraid that he'll be voted back to private practice if he rules that Santa Claus doesn't exist. The judge is saved by the mail when the post office delivers thousands of letters addressed to Santa Claus to the courtroom. The judge rules that the federal government's conclusion that Santa is real is binding on him. *Picturing justice*: "Santa's" attorney, Fred Gailey, quits his cushy law firm job to represent "Santa" for free and urges his friends to believe in the power of imagination. If Santa could really have this effect on lawyers, undoubtedly more people would believe in him. *Trial brief*: The film was remade in 1994, but the original is superior.

Whose Life Is It Anyway?, 1981. Richard Dreyfuss, John Cassavetes.

—■ —■

A trial crystallizes right-to-die arguments. Ken Harrison, a successful sculptor, is paralyzed from the neck down as the result of an automobile accident. Harrison is unwilling to spend years attached to tubes and watching television; perhaps he sensed the popularity of reality shows in the future. Harrison demands to be released from the hospital so he can die in peace. The hospital refuses, and at a hearing its psychiatrist testifies that Harrison's desire to die is itself evidence that he's not mentally capable of making that decision. *Picturing justice*: Judge Wyler pores over other judges' opinions before deciding that Harrison has a right to leave the hospital. This suggests the centrality of precedent in our legal system. *Trial brief*: In *Cruzan v. Missouri* (1990), the U.S. Supreme Court decided that competent patients have a right to refuse medical treatment. Yet no constitutional right to die exists, and at present only Oregon has a law that in very limited circumstances allows doctors to provide life-ending medication to terminally-ill patients who ask for it. The validity of the Oregon law was upheld by the Supreme Court in 2006.

Courtroom Comedies

Law and lawyers are so pervasive in American life and popular culture that they invite parody. Numerous courtroom comedies have responded enthusiastically to that invitation.

One way to produce laughs is to insert an "outsider" who doesn't know the rules into a highly regulated setting such as a courtroom or law school classroom, as in *My Cousin Vinny, Bananas, Legally Blonde, Trial and Error, The Advocate,* and *Disorder in the Court.* True to the pattern that courtroom films often use trials to explore social issues, comedies have commented on the role of women lawyers (*Legally Blonde, Adam's Rib, She Couldn't Say No*), the plight of the common man up against giant economic forces (*The Castle*), and male chauvinism (*How to Murder Your Wife*). The courtroom can also poke serious fun at really bad lawyer behavior (*From the Hip, Liar Liar*). These films are funniest when they play with familiar trial conventions, such as how to dress for court (*My Cousin Vinny*), how to take the witness oath (*Disorder in the Court*), how to phrase questions (*Trial and Error*), and how to break witnesses down on cross-examination (*Bananas, Legally Blonde*). These comedic films are a welcome respite from the often deadly serious courtroom genre.

Adam's Rib

Synopsis: Married lawyers turn a trial into a battleground for sexual equality.

MGM, 1949. Black and white. Running time: 101 minutes.

Screenplay: Ruth Gordon and Garson Kanin. Director: George Cukor.

Starring: Spencer Tracy (Adam Bonner), Katharine Hepburn (Amanda Bonner), Judy Holliday (Doris Attinger).

Academy Award nomination: Best Screenplay.

Rating:

The Story

Doris Attinger accosts husband Warren in the apartment of his mistress Beryl. After hurriedly consulting an instruction manual, Doris fires a gun wildly around the apartment. Doris means only to scare Warren and Beryl into stopping the affair, but she hits Warren with a stray bullet and is charged with attempted murder.

Prosecutor Adam Bonner insists to his wife, Amanda, that Doris had no right to take the law into her own hands. Amanda, also a lawyer, is equally adamant that Doris should benefit from the same "unwritten law" that protects husbands who shoot philandering wives. When Adam is assigned to prosecute Doris, Amanda decides to defend her.

At trial, Amanda's wit triumphs over Adam's conventional style. When Beryl claims that Warren was in her apartment only to peddle health and accident insurance, Amanda comments, "He showed remarkable foresight in this, wouldn't you say?" To prove that women are equal to men, Amanda calls women who testify to their successful careers. The last is a circus performer who demonstrates her strength by hoisting Adam above her head. It's Adam's high point in the trial. Finally, although Warren insists he was a good husband, Amanda forces him to concede that he regularly criticized Doris for being too fat, stayed out all night, and struck her. Warren points out that Doris often hit him when he was asleep: "This caused me great stress, also sleepless nights." However, Doris never stayed out all night: "I wish she had."

Amanda argues for equality of the sexes while asking the jurors to imagine Doris as a two timed husband, Beryl as a male lothario, and Warren as a wife. The jurors accept her unwritten-law argument and find Doris not guilty.

Meanwhile, the Bonners' marriage has been on trial along with Doris. After moving out, Adam returns to find next-door neighbor Kip with Amanda. Adam pulls a gun on them, forcing Amanda to scream that he has no right to take the law into his own hands. Satisfied that he has been proven right after all, Adam puts the gun into his mouth and takes a big bite out of it; it's made of licorice. As they meet with

Adam's Rib: Doris Attinger's (Judy Holliday) hat is not the only thing standing between Adam and Amanda Bonner (Spencer Tracy and Katharine Hepburn).

their accountant to discuss their joint tax return, Amanda and Adam realize they remain very much in love, proving that tax law is a potent aphrodisiac.

Legal Analysis

In this delightful comedy, the trial setting promotes sexual equality through witty banter and courtroom theatrics. Warren and Doris appear destined to reunite, so with Adam and Amanda also back together, the film supplies two happy endings for the price of one.

A great female cine-lawyer. Amanda is an able courtroom litigator, committed to Doris' defense, creative and emotional, yet sensitive in her arguments. Outside court, she can handle elegant parties and obnoxious neighbors with equal aplomb. When the film was made, very few women practiced law, and only a few obscure movies had featured women lawyers. Women lawyers are now common movie characters, but Amanda Bonner remains the most positive movie female lawyer role model of all time.

Doris' culpability. Even if Doris didn't intend to hurt Warren, she could still be guilty of attempted murder because spraying bullets around the apartment constituted reckless disregard for human life. Amanda might have urged the jury to convict Doris only of attempted manslaughter, a much less serious crime, because she acted in the "heat of passion" in a desperate effort to save her family. Adam's probable response would have been that Doris was not suddenly provoked, because she had trailed Warren for hours and expected to find him in Beryl's arms.

Amanda probably pinned her real hopes on jury nullification. Although attorneys cannot explicitly ask jurors to disregard legal rules, jurors have the inherent right to acquit defendants even if they are technically guilty. The jury in *Adam's Rib* heard lots of evidence about Warren's mistreatment of Doris, and he wasn't hurt all that badly. In the circumstances, the jurors might have decided to find Doris not guilty no matter what the rules said.

Can spouses actually represent opposing parties at trial? Some states formally forbid lawyer-spouses from appearing in court on behalf of opposing parties, especially in criminal cases. Underlying the ban is a concern about the appearance of impropriety and the risk that spouses will compromise their clients' interests. However, so long as lawyers disclose the situation to their clients and obtain their written consent, most states allow married lawyers to decide for themselves when they can effectively represent opposing interests.

In *Adam's Rib,* Amanda is able to push Adam's buttons in court in a way that no unrelated defense lawyer could have done. For example, during a heated courtroom exchange Amanda slyly refers to Adam by his pet name, "Pinky." Adam becomes flustered by the court reporter's questions about who Pinky is and whether Pinky ends in "y" or "ie." Thus, while the image of lawyers who litigate by day and conjugate by night is essential to the story of *Adam's Rib,* most lawyers try to avoid such situations.

Picturing justice. (1) Upset with Amanda's courtroom theatrics, Adam tells her that she's got "contempt of the law." "The law is the law whether it's good or bad. If it's bad, the thing to do is change it. Start with one law, then pretty soon it's all laws, then pretty soon it's everything, then it's me." Lawyers call this a "slippery slope" argument: One small misstep now will inevitably lead to a host of negative consequences. Adam's tirade, however, is more an avalanche than a slippery slope. (2) A drawing of a stage with curtains pops up at the beginning of the film and between scenes. The theatrical image may undercut

Amanda's strong image by reminding viewers that her character is more fantasy than reality.

Trial Brief

The so-called unwritten law that gave men the right to kill when they discovered that their wives were having an affair reflected old assumptions that husbands owned wives and were entitled to protect their property. The defense dates back at least to ancient Greece. Records exist of one case in which Euphiletus was charged with murder after killing his wife's lover. He argued that he should not be punished because the lover had seduced his wife and he had caught them in the lovemaking act, or as lawyers sometimes like to say *in flagrante delicto*. Surviving records don't indicate whether the Athenian jury bought the argument.

The unwritten law was once recognized by statute in Texas, Utah, and New Mexico. The statutes provided a complete defense to homicide if the husband caught his wife *in flagrante delicto*. Although no other states formally adopted the unwritten law, lawyers often successfully argued it to juries. In addition, juries sometimes accepted the defense when a father or a brother killed an unmarried daughter's or sister's seducer. Defense lawyers sometimes supplemented an unwritten law defense by trying to establish that killers were temporarily insane, as in the notorious 1906 trial of Harry Thaw for the murder of famous architect Stanford White (a former lover of Thaw's glamorous wife Evelyn Nesbit). Films depicting Thaw's case include *The Girl on the Red Velvet Swing* (1955) and *Ragtime* (1981). The unwritten law defense was rarely, if ever, successfully used by a wife who killed her husband's lover

Bananas

Synopsis: A nerd protests the Vietnam War and is tried for treason.

United Artists, 1971. Color. Running time: 82 minutes.

Screenplay: Woody Allen and Mickey Rose. Director: Woody Allen.

Starring: Woody Allen (Fielding Mellish).

Rating: ——◼ ——◼ ——◼

Bananas: Fielding Mellish (Woody Allen) finds little difference between a courtroom and a jungle.

The Story

Fielding Mellish participates in anti–Vietnam War demonstrations to impress a girl. When she dumps him, Mellish runs off to the small South American country of San Marcos and becomes part of a group of rebels trying to overthrow the latest in a long line of dictators. The revolution succeeds when the dictator mistakenly seeks assistance from the UJA (United Jewish Appeal) instead of the CIA, and Mellish becomes president of San Marcos. Mellish returns to the United States seeking foreign aid. His fake Fidel Castro–like beard fools no one, and he is charged with treason for having protested the Vietnam War.

A prosecution witness testifies unexpectedly that Mellish is a "warm, wonderful human being." However, according to the court reporter the witness testified that Mellish was "a rotten, conniving, dishonest little rat." Miss America performs a song and offers her opinion that Mellish is a traitor because his views are different from those of the president: "Differences of opinion should be tolerated, but not when they are too different." A final witness testifies that she heard Mellish make treasonous remarks. Mellish, who by this time is tied to his chair and gagged, mumbles unintelligible cross-examination questions at her. Nevertheless, she breaks down and confesses that she lied. Mellish is convicted by the pot-smoking jurors. The judge suspends the sentence on the condition that Mellish not move into his neighborhood.

Legal Analysis

Bananas creates laughs by lampooning features of the trial process as depicted in popular culture. For example, almost all the 271 *Perry Mason* television shows starring Raymond Burr featured Mason extracting a confession during cross-examination. Films in which aggressive cross-examinations induce witnesses to confess include *A Few Good Men* and *Young Mr. Lincoln.* Dramatic triumphs like these rarely occur in actual trials. Indeed, many cross-examiners are relieved if their questioning doesn't remind adverse witnesses that "your client also committed war crimes." *Bananas* spoofs the power of cross-examination by having the witness fall apart in response to unintelligible questions.

Flexibility of the courtroom genre. Like the practice of law itself, the courtroom film genre is chameleon-like, adaptable to whatever serious or comic points a filmmaker wants to make. As a result, *Bananas* simultaneously parodies the genre and other aspects of American culture. For example, Miss America's testimony is legally absurd while her canned manner of testifying and her stereotypical opinion satirize the beauty pageant industry. Similarly, by having a witness testify that Mellish is a "New York Jewish intellectual Communist crackpot," writer/director/star Woody Allen makes a humorous comment both about his own image and that of antiwar demonstrators.

Testimony by *pro se* litigants. Representing himself, Mellish testifies by asking questions while standing and then racing into the witness box to answer them. (*Lucky Partners,* a 1940 comedy, has a similar scene.) Fortunately, in actual cases self-represented litigants are usually allowed to testify in narrative form. In one recent trial, however, a *pro se* litigant in a discrimination case was required to state the question that she planned to ask herself before actually asking and answering it, so as to give the opposing lawyer the opportunity to object!

Did Mellish commit treason? No. Article 3, section 3, of the U.S. Constitution defines treason as (1) levying war against the United

States or (2) giving aid and comfort to an enemy. An enemy is a country against which the United States has declared war. Because the United States never declared war on Vietnam, Mellish could not have been convicted of treason under either rationale.

Conditions of probation. While probation often comes with strings attached, the condition that Mellish not move into the judge's neighborhood is not legitimate because it is not reasonably related to the activity giving rise to the conviction. The judge's order is, however, a humorous comment on a serious issue. Few communities want serious offenders (especially sexual offenders) released in their midst, resulting in often-bitter conflicts between rights of the community and rights of individuals.

Picturing justice. The court reporter's total alteration of a witness' testimony is a reminder that litigants are truly at their mercy, because appellate court judges cannot review what actually happened at trial, only what court reporters record as having happened.

The Castle

Synopsis: A tenacious Australian fights to keep his home from becoming a freight terminal.

Village Roadshow, 1997. Color. Running time: 82 minutes.

Screenplay: Santo Cilauro, Tom Gleisner, Jane Kennedy, and Rob Sitch. *Director*: Rob Sitch.

Starring: Michael Caton (Darryl Kerrigan), Charles "Bud" Tingwell (Lawrence Hammill).

Rating:

The Story

Just as a baby may have a face that only a mother could love, the Kerrigans live in a house that only they can love. The house abuts an airport runway and is built on toxic waste and under high-voltage power lines. It does, however, have room for their greyhounds. Then Airlink, a joint government/private company, announces plans to buy all the houses in the area to make way for a freight terminal. Head of household Darryl Kerrigan refuses to sell, though his greyhounds might have jumped at the offer.

Kerrigan asks the Administrative Appeals Tribunal to block the sale, but he represents himself and is hopelessly naïve. Asked by a starchy judge for his legal theory, Kerrigan replies that it's "obvious. . . . The law of bloody common sense. . . . A man's home is his castle. . . . You can't just walk in and steal our home. . . ." The result is obvious to the judge too, and he rules against Kerrigan.

Local solicitor Dennis Denuto appeals Kerrigan's case to federal court, but even in an inch of water Denuto would be out of his depth. Denuto claims that Airlink's demand is unconstitutional, but his only authority is "the vibes of the constitution." Unable to catch the vibes, the federal judge too rules against Kerrigan.

Lawrence Hammill, a retired queen's counsel (a QC is a particularly eminent barrister) who specializes in constitutional law, takes Kerrigan's case for free to the High Court in Canberra (Australia's Supreme Court). Hammill eloquently argues that property can be seized only on "just terms" and that taking a man's home to build a freight terminal isn't "just terms" because "you can acquire a house, but you can't acquire a home. Because a home is not just built of bricks and mortar, but of love and memories. You can't pay for it." The court decides in Kerrigan's favor. He continues improving The Castle and expanding his tow-truck business. Denuto moves on to fame and fortune, displaying an office nameplate announcing that he's "Dennis Denuto as Seen on TV." The Kerrigans' greyhounds are the big losers; unfortunately, they had no legal representation.

Legal Analysis

The Castle generates laughter while telling an inspiring story of a tenacious client and a laudable lawyer. Darryl Kerrigan fights for principle against mighty opponents and long odds. He argues to the Administrative Appeals Tribunal: "The law is supposed to be about justice and fairness. . . . This is not iffy. . . . It is right and fair that a family be allowed to live in its own house. That is justice." Law and justice are often miles apart (especially in most courtroom movies), but the High Court's decision in Kerrigan's case unites them. Kerrigan joins the pantheon of heroic movie clients who risk everything for a principle, along with such worthies as Bertram Cates in *Inherit the Wind* and Arthur Winslow in *The Winslow Boy*.

Lawrence Hammill's great skill and eloquence win a smashing victory. Hammill also turns out to be a great guy who graciously shares the glory with Denuto and befriends the working-class Kerrigans. Hammill deserves a place in the pantheon of lawyer heroes, along with Vinny Gambini in *My Cousin Vinny* and Atticus Finch in *To Kill a Mockingbird*. Dennis Denuto, on the other hand, should never be allowed within one mile of the courthouse.

Australian aborigines. In a frantic effort to make a legal argument in federal court, Denuto cites Australia's famous *Mabo* case, decided by the High Court in 1992. *Mabo* was the first case in which the High Court recognized that aborigines had valid claims for lands that were seized by white settlers. Historically, the lands occupied by aborigines were considered *terra nullius*, meaning they could be seized by whites at will. *Mabo* rejected the *terra nullius* fiction and ruled that the aborigines had to be compensated for their lost lands. The case turned Australian land law upside down, and its legal and political impact is still being felt.

Before his own land dispute, Kerrigan had probably never given a single thought to the plight of the aborigines, many of whom are stuck on the bottom rung of Australian society. However, disheartened by his loss in federal court, Kerrigan suddenly sees things from their point of view: "I'm really starting to understand how the aborigines feel. . . . Well, this house is like their land. It holds their memories. The land is their story. It's everything. You can't just pick it up and plunk it down somewhere else. This country has to stop stealing other people's land." Of course, the difference is that the state offered to compensate Kerrigan for his house; until *Mabo*, nobody ever thought about compensating the aborigines.

Compulsory acquisition. While the story of *The Castle* is quite stirring, it is legal nonsense. A person whose house is seized by the government through the process of compulsory acquisition (Americans call it "eminent domain") cannot stop the process. The property owner is entitled to fair compensation, but no more. Otherwise, public projects could never be built. There would be no highways, airports, or high-voltage power lines if a single stubborn property owner could stop the process.

The High Court's decision in Kerrigan's case is based on a provision in the Australian constitution. Section 51, paragraph 31, provides: "Parliament shall have power to make laws with respect to acquisition of property on just terms." Hammill argues: "How can forcible removal of a family, a good family, from their home have the blessing of our constitution? How can that be just terms?" However, this constitutional provision merely empowers the parliament to make laws for compulsory acquisition of property on just terms, meaning that property owners must receive fair compensation. The provision does not empower judges to stop a project because they consider it unjust.

Picturing justice. Denuto's appearance before the federal court is agonizing. He is terrified and completely unprepared. He shuffles frantically through his papers and cites a constitutional provision relating to copyrights. Hammill, on the other hand, is eloquent, well prepared, and utterly unflappable before the High Court, even when Denuto slips him a note offering him a glass of water in the middle of his argument. Thus the film reinforces what most viewers already believe: It sure helps if you have a great lawyer to argue your case.

Trial Briefs

1. The Administrative Appeals Tribunal, or AAT, is a unique Australian institution that allows parties to challenge every sort of administrative action. The AAT's jurisdiction includes the amount of compensation to be paid for a compulsory acquisition (as in Kerrigan's case), but it also covers disputes relating to revocation of professional licenses, veterans' benefits, deportation, taxation, and many others. The AAT provides an inexpensive forum where people can secure justice when they claim government has treated them unfairly. If they lose in the AAT, they can seek judicial review, as Kerrigan did. The AAT's procedures are informal, and many people represent themselves.

2. The Fifth Amendment to the U.S. Constitution provides: ". . . nor shall private property be taken for public use, without just compensation." In *Kelo v. City of New London* (2005), the U.S. Supreme Court interpreted this provision to mean that a city can seize private property and turn it over to private developers, so long as just compensation is paid and the seizure is for a public purpose, such as urban renewal. The 5-to-4 decision caused immediate controversy. In response to *Kelo*, many states considered amending their own constitutions to bar such takings. The freight terminal in *The Castle* apparently would have been owned by a government agency rather than by private parties, although private interests were financing it. The fact that private parties would profit from the seizure probably influenced the High Court decision that stopped the seizure of the Kerrigans' house.

From the Hip

Synopsis: A hotshot associate learns that trials are not always fun and games.

Columbia Pictures, 1987. Color. Running time: 95 minutes.

Screenplay: David E. Kelley and Bob Clark. Director: Bob Clark.

Starring: Judd Nelson (Robin "Stormy" Weathers), John Hurt (Professor Douglas Benoit).

Rating: ——⚖ ——⚖ ——⚖

The Story

"Stormy" Weathers fulfills a childhood (and popular-culture-fueled) ambition by becoming a first-year associate in a prestigious law firm: "When other kids were playing cowboys and Indians, I was playing plaintiff and defendant. I want to go to trial, I want to object and be sustained, I want to pace up and down and wave my arms around and pound on tables and do all that lawyer stuff."

Weathers schemes his way into his first trial representing Torkenson, a bank president who has been sued for slapping a colleague. Weathers' courtroom tactics consist of "trial and terror." He badgers the judge, engages in shoving matches with opposing counsel, hurls books containing the word "ass" around the courtroom, and disparages the plaintiff's sexuality. (Actually, the entertaining show was a complete phony, because Weathers and his opposing counsel choreographed it in advance.) When the jury rules in favor of Torkenson, Weathers becomes a media celebrity.

Professor Douglas Benoit is so impressed by Weathers' courtroom skills that he demands that the law firm assign his case to Weathers. Benoit is charged with murdering Liza Williams, a prostitute whose body has never been found. Benoit proclaims his innocence, but the facts are stacked against him. Williams was blackmailing Benoit, witnesses heard Benoit threatening Williams on the night she disappeared, and the police found a bloody hammer and Williams' bloody clothes under the front seat of Benoit's car. Weathers is reluctant to take on such a serious case, but Benoit pressures him into handling the defense.

Weathers' opening statement is unorthodox. He swings the hammer wildly, nearly decapitating a few jurors before smashing it into the

From the Hip: Stormy Weathers (Judd Nelson) and opposing counsel Matt Cowens (Richard Zobel) fake their courtroom theatrics.

counsel table. Demonstrating that she runs a tight ship, the judge orders Weathers to pay for table repairs.

Weathers' inexperience shows when he overlooks an obvious hearsay objection and allows Williams' mother to testify that her daughter said that Benoit made death threats. When Weathers mumbles a question softly in an effort to show that another witness has poor hearing, the witness repeats the question word for word. And when Weathers claims that if the witness had been in a bar late at night he must have been drunk, the witness retorts, "I had just arrived at the bar. I'm the night cleaner."

At this low point, Weathers suddenly morphs into the notorious Stormy, as though he were Superman emerging from a phone booth. He scores points by ridiculing an expert witness with irrelevant questions about bat guano. To counter a police officer's testimony that Benoit must have known that the hammer and clothes were under his car seat, Weathers pulls a caged rabbit from under the witness chair. Most dramatically, Weathers promises the jury that the murder victim will walk into the courtroom in fifteen seconds. She doesn't, but everyone looks expectantly at the courtroom doors. That gives Weathers a chance to argue to the jurors: "You all looked, and if you thought for the slightest fraction that she could come through that door, then you have a reasonable doubt."

* * *

SPOILER ALERT: You may not want to read further if you plan to see the film.

* * *

Finally understanding that Benoit is a psychotic killer, Weathers goads him into testifying and belittles his sexuality on the stand. Enraged, Benoit leaps at Weathers with the hammer. Having at last glimpsed the real Benoit, the jury convicts him of first-degree murder while the judge sentences Weathers to the slammer for ten days for contempt of court. Luckily Weathers didn't get ten days per antic or he would have ended up serving more time than Benoit.

Legal Analysis

From the Hip turns from a madcap parody to a serious commentary on the apparent conflict between law and morality. As a criminal-defense attorney, Weathers is obligated to provide Benoit with zealous representation and undivided loyalty, regardless of his feelings toward him. Yet once Weathers becomes convinced that Benoit is a sociopath, he asks himself "How can the ethical thing not be moral?" In the end Weathers betrays his client and settles for the moral answer over the ethical one.

The film teaches viewers that Weathers did the right thing. Senior partner Winnaker's approving smile, and girlfriend Jo Ann's congratulatory embrace, leave no doubt of that. Yet the film also suggests that most lawyers would have stuck by Benoit and tried to get him off. The message for the audience, therefore, is that most criminal-defense lawyers are immoral creatures who promote injustice and conceal the truth.

A harebrained experiment. Instead of pulling a rabbit out from under the police officer's chair, Weathers should have objected to the officer's testimony that Benoit must have known that the bloody articles were under the driver's seat. The opinion is improper because the jury is as capable as the police officer of drawing that conclusion. In any event, the caged-rabbit trick is improper. The officer spent only a few moments in the witness seat, whereas Benoit spent much more time driving his car around. Thus, the officer's unawareness of the rabbit is irrelevant to the question of whether Benoit knew about the items under his seat.

"Knock Knock" "Who's There?" "Nobody." Weathers' "the victim is about to walk through the door" ploy memorializes a mythical lawyer tactic. The myth's usual punch line is that the jurors realize the defendant is guilty because the defendant was the only one who didn't look at the door.

In the context of Weathers' defense, however, the tactic makes no sense. Weathers told the jury at the beginning of the trial that someone other than Benoit killed Williams, not that she is alive. Moreover, the argument is just plain silly. The jurors would have looked at the door if Weathers had said that Santa Claus was about to walk through it. So the fact that the jurors looked at the door doesn't suggest they doubted Benoit's guilt at all.

Picturing justice. According to the film, big law firms choose making money over ethical or dignified legal behavior. When Weathers' antics in the Torkenson case bring in new clients and increase profits, Weathers is made a partner. Of course, most big firms wouldn't dream of representing Douglas Benoit. They tend to specialize in representing big institutions or white-collar criminals, not accused murderers. Nor would a firm's supposedly busy partners sacrifice billable hours in order to loll about a courtroom watching Weathers.

Trial Brief

From the Hip was David E. Kelley's first major film project. Kelley was a former criminal-defense lawyer in Boston who went on to huge success as the creator and frequent writer of popular and often critically acclaimed television series about lawyers. They include *L.A. Law, The Practice, Ally McBeal, The Girls' Club, Picket Fences,* and *Boston Legal.* Kelley also created and often wrote several nonlawyer TV series, including *Chicago Hope* and *Boston Public.*

Legally Blonde

Synopsis: An apparent airhead excels in law school while trapping a witness into a murder confession.

MGM, 2001. Color. Running time: 96 minutes.

Screenplay: Karen McCullah Lutz and Kirsten Smith. Novel: Amanda Brown. Director: Robert Luketic.

Starring: Reese Witherspoon (Elle Woods), Luke Wilson (Emmett Richmond).

Rating: ⎯⎯▪ ⎯⎯▪ ⎯⎯▪

The Story

Elle Woods is an apparently ditzy sorority girl who never met a shade of pink she didn't like. Her boyfriend, Warner Huntington, is an intellectual snob who dumps her when he gets into Harvard Law School. To win him back, Woods applies to Harvard and amazingly is also admitted. She not only aced the law school entrance test, she also wowed the admissions committee with a video demonstrating her uncanny ability to recall soap-opera plots.

Woods is a dish out of water at Harvard, ostracized by her snooty classmates and kicked out of her first law school class. However, she's such a good student that Professor Callahan includes her on a team of students helping him to defend Brooke Windham. Windham is charged with murdering her older, wealthy husband. Woods' social savvy pays immediate dividends when a pool cleaner who testified that he'd been having an affair with Windham criticizes Woods in a hallway for wearing "last season's Pradas." Woods tells Callahan that only a gay man would know who designed her shoes, and Callahan uses the information to bully the witness into recanting his story.

When Callahan turns out to be a slimeball, Windham fires him and entrusts Woods with the cross-examination of Chutney, the victim's daughter. Chutney testifies that she came out of the shower to find Windham standing over her dead father holding a gun. Woods forcefully accuses Chutney of lying, because if Chutney had gotten her hair permed just hours earlier she wouldn't ruin it by showering. Chutney falls apart and confesses that she hates Windham and meant to shoot her but killed her father by accident. Just a typical day in court for a first-year cine-law student.

Legal Analysis

Law school and the courtroom are traditionally considered to be "male spaces" where success depends on such masculine traits as aggression and competitiveness. *Legally Blonde* portrays women as also able to succeed in these milieus while relying on female experiences and traits. For example, Woods breaks down Chutney's story through her knowledge of hair-care rules. Similarly, Woods regains her spiritual strength and bonds with her manicurist and a female law professor in the traditional "female space" of the beauty salon. By grounding these strong feminist images in a comedy rather than a drama, *Legally Blonde* softens them and perhaps makes them palatable to men as well as women. (By contrast, the stereotypical portrayal of the gay pool cleaner is regrettable.)

Square pegs in round holes. Like *My Cousin Vinny, Legally Blonde* generates humor by inserting eccentric characters into conventional settings. For example, Woods' parents are upset that she's going to Harvard after having been first runner-up in a summer beauty contest. It's safe to say that most parents whose children get into Harvard Law School would be more approving. And Woods' first law school class is a disaster because her college curriculum (consisting of courses such as "History of Polka Dots") didn't prepare her to expect a reading assignment for her first class.

Law school imagery. *Legally Blonde*'s images of law school perpetuate those depicted in earlier films, such as *The Paper Chase* and *Soul Man,* which also were set at Harvard Law School, or *The Pelican Brief,* which was set at Tulane. The films typically portray law school professors as intellectual terrorists who turn students' minds to mush so they can build them back up again. But in an era when professors advance within the ranks based at least in part on student evaluations of their teaching, and law schools rely on alumni to "give back," instructors are more likely to treat students as clients needing help than as adversaries to be intimidated.

The admissions committee ostensibly admits Woods because as a fashion major she provides "diversity." The scene cleverly turns diversity arguments in academia on their head. The value of diversity is usually a justification for admitting racial minorities or economically disadvantaged applicants, not wealthy white ones.

Picturing justice. Woods is a wonderful lawyer role model not only for her courtroom success but also for her personal values. She genuinely cares for others no matter what their status, an important trait for professionals who are supposed to be problem solvers. Woods brings muffins to the study group that rejects her, uses legal mumbo jumbo to help her manicurist regain custody of her dog from an abusive ex-boyfriend, and makes sure that Windham is comfortable in jail while awaiting trial. Viewers should root for Woods to retain her humanity after she graduates and begins practicing law.

Trial Brief

Amanda Brown, author of the novel on which the film is based, dropped out of Stanford Law School after two years. Elle Woods' first name is a play on Scott Turow's popular book *One L,* describing his experiences as a first-year Harvard Law School student.

My Cousin Vinny

Synopsis: A bumbling lawyer combines grits, burned rubber, and street smarts into a recipe for a successful murder defense.

20th Century Fox, 1992. Color. Running time: 120 minutes.

Screenplay: Dale Launer. Director: Jonathan Lynn.

Starring: Joe Pesci (Vincent Gambini), Marisa Tomei (Mona Lisa Vito), Fred Gwynne (Judge Haller), Lane Smith (Jim Trotter).

Academy Award: Best Supporting Actress (Marisa Tomei).

Rating:

The Story

College students Bill and Stan are driving cross-country to UCLA when they stop at a roadside convenience store in rural Alabama. Shortly thereafter, they are arrested for robbing the store and murdering the clerk. Bill's brash cousin, Vinny, agrees to represent Bill and eventually Stan, though he's never set foot in court and flunked the New York bar exam repeatedly before finally passing. Arriving with Vinny is his brassy fiancée, Mona Lisa Vito. Their demeanor and accents suggest that this is the first time they've left New York City or been so far from Chinese takeout.

No-nonsense Judge Haller is legitimately suspicious of Vinny's competence because Vinny has no idea how to dress for court or how to enter a plea of "not guilty." Vinny racks up contempt-of-court citations as often as Mona Lisa changes outfits, and he's often locked up with Bill and Stan. Lawyers are supposed to stay in contact with clients, but Vinny overdoes it.

My Cousin Vinny: Vinny Gambini (Joe Pesci) elicits expert testimony from Mona Lisa Vito (Marisa Tomei).

Vinny prepares for trial by going deer hunting with the prosecutor, Jim Trotter. Mona Lisa is furious; no doubt the deerskin section of her wardrobe is already full. When Vinny brags about how he used the trip to smooth-talk Trotter into giving him copies of the case file, Mona Lisa punctures his ego by pointing out that Alabama law required Trotter to do so. Vinny is so shocked that he pronounces a diphthong correctly.

At trial, three prosecution eyewitnesses place Bill, Stan, and their car at the convenience store right around the time of the robbery/murder. Vinny, a suddenly skillful cross-examiner, demonstrates that their identifications are worthless. However, Trotter's FBI agent seemingly sinks the defense. The agent is an expert on tire marks, and he testifies that the tire marks left outside the convenience store by the getaway car were made by Bill and Stan's car.

However, Vinny has one more schtick up his sleeve. He calls Mona Lisa to the stand, and she demonstrates expertise in automotive mechanics with the best explanation of ignition timing ever put on film. Mona Lisa then explains why Bill and Stan's car could not possibly have made the tire marks. So convincing is her testimony that Trotter happily asks for dismissal of the case.

Legal Analysis

My Cousin Vinny's trial resembles an exhibition basketball game between the hapless Washington Generals and the Harlem Globetrotters. Like the Generals, Judge Haller and prosecutor Trotter attempt to follow the rules of the courtroom "game." Like the Globetrotters, Vinny generates laughs by violating most of those rules, though usually unaware of what he is doing. Also like the Globetrotters, Vinny demonstrates that he can really play the game when he needs to.

Positive lawyer images. *My Cousin Vinny* creates humor within the context of normal courtroom procedures and good lawyer role models. Vinny knows almost nothing about courtroom fundamentals, but he genuinely cares for his clients, and his preparation and cross-examination skills pay off. Judge Haller is stern, but he tries to ensure that the defendants have competent counsel, and he gives both sides a fair hearing. Trotter prosecutes the case fairly, and genuinely believes that Bill and Stan are guilty. Allowing for the humor, almost all the characters reflect favorably on law, lawyers, and the legal system. Gibbons, a stuttering public defender who briefly represents Stan, is an exception. His inept cross-examination belies the ability of most public defenders, who generally do excellent work despite enormous caseloads.

Trial advocacy skills. While Vinny's courtroom missteps generate much of the film's humor, the film is satisfying because in crunch time he is an excellent advocate. For example:
- *Cross-examination technique.* Vinny demolishes a prosecution eyewitness' estimate that Bill and Stan were in the store for only the five minutes it took him to cook his grits by forcing him to admit that grits need twenty minutes to cook. Vinny first establishes that the witness likes his grits "regular," not "al dente," and that he didn't use instant grits. Either explanation could have supported the witness' initial five-minute estimate, and Vinny is careful to eliminate both before the witness can see why Vinny is asking the questions.
- *Eliciting an expert's opinion.* Mona Lisa testifies that the car that made the tire marks had "Positraction," a feature that Bill and Stan's car lacked. Vinny underlines the importance of this testimony by having her explain what Positraction is. He then asks her to point out how she can tell from a photo that the car that left the tire marks had Positraction. Attorneys often have difficulty offering expert testimony in such a clear and concise manner.

• *Preparation*. Before trial, Vinny interviews the three prosecution eyewitnesses, showing that courtroom effectiveness requires hard work. Vinny would have been out of luck had the witnesses refused to talk to him. Unlike civil cases, with their broad provisions for "pretrial discovery," criminal cases offer defense attorneys no means of communicating with uncooperative prosecution witnesses.

Eyewitness identification problems. The film's humor masks a serious problem with eyewitness identification. The three eyewitnesses honestly think that Bill and Stan entered and left the store about the same time the shots were fired. All three were wrong. While Bill and Stan were rescued by Vinny's (and Mona Lisa's) last-minute heroics, some criminal defendants have served years in prison before new information (often in the form of DNA evidence) proves that the eyewitnesses whose testimony put them there were mistaken.

Psychologists who study perception have identified factors that at least in experimental settings cause even the best-intentioned eyewitnesses to be wrong. Among the factors are: (1) stress hinders rather than sharpens perceptual ability; (2) people on the wrong end of a weapon typically look at the weapon and not the person holding it; (3) the accuracy of an identification is unrelated to a person's confidence in its accuracy; (4) and cross-racial situations negatively affect the accuracy of identifications. (See the discussion of *The Wrong Man* for further information about eyewitness identification procedures.)

Picturing justice. When the sheriff tells Bill (who thinks he was arrested for shoplifting a can of tuna fish) that he's charged with murder, a shocked Bill says questioningly, "I shot the clerk?" In court, the sheriff testifies that Bill confessed by saying "I shot the clerk." The scenes suggest how slight changes in words and even intonation can alter meaning.

Short Subjects

The Advocate (aka ***The Hour of the Pig***), 1993. Colin Firth, Nicol Williamson, Donald Pleasence. ▬▬█ ▬▬█ ▬▬█

In 1492 France, Richard Courtois finds out that practicing law in the countryside isn't quite the idyllic life he'd imagined. His first defense succeeds because the murder victim had seduced all the jurors' wives. His second client is eventually burned for being a witch, and his third client is a pig charged with murder. Finally a film in which the client and not the lawyer is a swine! *Courtroom highlight:* Courtois successfully defends the witch by demanding that the rats over which she supposedly cast a spell be subpoenaed. When the rats fail to appear in court, the charges are dismissed, producing a temporary victory for the witch. *Trial brief:* French lawyer Bartholomew Chassenee, one of the most successful lawyers of his time, represented a variety of animals, including dogs, rats, and even a swarm of locusts over the course of his career, and he wrote a treatise about animal trials in 1531. The last known European trial of an animal took place in Switzerland in 1906. Two brothers and a dog were charged with murder. The brothers must have had the better lawyer: They were sentenced to life in prison while the dog was sentenced to death. In Libya in 1974, a dog was tried for biting a human. It served a month in jail on a diet of bread and water.

Disorder in the Court, 1936. The Three Stooges. ⟶◼ ⟶◼

The Stooges bash courtroom conventions as well as one another. For example, Curly can't take the oath because he's simultaneously trying to obey the clerk's order to raise his right hand and the judge's order to remove his hat. When Curly can't find the words to describe a murder, the Stooges act out what happened. This allows Moe to squash Curly's head with a press, and Curly to use a pistol and a fire hose to trap a parrot that provides the vital evidence exonerating the defendant. It's no fun being a judge or a lawyer; they're the straight men.

Dreamboat, 1952. Clifton Webb, Ginger Rogers. ⟶◼ ⟶◼ ⟶◼

The movies literally put television on trial when an uptight college professor sues TV broadcasters to stop them from showing silent films in which he starred as a swashbuckling romantic hero. *Courtroom highlight.* The professor puts a TV set on the witness stand to demonstrate how tasteless editing and loud, cheap commercials have ruined his films and turned him into a laughingstock. *Picturing justice:* The professor argues that because television is such a powerful educational tool, the law must hold it responsible for its messages.

Going Bye-Bye!, 1934. Laurel and Hardy. ⟶◼ ⟶◼

After he's convicted, the brutish-looking Butch vows revenge on Laurel and Hardy, the key prosecution witnesses. When Butch escapes from custody, the boys find themselves in another fine mess. *Courtroom highlight*: Laurel objects to Butch's life sentence, asking the judge, "Aren't you going to hang him?" *Picturing justice*: It's risky for witnesses to testify against vicious criminals.

How to Murder Your Wife, 1965. Jack Lemmon. ——■ ——■

A murder trial portrays women as control freaks who trap men into marriage and then ruin their lives. Stanley Ford is a famous cartoonist who accidentally ends up married and miserable. He acts out a storyline in which his cartoon action-hero murders his wife, including dumping what looks like a human body into a cement mixer. When his wife runs home to mama and disappears, Ford is tried for murder. Ford boasts that he really killed his wife, and even the prosecutor is delighted when the all-male jury acquits him. *Courtroom highlights*: (1) When the henpecked defense attorney objects to his wife's testimony, she instructs him "not to interrupt me when I'm talking." (2) Ford's valet is so impressed by the prosecutor's cross-examination that he changes his mind and testifies that Ford is guilty. *Trial brief*: After Ford is acquitted, his valet tells him that he can kill his wife for real because double jeopardy will protect him. They apparently didn't cover criminal law in valet school, because killing his wife would be a separate act for which Ford could certainly be punished.

Liar Liar, 1997. Jim Carrey. ——■

Little Max's birthday wish that his father, Fletcher Reede, can't lie for an entire day comes true. Too bad Max didn't wish that Reede couldn't mug shamelessly every three seconds. The film tries to generate laughs by depicting lawyers as helpless if they can't tell lies, a cultural message that reinforces the public's contempt for lawyers. Reede represents a wife in a divorce trial, and the husband's evidence that she repeatedly violated her prenuptial agreement promise to remain faithful means that she should get none of his property in the divorce. Even though he has to tell the truth, Reede invalidates the agreement by proving that his client was a minor when she made the deal. *Courtroom highlight*: Max's wish compels Reede to object to his own leading questions. *Picturing justice*: After winning the case, Reede tells the judge: "I hold myself in contempt."

Serial Mom, 1994. Kathleen Turner. ——■

Beverly Sutphin, an outwardly normal housewife, murders people who offend her strange family. Sutphin successfully defends herself against murder charges, but after the verdict she beats one of the jurors to death for wearing white shoes after Labor Day. *Courtroom highlight:* The film tries to parody courtroom conventions and popular obsessions by showing a prosecution witness falling apart when Sutphin forces her to admit that she doesn't recycle.

She Couldn't Say No, 1940. Eve Arden. ——■ ——■

In a precursor to *Adam's Rib*, engaged lawyers Wally Turnbull and Alice Hinsdale represent the opposing parties in a trial for breach of promise to marry. Turnbull was happier when Hinsdale pretended to be only his secretary, complaining: "I made the mistake of wanting a wife who's just a wife. You want a career." After old-maid Pansy Hawkins testifies that cantankerous Eli Potter promised to marry her, Hinsdale charms Pansy during cross-examination by advising her on what colors to wear. Hinsdale also enchants the judge after a favorable evidence ruling, telling him, "It's a good thing you're here." It's an even better thing after the trial, because the judge is on hand to perform two marriage ceremonies. *Courtroom highlight:* Turnbull and Hinsdale argue over the meaning of Potter's answer of "Mebbe" to Pansy Hawkins' marriage proposal. *Picturing justice:* After the trial, Hinsdale will go back to being Turnbull's secretary—not the most inspiring conclusion for female viewers.

Trial and Error, 1997. Michael Richards, Jeff Daniels, Charlize Theron. ——■

Benny Gibbs advertises copper engravings of Abraham Lincoln for $17.99 and sends buyers a penny. Gibbs is charged with fraud, but his attorney Charlie Tuttle is too hung over to attend a preliminary court hearing. Tuttle's actor pal Ricky Rietti stands in for him, and then is forced by the judge to try the case. Rietti offers a junk-food defense, claiming that a lifetime of eating Tootsie Rolls diminished Gibbs' capacity to commit a crime. The jury concludes that the defense is just junk. *Courtroom highlight:* Excluded from the trial, Tuttle listens to the testimony electronically from his car and unsuccessfully tries to signal objections to Rietti by honking his horn Morse Code style. *Trial brief:* In the notorious Dan White case, a San Francisco jury concluded that because White had recently consumed Twinkies, he had not intended to kill two politicians. California subsequently abolished the defense of diminished capacity.

Trial and Error (aka **The Dock Brief**), 1962. Peter Sellers, Richard Attenborough. ——■ ——■ ——■

In this clever parody of barristers' ethics and skills, meek Herbert Fowle is on trial for murdering his wife because she laughed too much. Barrister Wilfred Morganhall has been waiting for years to try a case and is frustrated when Fowle tells him that he's guilty. Morganhall tells Fowle, "With no legal training at all, you've put your finger on the one fatal weakness in our defense." When Fowle points out that the man on whom Morganhall wants to pin the murder has an iron-clad alibi, Morganhall criticizes him for "putting all these difficulties in my way." Fowle is convicted but is later set free because of Morganhall's incompetence. *Courtroom highlight*: Fowle and Morganhall role-play various witnesses' testimony in an imaginary courtroom. *Picturing justice*: Fowle comforts Morganhall by telling him, "If I'd had a barrister who'd asked questions and made clever speeches, I'd be as dead as mutton."

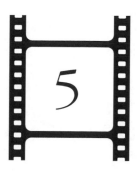

Corruption of Justice

It's often said that a good story requires a good villain, and this chapter presents an entertaining array of legal villains who have corrupted the justice system so that it cannot function properly.

Courtroom movies frequently attack the justice system as hopelessly corrupt and suggest that it can be easily manipulated by those who know which strings to pull, as in *Chicago* and *Devil's Advocate.* Evil political systems like the ones in *Judgment at Nuremberg, The Life of Emile Zola,* and *A Dry White Season* can also pollute justice. On a more everyday level, corruption results from betrayals by people we normally count on to uphold the law, such as prison officials (*Murder in the First*), law enforcement officers (*Night Falls on Manhattan, Sleepers, True Believer*), and judges (*And Justice for All, Night Court, The Star Chamber*). Of course, criminal defendants are readily available bad guys and may also corrupt justice by bribing and intimidating jurors, as they do in *Trial By Jury* and *The Juror.*

And Justice for All

Synopsis: A fiery criminal-defense attorney represents his nemesis, a judge accused of rape.

Columbia Pictures, 1979. Color. Running time: 119 minutes.

Screenplay: Valerie Curtin and Barry Levinson. Director: Norman Jewison.

Starring: Al Pacino (Arthur Kirkland), John Forsythe (Judge Fleming), Jack Warden (Judge Rayford).

Academy Award nominations: Best Actor (Al Pacino), Best Screenplay.

Rating: ——▪ ——▪ ——▪

And Justice For All: Arthur Kirkland (Al Pacino) makes a pointed opening statement.

The Story

The criminal justice system is a broken-down machine that dispenses only injustice and catastrophe. Judge Henry Fleming is privately a rapist but publicly a law-and-order zealot who believes that criminal defendants are the "scum of the earth who should be taken out and squashed like a cockroach." Judge Francis Rayford is a basket case: He wears a gun to court, eats lunch perched high on a window ledge, flies planes until they run out of fuel, and has no home life: "The last thing [my wife and I] did together was get married." Defense attorneys are equally lost souls: Jay Porter goes berserk after a murderer he'd successfully defended kills again.

In this bizarre system, the hapless defendants get nothing but unjust deserts. Jeff McCullaugh is imprisoned by mistake. Raped and beaten repeatedly by other inmates, McCullaugh goes mad and is killed by guards after taking hostages. Ralph Agee, a transvestite who participated in a robbery, is sentenced to prison because his lawyer failed to correct mistakes in a probation report. Dreading what awaits him in prison, Agee hangs himself.

Dedicated defense attorney Arthur Kirkland tries to maintain his sanity in the midst of this maelstrom. Kirkland and Judge Fleming have a hate-hate relationship, and Fleming once jailed Kirkland for throwing a punch at him. But when Fleming is charged with rape, he blackmails Kirkland into representing him. Fleming passes a lie-detector test, and an eyewitness supports his claim of innocence.

* * *

SPOILER ALERT: You may not want to read further if you plan to see the film.

* * *

Confronted by Kirkland with photos showing him engaging in sado-masochistic sex, Fleming gloats that he's guilty of rape but that he will never be convicted because of the phony exonerating evidence that he and his friends concocted. For Kirkland, Fleming's likely acquittal is the flaw that breaks the camel's back. Kirkland's opening statement tells the jurors: "We have a problem here . . . We want to win regardless of the truth, and we want to win regardless of justice. . . . Winning is every-thing." Referring to the alleged rape victim, Kirkland suddenly turns on Fleming: "The one thing that bothered me . . . was why? Why would she lie? . . . If my client is innocent, she's lying. . . . Yesterday I found out why she doesn't have a motive . . . because she's not lying. . . . The prosecution is not going to get that man today because I'm going to get him. My client, the Honorable Henry T. Fleming, should go right to fucking jail. The son of a bitch is guilty."

The spectators applaud Kirkland as the marshals hustle him out of the courtroom. As he sits on the courthouse steps contemplating his future, he's ignored by lawyers and others walking into the courthouse talking about their cases. Business continues as usual for the criminal justice system.

Legal Analysis

And Justice for All is too broad a parody to serve as a reasoned critique of American criminal justice. But as with most effective parodies, fair criticism lies beneath the exaggeration. The film accurately shows how the maelstrom of cases forces prosecutors and defense attorneys to dispose of almost all of them before trial, often by making hurried deals in courthouse corridors. Yet the system could not possibly func-tion unless most cases are plea-bargained instead of tried. Because judges are often appointed based more on whom they know than on what they know, there are too many harsh and tyrannical judges like

Judge Fleming on the bench (though hopefully no rapists!). And crime victims and criminal defendants, whose situations the system is supposed to address, are all too often merely supporting actors for the judges and lawyers, who are the system's stars.

Do you care enough to do your very best? For the most part, Kirkland is a positive role model. He cares about his clients and works tirelessly on their behalf. He accompanies an injured client to the hospital and tries desperately to keep the transvestite Agee out of prison. (Of course, it's unlikely that a participant in an armed robbery would be released on probation.)

The film suggests that good lawyers should care more about the good of the community than about their clients. Kirkland explodes when his role as a criminal-defense attorney forces him to attack the credibility of a truthful rape victim and defend a rapist who has acknowledged his guilt. Porter goes berserk when a client he had properly defended and gotten off on a technicality commits additional murders. As Kirkland tells Gail Packer, his lover who is also on the ethics committee, "Every day defense lawyers are out there protecting guilty people and getting them off, and they're not affected by it, it's not supposed to affect them. The difference is that Jay was affected by it. Isn't it ironic that the one lawyer who felt something should be brought up before your committee?"

Unethical heroes. Ironically, the film portrays the moment of Kirkland's professional downfall as his moment of greatest triumph. Denouncing Judge Fleming in open court will probably cost Kirkland his license to practice law. Criminal-defense lawyers are required to zealously defend even the most guilty of their clients, because every defendant has the right to force the state to prove guilt beyond a reasonable doubt. While Kirkland cannot call witnesses who he knows will commit perjury, he can and should cross-examine the woman who was raped and present other evidence that might cast doubt on Fleming's guilt.

Yet, as the spectators' applause signals, Kirkland's outburst makes him a hero. The film capitalizes on popular frustration with lawyers who try to free clients they know to be guilty. "The system" may require Kirkland to defend Fleming zealously, but not if, as Kirkland says, the system is out of order. Here and in films like *Criminal Law* and *Guilty as Sin*, lawyers become heroes when they try to convict the bad guys rather than defend them.

Picturing justice. (1) The film opens with exterior and interior photographs of a classic courthouse as children recite the Pledge of

Allegiance, which ends with "and justice for all." The remainder of the film mocks these core values. (2) Kirkland's grandfather asks him if he's an honest lawyer. Kirkland replies, "Being honest doesn't have much to do with being a lawyer, Grandpa."

Chicago

Synopsis: A murder trial is the path to musical fame and fortune.

Miramax, 2002. Color. Running time: 113 minutes.

Screenplay: Bill Condon. Based on the musical *Chicago* (1972) by John Kander, Bob Fosse, and Fred Ebb; on the films *Chicago* (1927) and *Roxie Hart* (1942); and on the play *Chicago* (1926) by Maurine Dallas Watkins. Director: Rob Marshall.

Starring: Renée Zellweger (Roxie Hart), Catherine Zeta-Jones (Velma Kelly), Richard Gere (Billy Flynn), Queen Latifah (Matron Mama Morton).

Academy Awards: Best Picture, Best Supporting Actress (Catherine Zeta-Jones), Best Editing, Best Sound, Best Art and Set Direction, Best Costume Design.

Rating: ——█ ——█ ——█ ——█

The Story

Aspiring cabaret singer Roxie Hart has tried to sleep her way to the top with Fred Casely, but she has remained on the bottom. When Casely walks out on her, Roxie guns him down and is charged with murder.

Mercenary jail matron Mama Morton connects Roxie with Billy Flynn, a spellbinding lawyer who has never lost a case—or followed the rules. Mama and Flynn turn Roxie into a media sensation by claiming that she is a repentant "fallen sinner" who shot Casely in self-defense. Flynn's other client, Velma Kelly, an entertainer who murdered the other half of her sister act, is jealous because Roxie is stealing her headlines.

Roxie's trial is literally a circus as the scenes morph seamlessly back and forth between a courtroom and a spectacle. Roxie enthralls the all-male jurors by showing them a bit of leg while tearfully telling the phony story that Flynn concocted for her. However, all seems lost for Roxie when D.A. Harrison calls Velma to read excerpts from Roxie's diary in which Roxie brags about killing Casely. Prosecutor Harrison is so grateful to Velma for allowing him to finally defeat Flynn that he's

Miramax/Photofest.

Chicago: Billy Flynn (Richard Gere) counsels Roxie Hart (Renée Zellweger).

dismissed all charges against her. Flynn then convinces the jurors that the diary excerpts are phony, no doubt planted there by Harrison. The jury finds Roxie not guilty, probably causing Harrison to wonder whether he or Perry Mason's foil Hamilton Burger has the longer losing streak.

With the trial over, Roxie is yesterday's news. She can't get a cabaret job. But Roxie and Velma as a double act—two murderesses singing and dancing on the same stage! There's an act that all Chicago has to see.

Legal Analysis

As entertaining as it is cynical, *Chicago* symbolizes popular culture's most enduring image of courtrooms as an arena in which style and creativity matter much more than truth and hard work.

The play's the thing. Helping Roxie commit perjury and creating a phony diary are illegal and unethical activities even by the standards of 1920s Chicago. But Flynn is successful not so much because of the story that he sells but because of the way he sells it. Outside of court, he creates an image for Roxie that ignites a media feeding frenzy. In the courtroom, Flynn senses when to hog the spotlight and when to focus the jury's attention on a witness. He uses the power of visual imagery by conducting demonstrations and acting out testimony. Flynn's techniques play as well to the jurors as to movie audiences, and *Chicago* suggests that the distinction between lawyers and actors may be finer than we would like to believe.

Pretrial publicity. Courtroom films "work" as entertainment because even their excesses are grounded in reality. Real as well as reel lawyers massage the public images of celebrity clients in an effort to influence jury verdicts. For example, before she went on trial for lying to federal agents about her dubious stock transactions, media star Martha Stewart appeared on scads of TV talk shows proclaiming her innocence. (In her case the pretrial publicity didn't help; she was convicted in March 2004 and went to jail.) Sadly, *Chicago*'s portrayal of lawyers' pretrial behavior in celebrity cases is not far from the truth.

Picturing justice. (1) An aerialist in the courtroom-circus rises into the air holding the scales of justice. Later, Flynn asks Roxie to "tell the audience . . . the jury, what happened next." The images suggest that justice and entertainment are synonymous. (2) Flynn tells Roxie's pathetic husband, Amos: "If Christ were alive today in Chicago and had five thousand dollars, things would have turned out differently." The scene suggests that justice is little more than a commodity that can be purchased only by the wealthy. (3) A convicted woman's execution is juxtaposed with a graceful ballerina's circus act, depicting capital punishment as simply a form of popular entertainment. Ironically, the woman who was executed was apparently the only innocent one on murderess' row. (4) Standing next to Roxie at a press conference, Flynn becomes a puppeteer and Roxie a puppet, mouthing Flynn's words.

Trial Briefs

1. Before writing her first play, *Chicago*, Maurine Watkins was a reporter for the *Chicago Tribune*, and she based the plot on two actual cases, one that she remembered from her childhood and one that she had covered as a reporter. In both cases, females accused of murdering their lovers were acquitted by all-male juries.

2. The character of Billy Flynn is based on William Fallon (1886–1927). Fallon acquired the nickname "The Great Mouthpiece"

because of the many mob figures he represented. He was the first lawyer to charge extremely high fees for representing gangsters. Fallon represented 126 defendants charged with murder and never lost a case. His tactics were often questionable. He was charged with jury bribery in 1924 and managed to escape conviction by depicting the prosecution as a witch hunt led by the famous publisher William Randolph Hearst. Fallon devoted much of his abbreviated life to debauchery and drinking. For more about Fallon's classic gambits, see the discussion of the film *The Mouthpiece* in the sidebar "Memorable Courtroom Demonstrations" in Chapter 8.

3. *Roxie Hart* (1942) is *Chicago*'s closest movie ancestor. A terrific comedy, *Roxie Hart* stars Ginger Rogers as Roxie Hart and Adolphe Menjou as Billy Flynn. The primary plot difference is that in *Roxie Hart,* Roxie's husband kills Casely but Roxie tells the police that she shot Casely in self-defense because the notoriety will be good for her career. Under the censorship rules then in effect, Roxie could not have been the killer because crime could never pay. Velma Kelly does not appear in *Roxie Hart.*

Chicago pays homage to *Roxie Hart* in a number of scenes. For example, in both films Billy Flynn mouths Roxie's words as she testifies, Roxie hikes up her skirt for the benefit of an all-male jury, and when the jury comes in two different sets of newspapers are ready for sale: one set with a headline blaring Roxie's guilt and the other set with a headline trumpeting Roxie's acquittal.

Judgment at Nuremberg

Synopsis: Nazi judges face justice after World War II.

United Artists, 1961. Black and white. Running time: 190 minutes.

Screenplay: Abby Mann. TV play: Abby Mann. Director: Stanley Kramer.

Starring: Spencer Tracy (Judge Dan Haywood), Marlene Dietrich (Frau Bertholt), Burt Lancaster (Ernst Janning), Richard Widmark (Colonel Tad Lawson), Maximilian Schell (Hans Rolfe), Judy Garland (Irene Hoffman Wallner), Montgomery Clift (Rudolph Petersen), William Shatner (Captain Byers).

Academy Awards: Best Actor (Maximilian Schell), Best Screenplay.

Academy Award nominations: Best Picture, Best Director, Best Cinematography, Best Actor (Spencer Tracy), Best Supporting Actor (Montgomery Clift), Best Supporting Actress (Judy Garland).

Rating:

Judgment at Nuremberg: Ernst Janning (Burt Lancaster) listens as his former mentor, Dr. Wieck, denounces him.

The Story

In 1948, after the conclusion of the main Nuremberg trials, four German judges go on trial for war crimes they committed during the Nazi era. The tribunal's chief judge is Dan Haywood, a judge from Maine who had recently been defeated for reelection. Three of the defendants are Nazi thugs who enthusiastically carried out the laws of the Third Reich. The fourth defendant, Ernst Janning, was a famous jurist and law professor who drafted the democratic Weimar constitution and who despised Hitler and the Nazis. Hans Rolfe, a masterful lawyer, represents all four defendants.

Seizing the opportunity to use a visual aid that would make most prosecutors drool, zealous prosecutor Lawson shows a ghastly film about the death camps. He also introduces documents signed by each of the defendants that approved the transfer of Germans to concentration camps under Nazi security laws. Rolfe unsuccessfully objects, complaining that there was no apparent link between these judges and the Holocaust and that the defendants, like most good Germans, did not know that the Nazi leaders had slaughtered millions of people in the camps.

The most important charge against Janning is that he convicted Feldenstein, a prominent elderly Jew, of violating racial-purity laws by having sex with a sixteen-year-old Aryan girl named Irene Hoffman. As Rolfe tries to badger Hoffman into admitting that she and Feldenstein had been lovers, Janning breaks the silence he maintained since the trial started. He admits that Feldenstein's trial was a sham: "I would have found him guilty whatever the evidence. It was not a trial at all, it was a sacrificial ritual in which Feldenstein the Jew was a helpless victim." He admits he was aware of the concentration camps: "Perhaps we weren't aware of the extermination of the millions, but we were aware of the extermination of the hundreds. Does that make us any the less guilty?"

Meanwhile, the Russians have blockaded Berlin. The authorities pressure Haywood and Lawson to go easy on the judges because the prosecutions are unpopular and the Americans need German cooperation against the Russians. Haywood is unmoved. By a 2-to-1 vote, the three judges find all four defendants guilty and sentence them to life imprisonment.

Legal Analysis

Judgment at Nuremberg raises profound questions about the role of a judge who is called on to execute unjust, even horrible, laws. Must a judge apply the law regardless of its content? If a judge objects to the morality of the laws, must he resign? Can he remain on the bench in the hope that he can apply the laws mercifully? Haywood's opinion is simple. A judge is guilty of war crimes if he executes laws that violate legal or moral principles accepted by civilized nations. These issues were particularly trenchant for audiences in 1961, when the film was released. Martin Luther King Jr. was leading the civil rights movement, and southern judges were enforcing Jim Crow laws.

The Nuremberg trials. The Nuremberg trials extended from 1945 to 1949. The first and most important of the trials was authorized by the London Charter of 1945. It condemned the leaders of the Third Reich who had survived the war, such as Hermann Goering. The judges came from the United States, Great Britain, France, and the Soviet Union—the four countries then occupying Germany. The charter and the trials established for the first time that international law applies to individuals, not simply to nations. They established the principle that international law prohibits the leaders of a country from committing war crimes against their own people. The trials affirmed that the victors in war could set up a tribunal and prosecute crimes occurring during the war. Finally, the Nuremberg judgments invalidated the "following orders" defense for subordinates who committed war crimes.

Nevertheless, the legal validity of the Nuremberg trials is still controversial. For example, the trials raise important issues about *ex post facto* laws (laws that define acts as crimes after the acts have occurred). The U.S. Constitution prohibits *ex post facto* laws. And it is not clear what gave the victorious allies jurisdiction to try cases in which Germans committed offenses against other Germans. But surely it is fair and just to hold the Nazis responsible for behavior that offended every norm of civilized human beings, even if such crimes had never before been defined or punished. After the war, many of the allies favored rounding up and shooting the top Nazis after hasty court-martials. It was better to prosecute them according to due process of law than to impose the summary justice that the victors have traditionally meted out after wars. The Nuremberg precedent (particularly rejection of the "following orders" defense) is critical in the effort to deter and to punish the international criminals of the present and future.

The criminal responsibility of a judge. At the conclusion of the trial, defendant Hofstetter argues: "I followed the concept that I believe to be the highest of my profession. The concept that says to sacrifice one's own sense of justice for the authoritative legal order, to ask only what the law is and not to ask whether or not it is also justice. As a judge I could do no other." Hofstetter is arguing what legal philosophers call positivism: The law is what it is, and the task of judges is to carry it out. The tribunal's judgment places judges in a terrible dilemma: Unless judges resign immediately after enactment of an unjust law, they are responsible under the Nuremberg rules if they execute the law, but they would be responsible under domestic law if they refuse to execute them.

Janning's responsibility: The criminal and moral responsibility of Ernst Janning is the central issue in *Judgment at Nuremberg.* He served as a Nazi judge and as minister of justice and probably helped more people than he hurt. Surely, if he had refused to judge the Feldenstein case another Nazi judge would have been glad to sit in his place. Haywood refuses to engage in this sort of pragmatic balance. In his judgment, Haywood says: "Janning, to be sure, is a tragic figure. We believe he loathed the evil he did. . . . If he and the other defendants had been degraded perverts . . . then these events would have no more moral significance than an earthquake or any other natural catastrophe. But this trial has shown that under a national crisis, ordinary, even able and extraordinary men, can delude themselves into the commission of crimes so vast and heinous that they beggar the imagination. . . . How easily it can happen."

Trial Brief

After the first Nuremberg trial against the top officials of the Third Reich, there followed twelve more trials conducted exclusively by American civilian judges. German defense lawyers were paid, housed, and fed by the American authorities. *Judgment at Nuremberg* is a fictionalized account of the third of these trials. Cases were also brought against industrialists, military personnel, concentration camp superintendents, and other less-prominent Germans.

The trial of the Nazi judges was presided over by James T. Brand of the Oregon Supreme Court. Ernst Janning is a composite of several of the Nazi judges or justice ministry officials who were defendants. One of the defendants had been a judge at Nuremberg and presided over a trial exactly like the Feldenstein case (the Katzenberger case). Four of the defendants received life sentences, six others received prison terms of five to ten years, and four were acquitted.

The Life of Emile Zola

Synopsis: Famed social critic Emile Zola exposes the Dreyfus affair and receives equal mistreatment from the French courts.

Warner Bros., 1937. Black and white. Running time: 116 minutes.

Screenplay: Norman Reilly Raine. Original story: Heinz Herald and Geza Herczeg. Book: Matthew Josephson. Director: William Dieterle.

Starring: Paul Muni (Emile Zola), Joseph Schildkraut (Alfred Dreyfus).

Academy Awards: Best Picture, Best Screenplay, Best Supporting Actor (Joseph Schildkraut).

Academy Award nominations: Best Actor (Paul Muni), Best Director, Best Original Story, Best Musical Score, Best Art Direction.

Rating: ——▪ ——▪ ——▪

The Life of Emile Zola: Colonel Picquart (Henry O'Neill) testifies in support of Emile Zola (Paul Muni).

The Story

Captain Alfred Dreyfus, a loyal French Jewish officer, is court-martialed in 1894, convicted, expelled from the army, and imprisoned on Devil's Island for sending the Germans a letter (the "bordereau") revealing French military secrets. A year later, Colonel Picquart, the French chief of intelligence, determines that a French officer named Esterhazy wrote the bordereau. However, with the army's honor and their own careers at stake, the general staff covers up the miscarriage of justice. Picquart is exiled. Esterhazy is court-martialed, but it's strictly a show trial and he is acquitted.

Famous muckraking author and social critic Emile Zola describes the sordid affair in a letter called *J'Accuse*. It's published in *L'Aurore*, and hundreds of thousands of copies are sold. The minister of war prosecutes Zola for criminal libel. The government tries to avoid reopening the Dreyfus affair by limiting the case to Zola's charge that the Esterhazy court-martial was fixed.

The presiding judge in Zola's trial is in the government's pocket. Uniformed officers pack the courtroom and address the judges and jury at will. Mobs surround the courtroom and scream their contempt for Zola. Zola cannot talk about the Dreyfus case. The judges support Esterhazy's refusal to answer questions. Zola's stirring closing argument is for naught, and the jury swiftly convicts him. He is sentenced to one year's imprisonment and a fine of three thousand francs. All in all, it's a great example of "rue" rather than "due" process.

After his appeal fails, Zola flees to England and continues to write about Dreyfus. Finally, a new minister of war unravels the cover-up and sacks various guilty officers. Dreyfus returns in 1899 and is restored to his former rank. The night before the triumphal ceremony, Zola dies of asphyxiation from a leaking coal stove.

Legal Analysis

Though civilian officials conducted Zola's libel trial, they managed to repeat the injustices of Dreyfus' military trial. These included a fixed outcome and absurd rulings that allowed the government to offer whatever evidence it wanted while tying Zola's hands. The film powerfully dramatizes two deplorable chapters in the history of French justice.

Criminal libel. The French Press Law of 1881 made truth a defense to a criminal libel charge, but Zola had the burden of showing that what he said in *J'Accuse* was true. Unable to cross-examine the government's witnesses or to talk about the Dreyfus case, Zola had no chance of satisfying this burden.

Criminal libel prosecutions were once common in the United States because they offered an alternative to duels. Truth was not a defense if a damaging statement was made with malicious intent. However, criminal libel is as extinct as dodo birds. Today, the target of a false statement whose reputation has been damaged can sue in civil court for money damages under the law of defamation. Under the famous case of *New York Times v. Sullivan* (1964), a "public figure" must prove that the defendant knew that his statements were false (or that he made them without regard for their truth). The *New York Times* case is a bulwark of the First Amendment. Without that case, public figures who didn't like being criticized could turn the tables on their accusers by bringing a libel suit and thus intimidate their critics into silence.

If the *New York Times* rule had been in effect in France at the time of the Zola case, the prosecution would have been required to prove not only that the *J'Accuse* letter was false but also that Zola knew it was false. This would have been impossible both because Zola believed his statements were true and because they actually were true.

Inquisitorial trials. In the French inquisitorial system, public prosecutors and the police first investigate serious crimes, much as in the United States. If they want to proceed, they turn the case over to a judge called the examining magistrate, or *juge d'instruction*. The magistrate then supervises the investigation and interviews the witnesses, including the accused. A dossier includes all the evidence and transcripts of interviews and is open to both sides. The defendant is represented by a lawyer at all stages of investigation and trial. A crime victim is entitled to become a party to a case and can compel prosecution even if the public prosecutor declines to proceed.

All cases go to trial, even if the defendant wants to plead guilty. No plea bargaining! The presiding judge determines which witnesses to call and questions them. (The film shows the lawyers more in control than would normally be true in a French trial.) Defendants are presumed innocent and must testify but are not placed under oath. In modern French practice, serious criminal cases are decided by a panel of three professional judges and nine lay jurors who all deliberate together on the question of both guilt and punishment. Eight votes are required to convict. The same jurors sit for an entire term of court rather than for brief periods, as in the United States. (The separate lay jury depicted in the film was abandoned in 1932.)

Trial Briefs

1. The film depicts Zola's trial and the hysteria surrounding it with reasonable accuracy. The trial took place over the course of two weeks in the spring of 1898. Anti-Semitism pervaded the Dreyfus and Zola cases from beginning to end, a fact that the movie downplays. The film *I Accuse!* (1958) portrays the Dreyfus case from the point of view of Dreyfus and his family rather than focusing on Zola.

2. Zola's conviction was reversed by the High Court of Appeal on a technicality: The prosecution was improperly instituted by the minister of war rather than by the members of the court-martial that acquitted Esterhazy. Instead of using the reversal as an excuse to quietly drop an embarrassing case, the government insisted on retrying Zola, and once more the court refused to hear evidence that Dreyfus was innocent. As a result, Zola did not contest the charges and fled to London. He

returned to France in 1899, eleven months later. Zola accidentally died of carbon-monoxide poisoning in 1902.

3. Dreyfus returned to France in 1899 after four years on Devil's Island. He faced a second court-martial and was again convicted and sentenced to ten years in prison. Zola and Theodore Roosevelt were among the world leaders who protested the second conviction. Ten days after the conviction, the president of the republic pardoned Dreyfus. Dreyfus was reluctant to withdraw his appeal because the pardon did not restore his honor, but he finally accepted it. In 1906 the High Court of Appeal threw out Dreyfus' second conviction and pronounced him innocent. Dreyfus was restored to his army rank and made a Knight of the Legion of Honor. He was shot and slightly wounded in 1908 during a ceremony transferring Zola's remains to the Pantheon. Dreyfus served in the French army during World War I and was promoted to lieutenant-colonel. He died in bed in Paris at the age of seventy-five in 1935.

Murder in the First

Synopsis: A lawyer blames Alcatraz for turning a prisoner into a murderer.

Warner Bros., 1995. Color. Running time: 122 minutes.

Screenplay: Dan Gordon. Director: Marc Rocco.

Starring: Christian Slater (James Stamphill), Kevin Bacon (Henri Young), Gary Oldman (Milton Glenn), William H. Macy (D.A. William McNeil).

Rating:

The Story

During the Depression, Henri Young steals five dollars from a post office and lands in Alcatraz, the forbidding "Rock" that typically housed the worst criminals—and people who waited until the movie started to unwrap their candy. In retribution for a failed escape attempt, associate warden Milton Glenn tortures Young and keeps him in solitary confinement for three years. Because this slightly exceeds the nineteen days in solitary that prison regulations allow, Glenn's boss, Warden James Humson, orders Young returned to the general prison population. Young immediately uses a spoon to kill the prisoner who snitched on the escape and is charged with murder.

Murder in the First: Henri Young (Kevin Bacon) is dragged away after his conviction.

Warner Bros./Photofest.

Young's case is assigned to inexperienced public defender James Stamphill. Stamphill turns out to be a bulldog who challenges both the establishment and his own supervisor by blaming the killing on Young's inhumane treatment. Stamphill also sneaks a hooker into Young's cell to try to rouse him from his near-catatonic state. Young can't perform, but the hooker's methods sure beat torture.

At trial, Stamphill tries to get Glenn to admit that he tortured Young. Glenn repeatedly claims convenient failures of memory, and the examination degenerates into a shouting match. A former Alcatraz guard helps out the defense by describing how he threw Young down a flight of stairs on orders from Glenn. However, the judge orders the jury to ignore the guard's testimony because Glenn had fired him. Warden Humson denies that Young was abused but admits that he rarely visited Alcatraz. Stamphill's final witness is Young himself. Young had intended to plead guilty, preferring the death penalty to doing more time in Alcatraz. On the stand, however, Young breaks down and says that the torture turned him into a weapon.

The jury convicts Young of involuntary manslaughter. The jurors save their fury for Humson and Glenn, pronouncing them guilty of crimes against humanity and demanding an investigation of Alcatraz. Before Stamphill can get Young transferred out of Alcatraz, he is found dead in his cell. Stamphill's voice-over tells us that the Young case resulted in the closing of Alcatraz's underground cells and the conviction of Glenn for prisoner abuse. Alcatraz closed for good in 1963 and was turned into a major tourist attraction. For another example of first-degree murder, check out the cost of a tour.

Legal Analysis

Associate Warden Glenn metes out the torture, but the film argues that Warden Humson (and by extension, viewers) are ultimately to blame for not paying attention to what happened inside Alcatraz. Though the film depicts conditions as they existed in Alcatraz more than fifty years earlier, its message to contemporary viewers is that public indifference to prisons leads inevitably to prisoner abuse. The message became especially relevant in the earliest years of the twenty-first century, when it was revealed that U.S. soldiers had secretly engaged in abuse of prisoners during the U.S. occupation of Iraq.

Young's guilt. Stamphill's "Alcatraz made him do it" claim doesn't constitute an actual defense. An insanity verdict would have fit the facts and have allowed the jurors to absolve Young of criminal responsibility, but Stamphill's not-guilty plea doesn't provide the jurors with that option. A verdict of voluntary manslaughter would also have been reasonable, on the grounds that Young acted in an uncontrollable heat of passion when, after serving three brutal years in solitary, he suddenly met up with the snitch. Another possibility is that three years in solitary so diminished Young's mental capacity that he was incapable of premeditation; this verdict would have produced a conviction of second-degree murder and not exposed Young to the death penalty. The involuntary manslaughter verdict makes little sense because that generally applies to unintentional but reckless behavior that results in another's death. Probably it represented a compromise between jury members who wanted to find Young not guilty and those who wanted to convict him of murder.

Life in prison. At the time of the events depicted in the film, judges typically gave free rein to corrections officials and ignored conditions inside prisons. By the time the film was made, the U.S. Supreme Court had decided that the Eighth Amendment's ban on "cruel and unusual punishment" applied to prisons. As a result, judges can order prison officials to correct hazardous or unduly harsh conditions. For example, judges have acted when presented with evidence of overcrowding, lack of access to medical treatment, failure to protect prisoners' safety, and inadequate facilities for prisoners in solitary confinement. Failure to provide hookers does not constitute cruel and unusual punishment, however.

Ignorance is amiss. A small gaffe, but one that frequently arises in courtroom films, occurs when Judge Clawson instructs the jurors to ignore the former prison guard's testimony about pushing Young down a flight of stairs at Glenn's behest. Apparently the judge thought the guard not credible because his testimony might have been payback to Glenn for firing him. But credibility decisions are for jurors to make, not judges. The judge's instruction was wrong.

Picturing justice: As Young is tortured and thrown into a dungeon, children sing a Christmas carol whose lyric refers to "tidings of comfort and joy." The ironic contrast emphasizes prisoners' isolation from society.

Trial Brief

The film begins by informing viewers that it is inspired by a true story, but the plot consists of at least as much fiction as fact. Henri Young did try to escape from Alcatraz and in 1941 was tried for murder for killing another prisoner. Young's defense was based on the brutality of confinement in Alcatraz, and he was convicted of involuntary manslaughter. The jury petitioned the judge to investigate conditions inside Alcatraz. Stamphill is an amalgam of a number of lawyers who represented Young.

However, Young was hardly the film's naïve orphan who was sent to Alcatraz for stealing a few dollars from a post office. He was convicted of bank robbery and imprisoned in Leavenworth, then transferred to Alcatraz because he was considered incorrigible. He had already served time in state prisons for burglary and robbery. Young was placed in solitary confinement while at Alcatraz, but whether it was for three weeks (as the Bureau of Prisons maintains) or three years (as the filmmakers contend) is uncertain because records no longer exist.

Young killed the victim long after Young was released from solitary. He did it with a knife in the prison laundry and not with a spoon in the mess hall (as shown in the film) or with a candlestick in the conservatory. The killing was likely the result of a lover's quarrel rather than an act of revenge for squealing about an escape attempt.

Young did not die in Alcatraz. He was transferred to the Medical Center for Federal Prisoners in Springfield, Missouri, where he served out his sentence in 1954. He was then transferred to a Washington state prison to serve time for a killing that took place during a robbery that he committed. Young was released in 1972, jumped parole, and disappeared.

Night Falls on Manhattan

Synopsis: An idealistic D.A. learns that two wrongs can make it right.

Paramount Pictures, 1997. Color. Running time: 114 minutes.

Screenplay: Sidney Lumet. Novel: Robert Daley. Director: Sidney Lumet.

Starring: Andy Garcia (Sean Casey), Richard Dreyfuss (Sam Vigoda).

Rating: ——🔨 ——🔨 ——🔨

The Story

Police officers Liam Casey and Joey Allegretto arrest dope dealer Jordan Washington after a ferocious shootout leaves three cops dead. The prosecutor at Washington's murder trial is Casey's son Sean, an idealistic neophyte.

Washington's lawyer is Sam Vigoda, whose surprising defense is that Washington shot the cops in self-defense. Washington had been paying off the cops for protection, and when he refused their higher demands they came to assassinate him. The jury quickly convicts Washington. His story seems outrageous, and Vigoda could perhaps have done a better job of preparing Washington to testify. Not only does Washington smile proudly when he testifies to gunning down the cops, but he also leaps over the witness box and attacks Sean during cross-examination.

Vigoda's pressure forces Internal Affairs to investigate, and Sean soon gets the bad news: Washington told the truth. In fact, Allegretto was one of the cops who extorted money from Washington. If that's not bad enough, Sean's father forged Washington's arrest warrant after the legitimate one expired. With all this dirt floating around, Sean and Vigoda agree to call it a wash. Sean protects his father by shredding the expired warrant. Vigoda keeps quiet, satisfied that Washington is in jail where he belongs and that the dirty cops will join him shortly.

Elected to the position of D.A., it's Sean's turn to welcome a new crop of prosecutors. He tells them that justice is not always black and white and that he has learned that sometimes not "breaking the law is more than just upholding the law." You can bet that they didn't learn this interesting tidbit in law school.

Legal Analysis

The film reprises the familiar question of whether the ends justify the means. Washington is evil, and the city is well rid of him. Yet if those who are sworn to uphold the law resort to illegal means, the legal and constitutional rules that protect privacy, prevent police misconduct, and guarantee fair trials are worthless.

The forged arrest warrant. Liam Casey didn't want to lose the chance to arrest Washington by taking the time to get a new arrest warrant after the old one had expired. Despite the importance the film attaches to Casey's behavior, his failure to obtain a valid arrest warrant would not invalidate Washington's arrest. At most, a judge might have thrown out any evidence the cops seized when they arrested Washington. Because they didn't seize any evidence, the lack of an arrest warrant wouldn't make any difference.

Washington's self-defense claim. Despite his criminal background, Washington had a right to respond to the cops' illegal use of deadly force with deadly force of his own. The cops' attempted assassination of Washington was obviously illegal, so Washington was legally justified in attempting to kill them before they killed him.

"I'm taking the Fifth!" During Washington's cross-examination, Sean asks him whether he ever killed anyone while building up his drug empire. Washington refuses to answer based on his Fifth Amendment privilege against self-incrimination. Washington has a right to take refuge in the Fifth Amendment when asked about his involvement in unrelated crimes. However, Washington's use of the privilege was unnecessary. Vigoda should have objected that Sean's question was irrelevant because the prior killings have nothing to do with the charges for which he is currently being tried.

Picturing justice. The film portrays prosecutors as the legal profession's bottom-feeders. It opens with a bored assistant to an assistant welcoming a freshly minted crop of prosecutors by telling them that they are there because they couldn't get a better job and that their real hope is to use the D.A.'s office as a stepping-stone to a job with a Wall Street law firm. In fact, this is untrue; entry-level prosecution jobs are highly sought after because they provide great trial experience. Later, a judge dozes off while Sean argues and a dinner date stomps out on him when he's delayed in court.

Trial Brief

Sidney Lumet, one of the greatest American directors, both wrote and directed *Night Falls on Manhattan*. Lumet specialized in legally oriented films, particularly those involving police corruption. He directed a number of trial films, including *The Verdict, 12 Angry Men,* and the vastly inferior *Guilty as Sin*. In addition, he directed *Q&A* (1990), *Prince of the City* (1981), *Serpico* (1973), and *Daniel* (1983), all of which involve themes relating to law and justice. Finally, he created the cable television series *100 Centre Street,* which also involved trials and judges. *Night Falls on Manhattan* was Lumet's twenty-ninth film set in New York City.

The Star Chamber

Synopsis: Angered by technicalities that allow dangerous criminals to go free, judges secretly turn to a hit man.

20th Century Fox, 1983. Color. Running time: 109 minutes.

Screenplay: Roderick Taylor and Peter Hyams. Director: Peter Hyams.

Starring: Michael Douglas (Judge Steven Hardin), Hal Holbrook (Judge Benjamin Caulfield).

Rating: ——▇ ——▇

The Story

A serial killer has robbed and killed five elderly victims, and a young boy has been brutally murdered. Judge Hardin has to dismiss charges against the serial killer because the cops illegally searched his garbage. Judge Hardin also has to free Lawrence Monk and Arthur Cooms, the alleged child-killers, because the cops stopped their van based on erroneous computer records.

A frustrated Hardin confesses to his wife, Emily: "I don't know if I can do it anymore. I don't know if I can look at one more face come into my

The Star Chamber. Judge Steven Hardin (Michael Douglas) must make difficult rulings excluding unlawfully seized evidence.

court expecting right and I've got to tell them wrong." Hardin's doubts about whether the legal system can produce justice grow when the murdered boy's father tells him that a second boy has been killed: "You go tell that father about your system. . . . You killed his son."

Hardin's mentor, Judge Caulfield, offers a solution. Caulfield convinces Hardin to join his secret cabal of judges that doles out and enforces death sentences to rectify the legal system's mistakes. The vigilante group consists of nine judges, turning it into a "Slew-preme Court." In Hardin's first case, the judges send their hit man after a killer whose conviction was reversed because the court reporter died while the case was on appeal. In a second case, the judges order the death of a killer set free by an ambiguity in a search warrant.

When Hardin brings the case of Monk and Cooms to the vigilantes, they order up two more deaths. But when Monk and Cooms turn out to be innocent (of the boy's murder, anyway), Hardin desperately tries to cancel the executions. The judges respond by making Hardin No. 3 on the hit man's list. Hardin survives beatings and a warehouse explosion, then helps a police officer listen in as the vigilantes discuss their next hit. Hopefully the cop has a search warrant. If not, a court may set the vigilantes free and they will have to order their own executions.

Legal Analysis

The film capitalizes on popular sentiment that criminals routinely go free because of mindless technicalities. Yet the film straddles both sides of the issue by arguing that neither the legal system nor vigilantism works. By turning itself into a thriller in which a meek Judge Hardin suddenly acquires the survival abilities of Agent 007, the film loses all pretense of serious criticism.

The Star Chamber. The title refers to an English court developed in 1347 to handle complex cases. The court took its name from the gilt stars in the ceiling of its courtroom. The term's negative connotation of unfair and arbitrary procedures dates from the reign of Henry VIII. He often used the court for trials of political dissidents. They were not afforded jury trials, and the court specialized in gruesome punishments like slit noses, severed ears, and bangers and mash for breakfast.

Fourth Amendment issues. Underlying the film is the "exclusionary rule," which prevents prosecutors from introducing unlawfully seized evidence in court. A companion rule that affected Judge Hardin's rulings is known as the "fruit of the poisonous tree," which means that in many situations prosecutors can't introduce evidence that results from illegally seized information.

The exclusionary rule has been a subject of continuing controversy, with many arguing that "the criminal shouldn't go free just because the constable erred." Others respond that the exclusionary rule deters police misconduct and that its value outweighs the occasional dismissal of criminal charges. The U.S. Supreme Court, which developed the rule in the first place, has somewhat reduced its influence. For example, the Court has ruled that if police officers conduct a search in good-faith reliance on a search warrant, the search is valid even if the warrant was in fact invalid (*United States v. Leon*, 1984). If the Court were to adopt a more general exception, allowing prosecutors to offer any evidence that results from a search carried out in good faith, the evidence in both of the cases that tormented Judge Hardin might be admissible. The police thought they were following the rules when they searched the garbage can and the van.

At the time the film was made, California rules required police officers to obtain search warrants before rummaging through garbage, and hopefully to bathe afterward. The U.S. Supreme Court later changed that rule, deciding that people do not have a reasonable expectation of privacy in their trash (*California v. Greenwood*, 1988). The police stop of Monk and Cooms' van would also be valid now, because the officers relied in good faith on computer records (*Arizona v. Evans*, 1995). Moreover, because of the mobility of cars compared with houses, judges tend to uphold most police stops and investigations of cars and their occupants.

Saving court reporters. In the interests of protecting court reporters, we should mention that their deaths do not affect case outcomes. One reason is that computers routinely make contemporaneous copies of transcripts. At any rate, a court reporter's transcript is just one method of proving testimony. Anyone who heard a witness testify (such as the judge, a clerk, an attorney, or a spectator seeking shelter from the rain) can testify to what the witness said in a later court proceeding.

Picturing justice. (1) Countering public sentiment that often equates criminal-defense attorneys with their scumbag clients, the demeanor of Monk and Cooms' attorney shows that he despises them. (2) When Hardin dismisses the charges against the serial killer, one side of his face is lit and the other side is dark, symbolizing the conflict between his duty to follow the law and his desire to achieve justice.

Suspect

Synopsis: A juror and a defense attorney find a killer and love during a deaf-mute's murder trial.

Columbia Pictures, 1987. Color. Running time: 121 minutes.

Screenplay: Eric Roth. Director: Peter Yates.

Starring: Cher (Kathleen Riley), Dennis Quaid (Eddie Sanger), Liam Neeson (Carl Anderson).

Rating: —◼ —◼

The Story

Law clerk Elizabeth Quinn is stabbed to death. The police find a knife and Quinn's purse in a nearby culvert inhabited by wild-looking derelict Carl Anderson. Shrewdly, they arrest him for murder. Rendered deaf and mute by a war-related illness, Anderson communicates with his attorney, public defender Kathleen Riley, with pen, paper, and occasionally fists. Anderson insists that Quinn was already dead when he found her body.

Slick political lobbyist Eddie Sanger unsuccessfully tries to get off the jury by mentioning during jury *voir dire* that Riley dyes her hair. (Maybe "multiple face lifts" would have been a better exit strategy.) Sanger rewards Riley for keeping him around with a secret phone tip that helps her attack prosecutor Charlie Stella's expert witness. Sanger then obtains valuable information by visiting Quinn's car, which the police have allowed to remain in the same commercial parking lot for two months. (Hopefully the police validate for parking.) Sanger also helps Riley break into government files. Sanger sure knows how to woo a lawyer, even if baleful Judge Helms becomes more suspicious of their activities by the minute.

* * *

SPOILER ALERT: You may not want to read further if you plan to see the film.

* * *

Sanger realizes that Judge Helms' car was parked in the same lot as Quinn's on the night she was murdered. Then, Riley breaks into Quinn's car (accumulating still more overtime charges) and finds an audiotape that the police thoughtfully left inside. The speaker confesses that he and Judge Helms took a bribe many years earlier. Sanger and Riley figure out that Helms killed Quinn to prevent the bribe from coming to light and derailing his expected promotion. Judge Helms is arrested, and Sanger and Riley head lustfully for her office.

Legal Analysis

Putting aside its implausible premise, *Suspect*'s most enduring image may be Judge Helms' motive for murder. Though he's already got it made as a trial judge, he wants to rise still higher in the legal system. Thus, even judges live in a dog-eat-dog world.

Suspect: Kathleen Riley (Cher) cross-examines while Charlie Stella (Joe Mantegna) waits his turn.

Public defender burnout. Other than the fact that the Potomac River does indeed run through Washington, D.C., perhaps the most accurate depiction in the film is Kathleen Riley as a tired and over-worked public defender. Elected officials get more mileage out of fund-ing prosecutors than funding criminal-defense attorneys. As a result, many public defenders carry excessive caseloads. Remarkably, on the whole, public defenders still manage to provide quality representation.

Commiserating with an equally drained colleague, Riley agrees that what keeps her going is the rare chance to defend an innocent client. However, few criminal-defense attorneys would measure success by the number of innocent clients they've successfully defended. Negotiating an advantageous plea bargain, finding an effective diversion program for a drug user, or arranging for counseling for a client who must serve time in jail are more common types of triumphs for publicly paid defense attorneys. Moreover, most criminal-defense lawyers find satisfaction in being part of a legal system that compels the state to follow fair proce-dures and prove guilt beyond a reasonable doubt.

Why can't jurors do that? Jurors have to do the best they can with the information that attorneys choose to introduce as evidence. If either side lacks the resources or the determination to investigate, or if both sides decide for strategic reasons to hold back information, the jury will base its verdict on incomplete information. Should jurors play a more active role? Some states now allow jurors to submit questions to the judge, who can pose them to the witnesses. However, no states allow jurors to investigate cases themselves, as Sanger does. (A juror also conducts an improper investigation in the classic film *12 Angry Men.*)

A gaffe a minute. *Suspect* presents an amazing array of misinformation about legal procedures. Here are some of the high (or low) lights.

• The basic plot is impossible. A public defender like Riley would never risk her career by accepting help from a juror. She also commits the crime of jury tampering, which would give her a chance to get close to many of her former clients by serving time with them.

• Riley didn't need to break into Quinn's car. Because the car might contain relevant evidence, the defense could inspect it at any time just by asking. In the unlikely event that the police refused permission, Riley could obtain a court order. Also, the police would not have overlooked the audiotape cassette; even the Keystone Kops would have found it.

• Sanger and Riley would not be able to find the case in which Judge Helms took a bribe in the *Federal Supplement.* The *Federal Supplement* compiles written opinions issued by federal trial-court judges. Because the case in which the bribe was taken was dismissed prior to trial, no written opinion would exist.

• Riley and Judge Helms have three *ex parte* (private) conversations about the case. Opposing counsel have a right to be included in all case-related conversations between judges and attorneys. Poor Prosecutor Stella might be searching for a better breath mint.

• Cross-examining the investigating officer, Riley asks whether he knows that 343 defendants were wrongly convicted of capital crimes and that 25 of them were executed. Riley doesn't provide the source of her figures, but given her trial skills she may be referring to just the clients who she's represented. At any rate, the question is improper for almost every reason that a question can be improper. Riley is not a witness and cannot insert information about other cases into the record. And the results of other cases are irrelevant to the issue of whether Anderson is guilty.

• Stella's cross-examination questions focusing on Anderson's violent past are improper. They invite the jury to infer that because Anderson committed violent acts in the past, he murdered Quinn. With few exceptions, character evidence rules forbid prosecutors from asking jurors to engage in this type of reasoning. (See "Sidebar: Character Evidence" in Chapter 10.)

• In his opening statement, Stella tells the jurors: "I've tried forty-three murder cases, and this one is the most senseless and indefensible." Apparently, he's not talking about the film's plot. However, he violates the "voucher rule," which forbids lawyers from asking jurors to base verdicts on the lawyers' backgrounds and experiences.

• In one scene, Riley suddenly throws an object to Anderson. He catches it in his left hand, demonstrating that he's left-handed and therefore not the killer. However, Riley's demonstration is improper. Anderson's catch is the equivalent of the testimony, "I'm left-handed," but he can't properly testify because he's not under oath and it's not his turn. Riley's ploy recycles a memorable scene from *To Kill a Mockingbird,* where Atticus Finch tossed an object to Tom Robinson to show that Robinson had no use of one arm.

Picturing justice. Their skills aside, Riley and Stella provide positive lawyer images. Riley is overwhelmed by the demands of her job and has no personal life, but she is deeply committed to her clients' welfare. Stella prosecutes because he honestly believes that Anderson is guilty, not for any ulterior motive.

Short Subjects

Coquette, 1929. Mary Pickford, Johnny Mack Brown. ——■ ——■

Dr. Besant is charged with murder after he kills his daughter Norma's adoring but poor sweetheart, Michael. Besant's lawyer convinces Norma to testify falsely that Michael had raped her, and then argues that Besant is not guilty under the "unwritten law." *Courtroom highlight*: After the D.A.'s ardent cross-examination reveals Norma's perjury, Besant picks up the loaded murder weapon from the exhibits table and kills himself. *Picturing justice*: Criminal-defense lawyers value winning more than justice. *Trial brief*: This was Mary Pickford's first "talkie," and she won the Academy Award as Best Actress. Most critics believe that the award recognized her for becoming "America's Sweetheart" during the era of silent films.

Devil's Advocate, 1997. Al Pacino, Keanu Reeves.
——■ ——■ ——■

Satan has come to earth as John Milton, the managing partner of a big New York law firm. Thus, the film engages in lawyer-bashing or Satan-bashing, depending on your point of view. Milton explains that law "puts us into everything. It's the ultimate backstage pass. It's the new priesthood, baby." Milton's protégé is Kevin Lomax, a superarrogant young lawyer who has never lost a case. Perhaps that's because Lomax has "hearing assist": he turns out to be Milton's son. Lomax successfully defends a murderer by putting on alibi testimony he strongly suspects is phony. In another case, Lomax demolishes a high school student's testimony that her teacher sexually molested her, even though Lomax is virtually certain that she's telling the truth. After Milton and Lomax have a fire-and-brimstone-filled falling out, Lomax mysteriously finds himself about to cross-examine the same student. This time, Lomax decides to withdraw from the case in open court. A journalist is amazed: "A lawyer with a crisis of conscience? It's huge." *Picturing justice*: Like many other films, *Devil's Advocate* sends the message that a criminal-defense lawyer who believes his client to be guilty should betray rather than defend the client.

JFK, 1991. Kevin Costner, Tommy Lee Jones, Joe Pesci. ▬▬■ ▬▬■

Perhaps the mother of all conspiracy films, *JFK* ridicules the Warren Commission's conclusion that Lee Harvey Oswald was the lone assassin of President Kennedy. New Orleans D.A. James Garrison unsuccessfully prosecutes Clay Shaw for being part of a conspiracy to assassinate the president. Filmmaker Oliver Stone conveys his opinion that the assassination was the work of the "military-industrial complex" through Garrison's lengthy closing argument. *Courtroom highlight*: Interspersed with the argument is actual footage from the famous "Zapruder film." *Picturing justice*: (1) Everyone in the courtroom listens raptly to Garrison's argument, suggesting to viewers that what he's saying is accurate. (2) Garrison argues, "Going back to when we were children, most of us in this courtroom thought that justice came into being automatically. . . . But as we get older we know this just isn't true. Individual human beings have to create justice, because the truth often poses a threat to power."

The Lady from Shanghai, 1947. Orson Welles, Rita Hayworth.
▬▬■ ▬▬■

Two sleazy law partners and a beautiful woman manipulate a love-smitten seaman in what many regard as a *film noir* classic. Lawyer George Grisby plans to escape to a new life by pretending to be dead and convinces Michael O'Hara to sign a written confession that he killed Grisby. In return, Grisby will give O'Hara enough money to allow him to run off with Elsa Bannister, the wife of Grisby's law partner Arthur Bannister. When Grisby turns up dead, O'Hara is tried for murder, and he's represented by Arthur. *Courtroom highlight*: Called as a prosecution witness, Arthur cross-examines himself. *Picturing justice*: O'Hara says that the lawyers are "like the sharks, mad with their own blood, chewing away at their own selves." *Trial brief*: The final shootout in a hall of mirrors is a film classic, and the montage is perhaps director Welles' critique of the criminal justice system.

Marked Woman, 1937. Humphrey Bogart, Bette Davis ——■ ——■

The courts are the last line of defense when politicians are in bed with the crooks. Gangster Johnny Vanning's chain of crooked clip joints is supported by political leaders and lawyers who "take advantage of every technicality of the law and who coach and buy perjured testimony." Mary Strauber and other "hostesses" entertain gamblers, and losers who can't pay end up dead in the river. Crusading D.A. David Graham tries to clean up both the city and the river, but the hostesses initially refuse to testify against Vanning because they believe that "the law isn't for people like us." They courageously decide to testify after Vanning murders Mary's sister and disfigures Mary's face. *Picturing justice*: Vanning's defense lawyer is a full partner in his criminal enterprise. *Trial brief*: The film was inspired by D.A. Thomas E. Dewey's successful prosecution of New York mob mastermind "Lucky" Luciano. While in prison, Luciano helped in the U.S. effort in World War II and as governor of New York Dewey pardoned Luciano and deported him to Italy.

Night Court, 1932. Walter Huston. ——■ ——■

Judge Andrew Moffett presides over night court, nobly declaring, "This court stands for honesty and decency and the protection of the poor people and the administration of justice." In fact, Moffett is as crooked and vicious as they come, perhaps the most thoroughly corrupt judge in movie history. He puts hungry beggars in jail while pocketing big bribes to dismiss criminal cases. To silence Mary Thomas, an innocent woman who got a look at his bank book, Moffett sends her to prison on a phony prostitution rap, sends her baby to an orphanage, and has her husband, Mike, beaten up and sent to South America. Meanwhile, special prosecutor Judge Osgood is closing in on Moffett. When Osgood is murdered, Moffett is the chief suspect. *Courtroom highlight*: The D.A. plays an incriminating tape of a meeting between Osgood and Moffett. Osgood hid a tape recorder in his humidor—high technology in 1932! (Ironically, Moffett didn't kill Osgood, but he's convicted and sent to prison anyway.) *Trial brief*: A film like *Night Court* could not have been made after 1934 because the Production Code (Hollywood's system of self-censorship) required that "special care" be exercised in the representation of law enforcement officers like prosecutors or judges. (See "Sidebar: The Production Code" in Chapter 3.)

Sleepers, 1996. Brad Pitt, Kevin Bacon, Dustin Hoffman, Robert DeNiro. ——■ ——■

Four teenage buddies end up in reform school after a prank goes awry. There they are brutally tortured by a sadistic guard. Years later, two of the buddies, now gangsters, gun down the guard and are prosecuted for murder. Luckily, a third buddy became a prosecutor and is assigned the case—and manages to lose it with the help of a supportive priest's perjured alibi testimony. In essence, the legal system aids and abets vigilante justice. *Picturing justice*: Defense lawyer Danny Snyder is a drunken incompetent who does as he's told. *Trial brief*: Lorenzo Carcaterra wrote the book and claims to be one of the four buddies. He asserts that the story is true, although names, dates, and places were changed. Many commentators doubt his claims, and Carcaterra has offered no evidence to back them up.

The Star Witness, 1931. Walter Huston. ——■ ——■

The prosecution of gangster Maxey Campo for gunning down two cops sends a message to viewers to stand up to hoodlums and foreigners. Members of the Leeds family see the shooting and identify Campo in the D.A.'s office but are too scared to identify him in court. Cantankerous Grandpa Leeds rescues his grandson from the gang, rushes into court, and identifies Campo, just as the judge is about to dismiss the case. Grandpa castigates his relatives: "If a lot of skunks are running the country it's not yours, it's theirs." *Picturing justice*: Justice and vigilantism combine as Grandpa knocks Campo to the courtroom floor as the spectators cheer. *Legal analysis*: Under some circumstances, judges and juries can base convictions on witnesses' pretrial identifications, even if the witnesses refuse to repeat the identifications in the courtroom.

Trial by Jury, 1994. Joanne Whalley, Gabriel Byrne. ──▪

The Juror, 1996. Demi Moore, Alec Baldwin. ──▪

Perhaps something was in the water during the mid-1990s, because both films concern mobsters who convince a juror to vote not guilty by threatening to kill her and her son. This plot is clearly not designed to make viewers feel good about serving on a jury. The films also capitalize on the popular conception that jury decisions are often irrational, as the threatened jurors manage to convince colleagues to join them in voting not guilty despite overwhelming evidence of guilt. Predictably, both films degenerate into improbable action stories, when the threatened jurors turn into vigilante superheroes and achieve with weapons the justice that the judicial process could not.

True Believer, 1989. James Woods, Robert Downey Jr. ──▪

The film implies that prosecutors and cops are willing to frame an innocent person for murder in order to protect a valuable informant. Eddie Dodd is a 1960s radical who defends the constitutional rights of drug dealers in court while sampling their merchandise in his office. Dodd obtains a new trial for convicted murderer Shu Kai Kim, and a few corpses and beatings later he secures Kim's freedom after his prosecutor testifies that the actual killer was a valuable informant. The prosecutor fails to explain how honest eyewitnesses could have mistaken the Korean Shu Kai Kim for the Colombian informant Arturo Esparza. *Picturing justice*: Dodd tells an idealistic new lawyer, "You want to be a criminal-defense attorney? Then know this going in. Everybody's guilty. Everybody." (Except for Shu Kai Kim, apparently.) *Trial brief*: Dodd's character is loosely based on San Francisco lawyer Tony Serra, and some scenes were shot in Serra's law office. The plot is a much-altered version of a matter that Serra once handled.

It's Just a Bunch of
Circumstantial Evidence

Cine-lawyers often deride the claims of their adversaries as based on "nothing but a bunch of circumstantial evidence." In fact, circumstantial evidence is a respectable means of proof on a par with its counterpart, direct evidence. Indeed, circumstantial evidence may have even greater probative force than direct evidence. To paraphrase the wise advice of a legal sage, "Everyone would accept dog tracks in the snow as evidence that a dog had passed by over the sworn declaration of ten witnesses who swore that it hadn't."

Circumstantial evidence is a form of proof whose value depends on an inference. We draw inferences routinely in everyday life, as when we assume that a smiling person is probably happy. Thus, there's nothing wrong with inferring that a masked person who dashed into a waiting car with a bag of cash probably robbed a nearby bank.

At the same time, circumstantial evidence is an excellent plot device because it often gives rise to conflicting inferences. For example, assume there's evidence that a bank teller saw a defendant charged with bank robbery in the bank the day before it was robbed. The prosecutor might argue that the teller's evidence supports an inference that the defendant was "casing the joint." Yet the defense attorney might counter that the teller's testimony disproves the defendant's guilt, because the defendant would never have entered a bank that he planned to rob the next day. In actual cases, judges and jurors have to decide which of these inferences is more likely to be true, and their decisions typically are shaped by numerous other items of evidence presented during the trial. Filmmakers can manipulate their audiences by choosing what pieces of circumstantial evidence to reveal and when to reveal them.

The films collected in this chapter demonstrate a variety of ways that filmmakers can use circumstantial evidence to create drama and suspense. Perhaps the audience knows "what really happened," yet strong circumstantial evidence leads the jurors in the wrong direction, as in *Fury* and *I Confess*. On the other hand, by choosing not to show crucial events, filmmakers can leave audiences in the quite realistic predicament of not knowing what really happened, as in *A Place in the Sun, Reversal of Fortune,* and *12 Angry Men.* Often, by selectively disclosing bits of circumstantial evidence, a film can lure the audience into the wrong conclusion about what actually happened; then the filmmaker springs the trap. *Witness for the Prosecution, Jagged Edge, Suspect,* and *Snow Falling on Cedars* are examples of this gambit. All in all, these films provide excellent circumstantial evidence of why courtroom films can be endlessly fascinating.

Fury

Synopsis: The survivor of an attempted lynching takes revenge on the lynch mob.

MGM, 1936. Black and white. Running time: 90 minutes.

Screenplay: Bartlett Cormack and Fritz Lang. Original story: Norman Krasna. Director: Fritz Lang.

Starring: Spencer Tracy (Joe Wilson), Sylvia Sidney (Katherine Grant).

Academy Award nomination: Best Original Story.

Rating: ——◼ ——◼ ——◼ ——◼

The Story

Joe Wilson drives to the small town of Strand to pick up Katherine Grant so they can marry. Before he gets there, he's arrested for participating in a kidnap-for-ransom plot. The serial number on a five-dollar bill in Wilson's pocket, and even a fondness for salted peanuts, link him to the crime.

Wilson is really stranded when lynch-mob fever takes over the town. The locals assume that arrested people are guilty and don't want to give Wilson time to find a lawyer, because "that's the racket of those big-time attorneys, helping these skunks beat the law." A mob descends on the jailhouse, setting it on fire and dynamiting it to bits. Grant and

Fury: D.A. Adams (Walter Abel) is not proposing marriage to Katherine Grant (Sylvia Sidney), but instead asking her to identify the fateful ring.

everyone else think that Wilson is dead, at just about the same moment that the capture of the kidnap gang proves his innocence. In fact, Wilson escaped.

Prosecutor Adams defies the town's leaders and charges twenty-two defendants with murdering Wilson. At trial, Adams condemns the mob as "a destroyer of a government that patriots have died to establish and defend." The trial is broadcast live to a rapt nation, giving Wilson the rare privilege of listening in on his killers' trial. The defense seems to be on a roll when all of Adams' witnesses provide the defendants with phony alibis and the sheriff says that the mob was made up of outsiders. Adams then shows a newsreel film depicting the defendants in the act of destroying the jail. Adams' clever strategy implicates the defendants and subjects the witnesses to perjury charges, though what jail he intends to put all of them in isn't clear.

Citing the *corpus delicti* rule, the defense attorney argues that the case must be dismissed because there's no proof that Wilson had actually died. Hearing this on the radio, Wilson provides the missing link by sending the judge an anonymous letter and a ring. The judge testifies that, according to the letter, the ring was found in the ashes of the jail, and Grant identifies the ring as Wilson's.

Grant figures out from a spelling mistake that Wilson wrote the letter, and she finds him and urges him to come forward. Wilson initially refuses. But as the clerk reads the jury's verdict pronouncing almost all the defendants guilty, Wilson walks into the courtroom and reveals his identity to the judge.

Legal Analysis

Made at a time when lynching still occurred and distrust of outsiders was rampant, *Fury* warned audiences that even ordinary towns were subject to a mob mentality. As in other overtly political films, the courtroom genre allows filmmakers to create drama and suspense by focusing on specific events, while the characters educate the audience through dialogue that raises wider social concerns. Thus, when Adams purports to talk to jurors about the scope of the lynching epidemic and Wilson tells the judge that mob violence undermines democracy, they address viewers directly while staying within the film's storyline. Yet the film pulls its punches by putting Strand into the Midwest and making a white male the target of the mob. In fact, most lynchings took place in the South, and the victims were almost always black males.

News-reel justice. At the time of *Fury,* photographs were routinely admissible in evidence. But the admissibility of a film, such as a news-reel, was less certain, because judges feared that jurors would be unduly swayed by the filmic "spectacle." However, judges soon decided to accept films as evidence of their contents on the theory that they were collections of individual photographs. (Effective legal arguments often suggest that what seems revolutionary is in reality quite familiar.) Of course, the lawyers would have to provide a foundation for admissibility by obtaining testimony from the filmmakers about when, where, and how the film was made.

When they first began to be admitted into evidence, films and photographs were no doubt considered to be better evidence of what really happened than live witnesses, who might easily be lying or mistaken. However, advances in technology render such faith in photographic evidence naïve. Aided by computers and digital processes, photographers and filmmakers can manipulate images to produce almost any desired effect.

The *corpus delicti* rule. This Latin phrase seems to connote that in a murder case the prosecution has to produce a dead body, and a good-looking one at that. However, the purpose of the *corpus delicti* rule is to prevent convictions based solely on defendants' own confessions. People sometimes confess to crimes they didn't commit because of a desire for attention or because of police coercion. As a result, the prosecution must prove by some means other than a defendant's own words that a crime took place and that the defendant committed it. However, the prosecution is not required to produce a dead body, just circumstantial evidence that a homicide occurred and that the defendant did it.

Role reversal. A sensible rule forbids judges from testifying at trials over which they preside. Thus, any conviction of the defendants would have been quickly reversed. The judge should have shown the letter and the ring to both sides. Grant's testimony that she gave the ring to Wilson, and its condition, would serve as circumstantial evidence that Wilson had died in the fire. However, the anonymous letter stating where the ring was found is inadmissible as evidence because its contents are hearsay.

Picturing justice. As a mob mentality sweeps over Strand, the camera focuses on a restaurant sign that reads "Calves Brains, 45 cents." The image suggests that mob activity subverts justice by turning people into animals, though the filmmakers might have been unfair to calves.

Trial Briefs

1. The great Viennese director Fritz Lang co-wrote and directed *Fury*. Lang also directed the classic film *M* (1931), which involved similar themes. In *M,* the police are hunting for a crazed killer of little girls. Their search disrupts the business of the local gangsters, so the mobsters capture the killer and put him on trial themselves. *Fury* was Lang's first American film after fleeing the Nazis. The harrowing lynch mob scenes in *Fury* must have drawn heavily on his personal experience at the hands of the Nazis. For example, the sheriff blames the whole fiasco on unknown people from out of town—which sounds quite a bit like Hitler blaming the Jews for Germany's troubles.

2. The film was first titled "The Mob" and then "Mob Rule," but Joseph Breen (head of the Hollywood self-censorship system) rejected both titles. Supposedly, MGM also softened the hard edges of the script, especially at the end. Louis B. Mayer detested Lang, so MGM released the movie without publicity in hopes it would flop so they

could get rid of Lang. Fortunately the critics immediately declared the film a classic.

3. The film is based on an incident that occurred in San Jose, California, in 1933. A mob dragged two accused kidnappers from their cells and hanged them in a public park. All the action was captured on newsreels. The governor of California, Sunny Jim Rolph Jr., refused to send in the militia and later declared that the lynching was the best lesson ever given the country. Nobody was charged with a crime.

I Confess

Synopsis: An accused priest's vow of silence prevents him from revealing the actual murderer's identity.

Warner Bros., 1953. Black and white. Running time: 95 minutes.

Screenplay: George Tabori and William Archibald. Original play: Paul Anthelme. Director: Alfred Hitchcock.

Starring: Montgomery Clift (Father Michael Logan), Karl Malden (Inspector Larrue).

Rating: ——▪ ——▪

The Story

In his church confessional, Father Michael Logan hears Otto Keller's confession to killing a lawyer named Villette. However, tenacious Inspector Larrue regards Father Logan as the prime suspect. Ruth Grandfort, Logan's precollar flame, tells Larrue that she was with Logan at the time of the murder. But her explanation that they met to talk about Villette's blackmail threat only adds "feud" to the fire. What Grandfort calls "alibi," Larrue calls "motive."

At trial, prosecutor Willy Robertson offers strong, circumstantial evidence of Father Logan's guilt. Witnesses saw a priest leaving Villette's home on the night of the murder. The police found a priest's cassock stained with blood of Villette's type hidden in a trunk in Logan's room. Keller, no stranger to sin already, adds perjury to his list by testifying that a distressed Logan came into the church shortly after the time of the murder. Logan denies committing the murder. He also denies that the bloody cassock is his, but he can't explain how it got into his trunk. Logan maintains his silence about Keller's confession.

I Confess: Father Logan (Montgomery Clift) can't explain how a bloody cassock got into his trunk.

The jury finds Father Logan not guilty, but it's an unpopular verdict and a mob soon forms around Logan. Either Logan is in danger or hundreds of people have decided to trust him with their confessions. Fearing the former, Mrs. Keller rushes forward and starts to shout out the truth. Perhaps she too should have taken a vow of silence, because Keller shoots her dead and flees. Quickly cornered by Larrue and Logan, Keller goes berserk and falsely accuses Logan of revealing his confession to the police. As the truth finally dawns on Larrue, the cops kill Keller.

Legal Analysis

The film is set in Quebec, but the investigation and trial are thoroughly American. As a suspect in the United States, Father Logan would have a constitutional right to remain silent. But as *I Confess* suggests, that right can't prevent the police and the jurors from drawing an inference of guilt if a suspect either cannot or will not explain away seemingly damning evidence.

Priests and penitents. The film's dramatic conflict grows out of Father Logan's decision not to reveal Keller's confession. During the investigatory phase of the case, the decision is rooted in Logan's conscience and his interpretation of the Catholic faith, rather than in a legal duty to remain silent. Other priests might interpret their religious obligations differently, especially when they become suspects.

Once formal legal proceedings get under way, Father Logan's obligations are measured not only by his conscience but also by a long-standing rule known as the "priest-penitent privilege." This alliterative doctrine aims to avoid conflicts between religious and legal obligations by providing that confidential communications between religious leaders (of all faiths) and members of their congregations cannot be disclosed. Keller would generally be regarded as the "holder" of the privilege, which means that Keller could have prevented Logan from testifying to what Keller told him even if Logan changed his mind and decided to disclose it.

In the film, Keller tells his wife about his confession. Ordinarily, publicizing an otherwise private conversation eliminates a privilege. However, Keller would be entitled to prevent his wife from squealing because a separate spousal communication privilege would apply. Keller is either very lucky, or he's an evidence expert masquerading as a lowly gardener.

Could Father Logan defend himself? Yes! Before Keller confessed to him, Father Logan saw Keller run into the church carrying a bundle of clothing. Logan's vow of silence should not extend to these preconfession events. Had Logan told Larrue what he saw, the right man would undoubtedly have ended up in the dock. Also, as a man of morality, one would expect Logan to urge Keller to salvage what remains of his soul by urging Keller to turn himself in.

Picturing justice. The film intermingles images of law and religion. For example, when Father Logan testifies a crucifix is visible on the courtroom wall behind him. The images suggest that, despite their power, neither institution can fully protect against injustice.

Trial Brief

In the original play, the priest is convicted and executed. While admittedly a downer, that ending would no doubt have increased the film's dramatic power. However, the Production Code (see "Sidebar: The Production Code" in Chapter 3) then in effect did not allow such an injustice, and Hitchcock evidently decided not to challenge the code.

The Hearsay Rule

The hearsay rule prevents a witness from testifying to an out-of-court statement that is offered for the truth of its contents. The idea behind the hearsay rule is that witnesses should tell their stories in court so that they can be cross-examined and judges and jurors can evaluate their truthfulness. In the United States, the hearsay rule is considered basic to the adversary system of trial and "Objection, hearsay!" is rightly one of the most common phrases that cine-lawyers utter. Viewers may think that hearsay evidence is like something that should be scraped off shoes, but in fact the rule has so many exceptions that witnesses frequently are allowed to testify to statements made by people who aren't in court. Here's how the hearsay rule would operate in some of the films this book discusses.

- In *Anatomy of a Murder,* Lieutenant Manion testifies that just before he shot Barney Quill his wife, Laura, told him that Quill had raped and beaten her. There's no problem with the hearsay rule, because what Laura told him isn't intended to prove that the rape actually took place but only to explain why Manion might have been temporarily insane when he shot Quill.

- In *Witness for the Prosecution,* the murder victim's housekeeper undermines Leonard Vole's alibi by testifying that she recognized Vole by his voice, talking to the victim in the house around 9:30 P.M. Again, there's no problem with the hearsay rule because the housekeeper's testimony isn't being used to prove that anything that Vole said was accurate, only that Vole was inside the house around the time of the murder.

- In *I Confess,* Keller admits to Father Logan that he killed a man, but Father Logan ends up charged with the murder. The hearsay rule might well prevent Logan from testifying that Keller admitted to him that he was the killer. However, if Keller were on trial for the killing, the "party admission" exception to the rule would allow Logan to testify that Keller admitted that he was the killer.

- In *Jagged Edge,* Jack Forrester is charged with killing his wife, Page, to prevent her from seeking a divorce that would leave him broke. Page's friend Virginia testifies that shortly before Page was killed, Page told Virginia that Jack was cheating on her. What Page told Virginia is admissible in evidence despite the hearsay rule because it isn't being used to prove that Jack was actually cheating. Instead, it is being used to prove that Jack had a motive to kill Page because she might well be planning to divorce him.

A Place in the Sun

Synopsis: A man is charged with murdering his unwanted and pregnant fiancée.

Paramount Pictures, 1951. Black and white. Running time: 120 minutes.

Screenplay: Michael Wilson and Harry Brown. Novel: Theodore Dreiser, *An American Tragedy*. Director: George Stevens.

Starring: Elizabeth Taylor (Angela Vickers), Montgomery Clift (George Eastman), Shelley Winters (Alice Tripp).

Academy Awards: Best Director, Best Screenplay, Best Cinematography, Best Costume Design, Best Editing, Best Musical Score.

Academy Award nominations: Best Picture, Best Actor (Montgomery Clift), Best Actress (Shelley Winters).

Rating:

The Story

Hailing from the disreputable side of the family, George Eastman goes to work for his wealthy Uncle Charles. Eastman begins a torrid romance with Alice Tripp, a poor assembly-line worker. Eastman gets Tripp "in trouble," and she pressures him to marry her. However, Eastman's secret new romance with the glamorous and wealthy Angela Vickers makes Tripp a decided liability.

Eastman takes Tripp to Loon Lake for what he tells her is a prehoneymoon. He rents a canoe and rows to an ominous, secluded inlet. As day turns to night, both the boat-rental cost and Eastman's frustration with his predicament rise precipitously. The conversation turns heated when Tripp suddenly stands up and the canoe overturns, spilling them both into the lake. Eastman swims to shore, but Tripp drowns. Eastman seems destined to marry Vickers until he's arrested for murdering Tripp.

A Place in the Sun: The D.A. (Raymond Burr) prepares to sink George Eastman's (Montgomery Clift) rowboat.

Tripp's pressure on Eastman to marry her furnishes D.A. Marlowe with ample evidence of motive. In addition, Marlowe presents evidence that Eastman and Tripp quarreled shortly before they got to Loon Lake; that Eastman rented the canoe under a false name; and that, according to the coroner, Tripp had been struck with a blunt instrument before she drowned. Eastman admits that he rented the canoe with the thought of drowning Tripp but insists that he couldn't follow through. When the canoe accidentally overturned, he claims he tried to save her.

Marlowe's impassioned cross-examination accuses Eastman of lying. Marlowe brings the canoe into the courtroom, and with Eastman seated in it ridicules his claim that he couldn't save Tripp. Marlowe concludes by smashing the oar to bits while accusing Eastman of murder. Marlowe's rowing technique needs work, but his trial technique is just fine. The jury convicts Eastman of murder, and he walks to the electric chair after Vickers tells him that she still loves him. That should help him feel better.

Legal Analysis

A Place in the Sun cuts away from the scene of Tripp's death at just the moment that the canoe overturns. The film contradicts prosecutor

Marlowe's version of events in two respects: The boat turned over accidentally, and Eastman didn't hit Tripp with an oar before it overturned. But he might have struck her once they were in the water, or she might have hit her head when the boat overturned. Either way, Eastman might have held Tripp underwater or he might be telling the truth when he said he tried to save her but couldn't. Thus, in the film, as in real trials, the jury (as well as film viewers) must decide what really happened based on incomplete information.

Although most of the circumstantial evidence favors the prosecution, some of it favors Eastman. For example, if Eastman had committed murder, he probably wouldn't have talked to the boatkeeper and to campers after he swam to shore. The proof problems on both sides would have made this an ideal situation for Eastman to make a deal with the prosecution and plead guilty to a lesser charge. At least, the jury should have been given the opportunity to convict him on a lesser included offense, such as second-degree murder or manslaughter.

Taking shore leave. Tripp may have drowned because Eastman didn't try to rescue her. Such conduct seems morally reprehensible, but it would not be murder. People other than Caped Crusaders have no general obligation to attempt rescues. This seemingly harsh rule spares people from having to choose between risking their own safety and being charged with a crime or required to pay damages if they fail to act.

Nevertheless, a duty to attempt rescue can arise when parties are in a "special relationship." For example, if Eastman and Tripp had been married, he would have been required to try to rescue her. Here, Tripp was pregnant with Eastman's child and they planned to marry. Moreover, Eastman took Tripp canoeing knowing that she couldn't swim. Thus his actions increased the risk that she might drown. Even if Eastman was not responsible for the canoe turning over, failing to attempt to save Tripp might have exposed him to a charge of involuntary manslaughter.

Publicity shy. Eastman's uncle agrees to pay for the defense attorneys after they and prosecutor Marlowe agree not to mention Vickers' name during the trial. As a result, the jurors hear occasional references to "another woman" but never learn who she is. Marlowe should never have agreed to such a deal because he could have bolstered his motive argument by calling Vickers as a witness and asking her to describe the intensity of her relationship with Eastman. At any rate, either side could have called Vickers, despite the agreement not to, because the bargain was legally unenforceable.

Picturing justice. (1) The film depicts the effect of class differences on the criminal justice system. For working-class people like Eastman, only disaster can result from seeking a "place in the sun" of wealth and power. Vickers' exalted social status keeps her name out of the trial entirely. (2) Dusting off a standard courtroom film gambit, prosecutor Marlowe figures that convicting Eastman will get him elected governor. Not if the taxpayers find out that he wastes government funds on oars that he immediately smashes to bits it won't.

Trial Brief

The film (and Dreiser's novel) is based on the true story of Chester Gillette, who was convicted of murdering his pregnant girlfriend, Grace Brown, in 1906. Gillette was executed in 1908.

Witness for the Prosecution

Synopsis: A turncoat witness destroys an alibi and a barrister's faith in his judgment.

United Artists, 1957. Black and white. Running time: 116 minutes.

Screenplay: Billy Wilder and Harry Kurnitz, adapted by Larry Marcus. Original story and play: Agatha Christie. Director: Billy Wilder.

Starring: Charles Laughton (Sir Wilfrid Robarts), Tyrone Power (Leonard Vole), Marlene Dietrich (Christine Helm Vole), Elsa Lanchester (Miss Plimsoll).

Academy Award nominations: Best Picture, Best Actor (Charles Laughton), Best Supporting Actress (Elsa Lanchester), Best Director, Best Film Editing, Best Sound.

Rating:

The Story

Irascible barrister Sir Wilfrid Robarts suffers from a bad heart and a smothering nurse, Miss Plimsoll. Her conversation is terminally cheerful, leading Sir Wilfrid to complain: "If I'd known how much you talked, I'd never have come out of my coma." Sir Wilfrid postpones retirement

Witness for the Prosecution: Sir Wilfrid Robarts (Charles Laughton) examines Leonard Vole (Tyrone Power).

in order to represent Leonard Vole, a war veteran charged with killing a wealthy widow, Emily French.

Prosecutor Myers offers powerful circumstantial evidence of Vole's guilt. Most damning is the testimony of Vole's "wife," Christine, who's allowed to testify because it turns out that she and Vole were not legally married. Christine demolishes Vole's alibi by testifying that on the night of the murder he returned home after 10:00 P.M., not at 9:30, as she had previously told the police. Christine also testifies that Vole admitted killing French. Sir Wilfrid refuses the judge's suggestion of a recess: "Pray, let the witness continue. We are all caught up in the suspense of this horror fiction. To have to hear it in installments might prove unendurable." Sir Wilfrid concludes Christine's cross-examination by commenting, "She's already violated so many oaths that I'm surprised the testament didn't leap from her hand when she was sworn here today."

With Sir Wilfrid's case looking worse than his E.K.G., he tricks Christine into admitting that she wrote a love letter to someone named Max describing her plan to rid herself of Vole by falsely implicating him in the murder. The prosecution's case collapses, and Vole is found not guilty. Yet Sir Wilfrid is troubled: "It's too neat, too tidy, altogether too symmetrical. That's what's wrong with it. It's not [the jury's] judgment that worries me, it's mine."

* * *

SPOILER ALERT: You may not want to read further if you plan to see the film.

* * *

Christine triumphantly tells Sir Wilfrid that Vole indeed killed French. Fearing that the jury would not believe her if she testified for Vole, she testified against him and, while in disguise, sold Sir Wilfrid the phony letter that allowed him to destroy her credibility. Christine embraces Vole, but he scorns her and embraces Diana, his new love. A furious Christine stabs Vole to death. In Sir Wilfrid's judgment, Christine was Vole's executioner, not his killer.

Legal Analysis

At the film's end, a voice-over advises viewers "not to divulge to anyone the secret of the ending." Hopefully, nobody did. The great acting and the double twist ending make *Witness for the Prosecution* one of the most entertaining courtroom pictures of all time. However, the movie nourishes popular suspicion that the trial process can be easily manipulated by clever people, like Vole and Christine. When he learns how he was deceived, Sir Wilfrid remarks: "The scales of justice may tip one way or the other, but ultimately they balance out." Perhaps so in the film, but perhaps not in real life.

Barristers and solicitors. As a barrister, Sir Wilfrid has a "right of audience" (he can appear as counsel) in the country's highest courts (the Crown Courts) so long as he wears a funny but very expensive wig. Vole is also represented by Mayhew, a solicitor who cannot appear in a Crown Court. A move has been afoot for some years to unify the profession. If solicitors are eventually allowed to appear in the Crown Courts, British wigmakers will be the big winners.

Spousal privileges. A long-standing rule allowed one spouse to prevent the other from giving harmful testimony. The rule supposedly protected family harmony. Most American states now give a spouse the right to testify against the other spouse but prevent lawyers from compelling them to do so. Had the newer American version of the rule been in effect in *Witness for the Prosecution*, Christine could have testified against Vole even if they were legally married.

A separate "marital communication" privilege bars testimony about private conversations between spouses. If Christine and Vole had been married, this second privilege would bar her from testifying that Vole told her he had bumped off French. Many American judges would probably rule that because Vole and Christine went through a marriage ceremony and lived together as husband and wife, he was a "putative spouse," which could prevent Christine from testifying to his confession.

The golden rule of cross-examination. After "mommy" and "daddy," the first phrase a future lawyer probably learns is "On cross-examination, never ask a question that you don't know the answer to." Sir Wilfrid pays dearly for violating this rule. Trying to undermine the testimony of French's testy housekeeper that she recognized Vole's voice through a thick door, Sir Wilfrid smugly suggests that the voices she heard probably came from a television drama. "It was not the television," retorts the housekeeper. "Why not?" asks Sir Wilfrid. "Because," she replies triumphantly, "the television was away being repaired that week." The zinger immediately drives Sir Wilfrid to his brandy-filled thermos.

Representing Christine. Sir Wilfrid plans to represent Christine at her upcoming murder trial. That provides a tidy ending to the film, but it could never happen. He would be a witness at her trial, and lawyers can't play both advocate and witness no matter how much they may want to.

Whoever does represent Christine would have a fair shot (or stab) at a conviction for manslaughter, a less-serious crime than premeditated murder. Her attorney would argue that she killed Vole in the heat of passion after he suddenly abandoned her. In fact, a jury might even find Christine not guilty of anything, because as a two-timing cheat who'd gotten away with murder, Vole "had it coming."

Picturing Justice. Sir Wilfrid interviews Vole while peering at him in the glare of a bright light that reflects off his monocle into Vole's eyes Sir Wilfrid concludes from the "monocle test" that Vole is telling the truth. (During her interview, Christine foils the test by closing the curtains to cut off the light.) While Sir Wilfrid is wrong, the scene nevertheless suggests that seasoned attorneys have the instinct to divine truth-tellers from liars. By contrast, psychological research suggests that visual cues to truth-telling like fidgeting or maintaining eye contact are often misleading. Skillful liars know how to manipulate such cues, but nervous truth-tellers often don't.

Short Subjects

The Case of the Howling Dog, 1934. Warren William.

Perry Mason defends an estranged wife charged with shooting her husband. Mason secures an acquittal by convincing the jury that the wife couldn't have been the murderer because the family dog charged at the shooter but wouldn't have gone after its own mistress. Mason secretly knows that the husband switched dogs days before the shooting took place, but he assures loving secretary Della Street that the verdict is just, because he's convinced that the wife shot in self-defense. *Courtroom highlights:* Mason tricks the dead husband's lover into admitting that she can write with either hand, and a cab driver into confusing Street with the wife. *Trial brief:* Warren William also starred as Perry Mason in *The Case of the Curious Bride* (1935), *The Case of the Lucky Legs* (1935), and *The Case of the Velvet Claws* (1936). In these films, Warner Bros. tried to capture the wisecracking ambience of the successful *Thin Man* films, but Mason's creator, Erle Stanley Gardner, detested the movies. He didn't like the fact that Mason was a drunk who didn't worry much about ethical constraints. In the subsequent radio and TV shows, Gardner always retained control of the Perry Mason character. On the television series and in numerous later movies made for television, Mason was played by Raymond Burr, who became totally identified with the character.

Dr. Crippen, 1962. Donald Pleasence.

Dr. Crippen is convicted of poisoning and dissecting his wife, Belle. The prosecution's ample circumstantial evidence includes Crippen's phony story that Belle left London for Chicago and his immediately shacking up with Ethel Le Neve, who wears Belle's finery all over London. Crippen's pregallows assertion to a priest that he accidentally gave Belle an overdose of a sedative is tardy, unconvincing, and unlikely to get him into heaven. *Picturing justice:* Le Neve stands outside the prison like the Angel of Death when Crippen is hung. *Trial brief:* In the actual case, Crippen was executed in 1910. Le Neve was charged with being an accessory after the fact but was acquitted.

Evelyn Prentice, 1934. William Powell, Myrna Loy.

Lawyer John Prentice argues for jury nullification on the grounds that a woman justifiably killed her abusive lover. Prentice's neglected wife, Evelyn, develops a friendship with Lawrence Kennard, who turns out to be a con artist. When Kennard demands money in exchange for her embarrassing letters, Evelyn fires a gun at Kennard and asumes she killed him. After Evelyn flees, Kennard's mistress, Judith Wilson, happens on the scene and is charged with murder. Evelyn convinces Prentice to defend Wilson. *Courtroom highlight:* After Evelyn confesses in mid-trial that she killed Kennard, Prentice browbeats his client Wilson into admitting that she shot Kenard. *Picturing Justice:* Prentice argues that Kennard's death "was an act of high justice" and continues, "And I ask you, gentlemen, in the name of that same high justice, to find him guilty by declaring Judith not guilty." *Trial brief:* In 1939, MGM remade the film almost line-for-line as *Stronger Than Desire.*

Legal Eagles, 1986. Robert Redford, Debra Winger, Darryl Hannah.

A defense lawyer and a prosecutor fall in love while carrying out such routine legal tasks as driving wildly through Manhattan, escaping from a locked warehouse moments before it explodes, and purloining insurance-company records. *Courtroom highlight:* After the prosecutor's opening statement, defense attorney Tom Logan asks the jurors whether they think the defendant is guilty. When all raise their hands, Logan tells the jurors that they're ignoring the presumption of innocence. *Legal analysis:* Among the countless ethical lapses in the film, Logan sleeps with a defendant while still a prosecutor and violates the Fourth Amendment by illegally searching a warehouse. Logan also violates conflict-of-interest rules by defending a person whom he had been prosecuting before the D.A. fired him.

The Murder Man, 1935. Spencer Tracy.

A murder trial conveys popular anger toward schemers who profited during the Great Depression. Spencer Halford, a shady financial adviser, is killed, and his business partner Mander is convicted and sentenced to death. Ace reporter Steve Gray gets a death-house interview with Mander and tells him angrily, "You killed people with your schemes and with your lies just as surely as if you'd shot them down in cold blood." Later that day Gray saves Mander with his last story, which describes how Gray killed Halford for preying on his family and thousands of others. *Picturing justice*: The police chief tells Gray's sweetheart to expect a light punishment because a jury is likely to sympathize with Gray's motive. *Trial brief*: Famous actor James Stewart had his first credited role in this film.

Nora Prentiss, 1947. Ann Sheridan. ——◼

Dr. Talbot uses a dead patient to fool his family into thinking that it was Talbot who died when his car exploded in flames. Talbot runs off with Nora Prentiss and assumes a new identity as Thompson. Years later, Talbot as Thompson is charged with setting off the explosion and murdering himself. The circumstantial evidence all fits, and Talbot is convicted and sentenced to death. Unwilling to be remembered as a philanderer, Talbot refuses Prentiss' pleas to reveal the truth. *Courtroom highlight*: Talbot's wife, Lucy, testifies that she's never before seen Talbot, whose face was disfigured after he ran off with Prentiss and became Thompson.

Physical Evidence, 1989. Burt Reynolds. ——◼

Jenny Hudson, a sexually harassed public defender, represents Joe Paris, a suspended cop accused of killing a nightclub owner. Hudson implausibly has unlimited time to run around with Paris and undermine the prosecution's strong circumstantial evidence while their initially icy relationship predictably blooms into romance. One judge warns Hudson, "I can do without the dramatics, counsel," but unfortunately there aren't any. *Picturing justice*: In a scene apparently left over from an old Preston Sturges film, the D.A. tries to search Hudson's home while Hudson, her boyfriend, and Paris rush around the house madly, each demanding that the others leave. *Legal analysis*: Hudson plans to offer evidence that people other than Paris had a motive to kill the nightclub owner. Defense attorneys often refer to this tactic as "blowing smoke," but evidence of motive alone is not adequate to support an argument that people other than the defendant committed a murder.

Reversal of Fortune, 1990. Ron Silver, Jeremy Irons, Glenn Close. ——◼ ——◼

Imperious Claus von Bülow is convicted of attempting to murder his wife, Sunny, by giving her an injection that left her alive but permanently brain dead. Urged by his new girlfriend to "get the Jew," von Bülow retains Harvard professor Alan Dershowitz to handle the appeal. Although appellate courts typically review only the written record of a trial, Dershowitz succeeds in convincing the Rhode Island Supreme Court to consider new evidence showing that the State's medical evidence was flawed. The court reverses the conviction. *Picturing justice*: Trying to motivate law students to work on the case of a man whom nearly everyone despises, Dershowitz argues that defending the rights of the guilty protects the rights of the innocent. Of course, it doesn't hurt that he gets paid plenty for doing the job. *Trial brief*: The film is based on a true story. The Rhode Island Supreme Court officially reversed the conviction because of errors made in the trial court, but it may well have been influenced by the troubling factual material that Dershowitz included as an appendix to his brief. Von Bülow was found not guilty after a second trial. He later divorced Sunny, who remained in a coma as of 2006.

Stranger on the Third Floor, 1940. Peter Lorre. ──■ ──■ ──■
After his testimony helps convict an innocent man of murder, reporter Mike Ward has a bizarre dream in which he's on trial for killing his obnoxious neighbor. When Ward wakes to find the neighbor murdered, he tells the police about his dream and about the ominous stranger he thinks killed his neighbor, as well as the victims in the murder trial. Ward's detailed description of the crime results in his being charged with both murders. Tracked down by Ward's fiancée, Jane, the stranger confesses his guilt to a cop moments before dying. *Picturing justice*: (1) In both the actual trial and the dream trial, the judge and jurors pay little attention to the defendants' claims of innocence. (2) The eerie dream trial appears to take place in hell. *Trial brief*: Many critics regard this film as the first authentic *film noir*.

They Won't Believe Me, 1947. Robert Young, Susan Hayward.
──■ ──■ ──■
Larry Ballentine, a philanderer, is charged with murdering his wife, Greta. Ballentine's defense that he wanted to but didn't actually kill Greta unfolds primarily in flashbacks. When everyone mistakenly concluded that the woman who died in a fiery auto accident was Greta, Ballentine decided to kill her for real and inherit her wealth. As he searched for Greta, he found her already dead at the bottom of a cliff.

Will the jury decide that Greta committed suicide, that she died accidentally, or that Ballentine pushed her off the cliff? He decides not to stick around to find out. As Ballentine tries to flee the courtroom, the bailiff shoots and kills him. Moments later, the clerk reads the jury's verdict: not guilty. *Picturing justice*: Just as the circumstantial evidence surrounding Greta's death is ambiguous, so is Ballentine's escape attempt. He might have tried to escape either because he knew he was guilty or because he thought he'd be unjustly convicted.

The Unholy Three, 1930. Lon Chaney, Harry Earles. ——■ ——■

Disguised as an old lady, con man and ventriloquist Echo runs a pet shop. He gains entry to the fancy houses he later burglarizes by fooling customers into thinking that his parrots can talk. When the wrong man is tried for burglary, a disguised Echo testifies to an alibi. *Courtroom highlight*: When Echo's voice slips during the D.A.'s vigorous cross-examination, the D.A. rips off Echo's wig and reveals both his scalp and the truth. *Trial brief*: (1) Popular-culture references can date a film in the same way that Carbon-14 can date an old piece of pottery. In this film, a character mentions that Echo "could make Coolidge talk." The U.S. president when the film was being made was Calvin Coolidge, whose nickname was "Silent Cal." (2) This was the famous Lon Chaney's last film. Chaney had made the silent-film version a few years earlier, and this was his only talkie.

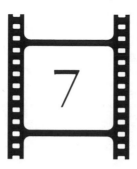

Uncivil Actions

Most courtroom movies depict criminal trials. This is hardly surprising given popular fascination with crime and the conflicts and suspense inherent in a criminal trial. Nevertheless, civil cases can generate plenty of drama too, whether they involve large numbers of people, like *A Civil Action, Class Action,* and *Runaway Jury,* or an individual seeking to right the scales of justice, as in *Libel, Mr. Deeds Goes to Town, The Rainmaker, The Verdict, The Castle, The Winslow Boy, North Country,* and *Brilliant Lies.* Of course, it helps if there's a pot of money at stake. Few people would pay a babysitter to go out and see the new film about a slip-and-fall case in small-claims court.

Films based on civil cases often depict sole practitioners hanging in against large corporate law firms. The David versus Goliath contest allows viewers to empathize with the little guy fighting against long odds. This recurring theme also opens the way for filmmakers to smear one of their favorite targets, greedy and unethical big-firm lawyers who think nothing of cheating and have the resources to drag out disputes until their opponents are exhausted, as in *A Civil Action, Class Action, Runaway Jury, The Rainmaker, Mr. Deeds Goes to Town,* and *The Verdict.*

Most of the films that pillory big law firms also slam greedy big business, another favorite target of Hollywood filmmakers. Many films depicting civil cases involve critiques of the civil justice process, including the contingent fee system (*A Civil Action*), ambulance chasing (*The Rainmaker, The Verdict*), discovery abuse (*A Civil Action, Class Action, The Rainmaker*), biased judges (*The Verdict, A Civil Action*), use of expert witnesses (*The Verdict, Mr. Deeds Goes to Town*), and easily manipulated jurors (*Runaway Jury, A Civil Action*). Some films, like *Erin Brockovich* and *A Civil Action,* also suggest that the adversarial trial process may be a poor way to determine issues of scientific truth. One thing is for sure: The civil trials shown in the movies are anything but civil!

A Civil Action

Synopsis: A lawyer ruins his life and his law firm trying to prove that chemical dumping poisoned a town's drinking water.

Paramount Pictures, 1998. Color. Running time: 112 minutes.

Screenplay: Steven Zaillian. Original book: Jonathan Harr. Director: Steven Zaillian.

Starring: John Travolta (Jan Schlichtmann), Robert Duvall (Jerome Facher), William H. Macy (James Gordon).

Rating: ——■ ——■ ——■

The Story

Jan Schlichtmann, a successful Boston personal-injury lawyer, is stuck with a complex case accepted by one of his partners. The case involves claims by parents living in nearby Woburn that chemicals dumped into a river polluted the town's drinking water and caused children to become sick and die. Schlichtmann wants to dump the case, but he changes his mind when he learns that W. R. Grace and Beatrice Foods operated factories along the river. These two huge firms have pockets even deeper than the river. Schlichtmann figures that when a jury hears the parents' pathetic stories, he'll get gold from them thar mills.

William Cheeseman represents Grace, and Jerome Facher represents Beatrice. Each is a partner in a Boston mega-firm, and their clients have the resources to keep Schlichtmann so busy running to court for pre-trial hearings and attending depositions that he cannot work on any other cases. In addition, he has to hire experts to prove that chemicals dumped by the two corporations migrated into the water supply and poisoned the children. It's not long before Gordon, Schlichtmann's creative accountant, runs out of tricks and the firm's financial resources are exhausted. The partners' houses are gone, and the office furniture is taken away.

The parents' emotional testimony also vanishes. Facher convinces Judge Skinner to bifurcate the trial. Before any of the parents can testify,

Paramount/Photofest.

A *Civil Action:* Jan Schlichtmann (John Travolta) is seriously overmatched by his adversaries, big-firm lawyers Jerome Facher (Robert Duvall) and William Cheeseman (Bruce Norris).

Schlichtmann first has to convince the jury that Grace and Beatrice poisoned the water. Schlichtmann can offer no evidence that Beatrice engaged in dumping, so it's dismissed from the case. Grace remains on the hook, but Schlichtmann is tapped out. He settles for $8 million, which, after deducting costs and fees, leaves each family with a paltry $375,000.

After the case concludes, Schlichtmann finally locates records proving that Grace and Beatrice poisoned the wells and turns them over to the U.S. Environmental Protection Agency (EPA), which goes after both companies with a vengeance. The factories are closed, and the companies have to pay fines and clean up the water. Schlichtmann must file for bankruptcy. After seventeen years of practicing law he's left with fourteen dollars and a portable radio.

Legal Analysis

A Civil Action is a bleak and depressing portrayal of important aspects of American civil justice. Consider its messages:

• Businesses care not a whit for the environment or people's health. They will lie and cheat and pay huge fees to big law firms to cover up their illegal activities rather than compensate victims of toxic-waste-dumping.

• Like the austere and intimidating Jerome Facher, elite lawyers work in big firms. Their activities include currying friendships with judges to secure rulings in their clients' favor and turning trials into wars of economic attrition that their underfinanced adversaries cannot win.

• Small-firm personal-injury lawyers are "bottom feeders." Schlichtmann may be able to win a case against an insurance company by schlepping clients to court in a wheelchair, but he's out of his league against "real lawyers" like Facher. In addition, he is materialistic and incompetent. He cares little for his clients' suffering and takes the Woburn case only because he thinks it's a gold mine.

• Trials are a terrible way to resolve complex environmental issues. The geologic and medical questions cannot be answered with any certainty under existing scientific methods. Moreover, toxic tort trials are unfair because they pit lawyers with limited financial resources against big businesses willing to invest endless dollars in their legal defense. Finally, jurors are expected to understand complex scientific testimony and are forced to answer unanswerable questions.

• The government enforces laws protecting citizens' health and welfare only as a last resort. The EPA takes action only after Schlichtmann turns over papers documenting years of chemical pollution and coverups.

These images lend a double meaning to the film's title. The case is "civil" because it's between private parties, but there's really nothing civil about it.

The importance of depositions. The film concentrates heavily on pretrial depositions, one of the most important (and most expensive) aspects of litigation. In a deposition, an attorney questions potential witnesses under oath. Depositions facilitate settlement because they allow attorneys to evaluate the strength of their case and that of their opponents. Depositions also help attorneys plan trial strategy. For example, after listening to a parent's emotional deposition testimony, Facher tells an associate, "These people can never testify. Nope." The deposition helped Facher to come up with the strategy that kept the parents off the stand.

Settlement sins. More than 95 percent of all civil cases are disposed of before trial, either by settlement or by pretrial motions. From the get-go, Schlichtmann planned to settle the Woburn case. Yet he mishandles the settlement negotiations by making an initial demand that is so excessive that Facher and Cheeseman walk out without bothering to make a counteroffer. Moreover, Schlichtmann's demand came as a complete surprise to his associates, and his clients knew nothing about it. Later, Schlichtmann rejects Facher's last-minute offer to settle the case against Beatrice for $20 million. Schlichtmann's behavior, as incomprehensible as it is unethical, suggests that he has become too personally and emotionally involved in the case to represent his clients properly.

Facher's class. Facher, like many lawyers, likes to bestow his wisdom on law students, and from time to time we see him lecturing in a trial-tactics class (at Harvard, of course). Facher tells the students that if they ever fall asleep in the middle of a trial, the first thing they should say upon awakening is "Objection!" In reality, mid-trial objections may disrupt an opponent's rhythm and annoy the jury, but they rarely influence the outcome of trials. When the admissibility of crucial evidence is seriously contested, judges often rule on the issue before the trial starts.

Facher also advises the students that they must never ask a "why" question when cross-examining a witness. Schlichtmann breaks this cardinal rule and pays the price. He asks John Riley, who ran the tannery owned by Beatrice, why he is so upset that the area around the plant is polluted. Riley answers: "That land has been in my family for three generations. That land to me is hallowed ground. When you ask me if I would be upset if someone came onto the land and desecrated it, land that is part of the town that I love, my answer to your question, Mr. Schlichtmann, is yes." Before the jury's eyes, Schlichtmann's "why" question turned Riley from a polluter into a saintly neighbor who champions conservation.

Picturing justice. Schlichtmann and Facher wait for the jury verdict in the hallway. Schlichtmann predicts, "They'll see the truth." Facher scoffs, "The truth? Oh, I thought we were talking about a court of law. Come on, you've been around long enough to know that a courtroom isn't the place to look for truth. If you're really looking for the truth, Jan, look for it where it is—at the bottom of a bottomless pit." Facher's comment, while cynical, is accurate insofar as it recognizes that the truth can never be known and that a trial is simply a set of procedures that ensure a reasonably fair system of dispute resolution.

Trial Brief

Jonathan Harr's best-selling book, on which the movie is based, is a riveting and detailed account of the Woburn case. Schlichtmann filed the complaint as co-counsel with a nonprofit legal organization, Trial Lawyers for Public Justice. When that group bailed out, he was left holding the bag. The EPA had investigated pollution in Woburn long before the lawsuit was filed, and Schlichtmann used its reports in preparing the case for trial.

At one point, Facher offered a settlement of $8 million. Schlichtmann counteroffered $18 million but never got a response. Facher never offered him $20 million in a courthouse hallway or anywhere else. W. R. Grace settled by paying the plaintiffs (and Schlichtmann) a total of $8 million. After the case concluded, Schlichtmann filed for bankruptcy and moved to Hawaii. After several years there, he moved back to Boston in 1993 and resumed practicing law.

In his book, Harr explains that two years after the verdict Facher's firm was found by the U.S. Court of Appeals to have violated its duty to turn over documents requested by Schlichtmann. The improperly concealed documents might have allowed him to prove that John Riley knew all along about illegal dumping. The movie makes no mention of Facher's seeming misconduct, perhaps to avoid legal action by Facher against the film's producers.

Class Action

Synopsis: A father and daughter square off in a trial involving an exploding car.

20th Century Fox, 1991. Color. Running time: 110 minutes.

Screenplay: Carolyn Shelby, Christopher Ames, and Samantha Shad. Director: Michael Apted.

Starring: Gene Hackman (Jed Ward), Mary Elizabeth Mastrantonio (Maggie Ward).

Rating: ——🔨 ——🔨 ——🔨

The Story

Jed Ward heads a small law firm devoted to exposing the sins of corporate America. His daughter Maggie Ward is on the fast track to partnership in Quinn, Califan & Lunt, a prestigious law firm that defends the

Class Action: Michael Grazier (Colin Friels) and Jed Ward (Gene Hackman) flex their veins over the admissibility of evidence.

interests of corporate America. Their career paths collide in a trial against Argo Motors for designing Meridian cars in a way that causes them to explode when struck by other vehicles. Jed realizes that proving the Meridian's design defects will be difficult, but he pursues the case because "I got a car that blows up. . . . I got a car company that doesn't give a shit. To me that makes a case." Michael Grazier, Maggie's supervisor and lover, allows her to spearhead the defense. She sees it as her big chance to strut her stuff for Grazier and senior partner Fred Quinn.

In a pretrial courtroom skirmish, Maggie complains about the huge burden of complying with Jed's request for information about the names and addresses of all Argo employees who helped design the Meridian. She is humiliated when Jed demonstrates how his single phone call to Argo's pension department revealed that Argo keeps up-to-date records on all current and former employees.

Maggie believes in her cause until she uncovers a "smoking gun." Dr. Pavel, a former Argo engineer, had submitted a report warning Argo that Meridians would explode if struck while the left turn signal was blinking. (Luckily, this defect would not endanger Los Angeles drivers, for they haven't used turn signals in years.) Argo ignored Pavel's warning, because it would cost much less to pay off claims resulting from exploding Meridians than to fix the problem. Jed is entitled to see Pavel's report, and Maggie wants to hand it over, but Grazier and Quinn insist on a "tsunami response." Jed will get the report, but buried and mislabeled in a truckload of worthless documents. In fact, Grazier destroys the report so that Jed can never see it.

Fed up with her supervisors' tactics, Maggie contacts Jed and together they arrange a courtroom double-cross. Jed tries to get Pavel to testify to the contents of his report, but he makes little headway, especially after Maggie nastily attacks Pavel's memory on cross-examination. Jed then puts Grazier on the witness stand to try to substantiate the report's existence, but Grazier evades his questions. Supposedly to clear up any doubts about the matter, Maggie asks Grazier point blank whether Pavel ever submitted the Meridian report, and Grazier answers "No."

Jed springs the trap with his last witness, an Argo risk-management expert ("bean counter") who establishes that Argo knew all about Pavel's report. The bean counter's revelation destroys Argo's defense and subjects Grazier to a possible perjury charge. In the judge's chambers, Quinn screams for a mistrial, claiming that Maggie turned over confidential information "in violation of every principle of ethics I know." Jed asks him, "Which one is that, Fred?" Jed then tells the judge about Grazier's destruction of records. Quinn is reduced to begging Jed to settle, offering millions of dollars. Jed smugly walks out, leaving Quinn dangling. Dancing happily together at movie's end, Jed and Maggie are a class act.

Legal Analysis

Class Action simplistically depicts law as a ying-and-yang profession. At one end of the spectrum are lawyers like Jed, who sacrifice wealth to protect "little guys" against greedy corporations. At the other end are the big civil-practice law firms who violate every rule of ethics in order to win victory for their evil and callous clients. Despite Jed's triumph, *Class Action* leaves no doubt that the little guys usually lose. Needless to say, lawyers in the real world don't have a monopoly on virtue or vice, whether they represent plaintiffs or defendants or whether they practice in large firms or solo.

Discovery wars. In the pretrial phase of lawsuits called "discovery," lawyers are supposed to turn over information about their cases to their adversaries. The hope is that the exchange of information will encourage settlements. However, the frequent effect of discovery is increased costs, delays, and endless bickering. Often, discovery enriches the lawyers (at least the lawyers at Quinn, Califan & Lunt who bill their clients by the hour) without contributing to finding the truth. The Quinn firm's "tsunami response" is an example of the sort of uncivil, scorched-earth litigation tactics that are all too common.

What's a girl to do? Grazier's destruction of Pavel's report is an extremely serious breach of legal ethics and even a criminal violation ("obstruction of justice"). His misconduct might well have led the judge to bar Argo from offering any evidence as to the Meridian's safety. The jurors would probably have been informed about his misconduct and no doubt would have taken out their anger on Argo in the form of huge punitive damages. (See films like *The Verdict* or *The Rainmaker* for other examples.) Argo in turn would probably have sued its lawyers for legal malpractice.

Once Maggie finds out that her supervisors destroyed Pavel's report, none of her choices is good. She might tell Argo about the consequences of destroying evidence and urge the company to provide Jed with another copy, or at least a summary. She might urge Argo to settle the case immediately to avoid disaster. If Argo refuses to settle or own up to the document destruction, Maggie could go to the judge and disclose what has happened. She should probably report Grazier's actions to the state bar association's lawyer disciplinary committee. She could withdraw from representing Argo and might even leave the firm.

All Maggie's choices are bad career moves. They will prevent her from becoming a partner and might very well end her career as a big-firm lawyer. The one thing that Maggie *can't* do is what she actually does. She sells out Argo by telling Jed what she knows and by executing a strategy that destroys both Argo and Quinn, Califan & Lunt. This breaches her duty of loyalty to Argo and is itself a career-ending breach of legal ethics.

Picturing justice. The film begins as Jed and Maggie try unrelated cases in adjoining courtrooms. Jed roams around the courtroom and speaks passionately on behalf of an environmentalist who rammed his truck into the offices of a polluting corporation. He calls for justice regardless of the law, provoking wild enthusiasm in the audience. Maggie, on the other hand, is dressed in a blue suit that looks like those of her male associates. She is coldly rational and anchored to the counsel table. She tells the court that emotions have no place in a court of law and that the wealth of her client should not matter. Needless to say, nobody applauds (other than her associates).

Maggie is a competent and hardworking lawyer. Yet her personal life is miserable. She can't sleep, and won't take a vacation. She hates what she has to do to succeed, telling a bartender about the "warm feeling you get from knowing you tore at least one person's heart out that day." She unwisely carries on a secret affair with a manipulative supervisor and insists on taking the Argo case to prove she's a better lawyer than her father. Her emotional entanglements cloud her judgment and are consistent with many of the negative stereotypes that often characterize female cine-lawyers.

Trial Briefs

1. The film is loosely based on the case of *Grimshaw v. Ford Motor Company* (1981), involving the faulty gas-tank design of the Ford Pinto. The jury awarded the plaintiff $2.5 million in actual damages and $125 million in punitive damages; the latter figure was reduced to $3.5 million on appeal. One of the documents offered in evidence in the *Grimshaw* case was an internal report prepared by a Ford employee stating that the cost of improving the safety of Pintos would be much higher than the cost of paying off the victims (or the families of the victims) who were hurt or killed in collisions. However, this sort of evidence should not have been so shocking. Manufacturers must constantly balance the cost of making improvements in their product against the hazards from the product, and they should not be forced to always design for safety regardless of the cost. Otherwise, every car would have to be designed like a Sherman tank.

2. A class action is a lawsuit brought to represent the interests of an entire class of people in a single case. Jed sensibly pursues the Argo case as a class action, because then he'd only need to offer the technical evidence about the Meridian's faulty design once. If the jury finds that the Meridian was negligently designed, then that issue is settled for all the victims, but each victim would still have to prove his or her damages separately.

3. The scenario of reputable lawyers deep-sixing harmful documents has actually occurred. A senior partner in one of Wall Street's most prestigious law firms (Donovan, Leisure) went to jail for contempt for lying about the existence of documents requested by the opposition. In fact, the very documents were in his briefcase. When this misconduct was ultimately discovered, the client (Eastman Kodak) was heavily sanctioned in an antitrust case and sued the law firm for malpractice. An associate who knew that the documents existed but didn't report that was fired, and his career was ruined.

Libel

Synopsis: A former POW is either Sir Mark Loddon or his killer.

MGM, 1959. Black and white. Running time: 100 minutes.

Screenplay: Anatole de Grunwald and Karl Tunberg. Play: Edward Wooll.
Director: Anthony Asquith.

Starring: Dirk Bogarde (Sir Mark Loddon/Frank Welney/No. 15), Olivia
de Havilland (Lady Margaret Loddon).

Academy Award: Best Sound.

Rating:

The Story

Sir Mark Loddon, Jeffery Buckenham, and Frank Welney were POWs
during World War II. Years later, Buckenham sits in a pub watching as
Loddon and his wife, Margaret, give TV viewers a tour of their mansion.
Buckenham was probably hoping to watch snooker, but what really
ticks him off is that he's certain that Welney killed Loddon during an
escape attempt. The sleazy Sunday *Gazette* publishes Buckenham's letter accusing Welney of masquerading as Loddon, and Loddon sues
Buckenham and the *Gazette* for libel.

Buckenham backs his claim with plenty of evidence. Welney and
Loddon resembled each other, and Welney was a ne'er-do-well who,
while a POW, constantly asked Loddon about his past life and once
spoke of eliminating Loddon and stealing his identity. Moreover, during
the escape attempt, Buckenham was returning from a food-scrounging
trip to the place where he'd left Loddon and Welney when he heard
gunshots. He saw one man run away wearing Welney's leather jacket,
and a body lying by the side of the river clothed in Loddon's British
army jacket. Finally, Dr. Schrott's testimony suggests that an anonymous
zombie-like man who has been under Schrott's care since the war is
the real Loddon. Buckenham's case convinces even Margaret that her
"husband" is actually Welney and that the ghastly patient whom Schrott
brings into the courtroom is Loddon.

* * *

SPOILER ALERT: You may not want to read further if you plan to see the film.

* * *

The patient's startling courtroom appearance unlocks Loddon's
memory. He testifies that he is indeed Loddon and that Schrott's

Libel: Sir Wilfred (Robert Morley) tries to persuade Lady Margaret Loddon (Olivia de Havilland) to testify for her husband.

ghastly patient is Welney. During the escape attempt, Welney attacked him but Loddon knocked him out. Because a British army jacket is a poor choice for teatime wear or when behind enemy lines, Loddon exchanged his jacket for Welney's leather one and ran off. To prove his claim, Loddon pulls a small medallion out of the lining of the patient's army jacket, which Schrott also brought to court. Margaret gave Loddon the medallion before the war, and only he could have known that it was there. Loddon and Buckenham happily reunite. Even Schrott should celebrate, because Loddon asks that the damages he collects from the *Gazette* pay for Welney's upkeep.

Legal Analysis

Libel's crackling courtroom scenes support a popular image of trials as filled with bombshell revelations that produce objective truth that all parties accept. Yet the adversary system often obscures rather than exposes the truth. *Libel* represents an aspiration that is more achievable on film than in everyday life.

The changing law of libel. The law of defamation protects people's reputations by providing recovery for false statements. False statements in written form (like Buckenham's letter) are called "libel," and those made orally are called "slander." Because written statements are likely to have a longer "shelf life" than oral ones, targets of libelous statements have traditionally been able to recover damages even if the statements have not caused them any economic harm.

However, because defamation law conflicts with the First Amendment's guarantee of free speech, Loddon would find it more difficult to collect damages if the case were tried in a contemporary American court. For one thing, Loddon could collect only if he could show actual harm to his reputation. Second, as a "public figure," Loddon could get damages only if he can prove that Buckenham made the false statement "maliciously," meaning with knowledge that it was false or without regard for whether it was accurate. Loddon would find it difficult to overcome this hurdle because Buckenham spoke to Loddon and examined him for a telltale scar before writing his letter. Finally, modern American libel law allows publishers to escape liability by printing adequate and timely retractions. Given deteriorating journalistic standards, tabloid publishers may decide to save time and space by including retractions in their celebrity stories.

Coming to a theater near you—Libel 2? Buckenham and the *Gazette* pulled off a neat two-for-one libel. After all, the letter also defamed Welney by claiming that he killed Loddon and was impersonating him. A lawsuit brought on Welney's behalf would raise an interesting issue of whether someone who's been brain-dead for fifteen years can be said to have a reputation. But the careers of many politicians suggest that this is quite possible.

Mr. Deeds Goes to Town

Synopsis: A big-city lawyer tries to steal the inheritance of a small-town eccentric.

Columbia Pictures, 1936. Black and white. Running time: 115 minutes.

Screenplay: Robert Riskin. Original story: Clarence Budington Kelland. Director: Frank Capra.

Starring: Gary Cooper (Longfellow Deeds), Jean Arthur (Babe Bennett).

Academy Award: Best Director.

Academy Award nominations: Best Picture, Best Actor (Gary Cooper), Best Screenplay.

Rating: ——◼ ——◼ ——◼

The Story

Longfellow Deeds of Mandrake Falls, Vermont, writes greeting-card poems. New York lawyer John Cedar tells Deeds that he's inherited his uncle Martin Semple's fortune. Deeds is more excited about the new mouthpiece for his tuba, and plans to give the money away.

Temporarily living in Semple's Manhattan mansion, Deeds learns that many of the Big Apple's elite are rotten to the core. Famous poets belittle him, perhaps because he knows more verses that rhyme with "roses are red" than they do. The president of the opera association demeans Deeds privately but expects him to cover the opera's financial losses. Newspaper reporter Babe Bennett pretends to care about Deeds, and he proposes marriage with a love poem that takes a sure sale away from a greeting-card company. Secretly, Babe's popular stories about Deeds' odd behavior turn him into a laughingstock.

Unable to convince Deeds to sign a power of attorney that would allow him to continue looting Semple's estate, Cedar files a petition claiming that Deeds is incompetent. Cedar asks that Walter, Semple's only other heir and a foolish wastrel whom Cedar can easily control, be put in charge of the money.

Deeds listens morosely as Cedar presents evidence of Deeds' foibles. He'll play the tuba in mid-conversation, he stopped traffic to feed doughnuts to a horse, and he jumped on a fire engine racing to a fire. Deeds also threw a haughty opera singer out of his house. (Judging from her size, Deeds should have immediately been added to the U.S. Olympic weightlifting squad.) The elderly Faulkner sisters come from Mandrake Falls to testify that Deeds is "pixilated." Dr. Von Haller, an eminent psychiatrist, testifies that Deeds is a manic-depressive, illustrating his testimony with a hokey chart that might have come from a first-grade primer, "Dick and Jane Learn About Mental Illness."

The judge is about to commit Deeds to a mental institution when Babe and a room full of unemployed workers urge Deeds to defend himself. The effect is like feeding spinach to Popeye. Deeds entertains the crowd while proving his competence. For example, Deeds shows that the Faulkner sisters think that everyone, including the judge, is

Mr. Deeds Goes to Town: Babe Bennett (Jean Arthur) speaks up on behalf of Longfellow Deeds (Gary Cooper) with Dr. Von Haller's chart in the background

pixilated—except them. Deeds concludes his case by slugging Cedar in the jaw. Perhaps Deeds thought that trials included "right cross" examination. The judge dismisses the petition, and Deeds and Babe embrace.

Legal Analysis

Ostensibly a comedy, the film probably struck many viewers as highly subversive. Cedar is greedy and dishonest, the sort of lawyer that people suffering through the Great Depression of the 1930s loved to hate. During his opening statement, Cedar denounces Deeds' plan to give away his money: "With the country incapacitated by economic ailments, and in danger with an undercurrent of social unrest, the promulgation of such a weird, fantastic, and impractical plan as contemplated by the defendant is capable of fomenting a disturbance from which the country may not soon recover."

Such harangues pit lawyers against common folk, such as Deeds and the unemployed workers who attend the competency hearing. Cedar implies that they are rabble and that only the elite like Cedar can pull the country out of its tailspin. In the end, Cedar is so powerless that he can't even prevail in a legal hearing against a nonlawyer. Thus, the film makes a strong argument in favor of folk wisdom and against centralizing power in elites such as lawyers.

Deeds' competence. Judges can appoint conservators to manage the property of people who lack competence to handle their own affairs. However, the film provides a very distorted image of conservatorship proceedings. For example:

• After Cedar files the petition, the police arrest Deeds and take him to an institution. But the police have no basis to arrest Deeds. He has not committed a crime, nor does he present an immediate threat to himself or others.

• Even if Deeds were incompetent, Walter would not qualify as a conservator. He has made a financial mess of his own life and has had no contact with Deeds. In the absence of a suitable close relative, a judge would appoint a professional conservator.

• Deeds is not incompetent. His eccentricities and desire to use his fortune to help the poor do not establish that he is incapable of managing his property. Even if Deeds is a manic-depressive, he is competent unless the effects of manic-depression render him unable to manage his property.

A conservatorship is a clumsy and costly way to deal with incompetence. (Durable powers of attorney or living trusts are cheaper and more convenient.) In addition to cost, conservatorship hearings are public and can result in the airing of a lot of dirty laundry. One of the most notorious examples involved the famous comedian Groucho Marx (1890–1977). Erin Fleming became Groucho's companion, manager, and nurse during the last years of his life. Fearful of Fleming's influence, Groucho's son Arthur went to court to seek appointment as Groucho's conservator. Arthur was successful, but the news stories recounting the evidence of Groucho's impaired physical and mental condition were devastating to the memory of a great comedian.

Picturing justice. As Cedar argues that Deeds' plan is dangerous and likely to lead to social uprisings, the camera focuses on the faces of the unemployed workers watching the hearing. The image aligns the workers with the viewers and suggests that Cedar's argument is an insult to all.

Trial Briefs

1. Cedar is a partner in the law firm of Cedar, Cedar, Cedar & Budington. The name is no doubt an homage to the author of the original story, Clarence Budington Kelland.

2. The film exemplifies the work of Frank Capra, one of America's greatest directors. During the Depression, Capra made numerous populist films glorifying the common man and attacking financial and political elites. For example, in *Mr. Smith Goes to Washington* a hick becomes a member of Congress and successfully challenges crooked legislators. *Meet John Doe* involves a struggle between a common man (a starving ballplayer who becomes famous as the result of a newspaper publicity stunt) and an aspiring fascist dictator. Finally, Capra's most famous film, the beloved *It's a Wonderful Life,* glorifies a generous small-town banker and vilifies a greedy industrialist.

3. The film was remade in 2002 as *Mr. Deeds.* The remake lacks the humor and charming innocence of the original, or even of *The Texas Chainsaw Massacre.* The remake at least spares both tuba players and the legal profession. Deeds never picks up an instrument, Cedar is a media mogul, and there are no courtroom scenes.

The Rainmaker

Synopsis: A fledgling lawyer and a paralawyer battle a greedy insurance company.

Paramount Pictures, 1997. Color. Running time: 135 minutes.

Screenplay: Francis Ford Coppola. Novel: John Grisham. Director: Francis Ford Coppola.

Starring: Matt Damon (Rudy Baylor), Danny DeVito (Deck Shifflet), Jon Voight (Leo F. Drummond), Danny Glover (Judge Tyrone Kipler).

Rating:

The Story

Rudy Baylor, fresh out of Memphis State's law school, has to start his own law practice when the disreputable lawyer who had employed him flees the country to avoid prosecution. Baylor inherits the services of Deck Shifflet, a self-proclaimed paralawyer (meaning that he knows enough law to have flunked the bar exam six times). Baylor has only one real client, Dot Black. Black had a family medical insurance policy written by Great Benefit Insurance, but when her son Donny Ray got leukemia, Great Benefit refused to pay for a bone-marrow transplant and Donny Ray died. The company rejected Black's claim seven different times,

The Rainmaker. Rudy Baylor (Matt Damon) summarizes the evidence against Great Benefit as client Dot Black (Mary Kay Place) looks on.

finally blowing her off with a letter calling her "stupid stupid stupid." Black's response is "lawsuit, lawsuit, lawsuit."

Great Benefit and its hired gun, Leo F. Drummond, provide Baylor with a doctored version of Great Benefit's claims manual and frustrate Baylor's efforts to depose Great Benefit employees by firing them. Nevertheless, Baylor tracks down former employee Jackie Lemanczyk, and her testimony devastates Great Benefit. The company paid her ten thousand dollars in exchange for resigning and promising not to say anything about Great Benefit's business practices or Black's claim. Lemanczyk also produces a complete claims manual, which instructs employees to deny all claims. Cross-examining Lemanczyk, Drummond adds injury to injury when he elicits her testimony that she was forced to have sex with various executives in order to win promotions. Great Benefit's CEO, Wilfred Keeley, also testifies, and Baylor forces him to admit that of more than 11,000 recent claims, over 9,000 had been denied. Well, at least the company didn't deny *all* claims!

Baylor and Black are ecstatic when the jury awards her actual damages of $150,000 and punitive damages of $50 million. However, Great Benefit quickly files for bankruptcy, and Drummond gives Baylor the bad news that the company has been looted. No one gets paid, not even Drummond.

Legal Analysis

A "rainmaker" is a lawyer who brings in lots of business. The irony of the term is that Baylor has no other real cases except Dot Black's, which he picked up while he was a student in a legal clinic. The Black case and its outrageous outcome so demoralize Baylor that he decides to abandon the practice of law. As he disappears into the sunset with his girlfriend, to make rain no more, Baylor muses that if he stayed he'd wake up one day and become Leo Drummond. "Each time you try a case, you step over the line. You do it enough times and you forget where the line is." When that happens, Baylor realizes, he'd become just another lawyer joke, another shark swimming in the dirty water.

Punitive damages. Normally, juries can award punitive damages for serious "quasi-criminal" misconduct, such as fraud, but not for a breach of contract. However, many states allow juries to award punitive damages against insurance companies for bad-faith refusals to pay a claim. The jury here was clearly justified in finding that Great Benefit acted in bad faith when it refused to pay for Donny Ray's treatment. The company provided Baylor with a doctored claims manual, refused almost all claims, and repeatedly stonewalled Black.

The ability of juries to sock corporate defendants with massive punitive damage awards is controversial. After all, punitive damages are a form of punishment, but defendants have none of the protections provided by the criminal law. Besides, punitive damages awards tend to be arbitrary. A jury can pick almost any number. Why not $500 million instead of $50 million?

In *State Farm Insurance v. Campbell* (2003), the U.S. Supreme Court limited a jury's ability to award punitive damages. The Court ruled that lower courts should not normally approve punitive damages that are in excess of ten times the compensatory damages. Indeed, if compensatory damages are substantial, punitive damages normally should not exceed them. Had this rule been in effect at the time of the Black lawsuit, the jury might have been limited to punitive damages of $150,000 (the amount of compensatory damages).

Dirty defense tactics. The film is unclear as to whether Drummond or Great Benefit is responsible for the defense's misconduct (such as deleting material from the claims manual, firing employees before their depositions, or bugging Baylor's office). Like many other films, therefore, *The Rainmaker* implies that big business and their lawyers are indistinguishable and that both are rotten. In reality, such gross misbehavior could be very costly to both Great Benefit and Drummond. For starters, Drummond might lose his license to practice. And Judge Kipler could have imposed heavy monetary sanctions on both of them and barred Great Benefit from introducing any evidence to contradict Black's claims. Thus, corporations and their lawyers have both moral and pragmatic reasons to follow the rules.

Follow that ambulance. Paralawyer Shifflet advises Baylor that if he doesn't get clients by chasing ambulances, he'll starve. The dynamic duo crash an accident victim's hospital room. The poor devil is in traction and in agonizing pain. He signs up as their client just to get rid of them. Such client solicitation is highly unethical and could have terminated Baylor's budding career before it ever got started. The rules prohibit face-to-face solicitation of strangers, particularly where a client is in such a physical or emotional state that he or she cannot be expected to exercise reasonable judgment. Ambulance-chasing scenes also appear in such films as *The Sweet Hereafter,* in which a personal-injury lawyer shows up in town after a horrible school-bus accident, and *The Verdict,* in which down-and-out attorney Frank Galvin hands out his business card at funerals.

Shoulda settled! After conferring with his client, Baylor rejects multiple settlement offers. That turns out to be a big mistake, though, because he winds up with a huge but worthless judgment. However, probably more than 95 percent of cases filed in court terminate before trial, usually by way of settlement. Trials are becoming increasingly rare events. The most important reasons are the high cost of litigation, the long delays in getting to trial, and the unpredictability of jury verdicts. In a contingent-fee case like Dot Black's, Baylor has an incentive to get his client to settle quickly because he'd be paying the costs of discovery and trial out of his own pocket.

Picturing justice. In the adversary system, well-heeled clients may pay huge fees to top lawyers, figuring that they'll win on talent even if the evidence is against them. Yet Baylor wins a huge judgment even though he hasn't a clue about how to try a case. (Collectors of improper leading questions may want to add Baylor's first question to Dot Black, which starts off "Now, you are the mother of Donny Ray Black, who recently died of acute myelocytic leukemia because the defendant, Great Benefit . . .") Thus, the film suggests that justice is powerful enough to protect even the worst courtroom bumbler, but reality may be far different.

John Grisham's Lawyers

John Grisham has become one of the world's best-selling authors during the past fifteen years with more than one hundred million copies in print. Most of his books have legal themes and are moderately suspenseful page-turners of little literary merit. Many of them read like screenplays that are tricked up as novels.

Grisham's novels, and the films made from those novels, consistently represent practicing lawyers as scum. The lawyers are almost always unethical, greedy, and arrogant. Prosecutors and big-firm lawyers are the worst of the worst. In *The Firm,* which was Grisham's first smash-hit novel, a respected tax-law firm turns out to be a murderous front for the mob. Prosecutor Roy Foltrigg in *The Client* is hyperambitious and supernasty. *Runaway Jury* presents both plaintiff and defense lawyers as greedy and unprincipled. Leo Drummond of *The Rainmaker* plays numerous dirty tricks on his opponents.

In Grisham novels that haven't yet made their way onto the screen, disgusting lawyers and judges are the norm. Consider, for example, Clay Carter and the other greedy plaintiff's lawyers in *The King of Torts,* Patrick Lanigan and his larcenous ex-partners in *The Partner,* the big-firm hired guns in *The Street Lawyer,* the avaricious probate lawyers in *The Testament,* and the ex-judges in *The Brethren* who run an extortion scheme from prison.

Almost the lone exception to the evil-lawyer trope is Grisham's first novel, *A Time to Kill.* Criminal-defense lawyer Jake Brigance is presented as an excellent lawyer and a decent human being, although Brigance's cronies, the prosecutors, and the judge are all pretty scummy.

A few Grisham lawyers are decent professionals and human beings. These include young lawyers who are just breaking into law practice and haven't yet been tainted by the profession, such as Rudy Baylor in *The Rainmaker* or Mitch McDeere in *The Firm.* Lawyers working for free also are treated favorably, such as Adam Hall in *The Chamber* or Reggie Love in *The Client.* Michael Brock and Mordecai Green in *The Street Lawyer* work selflessly for the homeless in a legal-aid office. Law students also come off well, such as Darby Shaw in *The Pelican Brief.*

U.S. lawyers are widely distrusted. Polling data suggest that the general public ranks lawyers below nearly all other occupations when it comes to trustworthiness. It was not always this way. Lawyers were reasonably liked and trusted until the mid-1970s, at which time their image began to plummet. It has never recovered. The public's hate affair with lawyers began well before John Grisham began to reflect it in his lawyer-trashing novels. Grisham struck gold when he started mining the deep vein of public distrust for lawyers. And nobody has done more than Grisham to reinforce this unfortunate and unfair portrayal of practicing lawyers as greedy and unethical.

Runaway Jury

Synopsis: The jury consultant from hell gets his comeuppance.

20th Century Fox, 2003. Color. Running time: 127 minutes.

Screenplay: Brian Koppelman, David Levien, Rick Cleveland, and Matthew Chapman. Novel: John Grisham. Director: Gary Fleder.

Starring: Gene Hackman (Rankin Fitch), John Cusack (Nicholas Easter), Dustin Hoffman (Wendell Rohr).

Rating: ——▇ ——▇

The Story

Celeste Wood sues Vicksburg Firearms, maker of an automatic weapon called the Performa 990, after a crazed ex-employee kills her husband in a workplace massacre. Wendell Rohr represents Wood because he wants to strike a blow against gun violence. Durwood Cable, the defense attorney, is a puppet whose strings are pulled by the gun industry and Rankin Fitch, a professional jury consultant.

Because a jury verdict against any one gun company would be devastating, the entire gun industry ponies up to pay for Fitch's services. His huge team compiles detailed bios on every juror in the pool. Nick Easter has been trying to get on a gun-case jury for a long time. With the help of his girlfriend, Marlee, Easter manages to get picked for the jury by hacking into the New Orleans jury commissioner's computer.

Easter manipulates the jury from the start. He ingratiates himself with the other jurors, gets them to pick a blind juror as foreperson, and

Runaway Jury: Durwood Cable (Bruce Davison) argues for his client, Vicksburg Firearms.

finds ways to get uncooperative jurors bumped off the panel. Once Fitch catches on, there's war between Easter and Fitch. This leads to chases, violence, and nasty, underhanded tricks, but Easter and Marlee stay one step ahead.

When the trial interrupts the thrills, Rohr offers evidence that Vicksburg was indifferent to who bought the Performa 990, an automatic weapon good only for killing lots of people quickly. Vicksburg rewarded dealers who sold large numbers of the guns to the same purchaser, who could then resell them to criminals. However, Rohr's key witness (a turncoat gun industry executive) vanishes—obviously another of Fitch's little tricks. Cable puts on the president of Vicksburg, who coldly testifies that gun violence isn't his problem.

Easter offers both lawyers the opportunity to pay fifteen million dollars for a favorable jury verdict. Rohr wavers but turns it down. Fitch goes for the deal and wires the money, but Easter double-crosses him and delivers a much larger verdict for the plaintiff.

Legal Analysis

The film brings to light arguments about whether juries and jurors are an important bastion of democracy (Rohr's view) or irrational and emotional clods who have no business deciding important and complex questions (Fitch's view). The American public retains great confidence in juries, and their presence undoubtedly helps to legitimate the legal system. By contrast, most countries do not use juries at all, and none uses them as much as the United States. Even England has dispensed with juries in all civil cases (except defamation) and in most criminal cases as well.

Jury consultants. Fitch is a caricature whose portrayal falsely implies that jury consultants snoop into people's backgrounds and threaten and bribe jurors. When clients can afford it, lawyers hire jury consultants to help them decide which juror characteristics (such as sex, age, or ethnicity) are most likely to help or hurt them. Consultants sometimes convene mock juries, paying people to provide feedback after listening to abbreviated trial presentations. The increasing prevalence of jury consultants in big civil and criminal cases raises serious issues about the fairness of the jury system, particularly if one side can afford consultants but the other side cannot.

The Second Amendment. Tormented by Rohr's cross-examination, Henry Jankle, Vicksburg's president, falls back on the Second Amendment to the Constitution, which states: "A well-regulated militia, being necessary to the security of a free state, the right of the people to keep and bear arms shall not be infringed." One view is that the Second Amendment refers only to the sort of organized state militias that existed in 1791 when the amendment was passed. Because we don't have citizen militias anymore, the argument goes, the Second Amendment is no longer applicable. However, the competing view is that the amendment means exactly what it says and prevents the government from interfering with gun ownership. So far, the U.S. Supreme Court has ducked cases that might give it an opportunity to clarify the meaning of the Second Amendment.

Liability of gun manufacturers. The liability of gun makers for deaths or injuries that their products cause is also uncertain, although it has little to do with the Second Amendment. Rohr's argument is the basis of most gun liability lawsuits: Manufacturers should be held liable for "negligent marketing" for failing to keep guns out of the hands of dangerous people. Gun makers typically respond with the argument that their products are legal and that they should not be held liable unless a gun is badly designed or manufactured. Gun makers also argue that tort liability would effectively drive them out of business and that their right to stay in business should be decided by legislatures and not juries. The gun industry has not yet been compelled to pay damages in cases of this kind, but the issues continue to be litigated all over the country. Constantly lobbied by gun enthusiasts, Congress is likely to enact legislation wiping out gunmaker liability lawsuits.

Picturing justice. Perhaps the best scene in the movie is a confrontation between Rohr and Fitch in the men's room. Rohr gives an idealistic spiel for the rights of gun victims and the rule of law, while Fitch expresses utter contempt for trials and juries.

Trial Briefs

1. In John Grisham's novel, the defendant was a cigarette company. It's unclear why the filmmakers switched to the gun industry as the scapegoat.

2. Though the two great actors Dustin Hoffman and Gene Hackman are old friends and former roommates, this is the first movie they've made together.

The Verdict

Synopsis: A boozed-out lawyer out-miracles an archdiocese in a medical-malpractice case.

20th Century Fox, 1982. Color. Running time: 128 minutes.

Screenplay: David Mamet. Book. Barry Reed. Director: Sidney Lumet

Starring: Paul Newman (Frank Galvin), James Mason (Ed Concannon).

Academy Award nominations: Best Picture, Best Actor (Paul Newman), Best Supporting Actor (James Mason), Best Director, Best Screenplay.

Rating:

The Story

Frank Galvin has spent so much time at the wrong kind of bar that his law practice has dwindled to a single medical malpractice case. Galvin represents the sister of Deborah Ann Kaye, who entered a hospital run by the Boston archdiocese to give birth and wound up permanently comatose, allegedly due to the anesthesiologists' malpractice.

The Verdict: Judge Hoyle (Milo O'Shea) and Ed Concannon (James Mason) gang up on Frank Galvin (Paul Newman).

On the eve of trial, the sight of Deborah Ann in her hospital bed awakens Galvin's professionalism, and he tells a nurse who asks him why he is there, "I'm her attorney." Galvin refuses defense lawyer Ed Concannon's settlement offer, because "if I take the money, I'm lost." Deborah, Ann Kaye's sister, is apparently more familiar with lawyers' ethical rules than is Galvin, because she is furious that he refused to settle without consulting her.

Meanwhile, Concannon assigns Laura Fischer to act as a sexual spy on Galvin and pays Galvin's medical-expert witness to disappear. Concannon advises Fischer about his philosophy of law practice: "You're not paid to do your best. You're paid to win. That's what pays for this office, for the *pro bono* work that we do for the poor. It pays for the type of law that you want to practice. It pays for my whiskey." At least Concannon's whiskey is decent.

Dr. Towler testifies that he gave Deborah Ann the proper anesthetic for someone who, as the admitting-room form indicated, had last eaten nine hours earlier. Consequently, he was not at fault for her coma. Galvin's substitute medical expert is a disaster. Bullied by Judge Hoyle, who takes over the questioning from Galvin, he admits that he didn't realize that Deborah Ann was anemic and that the time delay in restoring Deborah Ann's heartbeat may not have been negligent. Galvin angrily tells the judge, "If you're going to try my case for me, I wish you wouldn't lose it."

Galvin surprises Concannon with the testimony of Kaitlin Price, the admitting-room nurse. Price testifies that the form she filled out and gave to Towler indicated that Deborah Ann had last eaten an hour earlier and that Dr. Towler had forced her to change the one to a nine. Price has a photocopy of the unaltered form, but Judge Hoyle rules that both the copy and Price's testimony are inadmissible. Nevertheless, the jury rules in Deborah Ann's favor and asks for permission to award even more money than Galvin had asked for.

Legal Analysis

The Verdict uses the courtroom format to tell a story of personal redemption. Galvin's life is spiraling downhill until seeing his pitiful client makes him experience the power of a year's worth of AA meetings in a single moment. He turns into a lawyer on a moral mission, though admittedly he breaks a few rules and needs a lot of luck to pull off his mighty victory.

Honestly now! Deborah Ann's doctors used the wrong anesthetic for a reason that all of us can understand: They were exhausted after a long day of surgeries and didn't read the admitting-room form carefully. The jurors in *The Verdict* probably decided to punish the doctors not simply because they were careless but because they lied and tried to cover up their mistake. The film has plenty of real-life analogues. For example, juries have awarded huge punitive damages against cigarette companies after hearing evidence that they concealed research on the addictiveness of nicotine, and against pharmaceutical companies who covered up adverse research results while continuing to sell a drug.

Why not "The Directed Verdict"? Though Judge Hoyle's rulings were poppycock, they eliminated Galvin's evidence of negligence. Supposedly top-notch lawyer Concannon should have asked Hoyle to dismiss the case and to enter a directed verdict for the defense. Unfortunately for the archdiocese, its lawyer was played by "James" and not "Perry" Mason.

The best-evidence rule. In a sleepy backwater of evidence codes lies what has been traditionally called the "best-evidence rule." The rule generally requires parties to produce original documents. *The Verdict* is one of the few films to recognize the rule's dramatic potential. When

Nurse Price refers to her photocopy, Concannon objects, and Judge Hoyle rules that "a copy is inadmissible when the original is already in evidence." Poor Nurse Price angrily hung onto the photocopy for years, but it never gets out of her purse! Judge Hoyle was wrong, because a genuine dispute existed about whether Concannon's or Galvin's version of the form was accurate. Hoyle should have admitted both versions into evidence and left it to the jury to decide which version is accurate.

An ethical nightmare. *The Verdict* made many critics' lists of Top 10 Films of 1982, but it's also in the running for Most Lawyer Misconduct in a Single Film. (*Class Action* and *Jagged Edge* are strong competitors for that award.) Here are the lowlight highlights:

• Galvin solicits clients in funeral parlors, engaging in a prohibited form of ambulance-chasing.

• Galvin ignores the case until a few days before trial, violating his obligation to provide competent representation.

• Galvin breaks into a mailbox in order to track down Nurse Price's current address, violating various federal statutes.

• Galvin fails to ask his client whether she wants to accept settlement offers.

• Galvin has a private (*ex parte*) meeting with Judge Hoyle.

• Galvin was practicing law while a total alcoholic. Most cases of lawyer discipline concern substance-abusing attorneys. Apparently the rate of alcohol and drug abuse by lawyers is about twice that of the general population.

• In his closing argument, Galvin completely ignores the evidence (which doesn't exist anyway) and talks emotionally about his belief that the jurors have "justice in their hearts." The argument asks the jurors to base their ruling on factors other than the evidence and is improper.

• Concannon pays Laura Fischer to spy on Galvin. It's unclear why a hotshot like Concannon would risk his license on a case against a drunk who has done no work. Equally demeaning to female lawyers is that Fischer, a lawyer trying to return to Concannon's firm after taking a leave, is willing to do it.

• Concannon pads his legal fees outrageously by assigning enough associates to fill Harvard Law School to work on the case.

• Concannon pays Galvin's medical expert to disappear.

The woodshed. Concannon rehearses Dr. Towler's direct examination by questioning him in his office and offering suggestions for more-persuasive answers. (The term "woodshed" originated in the late 1800s, when attorneys would often meet with witnesses in woodsheds next to courthouses.) Such rehearsals are proper as long as attorneys don't change the substance of testimony. Despite his other ethical lapses, Concannon's preparation of Dr. Towler is within the rules. He helps Towler to testify more convincingly but does not alter the substance of his story.

Picturing justice. (1) Galvin takes Polaroid photos of Deborah Ann, comatose and pitifully hooked to numerous tubes as she lies in her hospital bed. The developing images symbolize Galvin's growing sense of professional responsibility. (2) After Concannon rehearses Dr. Towler's testimony, the doctor gives a confident grin. The moment nicely depicts the self-assurance that a good lawyer can instill in nervous witnesses.

Trial Brief

Judge Hoyle is a wonderfully misnamed character. In 1742, Edmund Hoyle produced a book compiling the official rules of popular games of skill and chance, and revised versions have been published ever since. In *The Verdict*, none of the judge's rulings are "according to Hoyle."

Short Subjects

Brilliant Lies, 1996. Anthony LaPaglia. ——∎ ——∎

The Australian antidiscrimination tribunal must resolve a he-said-she-said situation. Was Susie Connor sexually harassed by her boss, Gary Fitzgerald? Following unsuccessful attempts at conciliation, the tribunal conducts a hearing. Fitzgerald claims that nothing ever happened, but Connor describes a pattern of harassing phone calls and a brutal sexual act. There's plenty of lying and opportunism on both sides, but Fitzgerald folds after Connor's graphic testimony and settles for a handsome sum. Filmmakers seem uninterested in administrative trials (*Brilliant Lies* depicts the only one in this book), but in reality there are far more administrative than judicial trials. In Australia and Britain, administrative cases are typically heard by three-person tribunals, whereas in the United States they are generally heard by a single administrative-law judge.

North Country, 2005. Charlize Theron. ──■ ──■

Josey Aimes takes a job in a taconite mine that is a cesspool of sexually depraved male employees who resent and sexually harass the few female employees. Aimes' efforts to change the hostile culture make her a pariah even to female co-workers. A small-town lawyer agrees to sue the mine owners because he'd be the first to file a sexual harassment case as a class action. *Courtroom highlight:* The judge rules that the case can proceed as a class action during a hearing in which male and female co-workers who previously shunned Aimes rise up one by one to acknowledge the accuracy of her claims. *Picturing justice:* Aimes' mother angrily turns off the TV as Aimes and her daughter watch Anita Hill testifying before a congressional committee that U.S. Supreme Court nominee Clarence Thomas sexually harassed her. The scene links Aimes to Hill and suggests that they are both heroes for publicizing and fighting the injustice of sexual harassment. *Trial brief:* The film is based on the case of *Jenson v. Eveleth Taconite Co.* (1997). About ten years after the case began, it ended when fifteen employees and former employees accepted a settlement of $3.5 million. The federal court of appeals opinion excoriated the company's lawyers for "exercising senseless and irrelevant discovery and by making endless objections at trial."

The People vs. Dr. Kildare, 1941. Lew Ayres, Lionel Barrymore. ──■ ──■

Dr. Kildare performs emergency surgery at the scene of an auto wreck that saves the life of professional ice-skater Frances Marlowe. When Marlowe ends up paralyzed, she sues the hospital and Kildare for medical malpractice based on a theory of *res ipsa loquitur* ("I don't know what happened, but Kildare must have been careless."). Kildare and his mentor, Dr. Gillespie, discover that the paralysis is unrelated to the surgery and get her back on the ice. *Courtroom highlight:* Marlowe's lawyer plays on the jurors' emotions by having her testify in front of a huge photo blowup showing her in skating costume. *Picturing justice:* Marlowe's lawyer is overbearing and bombastic and is more interested in attacking the doctors than finding out the truth.

The Wreck of the Mary Deare, 1959. Gary Cooper, Charlton Heston. ──■

Once again, the formal legal system is not up to the task of doing justice. Salvage operator John Sands finds first officer

Gideon Patch alone at sea on a derelict ship. Patch plans to prove to a British Court of Inquiry that the ship's owner committed insurance fraud. When the owner's lawyer convinces the judge that Patch is all wet, Patch and Sands have to risk their lives by taking a midnight dive to prove that Patch was right. *Courtroom highlight*: The barrister representing the ship's owner attacks Patch's character so effectively that the judge does not take his testimony seriously.

Familiarity Breeds
Contempt (of Court)

Courtroom films often intertwine the personal lives of the lawyers and their clients. This device enables the filmmaker to add a subplot to a legal story while intensifying the characters' emotions and confronting the lawyers with ethical and professional conflicts. For example, in *Suspect* a public defender and a juror carry on an investigation while trying to conceal their budding relationship from the judge. In *Jagged Edge* the client manipulates the lawyer into falling in love with him; this adds depth to the story while gravely impairing her objectivity. In *The Letter,* the lawyer's friendship with his client's husband leads him to destroy evidence. And in *Adam's Rib,* married lawyers duke it out in court while trying to maintain a normal home life.

This chapter focuses on films in which the lawyers' personal connections to a case affect their actions. While exaggerated in films for dramatic effect, the issues are quite real. Lawyers often perform legal services for close relatives and friends, and they have to be careful that the personal relationships do not interfere with their ability to remain dispassionate enough to provide effective help.

Perhaps the biggest no-no for lawyers is to act on sexual feelings for clients. Apart from the small matter of violating ethical rules, lawyer-client sexual liaisons cloud lawyers' objectivity and almost always cost both the lawyer and the client dearly, as they do in *The Paradine Case, Jagged Edge,* and *Body of Evidence.* Lawyers also take risks when they represent parents (*Music Box, Madame X*) or friends (*The Young Philadelphians, Knock on Any Door, The Letter, Defenseless*) or people who have close relationships with their family (*A Free Soul*).

In addition to excessive personal attachment to clients, films have enmeshed cine-lawyers in their clients' lives in a variety of other ways.

At one extreme, lawyers are synonymous with their clients (*The Secret Six*) or have committed the very crimes with which their clients are charged (*The Unknown Man*). Lawyers can also get into trouble when they prosecute friends (*Manhattan Melodrama, Sleepers*) and when they realize that they've helped former clients escape justice and feel they must somehow rectify the error (*Music Box, Criminal Law, Guilty as Sin*).

Lawyers often have to figure out how to provide effective advocacy without identifying themselves too personally with their clients. In general, the films in this chapter send cautionary messages about the dangers of lost objectivity.

Jagged Edge

Synopsis: A lawyer horses around with a husband charged with murdering his wife

Columbia Pictures, 1985. Color. Running time: 108 minutes.

Screenplay: Joe Eszterhas. Director: Richard Marquand.

Starring: Jeff Bridges (Jack Forrester), Glenn Close (Teddy Barnes).

Academy Award nomination: Best Supporting Actor (Robert Loggia).

Rating:

The Story

Wealthy San Francisco newspaper publisher Page Forrester and her maid are brutally stabbed to death. Her husband, Jack Forrester, claims that the intruder who committed the killings also knocked him out. D.A. Krasny doesn't buy Forrester's story and charges him with murder. In short order, Teddy Barnes becomes Forrester's lawyer, horseback-riding partner, and lover. Supposedly tough and street-smart, Barnes unquestioningly accepts Forrester's claim of innocence.

Krasny's evidence shows that Forrester had a strong financial motive to kill Page, because her divorce plans would have left him penniless. Moreover, Forrester was an unfaithful womanizer who often lured women to his bed by taking them horseback riding. This information adds little to Krasny's case, but it does lead Barnes to throw a jealous hissy-fit. Finally, a janitor at the Forresters' country club testifies that he saw a jagged-edged hunting knife in Forrester's gym locker a

Jagged Edge: Teddy Barnes (Glenn Close) and D.A. Tom Krasny (Peter Coyote) debate the admissibility of evidence.

few months before the murder. Barnes produces another club member who testifies that a jagged-edged hunting knife was in his locker at around the same time. Either the janitor made a mistake or Forrester belonged to one of San Francisco's best-armed country clubs.

The latest in a series of anonymous notes leads Barnes to Julie Jensen. Jensen testifies that she was attacked by a man wielding a jagged-edged knife more than a year before Page and her maid were killed. Because both attacks were so similar and unusual, Jensen's testimony suggests that the same person was responsible for both. Because Krasny cannot link Forrester to the attack on Jensen, her testimony creates doubt about Forrester's guilt, and the jury finds him not guilty.

* * *

SPOILER ALERT: You may not want to read further if you plan to see the film.

* * *

Barnes wanders into a closet off Forrester's bedroom and finds an old typewriter. Practicing her typing, she realizes that Forrester's typewriter makes the same distorted "t" as in the anonymous notes. She realizes that Forrester authored the anonymous notes and sent them to her so that she'd connect with Jensen. Forrester had attacked Jensen and allowed her to live so that Jensen could exculpate him after he later killed Page.

Barnes reveals what she's found out to Forrester and goes home. As she lies in bed, a hooded man breaks into her house and approaches her with a jagged-edged knife. Barnes pulls out a gun from under the covers and kills Forrester.

Legal Analysis

Ethics rules in many states now absolutely prohibit sexual liaisons between lawyers and clients. Even if the affair wasn't banned, it gravely affected Barnes' judgment and deprived her of objectivity. She became an easy pawn in Forrester's manipulative scheme. Even worse, when she discovered that Forrester had carried on a series of affairs, she nearly ditched her client.

Reverse signature crime evidence. Julie Jensen's account of her attack is the evidentiary highlight of the trial. Normally prosecutors offer evidence of defendants' "signature crimes," arguing that if crimes are committed in a similar and unique way the same person must have committed them all. *Jagged Edge* cleverly turns the usual scenario upside down. The jury could reasonably conclude that the same man attacked both Jensen and Page. Thus, if Forrester didn't attack Jensen, he probably didn't attack Page either.

Forrester's motive for killing Page. Because the Forresters apparently did not have a "prenup" agreement, their property rights would be governed by California community-property laws. Forrester would be entitled to at least half the amount by which the publishing empire increased in value during the time of the marriage. And a plethora of wealthy San Francisco women were apparently anxious to read Forrester's fine print, so while divorce might end his career as a newspaper publisher, he'd have plenty of time to give horseback riding lessons. Thus, his motive to kill Page is weak.

Forrester's motive for trying to kill Barnes. Because Forrester had already been found not guilty, the double-jeopardy ban would have prevented Krasny from retrying Forrester for murdering Page and the maid. Moreover, the statute of limitations might have barred Krasny from prosecuting Forrester for attacking Julie Jensen. So Forrester's motive for seeking to kill Barnes is also weak.

***Ex parte* communications.** Many films feature improper mid-trial *ex parte* (off-the-record) meetings between a judge and an attorney for one of the parties. The *ex parte* conference in *Jagged Edge* takes place at the judge's house, where Barnes confides her misgivings about representing a hypothetical client who might be guilty. The judge appropriately tells her that representing guilty defendants is her job and that she should get back to work.

Picturing justice. Typical of the courtroom-thriller crossover genre, the jury gets it wrong and the lawyers are a mess. Krasny has a history of concealing exculpatory information, and he does it again by failing to disclose before the trial that the prosecution knew about the Jensen attack. The portrayal of Teddy Barnes is even more negative. Like many modern female cine-lawyers, she is impulsive, unethical, and incompetent. Supposedly a hard-nosed legal veteran, she claims to "know" that Forrester is innocent, almost immediately becomes his lover, then throws a tantrum when she finds out about his other conquests. Her family life is a mess. She carries on a feud with Krasny and improperly denounces him in front of the judge and the media after the trial concludes. Barnes is definitely not a good role model for women considering going to law school.

Music Box

Synopsis: A daughter represents her father, a loving family man accused of committing horrible war crimes.

Carolco, 1989. Color. Running time: 124 minutes.

Screenplay: Joe Eszterhas. Director: Costa-Gavras.

Starring: Jessica Lange (Ann Talbot).

Academy Award nomination: Best Actress (Jessica Lange).

Rating: ——◼ ——◼

The Story

Mike Laszlo is a naturalized citizen from Hungary living in Chicago with his daughter, Ann Talbot, a savvy criminal-defense lawyer, and her son, Mikey. The United States institutes proceedings to revoke Laszlo's citizenship and extradite him to Hungary to stand trial as a World War II war criminal. Laszlo convinces his reluctant daughter to represent him. He insists that he was a low-level functionary during the war and that Hungary is out to destroy him because he opposes its Communist leaders.

Music Box: Ann Talbot (Jessica Lange) argues that her father, Mike Laszlo (Armin Mueller-Stahl), is not a war criminal.

Prosecutor Burke offers evidence that Laszlo, then known as Mishka, was a leader of a Nazi-organized death squad known as Arrow Cross. A document expert testifies to the genuineness of an Arrow Cross identification card containing Laszlo's photo and signature. Holocaust survivors from Hungary testify to numerous brutal murders and rapes of Jews and gypsies that Mishka committed.

Burke's final witness, Pal Horvath, is to testify that Mishka was his Arrow Cross squad leader, but he is so ill that the parties have to travel to his hospital room in Budapest. We hope they flew economy, because Judge Silver rules that Horvath is too unreliable to testify. The ruling is based on affidavits bearing Horvath's signature identifying someone other than Mishka as the squad leader. Even though Horvath says that he's never seen the affidavits, Silver dismisses all charges against Laszlo.

* * *

SPOILER ALERT: You may not want to read further if you plan to see the film.

* * *

A ticket from a Chicago pawn shop leads Talbot to a music box that belonged to a former member of Mishka's Arrow Cross squad. Concealed in the music box are photos of Mishka committing war crimes. When

Talbot confronts her father with the photos, he mocks her and says she can never keep him away from Mikey. Talbot's revenge is to mail the photos to Burke, and Laszlo's past is soon front-page news.

Legal Analysis

Even though Talbot succeeds in having the charges against her father dismissed, *Music Box* illustrates why lawyers should be reluctant to represent close relatives. Before she finds out the truth, Talbot's emotional stake in her father's innocence leads her to embarrass prosecutor Burke by revealing that she knows that his drunk driving caused his wife's death. Had Burke been inclined to resolve the case amicably, Talbot's cheap (and erroneous) shot would have hardened his stance.

Talbot's emotional ties to her father cause her to overreact in the opposite direction when she mails the music-box photos to Burke. Even though the charges have been dismissed, lawyers have ethical duties to former as well as current clients. Thus, Talbot can't reveal information related to her father's case except under extreme circumstances not present here. For example, publicizing the photos was not necessary to prevent Laszlo from killing or severely harming another person. While Talbot's desire for vengeance is understandable and viewers are thrilled to see her provide a measure of retribution to Laszlo, her reactions explain why she should not have taken the case.

A defense verdict on a Silver platter. Perhaps influenced by the Budapest setting, Silver's pro-defense rulings were from "hunger-y." Burke had already presented three witnesses who testified that Laszlo committed war crimes. Thus, even if Judge Silver thought that Horvath wasn't believable, Silver had no business dismissing the charges.

Equally improper was Silver's ruling that Horvath could not testify. The affidavits, hidden in a box of marzipan, were given to Talbot by a stranger only the night before. Silver should have smelled a rat, as well as marzipan. He should have allowed Burke to question Horvath and show that his present recollection of Mishka's crimes was more credible than the affidavits.

Picturing justice. (1) As Talbot confronts her father with the truth, her ex-father-in-law, a patrician and anti-Semitic lawyer, complains to the press that the prosecution was a waste of taxpayer money and a misguided effort to "appease the liberal New York–Washington lobby." The contrast magnifies the difficulties of bringing war criminals to justice.

(2) Before the trial, Laszlo good-naturedly complains "Damn lawyers, they find out everything" when Talbot reveals that she's found out about a secret romance between her father and a woman at their church. The final revelations give Laszlo's complaint a deeper meaning.

Trial Brief

Joe Eszterhas, who wrote the screenplay, was born in Hungary and after World War II lived in refugee camps before moving to the United States. The Arrow Cross was a Hungarian political party that collaborated with the Nazis and was implicated in atrocities of the sort depicted in the film. The character of Laszlo is based on John Demjanjuk. Demjanjuk lived in the United States from 1951 to 1986, when he was stripped of his U.S. citizenship and extradited to Israel to stand trial for committing war crimes as a concentration camp guard known as "Ivan the Terrible." He was convicted and sentenced to death, but the conviction was set aside by the Israeli Supreme Court as based on mistaken identity.

Demjanjuk's U.S. citizenship was restored in 1998. The U.S. Justice Department brought him to trial a second time, alleging he took part in rounding up Jews in Poland and brutalized prisoners at different concentration camps. He was again convicted and stripped of his citizenship. In 2004, the second conviction was affirmed on appeal and in December 2005 an immigration judge ordered that he be deported to the Ukraine.

The Paradine Case

Synopsis: A beautiful murder defendant who may have poisoned her husband poisons her barrister's life.

United Artists, 1947. Black and white. Running time: 119 minutes.

Screenplay: David O. Selznick. Novel: Robert Hitchens. Director: Alfred Hitchcock.

Starring: Gregory Peck (Anthony Keane), Alida Valli (Maddalena Paradine), Ethel Barrymore (Lady Sophie Horfield).

Academy Award nomination: Best Supporting Actress (Ethel Barrymore).

Rating: ⚖ ⚖ ⚖

The Paradine Case: Anthony Keane (Gregory Peck) questions his client Maddalena Paradine (Alida Valli).

The Story

Exotic beauty Maddalena Paradine is charged with murdering her husband, Colonel Paradine. The colonel was rich, old, and blind, so Maddalena's motive for killing him is apparent. Her lawyer, Anthony Keane, is so spellbound that he immediately describes her as "noble and self-sacrificing."

Ignoring his client's explicit instructions, Keane tries to pin the murder on Andre Latour, the colonel's longtime valet. After Latour testifies for the prosecution that he saw Maddalena outside the colonel's bedroom door on the night he died, Keane's cross-examination is nasty and infuriating to Maddalena. Latour knew that he would receive a legacy on the colonel's death, and he had access to poison. Latour finally falls apart and admits that he and Maddalena were lovers. In love with Maddalena himself, Keane thinks he's well on his way to securing an acquittal while ridding himself of a rival for Maddalena's affections.

Maddalena testifies impressively in her own defense until word reaches the courtroom that Latour has committed suicide. Picking a bad time and place to confess, she admits while standing in the dock that she murdered the colonel, just as Keane's questions killed Latour and destroyed her life: "My only source of comfort is the hatred and contempt I feel for you." Humiliated, Keane resigns on the spot. Keane's wife, Gay, stands by him and praises his brilliance. Maddalena no doubt disagrees. She is convicted and sentenced to death.

Legal Analysis

Despite the emotional testimonial revelations, most viewers will figure out the truth long before Keene does. From the standpoint of courtroom drama, it's even more damaging that Keane fails to notice that the prosecutor's cupboard is virtually bare of evidence connecting Maddalena to her husband's death. For example, Maddalena may have wanted to escape marriage to an elderly blind husband, but, if so, that motive had existed for a long time and no evidence shows that she poisoned him. To create suspense, the film resorts to having Keane act as both prosecutor and defense attorney by investigating how Colonel Paradine died.

Who's in charge here? Keane's intense cross-examination of Latour effectively casts him in the role of possible murderer. However, while lawyers usually decide what questions they'll ask, inculpating Latour was a major strategic decision that Maddalena had the right to make. So long as she is competent to understand the consequences of her decision, Keane should have obeyed her instruction to protect Latour's innocence. If Keane thought that he couldn't effectively represent Maddalena in those circumstances, his option was to resign.

Silence is golden. Angered by Maddalena's instructions, Keane tells her that, after he's finished with Latour, "I shall put you in the box. You can say what you like there. My questions will be mine, your answers yours." Because the prosecution did not have enough evidence to convict Maddalena, Keane should have strongly advised her not to testify. While Keane could not have anticipated Latour's suicide and its destructive effect on Maddalena, defendants often do themselves more harm than good by testifying, and Maddalena is no exception.

Picturing justice: (1) Lecherous Lord Horfield, who presides over Maddalena's trial, is contemptuous of her throughout. As Horfield haughtily tells his wife that Maddalena will shortly hang, his face is framed by two long candles. The imagery suggests that Horfield's lack of empathy for Maddalena makes him as much a prisoner of the law as she is. (2)

Maddalena's and Keane's backs are to the camera when they are first seen, yet when we first see Keane's wife, Gay, she is facing the camera. The contrast suggests that, unlike the other two main characters, Gay is open and honest. The film ends with Keane facing Gay and looking directly into the camera, suggesting that Gay's love has redeemed him.

Trial Brief

While the courtroom scenes are done well, critics generally rate *The Paradine Case* as one of the lesser works of the great director Alfred Hitchcock. If so, its deficiencies may lie in backstage intrigues. The story was an "orphan project" that Hitchcock agreed to do only to fulfill his contract with David O. Selznick, the film's producer and writer. Selznick was in economic and psychological distress and repeatedly contradicted Hitchcock's creative decisions. For example, Selznick insisted that American actor Gregory Peck play the role of an English barrister and that the suave Louis Jourdan, rather than an "earthier" actor, play the role of Latour. Coincidentally, a character named David is murdered in the first minute of Hitchcock's next film, *Rope*.

The Young Philadelphians

Synopsis: A tax lawyer risks his social standing to defend a friend charged with murder.

Warner Bros., 1959. Black and white. Running time: 136 minutes.

Screenplay: James Gunn. Book: Richard Powell. Director: Vincent Sherman.

Starring: Paul Newman (Tony Lawrence), Robert Vaughn (Chet Gwynn).

Academy Award nominations: Best Supporting Actor (Robert Vaughn), Best Cinematography, Best Costume Design.

Rating:

The Story

Tony Lawrence has inherited the last name but not the money of one of Philadelphia's wealthiest and snobbiest families. Lawrence becomes

The Young Philadelphians. Tony Lawrence (Paul Newman) hones in on the uncertain olfactory nerves of George Archibald (Richard Deacon).

an associate in Philadelphia's most elite law firm, but he feels like he's working in a "high-class graveyard," and the hours are endless. When Lawrence shows an eccentric client how she can save a ton in taxes by donating appreciated stock instead of cash to charity, his career as a tax lawyer takes off.

Chet Gwynn, Lawrence's old pal and the alcoholic black sheep of a blueblood family, is charged with murdering his uncle and trustee, Morton Stearnes. Gwynn insists he's innocent and after much pleading convinces Lawrence to represent him.

Prosecutor Louis Donetti, Lawrence's law-school friend, proves that Gwynn had a financial motive to kill Stearnes and had written him a threatening note. Moreover, Gwynn had showed up at Stearnes' mansion drunk and with a gun just hours before Stearnes was shot. Finally, George Archibald, Stearnes' haughty butler, places Gwynn in the study, the room where Stearnes was killed. Stearnes handed empty drinking glasses to Archibald through the study door, and Archibald could distinguish the smell of Gwynn's cheap rye from that of Stearnes' well-aged Scotch.

Lawrence uses a classic courtroom demonstration to prove that Archibald's testimony stinks. Lawrence produces three cups of liquid and asks Archibald to sniff each carefully and identify its contents.

Archibald confidently testifies that the first cup contains cheap rye, the second contains expensive Scotch, and the third contains water. Archibald then takes a drink from the third cup and chokes on its contents: gin! A shaken Archibald admits that he could have been wrong on the night Stearnes died as well and that the sound that woke him minutes before he heard the gunshot could have been Gwynn leaving the property through the garden gate.

Lawrence solves the mystery of how Stearnes died by calling Dr. Shippen Stearnes, who knows where all the Stearnes family skeletons are buried. Shippen reveals that Stearnes had painful terminal cancer and that he probably used Gwynn's gun to commit suicide. The jury finds Gwynn not guilty; Lawrence wins by a nose.

Legal Analysis

Lawrence's willingness to represent his old friend Gwynn is understandable, but a murder trial isn't a recommended way to get that first trial experience under your belt. Lawrence should have at least associated an experienced criminal lawyer to do the heavy lifting.

Drinking problem. Lawrence's drinks demonstration is both risky and unnecessary. Lawrence should have concentrated on showing that Archibald's testimony is consistent with Lawrence's argument that Gwynn had been in Stearnes' study but left through the garden gate before the gun was fired. Similarly, Archibald must have been aware that his beloved employer was in great pain, and Lawrence should have asked him about that. Lawrence could have bolstered his contention that Morton took his own life without attacking Archibald's sniffer.

Picturing justice. *The Young Philadelphians* provides generally positive images of lawyers of the stuffy "gentlemen's club" variety. Despite his inexperience as a trial lawyer, Lawrence is as adept at finding holes in evidence as he is at finding loopholes in the tax laws. Lawrence's boss, Wharton, devotes a summer to writing a treatise on antitrust law and is not at all a supergreedy big-firm baddie. (Compare Wharton with the big-firm lawyers in such later films as *Devil's Advocate, Class Action, The Firm, Liar Liar,* and *The Rainmaker.*) The tax client's former lawyer graciously steps aside so that Lawrence can steal her for his firm. Prosecutor Donetti is honest and has a social conscience.

Memorable Courtroom Demonstrations

Demonstrations are often the highlight of courtroom films. A good demonstration can inject drama or comedy into a film while providing visual action as a counterpoint to a talky trial script. Here are a few films not covered elsewhere in *Reel Justice* that depict notable courtroom demonstrations:

The Awful Truth, 1937. Cary Grant, Irene Dunne.

With their divorce nearly final, the screwball Warriners battle in court over custody of their beloved dog, Mr. Smith. When the judge rules that Mr. Smith's own preference will decide the issue, both spouses try to outdo the other to convince Mr. Smith to jump into their arms. *Trial brief:* The film received six Academy Award nominations, including Best Picture, and received the award for Best Director.

Criminal Court, 1946. Tom Conway.

Crack criminal-defense attorney Steve Barnes cross-examines Brown, who falsely testifies that he "stood calmly by" when Barnes' client Marsh ran up to and gunned down the victim, who was next to Brown. Ignoring the judge's admonishments, Barnes angrily accuses Brown of lying, and the D.A. of knowingly suborning perjury. Finally, Barnes yells that he'll "take justice into my own hands" and yanks a gun out of his coat. Everyone in the courtroom, including Brown, dives for cover. Brown's reaction destroys his claim that he calmly observed the killing, and Marsh is acquitted.

The demonstration is based on one of attorney Earl Rogers' most famous courtroom stunts. As the *Los Angeles Times* described it the next day, "Buffalo Bill's hottest show was a tame performance compared with Earl Rogers in the Boyd trial yesterday. It was so effective that he drove the jury under the table and the audience out the fire escapes." *Final Verdict* (1991) is a made-for-TV movie depicting the alcohol-shortened life of Earl Rogers. Rogers was also the model for the alcoholic lawyer Stephen Ashe, who was played by Lionel Barrymore in *A Free Soul,* a film based on a novel written by Rogers' daughter, journalist Adela Rogers St. John.

The Mouthpiece, 1932. Warren William. ——■ ——■ ——■

Vincent Day, organized crime's favorite defense attorney, tries to get a prosecution witness to admit that he had been knocked out during a melee and therefore could not have seen Day's client commit a murder. The witness, an ex-boxer, claims that nobody could have knocked him out. Day slugs the witness as he leaves the witness stand, knocking him out with the aid of a weight concealed in his fist.

In the same film, Day's client is charged with murder, allegedly by poisoning his victim. To disprove the prosecution's claim that the vial the police found contained a deadly and quick-acting poison, Day dramatically drinks the vial's remaining contents. When nothing happens to Day, the jury acquits the defendant. Day, who had earlier drunk a protective liquid, then immediately has his stomach pumped.

The poison demonstration was performed in an actual case by William Fallon, a New York lawyer who acquired the nickname of "Mouthpiece for the Mob" in the first two decades of the twentieth century. Fallon is the model for the character of Billy Flynn in *Roxie Hart, Chicago,* and numerous other films (particularly those made in the 1930s) in which lawyers represented racketeers, such as *The Defense Rests* (1934). *The Mouthpiece* was remade as *The Man Who Talked Too Much* (1940) and *Illegal* (1955).

A Night of Adventure, 1944. Tom Conway. ——■ ——■

While examining a glove expert, the prosecutor has the defendant put on the glove that the murderer dropped at the crime scene. The expert testifies that the wear lines on the glove show that it is an exact fit. Defense attorney Latham then tries on the same glove, and the expert has to concede that it fits him too. The film is a remake of *Hat, Coat, and Glove* (1934). Perhaps the prosecutors in the famous 1995 murder trial of O.J. Simpson watched this demonstration as part of their trial preparation. They asked Simpson to try on a glove that the police found at the murder scene. The ploy backfired when it became apparent that it was much too small for Simpson's hand. Defense attorney Johnny Cochran's follow-up argument became one of the trial's mantras: "If the glove don't fit, you must acquit."

Mountain Justice, 1937. George Brent. ——■ ——■

A hillbilly defendant denies that the rifle from which a shot was fired belonged to him. With the defendant seated at the counsel table as the trial nears its end, the prosecutor suddenly picks up the rifle, turns to the defendant, and asks him, "Do you want to take your rifle home with you?" The defendant gladly accepts it, and the jury quickly convicts him.

The following films are discussed elsewhere in *Reel Justice,* and each contains a memorable courtroom demonstration:

- *The Young Philadelphians* (testing butler's olfactory ability)
- *Philadelphia* (visibility of AIDS lesions in a mirror)
- *Adam's Rib* (female strength)
- *From the Hip* (survival of murder victim)
- *Beyond a Reasonable Doubt* (pipe marks)
- *To Kill a Mockingbird* (catch a glass)
- *Trial* (in the spotlight)
- *A Place in the Sun* (don't rock the boat!)
- *My Cousin Vinny* (how many fingers?)
- *Knock on Any Door* (testing a bartender's memory)
- *The Unholy Three* (hair loss)
- *Eight O'Clock Walk* (music sets off maniac)

Short Subjects

Body of Evidence, 1993. Madonna, Willem Dafoe. —■

In this sleazy film, T&A certainly doesn't stand for Trial Advocacy. Kinky playgirl Rebecca Carlson is tried for murdering her elderly lover in order to inherit his fortune. Carlson's M.O. was to induce a heart attack by slipping her man cocaine while engaging him in strenuous sex. The M.O. leads to defense attorney Frank Dulaney investigating Carlson's sexual prowess in elevators and car parks. As in *Witness for the Prosecution,* a set-up witness hoodwinks the jury into an acquittal, but justice triumphs outside of court. *Courtroom highlight:* A previous lover's graphic testimony that Carlson used the same method in an unsuccessful effort to inherit from him is a good example of permissible "signature crime" testimony. *Picturing justice:* The attorneys repeatedly shout out silly objections, and the judge responds with anger and sarcasm. At one point, the judge clears the courtroom after the spectators misbehave, thus cutting down on the costs for extras.

Criminal Law, 1988. Kevin Bacon, Gary Oldman. ────▪

Successfully undermining the testimony of the prosecution's eyewitnesses, defense lawyer Ben Chase gets Martin Thiel acquitted of a brutal rape-murder. After several similar crimes occur, Chase realizes that Thiel is guilty of all of them. Although he agrees to continue to represent Thiel, Chase plots with the police to trap him. *Picturing justice*: Though Chase's associate reminds him that "guilty is for juries and justice is for God," the film panders to the popular view that lawyers should betray scummy clients rather than defend them.

Defenseless, 1991. Barbara Hershey, Sam Shepard. ────▪

Ellie Seldes is tried for the gory murder of her husband, Steven. Because zero evidence links Ellie to the crime, defense lawyer T. K. Katwuller manages an acquittal. However, to describe the convoluted plot in this way is like saying "World War II started and later it ended." It turns out that Steven and Katwuller had been lovers, the police later find evidence suggesting that Katwuller was the murderer, and Katwuller has two simultaneous near-death experiences as a psychopath tries to shoot her while she dangles precariously from a cable high above an empty elevator shaft. And there's more—oh, so much more. *Courtroom highlight*: Cross-examining a police officer, Katwuller uses her inside knowledge of how Steven was killed to destroy the officer's credibility. *Picturing justice*: Katwuller's apartment is a mess, just like her personal life and this film.

A Free Soul, 1931. Lionel Barrymore, Norma Shearer, Clark Gable. ───▪ ───▪ ───▪

It's "Bluster's Last Stand" for brilliant but alcoholic lawyer Stephen Ashe. When Ashe's client, notorious gangster Ace Wilfong, becomes abusive to Ashe's daughter Jan, Jan's ex-fiancée, Dwight Winthrop, kills Wilfong and is tried for murder. *Courtroom highlight*: With the defense going badly, Jan hauls her drunken father out of the gutter and into the courtroom. Ashe argues that Winthrop isn't guilty because "when [Wilfong] threatened the rest of her life, her father wasn't there to protect his daughter. All this Dwight Winthrop knew . . . and the poor boy went insane. . . . Stephen Ashe is guilty and nobody else." With that, Ashe collapses and dies on the courtroom floor. *Picturing justice*: Demonstrating that lawyers do not always like their clients, Ashe tells Wilfong: "The only time I hate democracy is when one of you mongrels forgets where you belong." *Trial brief:* The film is based on a novel by journalist Adela Rogers St. John. The characters of Jan and Ashe are based on Adela and her father, famous California lawyer Earl Rogers. For more about Rogers, see "Sidebar: Memorable Courtroom Demonstrations" in this chapter.

Guilty as Sin, 1993. Rebecca De Mornay, Don Johnson. ——■ ——■

David Greenhill, a handsome gigolo charged with killing his wife smooth-talks Jennifer Haines, a supposedly top-notch lawyer, into believing in his innocence. When Haines realizes that Greenhill is a serial killer planning to make her his next victim, Haines decides to let ethical rules take the hit instead. Fans of recycled plot devices should watch for a female lawyer who's too trusting of her client (*Jagged Edge*); a lawyer trying to achieve justice by betraying a client she's certain is guilty (*And Justice for All, From the Hip*), a defendant trying to avoid a guilty verdict by creating and then demolishing prosecution evidence (*Chicago*); or a lawyer and client struggling to the death (*Jagged Edge*, either version of *Cape Fear*). *Picturing justice:* The sleazy perjury that Haines offers on Greenhill's behalf belies the majesty of the marbled courtroom.

Madame X, 1937. Warren William. ——■ ——■ ——■

Raymond Fleuriot grew up thinking that his mother was dead, and doesn't realize that Madame X, the anonymous alcoholic he's defending against a charge of murder, is his mother. Fleuriot's father, a famous lawyer, had banished Madame X for having an affair, and she killed to prevent a con man from telling Fleuriot that she was still alive. *Courtroom highlight:* Not realizing that the man he's condemning is his father, Fleuriot argues that "this husband should be here on trial, for he is without heart, without soul. Who is this God-like man who wouldn't give a fellow creature one more chance?" *Picturing justice:* Before finding out the identity of Fleuriot's client, his father advises Fleuriot that "All you can do is your best. After all you're a lawyer, not a doctor. If your client is a woman, find some man and blame it on him." *Trial brief:* A boon to hankie manufacturers, the story has formed the basis of numerous films, including a 1966 version starring Lana Turner. An early talkie variation is *Scarlet Pages* (1930), in which a female defense attorney successfully defends the illegitimate daughter she had abandoned years earlier. Another close cousin is *The Secret of Madame Blanche* (1933; Irene Dunne). Here, a mother is charged with murder after she implicates herself in a killing that she realizes was committed by her long-lost son. When the son realizes that the defendant is his mother, he confesses to the killing in the courtroom and goes to jail. If there's yet another remake, they might call it *Madame Y* but spell it differently: "Why?"

Manhattan Melodrama, 1934. Clark Gable, William Powell, Myrna Loy. ──■ ──■

Jim Wade becomes a prosecutor and governor of New York, while Blackie, his childhood chum, becomes a gangster whom Wade reluctantly convicts of murder. After Wade finds out that Blackie killed to protect a secret that would have ruined Wade's political career, Wade tries to commute the sentence. Blackie refuses: "If I can't live the way I want, at least let me die when I want." Wade resigns as governor. *Picturing justice*: With audiences very aware of the carnage that had accompanied the recently ended Prohibition, Wade argues to the jury: "Either we can surrender to an epidemic of crime and violence . . . or we can give warning to the hosts of other murderers and gangsters that they are through." *Trial briefs*: (1) Notorious gangster John Dillinger was leaving a Chicago theater after watching this film when FBI agents gunned him down. (2) This was the first film to pair William Powell and Myrna Loy; they went on to star as detectives Nick and Nora Charles in the very successful *Thin Man* detective films.

The Secret Six, 1931. Clark Gable, Jean Harlow. ──■ ──■

When bootleggers become more powerful than the courts, it's time for a secret group of community leaders to intervene. *Courtroom highlight*: After defense lawyer Newton secures an acquittal by bribing the jurors, the judge angrily tells the jurors that he has "never seen a more outrageous miscarriage of justice." *Picturing justice*: Newton is both the mouthpiece for and the brains in charge of the bootleggers. *Trial brief*: The film was banned in a number of cities because of its excessive violence and its depiction of the entire bootlegging process from distillery to consumer.

The Unknown Man, 1951. Walter Pidgeon. ——■ ——■

Brad Mason is so upset after securing the acquittal of guilty killer Rudi Walchek that he decides to hunt down Walchek's crime boss. When the boss turns out to be the well-connected Andrew Layford, Mason kills Layford with Walchek's dagger. Ironically, Walchek is charged with killing Layford, and Mason again defends him. This time Walchek is convicted. To rectify what he regards as an injustice, Mason visits Walchek in jail with the dagger and turns his back so that Walchek can kill him. *Courtroom highlight*: Mason's questions to witnesses reveal to prosecutor Bucknor that Mason killed Layford. *Picturing justice*: Standing in for Mason as the speaker at a law school graduation, Bucknor tells the new lawyers-to-be that law is not synonymous with justice: "The law may make mistakes, but justice never. So reach out for justice."

Prejudice on Trial

Prejudice, most commonly based on race, is an unfortunate but enduring part of human existence, and it has always been reflected in the U.S. justice system. For decades, juries consisted only of white men, and in *Plessy v. Ferguson* (1896) the Supreme Court held that racial segregation was constitutional. Only in 1954, in *Brown v. Board of Education,* did the Court reverse that historic error. Since that time, the passage of numerous civil rights laws and countless judicial decisions have gone a long way in eradicating the shadow of racism from the American justice system, but most people would concede there is still a long way to go.

It is not surprising that courtroom movies often reflect and critique racial attitudes. Sometimes, as in *Judge Priest*, racial stereotypes are taken for granted and now-embarrassing portrayals of African-Americans are simply part of the "wallpaper" in front of which the story unfolds. In a few films dating back to the middle of the twentieth century, pioneering filmmakers confronted the realities of courtroom prejudice, as in *Pinky* and *Trial.* And by focusing on the prejudice of British colonials against Asians, *The Letter* demonstrated that racism is hardly unique to the United States.

As the civil rights movement picked up steam, courtroom movies of the 1960s, including *Sergeant Rutledge,* challenged racial prejudice in the courtroom. One of the finest films ever made, *To Kill a Mockingbird,* is the definitive statement about racism in the justice system of the Deep South. More-contemporary films have returned to these themes, both exploring racism in earlier times (*Amistad, Sommersby, Snow Falling on Cedars*) and raising questions about whether racial elements still pervade today's system of criminal justice (*A Time to Kill, Bonfire of the Vanities*).

There is something about human nature that hates and fears "the other." Multiple forms of prejudice are reflected in such films as *Philadelphia* and *Midnight in the Garden of Good and Evil* (homophobia); *They Won't Forget* (southern antipathy toward Yankees); *A Cry in the Dark* (religion); *Inherit the Wind* (evolutionists); *Fury* (outsiders); and *Johnny Belinda* (physically challenged individuals). All these films highlight the ways that prejudices in the world project into the legal system and the courtroom.

Amistad

Synopsis: A U.S. Supreme Court decision frees illegally enslaved Africans.

Dreamworks, 1997. Color. Running time: 153 minutes.

Screenplay: David Franzoni. *Director*: Steven Spielberg.

Starring: Matthew McConaughey (Roger Baldwin), Anthony Hopkins (John Quincy Adams), Djimon Hounsou (Cinque).

Academy Award nominations: Best Supporting Actor (Anthony Hopkins), Best Cinematography, Best Costumes, Best Original Score.

Rating:

The Story

In 1839, slave traders capture a group of Africans and ship them to Havana. Ruiz and Montes purchase the slaves and secure documentation falsely stating that the Africans were Cuban. The new owners transport them to another Cuban port in the *Amistad*, but the Africans seize the ship and kill the crew. Ruiz and Montes survive and fool the captives into sailing to Long Island, where the U.S. Navy captures the ship.

The African captives are tried for piracy and murder in a Connecticut federal court. In the same case, Ruiz and Montes ask the judge to award them title to the captives, claiming they were legally purchased in Havana. They have heavyweight backing from the government acting for Queen Isabella II of Spain (Cuba was then a Spanish colony) and U.S. President Martin Van Buren, who fears loss of the South in the upcoming election if the captives go free. The sailors who captured the *Amistad* also assert ownership of the ship and the captives, perhaps mistakenly thinking that their motto is "Join the Navy and Seize the World."

DreamWorks/Photofest.

Amistad: John Quincy Adams (Anthony Hopkins) argues the *Amistad* case to the Supreme Court as the bust of his father looks on.

A young local attorney, Roger Baldwin, defends the captives. Rejecting the high-flown rhetoric of the local abolitionists, Baldwin's narrower theory is that though blacks born in Cuba are legally slaves, his clients were from Africa and thus were illegally seized. As free men, Baldwin argued, the captives were defending their rights when they mutinied and took control of the ship. After Cinque, the Africans' leader, testifies through an interpreter to the horrible story of how the captives ended up on Long Island, the judge rules that the Africans are not guilty of any crimes and are not the property of anyone. Indeed, he arrests Ruiz and Montes for presenting fraudulent documents to the court.

The Africans' celebration is short-lived as the government appeals to the Supreme Court. Baldwin persuades former president John Quincy Adams to argue the case. Adams' eloquent argument proves persuasive, and with one dissenting vote the Supreme Court rules in favor of the Africans. Cinque and the other Africans are returned to Sierra Leone, but civil war has destroyed their villages and their families are gone, perhaps also sold into slavery.

Legal Analysis

The U.S. Supreme Court's decision in the *Amistad* case was surprising in light of the intense political pressure to return the slaves to their Spanish owners. President Van Buren asserted that the treaty between the United States and Spain required their return, and the Court usually defers to the executive branch in matters of foreign relations. In addition, a decision favoring the captives had the potential to trigger serious domestic repercussions because it concerned a murderous slave rebellion. Even though a majority of the justices were themselves slave owners, the Court defied the president and freed the captives.

Justice Story (played by then-retired Supreme Court Justice Harry Blackmun) delivers his opinion in a dry tone that belies its emotional impact. Story declares that the Africans "cannot be considered merchandise but are rather free individuals with certain legal and moral rights, including the right to engage in insurrection against those who would deny them their freedom."

Of course, the Court did not question the institution of slavery in the United States or in Cuba. Its decision did nothing to help the millions of men and women who were enslaved. Quite a few years later, in the notorious *Dred Scott* case (1857), the Supreme Court held that American slaves could not be treated as citizens, even if they escaped to free states. Nevertheless, the *Amistad* case is one of the greatest civil rights decisions in the history of the Supreme Court and a monument to its independence from the executive branch.

Adams' argument. Adams begins by noting that his colleague Roger Baldwin had argued the case so completely that he had scarcely anything left to say. In fact, however, he has plenty to say. Noting that the case seemed at first to involve mundane details of property, Adams said: "This is the most important case ever to come before this Court because what it in fact concerns is the very nature of man." He points to the political background of the case and heaps scorn on Queen Isabella II, Van Buren, and the institution of slavery.

Adams wonders how the Court might deal with that "annoying" document, the Declaration of Independence, and its resounding statement that "all men are created equal." He has a modest suggestion: He tears the document into shreds. Touching the busts of the founding fathers (including that of his own father, the second president, John Adams) and calling on them for guidance, Quincy Adams declares:

"We've been made to understand . . . that who we are *is* who we were. . . . Give us the courage to do what is right. And if it means civil war, let it come. And when it does, may it be finally the last battle of the American Revolution."

The legal issue in the *Amistad* case. If the captives were from Africa, their seizure was illegal because the United States had banned the slave trade. They were free men who were entitled to defend their freedom, even by seizing the ship and murdering the crew.

If, on the other hand, the captives were from Cuba, their purchase by Ruiz and Montes would have been legal and they could be viewed as mere cargo on the *Amistad*. They would not be entitled to seize the ship because they had no freedom to defend. Under article 9 of the 1795 treaty between the United States and Spain, they should be returned to their lawful owners.

Thus Cinque's testimony in the district court that the captives were seized in Africa is critical. His testimony allows both courts to look behind the fraudulent documentation offered by Ruiz and Montes. At first, Baldwin has no way to prove the truth because of the language barrier. Desperate to find someone who could translate, Baldwin walks the docks counting loudly in Mende, until a man who speaks both languages comes forward. Finally, Cinque is given a voice. Even the government's handpicked judge could not resist the forcefulness of Cinque's testimony about the indescribably brutal transport of the captives from Africa to Havana.

Picturing justice. The film focuses on two great lawyers whose skill and dedication stopped the governments of the United States and Spain in their tracks. Without the work of these lawyers, the voiceless Africans would have been either hanged or returned to slavery. (As usual, Hollywood concentrated more on the white heroes of the story than the black ones.) Baldwin destroyed his own law practice in his tireless work on behalf of the Africans in the district court. And Adams, who was scorned as a pitiful has-been former president who snoozed his way through sessions of Congress, rose to great oratorical heights in his Supreme Court argument.

Trial Briefs

1. The account in the film of the *Amistad* case is substantially correct, although many details have been left out or simplified. In the real

case, Adams' argument lasted eight and a half hours, quite a contrast to the modern Supreme Court, where arguments are usually limited to thirty minutes. Some of Adams' argument in the film is fictitious. For example, he didn't tell tales about Cinque or welcome the Civil War. It is interesting that one of the captives was found to have been born in Cuba and was returned to his owner there.

2. Roger Baldwin was a grandson of one of the signers of the Declaration of Independence. He later became governor of Connecticut and a U.S. senator. One of his co-counsels in the case was Seth Staples, who founded the Yale Law School.

3. Barbara Chase-Riboud sued Dreamworks and Steven Spielberg, claiming that *Amistad* had been copied from her book *Echo of Lions*. The federal district court refused to halt the opening of the film. Later Chase-Riboud dropped her lawsuit and praised the film, but whether she got any money has never been disclosed. Many believe that the litigation seriously damaged *Amistad*'s Academy Award prospects.

The Letter

Synopsis: A lawyer must decide whether to destroy incriminating evidence on his client.

Warner Bros., 1940. Black and white. Running time: 95 minutes.

Screenplay: Howard Koch. Original short story and stage play: W. Somerset Maugham. Director: William Wyler.

Starring: Bette Davis (Leslie Crosbie).

Academy Award nominations: Best Picture, Best Director, Best Actress (Bette Davis), Best Supporting Actor (James Stephenson), Best Cinematography, Best Musical Score, Best Editing.

Rating

The Story

Leslie Crosbie and her husband, Robert, are British expatriates who own a Malaysian rubber plantation. While Robert is away, Leslie shoots and kills another ex-pat, Geoff Hammond, supposedly to prevent Hammond from raping her. Hammond is a pariah for marrying a Eurasian woman, so the British colonials happily accept her story.

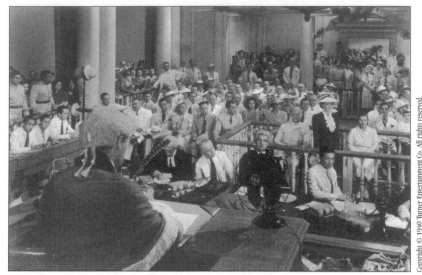

The Letter: Leslie Crosbie (Bette Davis) is protected by the letter of the law.

Lawyer Howard Joyce, Robert's close friend, is confident of a not-guilty verdict until he's handed a copy of a letter written by Leslie to Hammond. The letter makes clear that Leslie and Hammond were lovers and that she killed Hammond when he tried to break off their affair. Leslie implores Joyce to buy the letter from Hammond's widow, and he reluctantly agrees, in order to spare Robert from finding out about Leslie's affair.

With the letter out of the way, Leslie is swiftly acquitted. Robert then tells Leslie of his plans to buy another rubber plantation. Robert should have checked his bank statement. Leslie confesses that she used all their savings to buy the incriminating letter. Robert is inclined to forgive and forget, but Leslie can't face another couple of decades surrounded by rubber trees. Sensing the fate that awaits her, she wanders into her garden and is stabbed to death by Hammond's widow. At least Leslie got both the farmer and the letter.

Legal Analysis

The subtext of *The Letter* is the contempt of the British colonials for the Asians with whom they live and work. For example, no Asians attend the party that celebrates Leslie's acquittal. Also, Joyce diminishes

Hammond's character in the English jury's eyes by letting it drop that Hammond married a Eurasian. The feelings were mutual: Hammond's widow forces Leslie to pick the letter up off the floor after Leslie hands her the money.

Dread letter day. Joyce's ethical responsibility to Leslie means that he cannot reveal the letter's existence to the police. By the same token, Joyce cannot take action that makes it more difficult for the police to find out about the letter themselves. Thus Joyce violated legal ethics when he bought and destroyed the letter.

No questions. While lawyers cannot knowingly present perjured testimony, defendants have the right to testify. Joyce should have simply called Leslie to testify and let her tell the story in her own words, without questioning her. Instead, Joyce gets himself in further ethical hot water by eliciting her phony story and arguing its accuracy.

Anything for a friend. Joyce at first refuses Leslie's plea to purchase the letter. He tells her, "I've always looked on myself as an honest man. . . .A lawyer has a duty to his profession and to himself. No, I can't do what you ask." Leslie convinces Joyce to change his mind by appealing to the devastating impact her conviction would have on his close friend, Robert. Like other films (such as *Music Box*), *The Letter* illustrates why lawyers should be reluctant to handle cases involving close friends or relatives. Joyce's ethical gaffe might cost him his career if Hammond's widow decides to reveal the transaction.

Picturing justice. In nearly every scene, the dilemmas faced by Leslie and Joyce are magnified by strong vertical and horizontal lines that seem to trap them in a grid. The horizontal lines are often shadows cast by the window slats used as blinds in the plantation houses. The grid also suggests the oppressive and racist British colonial society of Malaya.

Trial Briefs

1. In Somerset Maugham's original story, Leslie lives and declares that she still loves Hammond. The story had to be changed because under the Production Code, Hollywood's system of self-censorship that was in effect from 1934 to 1968, sex outside marriage had to be punished, generally by disgrace or death. Also, crime could never pay, and Leslie had committed adultery and murder.

2. *Wyler's direction. The Letter* is enhanced by the stunning music of Max Steiner and the expressionistic direction of the great William Wyler. The film opens with a justly acclaimed tracking shot. As the credits roll, a rubber plantation is bathed by brilliant moonlight. The camera travels from a rubber tree dripping its precious sap into a bucket, to a group of plantation workers, sleeping in hammocks or playing instruments, to a white cockatoo roosting on a roof. Suddenly a shot rings out from the house. The bird takes flight. A man staggers through the doorway and falls down the stairs. A woman follows him out, holding a pistol. She fires five more times into his fallen body. The camera closes in on her expressionless face. Clouds blow in front of the moon. Later, during the film's courtroom scene, the figures in the foreground and the background are in perfect focus. Wyler was a proponent of deep-focus cinematography. Wyler also directed *Counsellor-at-Law* (1933), one of the best depictions ever made of the life of a lawyer.

Philadelphia

Synopsis: A gay lawyer sues a law firm for illegally firing him because he had AIDS.

Tristar, 1993. Color. Running time: 125 minutes.

Screenplay: Ron Nyswaner. Director: Jonathan Demme.

Starring: Tom Hanks (Andrew Beckett), Denzel Washington (Joe Miller), Jason Robards (Charles Wheeler), Mary Steenburgen (Belinda Conine), Antonio Banderas (Miguel Alvarez).

Academy Awards: Best Actor (Tom Hanks), Best Original Song (Bruce Springsteen).

Academy Award nominations: Best Original Screenplay, Best Original Song (Neil Young), Best Makeup.

Rating:

The Story

Andrew Beckett is a senior associate at the elite Philadelphia law firm of Wyant, Wheeler and seemingly on the fast track to partnership. Beckett tried to prevent the other lawyers from finding out that he is gay and infected with the deadly AIDS virus. The firm fires Beckett,

Philadelphia: All things considered, Andrew Beckett (Tom Hanks) and Joe Miller (Denzel Washington) prefer trial in Philadelphia.

asserting that his work was generally mediocre and that he had misplaced a complaint in an important case. Beckett claims that those reasons are phony and sues the law firm for illegal discrimination.

Beckett asks Joe Miller, a former adversary, to represent him. Miller turns him down because he is homophobic and also because he is reluctant to take on the powerful Wyant, Wheeler firm. Later, after he sees Beckett all alone in a law library, shunned by other patrons and the librarian, Miller agrees to take the case.

By the time the case goes to trial, Beckett is dying. Miller offers evidence that Beckett was a highly competent lawyer and that one of the firm's partners recognized the lesion on Beckett's face as a symptom of AIDS. Beckett describes his admiration for senior partner Charles Wheeler, his former mentor. "He was the kind of lawyer I thought I wanted to be, . . . possessed of an encyclopedic knowledge of the law, a razor-sharp litigator, . . . gifted at bringing out the very best in others, an awesome ability to illuminate the most complex of legal concepts to a colleague, a courtroom, the man in the street. . . ." However, Beckett admits that he tried to conceal his sexual orientation from the partners because he overheard them making jokes about gays.

Miller asks Beckett what he loves about the law. He answers, "What I love the most about the law . . . is that every now and again, not often but occasionally, you get to be a part of justice being done." Of course, Beckett's own lawsuit is just such a case.

Defense lawyer Belinda Conine offers evidence that the partners did not know that Beckett had AIDS and that, as Wheeler testifies, the firm was "waiting for the promise to kick in and deliver, but ultimately we could no longer ignore the gap between the reality and the promise."

The jury struggles with the case. The clinching argument is made by a juror who seems to be an expert on military aviation. He mocks the idea that the firm regarded Beckett as mediocre yet assigned him to work on a critical case. The jury awards Beckett a fortune in back pay and punitive damages. Beckett lives long enough to celebrate victory in his hospital room, then tells his partner, Miguel Alvarez, that he's ready to die.

Legal Analysis

When *Philadelphia* came out (so to speak), AIDS meant certain death. The film sends a message of compassion for AIDS victims and argues that they should be protected from discrimination in the workplace. This dual meaning is most apparent during Miller's opening statement. Miller tells the jurors that when the partners realized that Beckett had AIDS, they panicked. He continues, "Now, the behavior of Andrew Beckett's employers may seem reasonable to you. It does to me. After all, AIDS is a deadly, incurable disease. But no matter how you come to judge Charles Wheeler and his partners in ethical, moral, and human terms, the fact of the matter is when they fired Andrew Beckett because he had AIDS. They broke the law." By acknowledging that fear of AIDS is reasonable and widespread, Miller makes it possible for jurors and viewers to conclude that Beckett should be protected against discrimination without changing their attitudes toward homo-sexuality or toward AIDS.

Three faces of law. The tragic but uplifting story of *Philadelphia* centers on three talented Philadelphia lawyers.

• Andrew Beckett is the most positive portrayal of a homosexual lawyer in movie history. Despite his illness, he wants to continue working and he maintains a loving, mutually supportive relationship with his own family and with Alvarez.

• Joe Miller is probably the most favorable and balanced representation of an African-American lawyer who has ever appeared in the movies. He's a hustling personal-injury lawyer who's always looking for clients (he advertises on TV, and his office window has "toxic torts" emblazoned on it), but he handles the Beckett case with great skill and empathy. Like Beckett, Miller has a warm and satisfying personal life.

• Charles Wheeler is a respected senior partner and Beckett's idol. But Wheeler can't overcome his bigotry against homosexuals and his irrational terror of the AIDS virus. This man of wisdom makes fatal errors of judgment. He furnishes perjured testimony at the Beckett trial. Even worse, he foolishly refuses to settle the case, thereby exposing his firm to a crushing financial liability and destroying its cherished reputation.

Miller's redemptive moment. Miller passes on representing Beckett until they both happen to be doing research in the "Attorneys Only" section of the law library. Miller, who is black, observes a white patron looking at him in a way that suggests that Miller couldn't be an attorney and so has no right to be there. At nearly the same moment, Miller observes a librarian rudely trying to move Beckett to a private research room. The juxtaposition makes Miller realize that Beckett is a victim of discrimination just as African-Americans have been. The scene also furthers the film's political message, as it analogizes a form of discrimination that most viewers agree is wrong (racial discrimination) to a form that in the early 1990s was more debatable (discrimination based on AIDS).

The two hemispheres of law practice. Sociologists of the legal profession identify two separate worlds within the law. The members of each group have little to do with one another and seldom meet except in court. The first tier consists of lawyers who practice in large firms and represent big institutions. When they appear in the movies, the lawyers in such firms are always treated as villains, as in *Philadelphia* as well as *The Verdict, The Firm, The Rainmaker, Devil's Advocate, Class Action, Liar Liar,* and *Regarding Henry*.

The second tier consists of lawyers who represent ordinary people and small business, such as most criminal-defense, family, or personal-injury lawyers. They usually practice in small firms or alone, like Joe Miller. Lawyers from the second tier are sometimes presented favorably in the movies, especially when they challenge arrogant prosecutors, as in *The Client* or *A Time to Kill,* or when they take on first-tier firms in court, as in *A Civil Action, Erin Brockovich,* and *Class Action.*

Over the top. In its zeal to score political points and remain entertaining, *Philadelphia* contains some ludicrous scenes. While questioning his own witness, Miller suddenly asks him whether he's a homosexual. He then makes a speech piling on the nasty, demeaning epithets: Are you a fairy? A faggot? Miller's explanation to the judge that all he's trying to do is get the common loathing of homosexuals out in the open is silly. The witness' sexual orientation has nothing to do with the case, nor can Miller give a speech in the middle of the trial. Miller undoubtedly succeeds, however, in teaching new antigay epithets to teenage film viewers.

Defense attorney Conine also drags thoroughly irrelevant material into the courtroom. While cross-examining Beckett, she asks whether he has seen movies at a pornographic gay cinema and whether he had sex with customers there. This highly prejudicial material has nothing to do with the issues in the trial, and the judge should have excluded it.

Mirror, mirror on the wall. Filmmakers often try to juice up talky trial films with visual courtroom demonstrations. In *Philadelphia*, defense lawyer Conine uses a mirror in an attempt to disprove Beckett's claim that he was fired after a partner noticed a lesion on his face. Conine holds a mirror up to Beckett's face and asks if he can see any lesions. Although Beckett has a small lesion, he admits that he can't see it in the mirror. Miller leaps on this golden opportunity. He asks Beckett to remove his shirt and see if he can spot any lesions in the mirror. Beckett reveals a chestful of sickening lesions. The faces of the jurors suggest that this is a turning point in the trial.

Conine's demonstration was irrelevant because the issue is whether Beckett had a visible lesion when he was fired, not whether one is currently visible. Miller's counterdemonstration is equally irrelevant, and it appeals to the jurors' passion rather than their reason. Still, once Conine made the fatal mistake of raising the issue of lesions, she opened the door to Miller's devastating riposte.

Picturing justice. (1) The partners of Wyant, Wheeler sit together at the defense-counsel table with their lawyers. The partners are all elderly and white, dressed in expensive suits. At the plaintiff's table, Miller and Beckett sit alone. Conine paints exactly the wrong picture for the jury of a big, affluent law firm beating up on a dying plaintiff. In addition, Conine's smirking, condescending manner makes her seem insincere. (2) As Miller tries to prepare a desperately sick Beckett for his direct testimony, Beckett translates for him a tragic aria sung by Maria Callas from the opera *Andrea Chenier*. This brilliant and deeply moving scene suggests that the concerns of the lawyer and the client have moved far apart.

Trial Briefs

1. The film was based primarily on the case of a New York City lawyer named Geoffrey Bowers who was fired by the mega-firm of Baker & McKenzie. Seven years after his death from AIDS at the age of thirty-three, Bowers' family won a $500,000 award from the New York State Department of Human Relations. Baker & McKenzie appealed, and the case was settled in 1995 for an undisclosed sum. Later, Bowers' relatives sued the makers of *Philadelphia,* claiming that the filmmakers had reneged on their promise to compensate them for providing details about Bowers' life. Seven days into the trial, the film's producer settled the case for a figure in the "mid-seven-figure range" and acknowledged that the film was inspired in part by Bowers' life.

2. The film was also based on a real case in Philadelphia. Hyatt Legal Services (a law firm offering low-cost standardized legal advice) fired a lawyer named Cain after discovering that he had AIDS. In the path-breaking case of *Cain v. Hyatt* (1990), the court held that firing an employee because he had AIDS was illegal and that prejudice and misinformation about the disease could not be the basis for discrimination. The *Cain* decision is still followed today under the federal Americans with Disability Act. As long as employees with HIV can continue to do the work (with reasonable accommodation for the illness, such as time off for medical treatment), employers are not permitted to discharge them.

Pinky

Synopsis: A black woman gets a surprisingly fair shake from a southern judge.

20th Century Fox, 1949. Black and white. Running time: 102 minutes.

Screenplay: Philip Dunne and Dudley Nichols. Novel: Cid Ricketts Sumner. Director: Elia Kazan.

Starring: Jeanne Crain (Pinky), Ethel Barrymore (Miss Em), Ethel Waters (Granny).

Academy Award nominations: Best Actress (Jeanne Crain), Best Supporting Actress (Ethel Barrymore), Best Supporting Actress (Ethel Waters).

Rating: ———🔨 ———🔨

Pinky: After Pinky (Jeanne Crain) won her probate case, Dr. Thomas Adams (William Lundigan) pleads with her to leave the South, but she stays with her Granny (Ethel Waters).

The Story

Patricia "Pinky" Johnson is a light-skinned black woman who was raised by her Granny in rural Alabama before moving to Boston and becoming a nurse. She passed as white and became engaged to a white doctor. Undecided about whether to go through with the marriage, Pinky returns to Alabama, where local whites demonstrate that they've kept racism alive and well in her absence.

Miss Em, an imperious white woman, is a property-rich but cash-poor widow. She has serious heart problems, and Granny shames Pinky into nursing her. Pinky and Miss Em come to trust each other. Shortly before her death, Miss Em executes a lengthy handwritten will leaving her house and land to Pinky. This infuriates Miss Em's sole relative, Melba Wooley, who contests the will. Reluctantly, Judge Walker, a retired judge and friend of Miss Em, agrees to represent Pinky.

Stanley, Wooley's lawyer, argues that Pinky exerted undue influence over Miss Em and that Miss Em was not mentally competent to make a will. Walker responds that the only reason for the will challenge is that whites cannot tolerate a Negro inheriting property from a white.

Things look grim when Pinky's key witness, Dr. Joe McGill, doesn't show up for the trial. Dr. McGill witnessed Miss Em's will and was its executor, but he decides that making a house call is a better option than getting embroiled in a racial controversy. Melba Wooley testifies to a conversation in which Miss Em said she was thinking about a will and Pinky said in a threatening voice that Miss Em should do it now if she was ever going to. Wooley also testifies that Miss Em had been doped and was out of her mind half the time.

Judge Shoreham rules that Miss Em was in full possession of her faculties when she wrote the will and that Wooley failed to prove undue influence. Rather than sell the property and move west with her fiancé, Pinky stays in town. She converts Miss Em's old house into a combination medical clinic and school for local black children.

Legal Analysis

Judge Shoreham's decision establishes that a good judge can and should surmount the ignorant passions of the locals, who whoop and cheer at his evidence rulings in Wooley's favor. Had Pinky's case been tried before a local jury, there is little doubt that Wooley would have come away the winner. Shoreham's decision stands in stark contrast to the racist jury verdict in *To Kill a Mockingbird*.

Racism in the movies. Made in 1949, *Pinky* was among the first films to dramatize the blatant racism of the Deep South. Wherever Pinky goes, she encounters the contempt and hostility of the white population. She narrowly escapes being raped by a couple of rednecks. Melba Wooley pushes ahead of Pinky in a store, and the store-keeper raises the price Pinky has to pay for a veil to wear to Miss Em's funeral.

Pinky was also an important breakthrough in featuring a black character who was a trained nurse. Before *Pinky*, black characters were represented in stereotypical fashion in movies intended for main stream white audiences. They were usually loyal but fawning servants (as in *Gone with the Wind*), comic fools (as in the many roles played by Stepin Fetchit, including a character in the courtroom film *Judge Priest*), or savage brutes (as in *Birth of a Nation*). Black characters were almost never ordinary people with ordinary problems. Referring to the fact that the only roles available for a black actress were as maids, Hattie McDaniel (who played Mammy in *Gone with the Wind*) remarked that she'd rather play a maid than be one.

From a contemporary perspective, one can quarrel with the treatment of the racial issues in *Pinky*. Several of the black characters in the film are crude Negro stereotypes. The film suggests that Pinky could never be happy if she continued passing as white and married a white man. Only black children attend Pinky's school, which suggests that blacks should be attending segregated rather than integrated schools. Of course, *Pinky* was made five years before *Brown v. Board of Education* outlawed school segregation; nobody thought in 1949 that segregation would soon become illegal. On a more practical note, the local whites would never have permitted an integrated school, so Pinky's school benefited the local black kids in the only way that was then possible.

Will challenges—what was wrong. Although the will contest is entertaining, it is legally inaccurate. Miss Em's will was not legally valid—but for reasons different than those argued by Wooley. Miss Em's will was written entirely in her own handwriting, so it would have been valid in many states even if it had not been witnessed (this is called a "holographic will"). In most states that allow holographic wills, the fact that Dr. McGill's signature also appears on the document would not invalidate it (even though it is not in the decedent's handwriting). However, Alabama has never recognized holographic wills. As a result, the will is valid only if it is properly witnessed. Like all other states, Alabama requires the signature of at least two witnesses. Because there was only one, the will is invalid.

Will challenges—what was right. Stanley argued that Miss Em lacked the mental capacity to make a will. Essentially this argument boils down to whether Miss Em understood how she was disposing of her property. Because Miss Em wrote out a detailed, multipage document in her own handwriting, it is obvious that she had more than enough mental capacity to make a will. The fact that she might have taken sedatives at other times wouldn't matter.

Stanley's undue influence argument was equally weak. To establish undue influence, he had to show that Pinky had coerced Miss Em into doing what Pinky wanted instead of what Miss Em wanted. However, Stanley's proof on this issue was not convincing. For example, Pinky wasn't even present when the will was written. Instead, Judge Shoreham was convinced by Walker's argument: Miss Em left the property to Pinky because she was grateful that Pinky had nursed her and she had no other way of paying.

Picturing justice: Pinky's lawyer, Judge Walker, chose to confront the town's blatant racism rather than ignore it. In his opening statement, Walker said: "What is done in our courts in cases such as this has become a matter of moment in the eyes of the world. Let us examine our conscience. Let us look into our attitudes and traditions. Let us take care lest it be said of us that here there is neither law nor justice."

Trial Brief

Two years before *Pinky,* director Elia Kazan made *Gentlemen's Agreement,* starring Gregory Peck. *Gentlemen's Agreement* was the first and probably the best movie ever made about anti-Semitism, an issue that had historically been ignored in Hollywood films. Kazan took over the filming of *Pinky* when his idol John Ford withdrew after shooting for ten days. Ford claimed that he was sick with shingles, but it wasn't true. In fact, Ford and actress Ethel Waters couldn't stand each other and Ford didn't want to continue. It may also be that he was uncomfortable with the racial politics of the film. Zanuck begged Kazan to come to Hollywood and finish the picture. Kazan threw out Ford's work and started fresh.

Snow Falling on Cedars

Synopsis: A murder trial has its roots in the Japanese internment of World War II.

Universal Pictures, 1999. Color. Running time: 127 minutes.

Screenplay: Ron Bass and Scott Hicks. Original book: David Guterson. Director: Scott Hicks.

Starring: Ethan Hawke (Ishmael Chambers), Rick Yune (Kazuo Miyamoto), Max von Sydow (Nels Gudmundsson).

Academy Award nomination: Best Cinematography.

Rating:

The Story

Caucasian and Japanese communities coexisted uneasily for many years before World War II on an island in Puget Sound. That ended when the entire Japanese population was hauled away in 1942 to Manzanar, an internment camp in the California desert.

Before the war, the Miyamoto family made a deal to buy seven acres of island farmland owned by the Heine family. Because Washington law prohibited Asian noncitizens from owning land, the informal deal was unrecorded. The idea was that after all payments had been made, Heine Sr. would convey the land to Kazuo Miyamoto, who had been born in the United States and thus was a citizen. But the Japanese relocation caused the Miyamotos to miss their last two payments. After the war ended, Miyamoto returned to claim his land, but Heine Sr. had died. Heine's widow refused to honor the deal and instead returned the Miyamotos' money to them. Later, Carl Heine Jr. repurchased the property and had to decide whether to sell the disputed seven acres to Miyamoto.

In 1950, both Miyamoto and Carl Heine Jr. were fishermen. One very foggy night, Heine drowned, and Miyamoto is charged with his murder. Prosecutor Alvin Hooks offers the following circumstantial evidence along with a generous sprinkling of reminders to the jury about Pearl Harbor and Japanese inscrutability:

• Miyamoto was antagonistic to Heine because Heine had so far refused to sell him the land.

• Miyamoto was the last person to see Heine alive; he'd been on Heine's boat to loan him a battery shortly before Heine died.

• Blood found on Heine's fishing gaff matched Heine's blood type.

• Heine suffered a severe head wound that could have been made by the gaff, and Miyamoto was expert in Japanese stick fighting.

• When first questioned, Miyamoto and his wife, Hatsue, lied when they told the police that Miyamoto had not been on Heine's boat on the fateful night.

Miyamoto and Hatsue testify that Miyamoto saw that Heine was in distress and so loaned him a battery, using Heine's gaff to help install it. Heine was grateful for the help and told Miyamoto that he would sell him the land. Heine started up his boat and Miyamoto left, thinking all was well.

* * *

SPOILER ALERT: You may not want to read further if you plan to see the film.

* * *

Ishmael Chambers, a journalist who as a teenager had been in love with Hatsue, discovers that a large freighter had been in the channel about the time that Heine drowned. He reports this information to the sheriff while the jury deliberates. Further investigation reveals that the freighter's wake probably caused Heine to fall off his boat's rigging onto a rail and then into his fishing net, where he drowned. Over Hooks' objection, the judge halts jury deliberations and dismisses the case.

Legal Analysis

The back story to a murder trial allows the filmmakers to portray racial interactions and prejudice during a particularly difficult period in U.S. history. The poignant scene that will probably stick longest in viewers' memories is the silent march of the Japanese people to the ferry that would take them away to an unknown fate.

The Japanese exclusion. In 1942, President Franklin Roosevelt issued Executive Order 9066. This order required that all persons of Japanese descent on the West Coast be shipped to remote camps, where they would be interned during the war. (Some internees, like Kazuo Miyamoto, were allowed to volunteer for military service; they fought with great bravery on the European front.) More than 100,000 people were wrenched from their homes and their lives. What happened to the Miyamotos' farmland (as well as Ishmael's and Hatsue's doomed romance) was typical of untold thousands of stories of ruined lives and businesses.

The exclusion order occurred soon after the surprise bombing of Pearl Harbor. Yet no person of Japanese descent was ever suspected, let alone convicted, of subversive activity. Today, most people agree that the Japanese exclusion was one of the most racist government actions in American history.

Yet all efforts to overturn the exclusion in the courts failed until long after the military emergency was over. During wartime, judges felt unable to challenge the government's authority. In *Korematsu v. United States* (1944), the Supreme Court upheld the conviction of a man who had violated the military order that all Japanese must report to the camps. The Court ruled that military necessity justified the action. The same day as *Korematsu* was decided, the Supreme Court ordered the internship ended because there was no statutory authority for its continuance. *Ex parte Endo* (1944). That's when the Japanese were allowed to return to their homes.

Forty years later, a federal court ordered that Fred Korematsu's conviction be vacated because of government misconduct regarding the submission of false information to the Supreme Court in the 1940s (*Korematsu v. United States*, 1984). In 1988, Congress enacted a law apologizing for the internment program and providing for monetary reparations.

Alien land laws. Washington's alien land law prohibited non-U.S. citizens who were not eligible for citizenship from owning, leasing, or even sharecropping land. And guess what? Chinese and Japanese residents were ineligible to become citizens; only "free white persons" could become naturalized citizens. An attempted transfer to an ineligible alien was a criminal offense, and any land sold or leased to ineligible aliens had to be forfeited to the state. Similar laws in many western states prohibited Asian noncitizens from securing professional licenses or fishing licenses. As a result, the Miyamotos and Heines had to get around the law by entering into an unrecorded land contract that left the Miyamotos vulnerable to forfeiture when they couldn't make the final payments. Beginning in 1948, both state and federal courts began to strike down alien land and licensing laws as a violation of the equal protection clause of the Fourteenth Amendment, and they have long since passed into history.

Picturing justice. Defense lawyer Nels Gudmundsson is a memorable character who deserves to be compared to Atticus Finch in *To Kill a Mockingbird*. Gudmundsson must confront intense racial hatred against the "Japs." He was old and frail but nonetheless very effective in his cross-examination and his closing argument. He tries to neutralize the prejudice against his client by arguing that, though it's a small trial in a small place, all humanity is on trial. However, but for Ishmael's timely detective work, Miyamoto would undoubtedly have been wrongly convicted of murder.

Sommersby

Synopsis: An alleged murderer has to choose between being hung as an enlightened hero or walking free as a cowardly con man.

Warner Bros., 1993. Color. Running time: 114 minutes.

Screenplay: Nicholas Meyer and Sarah Kernochan. Story: Nicholas Meyer and Anthony Shaffer. Based on the film: *The Return of Martin Guerre*. Director: Jon Amiel.

Starring: Richard Gere (Jack Sommersby), Jodie Foster (Laurel Sommersby), James Earl Jones (Judge Barry Isaacs).

Rating: ——▪ ——▪ ——▪

Warner Bros./Photofest.

Sommersby: Jack Sommersby (Richard Gere) questions his wife, Laurel (Jodie Foster)—or is she?

The Story

Believed to have died in the Civil War, Confederate soldier Jack Sommersby gets a hero's welcome when he returns to his family and farm in Tennessee. However, his wife, Laurel, and some of the townsfolk are suspicious of his real identity. One clue is that Sommersby's feet have shrunk—not a typical by-product of war. Even more telling, the Sommersby who went away was an ignorant, abusive bigot. The returning Sommersby is kind, generous, and interested in Greek literature. Still, having slept in an empty bed for six years, Laurel doesn't want to ask too many questions. Besides, the alternative is Orin Meecham, a violent bumpkin who'd been helping Laurel plow the fields in the hope of doing additional plowing as her husband.

Sommersby realizes that failure to grow tobacco is hazardous to his wealth. He forms a tobacco-growing cooperative and makes deals to sell portions of his farm to sharecroppers, including former slaves. However, the good times end when Sommersby goes on trial for a murder that occurred before he went off to war. Prosecution witnesses identify him as the man who gunned down Charles Conklin after they fought over a card game. Webb, the defense attorney, seeks to prove that the defendant is not the real Jack Sommersby. Laurel testifies that the defendant is an imposter and not her husband. Folsom, a farmer from another county, identifies Sommersby as Horace Townsend, a con man who deserted from the army and later absconded with school funds.

* * *

SPOILER ALERT: You may not want to read further if you plan to see the film.

* * *

Grabbing defeat from the jaws of victory, Sommersby dismisses his lawyer and takes over the defense. He baits Folsom into making a racist diatribe against the black judge, leading the judge to throw Folsom in jail and strike the entirety of his testimony. Sommersby then recalls Laurel and argues to her that if he's not Jack Sommersby their newborn is a bastard and the sharecroppers would have to give back their land. He verbally bullies her into admitting that he is indeed her husband. With identity no longer an issue, Sommersby is convicted.

Awaiting execution, Sommersby admits to Laurel that he'd been a POW with the real Jack Sommersby and learned about his past. However, despite Laurel's anguished pleas to tell the truth, Sommersby refuses to give up "the only thing I've ever done that I'm proud of" and goes to the scaffold.

Legal Analysis

In this romantic tragedy, Laurel and the local farmers were content to live with ambiguity. Whoever he was, the new Jack Sommersby was a good man who had brought prosperity and land ownership to all. However, trials abhor ambiguity as much as nature abhors vacuums. Forced to take a definite position, the defendant makes the moral choice to insist that he is Sommersby, thereby legitimating his daughter and upholding the legality of the land-sale contracts.

What's in a name? The film deceptively makes the trial's outcome depend on the defendant's name. If the jurors believe the prosecution witnesses' testimony that the defendant was the shooter, then the defendant is guilty no matter what name he went by at the time. That is, the prosecution witnesses identified a *person,* not a *name.* Thus, defense attorney Webb should have tried to cast doubt on the accuracy of their identifications rather than try to prove that the defendant's real name was Horace Townsend.

Have his case and eat it too. Whenever possible, attorneys develop fallback arguments. Here, Webb should have been prepared to argue that even if his client is Jack Sommersby, he shot Conklin in self-defense. Even if the evidence doesn't quite show that Sommersby reasonably thought that Conklin was about to kill him, the jurors might have accepted the argument as a peg on which to hang their sympathy.

Webb might have put forward additional fallback arguments. He could have argued that the shooting was not premeditated and therefore at most constituted second-degree, and not first-degree, murder. (Tennessee had enacted a law establishing degrees of murder in 1829.) In addition, Webb could have argued that his client was guilty of nothing more than manslaughter, as he shot in the "heat of passion" that resulted from a vicious fight. Had the jury reached either of these verdicts, the defendant might have pulled a relatively short jail term instead of the end of a rope.

Trial Brief

It is possible (though unlikely) that a black judge would have presided over Sommersby's trial. Following the Civil War, the occupying Union army placed blacks in many government offices, installing some as justices of the peace. For the most part these black office holders were "carpetbaggers" from the North, since few former slaves had sufficient educational background to succeed in public office.

By the late 1870s, the Union army ceased its occupation. Without its protection, many black public officials in the South were attacked and driven from their offices. More than one hundred years would pass before southern blacks, aided by federal civil rights and voting rights laws and aggressive enforcement by federal troops, could start to reclaim the power they had in the years immediately following the Civil War.

They Won't Forget

Synopsis: An ambitious southern D.A. exploits anti-Yankee prejudice to convict a northerner of murder.

Warner Bros., 1937. Black and white. Running time: 94 minutes.

Screenplay: Robert Rossen and Aben Kandel. Novel: Ward Greene.
Director: Mervyn LeRoy.

Starring: Claude Rains (Andy Griffin), Edward Norris (Robert Hale),
Lana Turner (Mary Clay).

Rating:

The Story

Decades after the Civil War ended, locals in the small southern town of
Flodden still haven't accepted its outcome. Mary Clay, a student at
Buxton Business College, returns to the school to retrieve her vanity
case and is murdered. In the building when Mary was killed were the
black janitor, Tump Redwine; the proprietor of the school, Carlisle
Buxton; and Mary's teacher Robert Hale, a northerner who had
recently moved to Flodden.

For politically ambitious D.A. Andy Griffin, Hale's presence at the
school is a godsend. He'd score no points by convicting Redwine,
because any law student could manage that in Flodden. Instead, Griffin
charges Hale with the murder, hoping to ride the conviction all the
way to the U.S. Senate. Flodden journalist Bill Brock sensationalizes the
case, ruthlessly exploiting the anti-Yankee angle. Northern papers
respond in kind, trashing southern justice and hiring northern lawyer
Michael Gleason to defend Hale.

Griffin's case against Hale is based entirely on circumstantial evidence:

• There was a blood spot on Hale's jacket; he claims that he was cut
by the barber when he got a shave on the afternoon of Mary's murder.
The barber gazes at the intensely hostile crowd in the courtroom and
denies that he cut Hale.

• Hale was planning to leave town as soon as possible.

• Hale was extremely nervous when the police arrested him.

• Mary's friend Imogene testifies that Mary was infatuated with
Hale. However, nobody can testify that Hale had any interest in Mary
other than as a student.

• Mary's boyfriend Joe Turner had a date with her and came to the
school when she didn't show up. Hale, acting strange and nervous, prevented him from entering the building.

• Tump Redwine continually and pitifully denies that he killed
Mary. He testifies that he was sleeping in the basement when he heard
the elevator buzz. He brought the elevator to the first floor, where
Mary was killed. There he saw Hale looking scared. Because the movie

They Won't Forget: Prosecutor Andy Griffin (Claude Rains) argues with defense attorney Michael Gleason (Otto Kruger).

depicts what actually happened, viewers know that Redwine's testimony was false. He did not see who buzzed for the elevator. The perjured testimony was cooked up for Redwine by his lawyer. On cross, in one of Gleason's few successful moments, Redwine recants his story, but the damage is done.

Hale makes an unsworn statement to the jury denying any involvement in Mary's death, but he is stiff and unconvincing. Gleason's closing argument is pathetically weak. He argues that the only witnesses against Hale were "hatred, fear, and prejudice," but these are witnesses that the jury probably found quite believable. Griffin's closing, by contrast, is filled with emotion and exaggeration. Hale is convicted and sentenced to death. Governor Mountford bravely commutes the sentence to life imprisonment, knowing that this act will end his political career. As Hale is transported to prison, a mob led by Mary's brothers stops the train, and Hale is lynched.

In the final scene, Griffin promises Mrs. Hale that the lynch mob will be prosecuted, but there's no realistic chance of that. After she leaves, Brock and Griffin reflect on the case and wonder whether Hale really did it.

Legal Analysis

The film's dramatic depiction of prejudice and injustice never reveals Mary's killer. In all likelihood, a jury less subject to local prejudice would have come away with more than a reasonable doubt about Hale's guilt. Tump Redwine's testimony was conflicting and unbelievable, and the barber shaved the truth even more closely than he did Hale. The rest of the circumstantial evidence was as consistent with innocence as guilt. For example, the fact that Hale was planning to leave town was suspicious, but he had ample reason for doing so. He and his wife were unhappy in Flodden (who wouldn't be?), and Buxton had humiliated him in front of the class on the day of Mary's death. Justice took a back seat to the toxic mixture of Griffin's political ambition, Gleason's weak representation, Brock's irresponsible journalism, and the town's intense anti-Yankee animosity. Only the governor grasped the stunning injustice, but the lynch mob trumped the governor's brave decision to commute the death sentence.

Hale's statement. Criminal defendants often stand on their right not to testify to avoid having to undergo cross-examination and to prevent juries from finding out about any prior convictions. Jurors are told not to draw any negative inference from a defendant's failure to testify, but they often do so anyway. At the time of the Hale case, some states permitted a defendant to make an unsworn statement to the jury. If the statement was false, the defendant could not be prosecuted for perjury. In addition, the defendant could not be cross-examined, and his prior convictions were inadmissible. The procedure made it more likely that the jury got to hear the defendant's version of events. Unfortunately, Gleason failed to adequately prepare Hale, and his poorly delivered statement did him more harm than good in the eyes of the jury.

Trial Brief

They Won't Forget is closely based on the Leo Frank case, which took place in Atlanta between 1913 and 1915. In many respects, that highly publicized trial could easily compete with the O. J. Simpson case or the Lindbergh baby kidnapping case as the trial of the twentieth century.

Frank was a Jewish man who moved from New York to Atlanta to manage a pencil factory. Mary Phagan, age thirteen, worked there (child labor was permitted at the time). She entered the building on Saturday (which was Confederate Memorial Day) to pick up her pay and was mysteriously murdered. Frank was working in his office at the time. As in the film, a Negro janitor named Newt Lee discovered the body, but there was a second black man, Jim Conley, who does not appear in the film. Conley worked as a sweeper at the factory and was also present. Conley changed his story several times.

At the trial, Conley testified that Frank killed Mary Phagan and that Conley helped him try to conceal the crime. This was by far the most damaging evidence against Frank. (Conley received a short, one-year sentence in return for his testimony.) An idealistic lawyer (William Smith) helped Conley prepare his testimony. Smith later decided that Conley was lying and went over to Frank's side. Those who have studied the case believe that Conley was the killer of Mary Phagan (he was drunk and probably tried to steal her pay and killed her accidentally).

An intense wave of anti-Semitic hatred swept over Atlanta aimed at Leo Frank. Various political and journalistic figures whipped up popular hatred against him. Northern papers (and one of the Atlanta papers, which was owned by William Randolph Hearst) rallied to Frank's cause and caustically criticized southern justice. All this criticism only intensified the feelings of Georgians against Frank. As in the movie, a politically ambitious prosecutor, Hugh Dorsey, was determined to convict Frank. Although Frank had capable attorneys, they made some serious tactical blunders at the trial. Like Hale, Frank made an unsworn statement to the jury, which did him more harm than good.

Frank's conviction was upheld on appeal to the Georgia Supreme Court, and the U.S. Supreme Court denied review. (Justices Holmes and Hughes dissented on the basis of the mob atmosphere inside and outside the courtroom.) In a letter released after his death, trial judge Leonard Roan indicated that he had severe doubts about Frank's guilt and urged Governor Slaton to grant clemency.

Slaton courageously commuted the death sentence. (Slaton was the law partner of one of Frank's lawyers.) Shortly thereafter, a mob of respectable citizens entered the prison without firing a shot, dragged Frank away, and lynched him. Nobody was ever prosecuted for the lynching. The case revived the Ku Klux Klan in Georgia and was instrumental in the formation of the Anti-Defamation League. Dorsey ultimately became governor of Georgia. The filmmakers obviously were reluctant to confront the issue of anti-Semitism. Therefore they changed anti-Jewish prejudice into anti-Yankee prejudice.

A Time to Kill

Synopsis: A white lawyer defends a black father who killed his daughter's white rapists.

Warner Bros., 1996. Color. Running time: 149 minutes.

Screenplay: Akiva Goldsman. Novel: John Grisham. Director: Joel Schumacher.

Starring: Matthew McConaughey (Jake Brigance), Kevin Spacey (Rufus Buckley), Samuel L. Jackson (Carl Lee Hailey), Sandra Bullock (Ellen Roark).

Rating: ——■ ——■ ——■

The Story

Two drunken Canton, Mississippi, rednecks brutally rape Tonya, a ten-year-old black girl, and leave her for dead. They are swiftly arrested, but Tonya's father, Carl Lee Hailey, fears that a southern jury will let them off. He shoots and kills them on the courthouse stairs on the way to their arraignment. Hailey also accidentally wounds Deputy Sheriff Looney, who loses his leg.

Jake Brigance is an inexperienced but cocky sole practitioner who is struggling to make ends meet. Brigance decides on an insanity defense for Hailey, knowing it's weak but trying to give sympathetic jurors a place to hang their hats. Ambitious prosecutor Rufus Buckley is confident that it won't be their hats that the jurors decide to hang. For Buckley, it's a case of Southern Comfort. Brigance is a neophyte, the jury is all white, the KKK is on the march, and Judge Omar Noose is up for election.

The trial features dueling shrinks of dubious credibility. As a favor to Brigance's mentor, Dr. Bass testifies that Hailey was insane at the time of the shooting. Unfortunately, Bass has to admit that he was once convicted of statutory rape. Dr. Rodeheaver testifies that Hailey was sane, but Brigance discredits him by showing that in forty-six trials he's never found a single defendant insane, even the ones he gets paid to treat at his psychiatric hospital.

Hobbling to the stand, Deputy Looney testifies that Hailey was right to kill his daughter's rapists. Hailey testifies that he felt "outside himself" when he killed the rapists. Buckley's cross causes Hailey to lose his cool and shout that the rapists deserved to die. This undermines the

A Time to Kill: Jake Brigance (Matthew McConaughey) argues with his client, Carl Lee Hailey (Samuel L. Jackson), as crony Harry Rex Vonner (Oliver Platt) looks on.

insanity defense by suggesting that Hailey was very much inside himself when he fired.

Brigance's stirring closing argument turns the case around. He asks the jurors to close their eyes and imagine the tortures inflicted on Tonya. Then, he says, imagine if she'd been white—perhaps their own daughter. The implication, of course, is that if a white man killed a black man who had raped his daughter, he'd be acquitted by any southern jury. The jury, which had been leaning strongly toward conviction, acquits Hailey.

Legal Analysis

A Time to Kill updates *To Kill a Mockingbird,* the classic film about southern racism. In both films, courageous white lawyers endanger themselves and their families by defending unpopular black defendants before all-white juries. The difference, of course, is that in *Mockingbird,* Tom Robinson was innocent but was convicted, whereas in *A Time to Kill,* Hailey was guilty but was acquitted. This suggests that conditions have changed and that a black man who kills a white person can be treated sympathetically in a courtroom in the modern

South. The statistics belie this conclusion, however. Blacks who kill whites are much more likely to get the death penalty than whites who kill blacks or blacks who kill blacks.

Speech impediment. Brigance's closing argument was effective but improper. He referred to numerous facts that were not part of the record. He also flat out asked the jury to acquit Hailey because he was morally right regardless of his sanity. Jurors in criminal cases have the ultimate power to ignore the law, and the prosecution cannot appeal an acquittal. However, defense attorneys cannot explicitly urge jurors to exercise this power.

Disclosure of Hailey's plan to kill. Before the killing, Hailey visits Brigance and strongly implies that he's planning to kill the rapists. Brigance says nothing to the sheriff about the threat. As a general rule, attorney-client communications are confidential, and lawyers cannot disclose them to anyone. However, ethics rules in most states permit but don't require attorneys to disclose confidential information in order to prevent clients from committing a crime. Under such a rule, Brigance could have disclosed Hailey's plans to the sheriff, who might have prevented the killings. Instead, he kept quiet and let events take their course.

Putting in a good word. Citing the excessive and negative publicity about the case, Brigance asks Judge Noose to move the trial out of Canton. Buckley, on the other hand, wants the case to stay in Canton because its population is only 30 percent black and therefore he has a better chance of ending up with an all-white jury. To improve the likelihood that Noose will deny Brigance's request, Buckley has members of the legislature call Noose and advise him to leave the trial right where it is. Noose also discusses the case with a state supreme court justice, who advises him that the court will uphold his refusal to move the trial. Of course, all this back-door conversation is highly improper and a demeaning image of the legal system at work.

Peremptory challenges. Attorneys are allowed a limited number of peremptory challenges, meaning they can remove jurors without stating any cause. Buckley challenges all the black jurors in the panel. The U.S. Supreme Court's decision in *Batson v. Kentucky* (1986) forbids lawyers to challenge jurors in a civil or criminal case because of their race or sex. The *Batson* rule can be difficult to enforce in practice because lawyers can easily claim a nonracial or nonsexual reason for challenging a particular juror. Assuming the trial took place after 1986,

Judge Noose should at least have compelled Buckley to explain the reasons for his challenges.

Psychiatric evidence. Doctors Bass and Rodeheaver give expert witnesses a bad name. Bass obviously doesn't believe his own testimony, and Rodeheaver has yet to find a defendant who's insane. However, Rodeheaver is correct when he testifies that Hailey was sane at the time of the killing. Under the *McNaghten Rule,* a criminal defendant is insane if he cannot tell the difference between right and wrong. Hailey carefully and coldly premeditated the murder and understood perfectly well what he was doing and what the consequences would be. It was a revenge killing, pure and simple, and motivated by fear that the redneck rapists might otherwise escape justice.

Picturing justice. Brigance takes the Hailey case for a low fee because he hopes it will help build his reputation. He does a great job and stands up to intimidation and physical danger. His supporting team, however, is less favorably portrayed. His mentor, Lucien Wilbanks, is a disbarred drunkard. Harry Rex Vonner provides moral support but is extremely cynical and more than a bit sleazy. Ellen Roark, a law student who volunteers to assist Brigance because she opposes the death penalty, does excellent work but also demonstrates superior breaking-and-entering skills and a desire to seduce Brigance.

Short Subjects

Bonfire of the Vanities, 1990. Tom Hanks, Melanie Griffith, Morgan Freeman. ——■ ——■

A black minister hungry for fame goads a D.A. hungry for higher office into pursuing criminal charges against Sherman McCoy, a wealthy, white bond dealer hungry for love. McCoy and his mistress miss a highway turnoff, end up in a dangerous neighborhood, and run over a black would-be robber while speeding away. The black Judge White, a beacon of integrity, dismisses the charges when McCoy plays a recording of his mistress admitting that she was driving the car. *Courtroom highlight:* Judge White reminds the angry crowd that had just called him a racist pig, "Justice is the law, and the law is man's feeble attempt to set down the principles of decency." *Picturing justice*: As Sherman McCoy is booked, music from the opera he'd seen the night before plays in the background. The opera is *Don Juan in Hell*. McCoy's experience in the criminal justice system is equally hellish.

Fried Green Tomatoes, 1991. Kathy Bates, Mary-Louise Parker, Mary Stuart Masterson, Stan Shaw. ——■ ——■

In 1930s Alabama, Ruth Jamison's racist and abusive ex-husband Frank Bennett is killed while trying to abduct their child. Black laborer Big George and Ruth's best friend Idgie Threadgoode conceal the body by serving Bennett up as BBQ and are charged with murder. *Courtroom highlight*: Reverend Scroggins surprises the defendants by testifying to a phony alibi, convincing the judge to dismiss the charges. Scroggins, a strict fundamentalist, avoids committing a sin by secretly substituting a copy of *Moby-Dick* for the Bible when taking the witness oath. *Picturing justice:* The film scorns the racist prosecutor by turning his questions into loud unintelligible background noise.

Johnny Belinda, 1948. Jane Wyman, Lew Ayres. ——■ ——■

Belinda MacDonald is raped by Locky McCormick and gives birth to Johnny. The local leaders believe that Belinda, who can't hear or speak and is known around town as Dummy, is unfit to raise a child. Assuming that Johnny's father was Belinda's friend Dr. Richardson, they authorize McCormick and his wife, Stella, to adopt Johnny. When McCormick tries to snatch Johnny from Belinda, she shoots him and is tried for murder. *Courtroom highlight*: Stella reveals that McCormick raped Belinda and that he tried to take Johnny by force. *Picturing justice*: The prosecutor is a thundering bully who impugns Dr. Richardson's character and castigates Belinda for her inability to understand the court-provided interpreter. *Trial brief*: Jane Wyman won the Academy Award as Best Actress for her performance as Belinda. Her acceptance speech, perhaps the shortest ever, consisted of "I won this award by keeping my mouth shut and I think I'll do it again."

Judge Priest, 1934. Will Rogers. Director: John Ford. ——■ ——■ ——■

Judge Priest follows the spirit rather than the letter of the law while puncturing bigoted egos in a small Kentucky town. When obnoxious prosecutor Mayhew challenges Priest's fairness, he steps down temporarily, appoints another judge, and assists in the defense of Bob Gillis, a stranger who is charged with assaulting a local. Gillis testifies that he acted in self-defense, but he's not believed until Priest elicits testimony from the local minister that Gillis was a Confederate war hero whose honesty is beyond question. Gillis ends up leading the town's Confederate Day parade. *Courtroom highlights*: Judge Priest reads the comics page while Mayhew pleads for a harsh sentence, and a juror repeatedly spits tobacco juice at Mayhew during Gillis' trial. *Picturing justice*: Priest's sister-in-law Carrie says that a young woman is not marriage material because she was born out of wedlock and reminds Priest that "the name of Priest means something in Kentucky." The judge responds, "I've never heard that it meant intolerance."

Midnight in the Garden of Good and Evil, 1997. Kevin Spacey, John Cusack, Jack Thompson, Jude Law. ———■ ———■

In blackjack, the house often wins because players bust before the dealer has to draw cards. Similarly, in this atmospheric film filled with eccentric (though sometimes tiresome) southern characters, defendant Jim Williams beats a murder rap because a police detective commits perjury before Williams has to. The trial serves as a platform for depicting the cultural mores of Savannah, Georgia, especially attitudes toward homosexuality. *Nouveau riche* antique dealer Williams is charged with murdering his violent younger lover, Billy Hanson. Williams claims self-defense, but the absence of gunpowder residue on Hanson's hand undermines that claim. Aided by a reporter, the defense attorney proves that the detective lied about the investigation in an effort to cover up sloppy police work. Saved from having to account for the absence of residue, Williams lies about his sexual relationship with Hanson and conceals the fact that Hanson never got off a shot. *Picturing justice*: Asked by the reporter what really happened, Williams responds: "Truth, like art, is in the eye of the beholder." *Trial brief*: Sonny Seiler, the defense attorney for Jim Williams in the actual 1981 trials (four trials were held!), plays Judge White in the film. Jack Thompson plays the defense attorney both in this film and in *Breaker Morant*.

Murder!, 1930. Herbert Marshall. Director: Alfred Hitchcock. ———■ ———■ ———■

Famous actor Sir John Menier reluctantly votes to convict actress Diana Baring of brutally killing Edna Druce. As a noose's shadow signals Baring's impending execution, Menier cleverly reveals to cross-dresser Fane that he's figured out that Fane killed Druce to prevent her from revealing to Baring that he is a "half-caste." In a stunning sequence, Fane saves Baring's life and remedies the formal legal system's mistake during his trapeze act by forming a rope into a noose and jumping off his platform. *Courtroom highlights*: (1) As if they were watching a tennis match, the jurors in unison turn their heads back and forth as they listen to testimony and counsel's arguments. (2) During deliberations, the jurors hound Menier into voting for conviction by giving snippets of evidence and then in unison repeatedly saying, "Any answer to that, Sir John?" *Picturing justice*: The film ends with the curtain falling on Menier's new play, linking the courtroom and the theater in a way that suggests that trials are highly theatrical events. *Trial brief*: This early talkie portrayed sexuality and racism in an open way that film production codes would soon forbid.

A Passage to India, 1984. Judy Davis, Victor Banerjee, Peggy Ashcroft. Novel: E. M. Forster. ──■ ──■

During the colonial period of the 1920s, the British occupiers' racist attitudes toward Indians, and Indians' resentment of the British, crystallize around the trial of Dr. Aziz for the attempted rape of British tourist Adela Quested. *Courtroom highlight*: Adela repudiates the prosecutor's suggestive questions and infuriates her compatriots by withdrawing the accusation. *Picturing justice*: (1) Inside the courtroom, the British sit downstairs while the Indians sit in the upper galleries. (2) Though it's uncertain what happened between Aziz and Adela during a visit to the mysterious Marabar Caves, Aziz becomes a local hero by escaping British justice. *Trial brief*: The film was nominated for eleven Academy Awards (including Best Picture) and won two of them.

Sergeant Rutledge, 1960. Jeffrey Hunter, Woody Strode. Director: John Ford. ──■ ──■ ──■

The film depicted racism in the Old West for Martin Luther King–era audiences. Buffalo soldier Sergeant Braxton Rutledge is court-martialed for killing a white woman and her father. Rutledge claims that he found the woman already dead and that he shot her father in self-defense. He then fled out of fear that as a former slave he'd be presumed guilty. A heroic figure, Rutledge protects a woman from a possible Apache attack and while under arrest saves his military captors from an ambush.

Courtroom highlight: Defense attorney Cantrell literally beats a confession out of a surprise witness. Prosecutor Shattuck might have objected that "Counsel is bleeding the witness." *Picturing justice*: (1) The judges drink whiskey and play poker during the trial. (2) Shattuck, a racist, castigates Cantrell for trying to pin the killings on a white man.

Trial, 1955. Glenn Ford, Arthur Kennedy. ———■ ——■ ——■

This Cold War–era film condemns racial prejudice while warning youths about the evils of communism. Angel Chavez, a poor Mexican-American teenager, is tried for murder when the wealthy white girl he'd been embracing suddenly dies. Chavez is nearly lynched. Defense attorney Barney Castle is a Communist who secretly wants Chavez convicted and sentenced to death so he will serve as a martyr and a source of contributions. Thus Castle agrees to let law professor David Blake try the case, figuring he'll lose it because he has never tried a case. Blake's courtroom savvy forces Castle to try to regain control. *Courtroom highlight*: Blake puts a car spotlight in front of the prosecution's eyewitness, and the ensuing demonstration destroys the witness' claim that he saw what happened by shining his spotlight in the direction of the dead girl's scream. *Picturing justice*: (1) The D.A. and the black judge are sympathetic and fair-minded. (2) Blake needs to try a case because his dean insists that he can't be a law school professor unless he has actual courtroom experience. (This requirement would empty the halls of modern academia in a hurry!)

The Death Penalty

Only a small percentage of convicted murderers in the United States are sentenced to death, and of those only a small percentage are actually executed. In 2004, for example, there were more than 3,400 people on death row but only 59 executions. Indeed, since the U.S. Supreme Court's 1976 decision in *Gregg v. Georgia* upholding the constitutionality of narrowly drawn death-penalty laws, less than a thousand people have been executed. Six states—Texas, Virginia, Louisiana, Florida, Missouri, and Georgia—have accounted for about 70 percent of those executions.

Nevertheless, the death penalty remains the subject of intense debate. Proponents argue that it deters murderers and is an appropriate form of retribution, while opponents argue that it is immoral, ineffective as a deterrent, and unfairly administered. Capital punishment is also very expensive, and delays of ten to fifteen years between the death sentence and execution are common. Most countries have abolished the death penalty; there are significant numbers of executions only in the United States, China, and some Middle Eastern countries.

For filmmakers, the death penalty is both a source of drama and an opportunity to affect popular opinion. The films covered in this chapter, and numerous others not included in this book (because they lack substantial trial scenes), have generally portrayed the death penalty as unjust or barbaric. For example, in the movies, innocent people are frequently executed, as in *The Green Mile, Dancer in the Dark, Let Him Have It,* and *Paths of Glory*. Films sometimes portray capital punishment as a primitive relic of less-civilized times (*Compulsion*) or unfairly based on race or class (*Knock on Any Door*). Films also send an anti-death-penalty message by portraying executions in grisly detail, as in *I Want to Live!, The Green Mile,* and *Dead Man Walking,* and may suggest that the death-penalty process is highly unjust because of inept trial counsel or political pressure on state governors, who always deny clemency (*Dead Man Walking*). Finally, films may send a message that murderers who have been rehabilitated while in prison shouldn't be executed, as in *Dead Man Walking* and *Last Dance*.

Balanced against anti-death-penalty films are a large number of vigilante films, such as *The Star Chamber* and *The Onion Field,* that send a message that the legal system is ineffective and that loathsome killers avoid execution. Consequently, some films propose that the police (*Dirty Harry*) and ordinary citizens (*Death Wish, In the Bedroom*) take the law into their own hands by tracking down and killing murderers. Thus, the movies represent all sides of the capital-punishment debate, but the balance is clearly on the side of abolishing the death penalty.

Beyond a Reasonable Doubt

Synopsis: A plan to expose the dangers of capital punishment by convicting an innocent man of murder goes awry.

RKO, 1956. Black and white. Running time: 80 minutes.

Screenplay: Douglas Morrow. Director: Fritz Lang.

Starring: Dana Andrews (Tom Garrett).

Rating:

The Story

Newspaper publisher Austin Spencer opposes capital punishment, particularly when convictions are based on circumstantial evidence. To dramatize the risk of convicting an innocent person, Spencer and prospective son-in-law Tom Garrett secretly plant evidence around town implicating Garrett in the unsolved murder of Patty Gray. The plan is that after Garrett is convicted and sentenced to death, Spencer will whip up popular sentiment against the death penalty by proving that the case was a phony. Garrett's reward is that, as an author, he'll turn the story into a sure-fire best-seller. Garrett is soon arrested, and prosecutor Roy Thompson has an easy time convicting him. Pity defense attorney Wilson. He may have claimed that past clients were wrongly convicted by planted evidence, but probably never when his own clients were the gardeners.

Beyond a Reasonable Doubt: The D.A. (Philip Bourneuf) reaps what Tom Garrett (Dana Andrews) has sown.

Garrett is probably the most relaxed defendant ever to be convicted of capital murder. However, when a fiery car crash kills Spencer and destroys all the photos and other records of the phony scheme, Garrett is terrified. He reveals the plan to Wilson and his fiancée, Spencer's daughter Susan, and pleads with them to convince Thompson of his innocence.

* * *

SPOILER ALERT: You may not want to read further if you plan to see the film.

* * *

With Garrett's execution hours away, Wilson finally finds documents that convince Thompson that Garrett is innocent. As Thompson calls the governor to arrange for a pardon, Garrett's slip of the tongue reveals to Susan that he killed Gray. With marriage to Susan in the offing, Gray became an inconvenient part of his past. Spencer's plan was a great chance to eliminate Gray and get away with it. Unsure at first about what to do, Susan finally decides to report the truth to the D.A. As the governor is poised to sign Garrett's pardon, the phone rings, the governor answers, and puts the pen down. Moments away from walking free, Garrett walks toward his execution.

Legal Analysis

Spencer opposes death sentences based on circumstantial evidence, that favorite whipping boy of courtroom films. However, eyewitness testimony is just as likely to convict an innocent person as circumstantial evidence, and in fact circumstantial evidence is often quite reliable. Many prisoners who were saved from execution by DNA evidence were convicted on mistaken eyewitness testimony.

Mandatory death sentences. As in *Beyond a Reasonable Doubt,* the death penalty was once automatic in many states if a defendant was convicted of murder. An unintended consequence was that jurors might refuse to convict in close cases or in cases involving sympathetic defendants. Today, the death penalty is no longer automatic. Jurors must consider lists of "aggravating" and "mitigating" factors when deciding whether or not to impose a death sentence. However, the inevitable result is disparity in sentencing. Whether a murderer is sentenced to death depends on such factors as the state where a conviction takes place, the quality of the legal defense team, and the races and ethnicities of the killer and the victim.

Playing with matches. An eyewitness testifies that the man who drove off with Gray on the night she was killed was smoking a pipe. Thompson resorts to a clever courtroom demonstration to prove that Garrett smokes a pipe. He asks a pipe smoker among the jurors to light up. The juror uses a book of matches, then tamps down the lit tobacco with the matchbook cover. Thompson calls everyone's attention to the round, dark smudge on the juror's matchbook cover and points out that it matches the marks on the matchbook covers that the police found strewn all over the floor of Garrett's garage.

In a modern-day courtroom, Thompson himself might well get arrested for "aiding and abetting smoking in a public building." But Thompson's experiment is improper for other reasons. Though the juror doesn't speak, his actions are the equivalent of testimony that "this is the process of lighting a pipe." While jurors may often want to "pipe up" in mid-trial, a person cannot serve both as a juror and as a witness in the same case. Thompson should either have called an expert witness to testify to the source of the smudge marks found on the matchbook covers in Garrett's garage, or simply have trusted to the jurors' examination of Garrett's matchbook covers to conclude that the smudges were made during the pipe-smoking process.

Picturing justice. Prosecutor Thompson tells his assistant, "I can't let myself be swayed emotionally. Whatever happens in this case has got to be based on facts and the law, not on how people feel." Thompson's words echo the message of many films that human emotions are irrelevant to the application of laws. In fact, the emotional reaction of judges and jurors often determines case outcomes.

Trial Brief

Fritz Lang (1890–1976) was one of the world's most highly regarded directors. Before Lang fled Hitler's regime in Germany, he made the masterpiece *M* (1931). *M* is a dark film based on a real serial child-killer. The police so disrupt gangland activities in the course of hunting for the killer that the mobsters hunt him down themselves and put him on trial. Lang's first Hollywood film was *Fury* (1936), discussed in Chapter 6. *Beyond a Reasonable Doubt* is characteristic of Lang's favorite themes: crime, cruelty, and suspense.

Compulsion

Synopsis: After two psychotic intellectuals commit a supposedly perfect murder, their attorney tries to spare them from the death penalty.

20th Century Fox, 1959. Black and white. Running time: 103 minutes.

Screenplay: Richard Murphy. Original book: Meyer Levin. Director: Richard Fleischer.

Starring: Orson Welles (Jonathan Wilk).

Rating: ——▮ ——▮ ——▮

The Story

Artie Straus and Judd Steiner are wealthy college students who think of themselves as intellectual supermen who are not bound by society's rules. To prove their superiority, they murder and disfigure a young boy named Paulie Kessler. However, their careful plan goes awry when Steiner leaves his fancy designer glasses at the murder scene. The glasses lead the police to Steiner and Straus. Despite their haughtiness,

Compulsion: Harold Horn (E. G. Marshall) and Jonathan Wilk (Orson Welles) argue the fate of two thrill-killers.

prosecutor Harold Horn adroitly tears apart their phony alibis and charges them with murder.

The defendants' fathers retain famous criminal-defense lawyer Jonathan Wilk. Though Wilk has devoted his career to opposing wealth and power, he takes the case because "the rich have the same right of defense as the poor." With his clients' conviction inevitable, Wilk pleads them guilty. Wilk's tactic eliminates the jurors (who seem to be looking forward to a double execution) and puts the sentencing decision in the judge's hands alone.

In a presentencing hearing, Wilk presents extensive psychiatric testimony that Steiner and Straus are mentally ill. Wilk then delivers an eloquent and impassioned plea for his clients' lives. He acknowledges that the killing was brutal and senseless. Perhaps the defendants' great wealth explains their problems, and it certainly accounts for Horn's desire to execute them: "I've heard nothing but the cry of blood in this room. . . . If you hang these boys, it will mean that in this country of ours a court of law could do nothing more than bow down to public opinion. . . . Your Honor, if these boys must hang, you must do it. It must be your own cool, deliberate, premeditated act. . . . If there's any way to kill evil, it's not by killing men. . . . This is a Christian community, so called. Is there any doubt that these boys would be safe in the hands of the founder of the Christian religion? . . . If killing these boys would bring [Paulie Kessler] back to life, I'd say let them go. I think their parents would say so too. . . . I'm asking this court to shut them in a prison for life. Any cry for more goes back to the hyena. . . . This court is told to give them the same mercy as they gave their victim. Your Honor, if our state is not kinder, more human, and more intelligent than the mad act of these two sick boys, then I'm sorry that I've lived so long."

After describing in detail how the state would carry out the executions, Wilk responds to Horn's argument that executing Straus and Steiner would put an end to killing: "The world has been one long slaughterhouse from the beginning until today. . . . Why not think instead of blindly shouting for death? . . . Your Honor, if you hang these boys, you turn back to the past. I'm pleading for the future. . . . I'm pleading not for these two lives but for life itself."

Wilk's strategy succeeds. The judge sentences Steiner and Straus to terms of life (for murder) and ninety-nine years (for kidnapping). But as they pass by Wilk on their way out of the courtroom, Steiner and Straus show no remorse and are contemptuous of him rather than grateful.

Legal Analysis

Lacking sympathetic defendants or a grisly visual depiction of the execution process, *Compulsion*'s anti-death-penalty message relies on the power of Wilk's verbal argument. *Compulsion* is the ultimate anti-death-penalty film because it argues that capital punishment is inappropriate even in the context of a horrific crime and loathsome defendants.

Judge or jury? Present-day criminal procedures make Wilk's bold strategy to eliminate the jury's role in sentencing unnecessary. A jury's vote for death is only a recommendation to the judge, who has the power to give a lesser sentence. (By contrast, a jury's vote for a sentence lighter than death is binding on a judge.) Thus, in a capital case a defense attorney can try to convince the jury not to give a death sentence, and if unsuccessful can plead to the judge for a lesser sentence.

Who stole my trial? Though Wilk's strategy succeeded, ethics rules require attorneys to let clients decide whether to plead guilty or go to trial. Wilk doesn't even bother to discuss his strategy with his clients' parents—possibly a serious mistake, because they are paying his legal fees. Even if he had, Straus and Steiner are his clients, and they are the ones who must decide what to do.

Equally improper, at least under present standards, is the judge's immediate acceptance of the guilty pleas. It's hard to plead guilty these days! Judges have to ensure that defendants are advised of the various rights that they give up by pleading guilty and also have to question defendants about what happened, in order to satisfy themselves that the defendants are in fact guilty. A defendant who insists "I didn't do it but I'm pleading guilty just to get this over with" will have to go to trial.

Is the insanity rule insane? The film effectively questions the legitimacy of the legal system's definition of insanity. Under the widely used M'Naghten Rule, defendants are legally insane if they don't know what they're doing or if they can't tell right from wrong. Straus and Steiner were legally sane under this definition because they obviously knew the difference between right and wrong and killed Kessler just to see if they could get away with it. However, Wilk's psychiatrists emphasize that "knowing right from wrong" is not a psychiatric diagnosis. The expert testimony presented in the film leaves no doubt that Straus and Steiner suffered from serious mental illnesses. But whether the law should regard them as legally responsible for their acts is a far more complex question than the M'Naghten Rule suggests.

Picturing justice. From time to time the camera focuses on prosecutor Horn as he listens to Wilk's plea to spare his clients' lives. On each occasion, Horn appears to be embarrassed by his own cry for the death penalty. Moreover, Horn initially rises as if to respond to Wilk's arguments, then apparently thinks better of it and sits back down. Horn's demeanor and behavior reinforce the film's anti-capital-punishment theme.

Trial Brief

Compulsion is a largely factual account of the Leopold and Loeb case, which took place in Chicago in 1924. Nathan Leopold was a law student, and Richard Loeb was at the time the youngest person ever to have graduated from the University of Michigan. Leopold and Loeb kidnapped and killed fourteen-year-old Bobby Franks, who was simply in the wrong place at the wrong time. In their confessions, Leopold and Loeb each accused the other of carrying out the killing.

Clarence Darrow ("Wilk") represented Leopold and Loeb, and as depicted in the film he abruptly changed their pleas to guilty. Many authorities consider Darrow's final argument to be the most eloquent attack on capital punishment ever given in an American courtroom. Wilk's spellbinding speech in the film lasts about fifteen minutes, an improbably long monologue for the attention spans of present-day audiences. Darrow's actual argument went on for twelve hours and spanned two days. It was released to the public on a phonograph record.

Omitted from the film entirely is prosecutor Robert Crowe's responding argument. Crowe ridiculed Darrow's attempt to shift responsibility for the crime to the defendants' wealth and upbringing and referred to Darrow as "the distinguished gentleman whose profession it is to protect murder."

Leopold and Loeb were lovers, a fact that the film only slightly hints at. Hollywood movies were prohibited by the Production Code (a system of self-censorship that was in effect from 1934 to 1968) from dealing with homosexual themes. The erotic nature of Leopold and Loeb's relationship was played up by the press and in part accounted for the public's revulsion toward the defendants. Darrow addressed the sexual elements of the crime at length in his closing argument. He even asked Sigmund Freud to testify, but Freud was too ill to come to Chicago.

Loeb died in prison in 1936 after being stabbed by another inmate. Leopold was eventually released in 1958 after serving thirty-three years in prison. Robert Crowe wrote a letter supporting his release. Leopold was a model prisoner who taught in the prison school, worked in the prison hospital, and learned twenty-seven languages. He eventually married and moved to Puerto Rico, where he worked as a teacher and wrote a book, *Birds of Puerto Rico*. Leopold died of natural causes in 1971.

The Leopold and Loeb case inspired at least two additional films. *Rope* (1948), directed by Alfred Hitchcock, describes a murder committed by two students who think they are supermen and is filmed in real time (that is, the story is told virtually without interruption). *Swoon* (1992) emphasizes the homosexual elements of the story and treats the murder of Bobby Franks as an act of sadomasochism.

I Want to Live!

Synopsis: A destitute mother convicted of murder goes to the gas chamber protesting her innocence.

United Artists, 1958. Black and white. Running time: 120 minutes.

Screenplay: Nelson Gidding and Don Mankiewicz. Director: Robert Wise.

Starring: Susan Hayward (Barbara Graham), Simon Oakland (Ed Montgomery).

Academy Award: Best Actress (Susan Hayward).

Academy Award nominations: Best Director, Best Adapted Screenplay, Best Cinematography, Best Sound Direction, Best Editing.

Rating: ——▪ ——▪ ——▪

The Story

Barbara Graham is a prostitute with an infant and an abusive, drug-addicted husband. Her life goes from bad to cursed when she's arrested along with small-time hoods Santo, Perkins, and King for robbing and killing Mabel Monahan, a crippled widow. The cops question Graham for hours without food or respite, but Graham refuses to confess and rat on the others, even though a cop promises to set her free if she does. Her demands to talk to a lawyer are ignored.

King takes the deal, and at trial he testifies that Graham gained them entry to Monahan's house by asking to use her phone. The gang ransacked the house while Graham pistol-whipped Monahan. The D.A. also offers evidence that Graham asked Ben Miranda, an undercover cop, to testify to a phony alibi. Miranda tricked Graham into confessing on tape that she took part in the robbery. Nevertheless, Graham testifies that she was at home when the murder took place. The jury doesn't buy it and quickly convicts Graham, Santo, and Perkins of first-degree murder. All are sentenced to die in the gas chamber.

Ed Montgomery, a newspaper journalist who had previously dubbed Graham "Bloody Babs" and led the anti-Graham media circus, has a change of heart and tries to overturn her conviction. However, all Graham's appeals are denied. She is moved to death row, and the film depicts every detail of preparing the gas chamber for the executions. Almost cruelly, Graham's execution is delayed twice, once as she's entering the gas chamber. But the postponements are only momentary, and Graham is put to death. A prison guard tells her, "When you hear the pellets drop, breathe deep, and it will be easier that way." Graham's last words are "How would you know?"

I Want To Live!: The D.A. (Bartlett Robinson) helps to send Barbara Graham (Susan Hayward) to the gas chamber.

Legal Analysis

The gas chamber itself is perhaps the film's star. At its first appearance, prison officials slowly (almost lovingly) undrape it. When they are done, it is clearly "ready for its close-up." After the gas chamber's dramatic entrance, the film slowly and carefully depicts each step in the execution process, including preparation of the cyanide pellets and the acid into which they drop. The details emphasize the horror of the death penalty and heighten the viewer's sense that Graham was unjustly convicted and executed.

Police trickery. The film's most dramatic courtroom moment occurs when Miranda testifies for the prosecution. If the jury had any reason to disbelieve King because of his deal with the prosecution, Graham's disastrous bargain with Miranda sealed all doubts. Miranda would not be allowed to testify against Graham today (and the tape recording would be inadmissible) because she had an attorney at the time that he contacted her. By failing to identify himself as a police officer, Miranda interfered with Graham's right to counsel.

So long as they don't interfere with suspects' right to counsel, police officers can still use the other forms of trickery depicted in the film. For example, one cop falsely tells Graham that she should confess because Santo and Perkins were spilling their guts and blaming her for Monahan's death. If the cop's lie induced Graham to confess, her confession would be admissible in evidence. Similarly, Graham was wise not to confess in exchange for a cop's promise to drop the charges against her. Those decisions are made by prosecutors, not police officers.

Was Graham guilty of capital murder? First-degree murder generally requires a prosecutor to prove that a killing was premeditated. In this case, the plan was probably to rob Monahan but not kill her. However, when a death occurs as part of an inherently dangerous crime such as robbery, the felony-murder rule renders it first-degree murder. The prosecution does not have to prove premeditation. Thus, Graham's conviction of capital murder was legally proper.

Death-penalty tropes. The film makes use of numerous devices to encourage viewers to oppose the death penalty. First, the film suggests that Graham may have been innocent of the crime. Of course, the possibility that an innocent person will be put to death is one of the strongest arguments against capital punishment. In recent years, many persons condemned to death have been found to be innocent as the result of DNA analyses or dedicated investigative work. Second, the film humanizes Graham, causing the viewer to identify with her and therefore be distressed by her death. The visit with her little boy just before the execution is truly heartrending. The fact that Montgomery, apparently an independent journalist, believes in Graham also leads viewers to empathize with her. Third, her conviction seems tainted by questionable police tactics and by inept legal representation. Fourth, the almost obsessive concentration on the details of the gas chamber makes the process seem ghastly. Because executions are not the public spectacles they were in previous centuries and aren't televised, the movies are the only way that ordinary people can experience the horrible process. Fifth, the constant stays and last-minute legal maneuvering seem cruel to the prisoner.

Picturing justice. (1) Graham is sitting in the dentist's chair when she learns that her appeal has been turned down. Her arms and hands are in the same position they will be in when she is strapped to the chair in the gas chamber. (2) The film sends mixed messages about criminal-defense lawyers. Graham's trial lawyer, Tibrow, is a spineless jellyfish who rushes up to the bench after Miranda testifies to make sure that the judge and prosecutor know that Graham deceived him. By contrast, Matthews, the lawyer who works on Graham's appeals, does everything he can to save her life.

Trial Briefs

1. The California Supreme Court unanimously affirmed the convictions in 1954; all further federal appeals, including to the U.S. Supreme Court, were unsuccessful. According to the California court's decision, there was evidence that Barbara Graham pistol-whipped Mabel Monahan. However, the victim was also strangled, and the coroner listed the official cause of death as asphyxiation. Graham's oblique comment to her phony alibi partner that he didn't have to worry about anyone else coming forward led police to suspect that Graham participated in the elimination of a potential witness named Baxter Shorter. The police originally arrested Shorter in connection with Monahan's murder, and his information led them to Santo, Perkins, King, and Graham. Shorter disappeared and was never seen again.

2. Under present procedure, capital cases include a guilt phase and a penalty phase. During the penalty phase, Graham would have been able to present the jury with substantial mitigating evidence that might have lessened the punishment. When Graham was a child, her mother was in prison, and with no father in sight she was passed around from one relative to another. By the time she was a young teenager, Graham was in the same youth prison that had housed her mother, and when she was released she turned to prostitution and drugs. She was thirty-one years old when she was executed, one of four women who have been executed in California.

Knock on Any Door

Synopsis: A hooligan whose credo is "Live fast, die young, and leave a good-looking corpse" has a chance to achieve all three goals when he's tried for murder.

Columbia Pictures, 1949. Black and white. Running time: 100 minutes.

Screenplay: Daniel Taradash and John Monks Jr. Original story: Willard Motley. Director: Nicholas Ray.

Starring: Humphrey Bogart (Andrew Morton).

Rating: ——▮ ——▮ ——▮

The Story

Nick Romano is charged with robbing a bar and killing a police officer while attempting to escape. Romano's nickname is "Pretty Boy," and his rap sheet is "pretty long." Andrew Morton is a lawyer who has for years tried to help Romano succeed at something other than getting arrested. Morton passes up a partnership offer in order to defend Romano.

Prosecutor Kerman opens the trial with a hysterical attack on Romano's character, calling him "a jailbird, a moocher for whom the police lineup is a weekly routine, a skid-row Romeo, an outcast, a hoodlum killer." Morton objects only to the phrase "hoodlum killer," apparently hoping the other adjectives will raise Romano's esteem in the eyes of the ladies he's worked hard to keep on the jury.

Morton responds by telling the jury that Romano's sordid past isn't pertinent to the charges. Nevertheless, Morton recounts that past in detail, luckily through flashbacks that save his voice for the rest of the trial. After Romano's father died in prison, Romano lived in a slum that "can take a fine, sensitive kid and twist him and turn him." He was always in trouble, and when he ran out on his wife, Emma, she committed suicide. With Kerman seeking the electric chair for Romano, Morton probably hopes that Romano's tragic story doesn't leave a "fry" eye among the jurors.

Both sides' witnesses are shaky. The bartender, Swanson, identifies Romano as the robber but cannot remember talking to Morton even though Morton "accidentally" spilled wine on him when he interviewed Swanson before trial. Two other prosecution witnesses testify that they saw Romano running away from the scene of the shooting, but they are vagrants to whom Kerman has made regular payments in exchange for their testimony. Romano's friend Juan contradicts his statement to the police that he saw Romano shoot the police officer, claiming that he'd said that only because the police threatened to deport him. Morton's two alibi witnesses are no better, contradicting each other as to the kind of beer they were drinking.

* * *

SPOILER ALERT: You may not want to read further if you plan to see the film.

* * *

Knock on Any Door. Andrew Morton (Humphrey Bogart) observes that the hat fits himself as well as Pretty Boy Romano (John Derek).

Romano chooses to testify, and his decision is fatal. Romano confesses to the robbery and murder after Kerman repeatedly accuses him of causing Emma's death. Morton changes the plea to guilty and tries to save Romano's life. He admits, "Nick Romano is guilty, but so are we and so is that precious thing called society. . . . Until we do away with the type of neighborhood that produced this boy, knock on any door and you may find Nick Romano. If he dies in the electric chair, we killed him." The plea fails, and as Romano walks to the electric chair he goes out a good-looking corpse by stopping to comb his hair.

Legal Analysis

Morton's argument to the judge and the film's viewers is based on "sociological determinism," a concept that extreme poverty and slum life can turn a good kid into a vicious criminal killer. Considering the continuing power of criminal gangs in the ghettos of America's cities, the film's message resonates as strongly now as in 1949. Morton argues a version of what in later years came to be known as "the abuse excuse," although his argument is an effort to lessen the severity of Romano's punishment rather than to diminish his legal responsibility for killing the police officer.

A friend in need . . . probably shouldn't be a client. Morton's lengthy friendship with Romano clouds his judgment. After years of trying to be a father figure to him, Morton wants desperately to believe that Romano is innocent. A more-objective lawyer would no doubt have probed more deeply into his story and, given the weakness of Kerman's case, would have urged Romano not to testify.

Open and shut. Kerman's opening statement vilifies Romano's past in an effort to rouse the jurors' anger, while Morton recounts Romano's past in an effort to gain the jurors' sympathy. Both openings are improper, because Romano's past behavior is largely irrelevant and an opening statement is supposed to be a lawyer's preview of evidence to come. The judge should have silenced both lawyers immediately.

Morton's effectiveness. Morton did a good job of casting doubt on the credibility of Kerman's eyewitnesses. Morton should have followed up by asking the judge to dismiss the charges on the ground that Kerman's evidence was not strong enough to prove Romano guilty beyond a reasonable doubt. Moreover, Morton's litany of Romano's past misdeeds might well have backfired with the jurors. They may have concluded that Romano is just the type of person who would have robbed a bar and killed a police officer. Finally, Morton should have objected to Kerman's frenzied attack on Romano for causing Emma's death. Her death is irrelevant, and, more than improperly "badgering" Romano, Kerman rains down a whole zoo on his head.

A wine mess. Morton casts significant doubt on the bartender's credibility by showing that he can't recall seeing Morton even though he spilled wine all over his shirt. (Morton's ploy also reinforces a general belief that lawyers are sneaky.) However, Morton may have wasted a good glass of wine, because Kerman could have objected that the wine trick was irrelevant. The judge might have ruled that the conditions under which the bartender saw the robber and Morton were so different that his inability to remember Morton in no way undermines his identification of Romano.

Bad-guy blues. Because all the witnesses are a bit seedy, Kerman and Morton bash each other's witnesses with such past sins as doing time in jail and reform school, and convictions for begging and selling pornography. Years ago, trial rules tended to allow this sort of mud-slinging. However, to the chagrin of supermarket tabloids, it's no longer proper in the courtroom. Trial rules today generally prevent attorneys from dredging up opposing witnesses' past misdeeds.

Picturing justice. As Romano walks to the electric chair, doors open and he walks toward a brilliant white light. The light symbolizes the justice and peace that Romano never found on this side of the door, in the harsh conditions in which he grew up.

Trial Brief

The film was made by Humphrey Bogart's production company and strongly reflected Bogart's political views. Bogart also played a crusading district attorney (supposedly based on Thomas Dewey) in *Marked Woman*. One of Bogart's greatest roles was as Captain Queeg in *The Caine Mutiny,* in which he falls apart under cross-examination. Originally Marlon Brando was slated to play Pretty Boy Romano, but Brando withdrew after the death of producer Mark Hellinger, so John Derek (a far weaker actor) got the role. *Knock on Any Door* was an early film of director Nicholas Ray, who specialized in making films about psychological misfits and losers. Later Ray films include *In a Lonely Place,* which also starred Bogart as a paranoid and violent screenwriter, but he was most famous for *Rebel Without a Cause*.

S I D E B A R

Character Evidence

Cine-lawyers are often allowed to assail adverse witnesses with evidence of their past misdeeds. However, character evidence rules generally prevent this form of attack. Underlying the rule forbidding character evidence is the philosophy "We judge the act, not the actor." For example, a prosecutor cannot prove that a defendant committed an armed robbery by offering evidence that the defendant has a reputation for violence or that the defendant has committed other robberies. Here are some of the films in which the character-evidence rules would come into play.

- In *Suspect,* prosecutor Stella attacks a murder defendant by showing that the defendant had previously beaten a man with a shovel and attacked a congressional aide. Character-evidence rules would prevent this attack.
- In *Knock on Any Door,* prosecutor Kerman offers evidence that a murder defendant behaved so abusively toward his wife that she committed suicide. Character-evidence rules would bar this evidence.
- In *Body of Evidence,* a woman is charged with murder for causing her husband to have a fatal heart attack by giving him drugs and then engaging him in aggressive sex. The prosecutor offers evidence that the defendant tried exactly the same ploy with a previous lover. Evidence of the previous attempt is admissible, because the previous act is not a general attack on the defendant's character but rather evidence of the defendant's highly unique *modus operandi.*

Short Subjects

Dancer in the Dark, 2000. Björk, Catherine Deneuve.

Selma Jezkova is nearly blind and toils to earn enough money to purchase an operation for her son to save his sight. Her neighbor, a policeman, steals her cash hoard. The two get into a struggle, and Selma shoots him with his own gun more or less accidentally and takes back the money. Before she's arrested, she secretly pays for her son's operation. At her murder trial, she cannot tell the truth because she is afraid that the operation money will be used for her defense or returned to the victim's family. She is convicted, sentenced to death, and hanged. The usual anti-death penalty tropes are all present, such as the sympathetic prison guard, incompetent representation at her trial, and a macabre execution scene. *Picturing Justice*: Incongruously, during her trial and on death row Selma breaks into song and dance routines. These highlight the absurdity of the use of capital punishment in a case that calls for a far less severe penalty.

Eight O'Clock Walk, 1952. Richard Attenborough.

Although he's innocent, strong circumstantial evidence makes Tom Manning's "eight o'clock walk" to the gallows for killing a little girl seem imminent. Implausibly, Manning's barrister, Peter Tanner, spots another little girl holding the same candy as the dead girl. He realizes that one of the witnesses is in fact the murderer and induces him to confess on the witness stand. *Courtroom highlight*: Tanner calls on a street musician to play the same tune about the Old Bailey that the dead girl was singing when she was killed, which causes the maniac to break down and confess on the witness stand. *Picturing justice*: Tanner's father is the prosecutor, and the two fight each other vigorously in court but go off arm-in-arm after the trial is over.

The Onion Field, 1979. James Woods. Book: Joseph Wambaugh.
—■ —■ —■

This film, accurately depicting real events, illustrates how costly the death penalty is to administer. In 1963, Gregory Powell and Jimmy Smith kidnap Los Angeles policemen Ian Campbell and Karl Hettinger. In a distant onion field, Powell kills Campbell, but Hettinger escapes. The state seeks the death penalty, but after years of trials, appeals, and retrials, both killers are sentenced to life in prison. Demonstrating the power of pop culture to affect reality, Powell's parole date was canceled after the film was shown on television. *Picturing justice*: In utter frustration at another delay, prosecutor Halpin declares that he plans to quit the law: "I'm finished. . . . Campbell's forgotten. He may as well never have lived. Hettinger's a ghost. Only the legal process has meaning." *Trial briefs*: (1) Halpin didn't quit and went on to a long and successful career as a prosecutor. (2) Hettinger became a Kern County supervisor and died in 1994. (3) Smith was paroled in 1982, but in 2005, at the age of seventy-four, he was sent back to prison for a parole violation.

Wives Under Suspicion, 1938. Warren William. Director: James Whale. —■ —■

Merciless D.A. Jim Stowell so delights in obtaining death penalties that he moves a skull-shaped bead on his "death abacus" after each execution. But when Stowell's personal life begins to parallel that of the defendant he is prosecuting for murder, Stowell decides that justice does not require that all killers be put to death. *Picturing justice*: A series of shots traces electrical wires from their source to the execution site.

Military Justice

Films usually portray military justice as a blend of about nine parts military and one part justice. With the military mission on the front burner and justice relegated to the back burner, procedural protections of civilian trials often give way to hurried court-martials that protect the top brass and maintain discipline.

Many films depict the injustice created by "command influence," whereby the top brass makes sure that court-martial judges and lawyers reach the "right result," as in the films *Breaker Morant, Billy Budd,* and *Paths of Glory*. Filmmakers also use court-martials to dramatize difficult legal issues that arise in combat settings, such as whether soldiers must follow illegal orders (*A Few Good Men, Breaker Morant*) or whether the rules protecting civilians must be observed when the lives of military personnel are at stake (*Rules of Engagement*). *The Caine Mutiny* questions the right of naval officers to seize command of a ship from a mentally ill captain, and *The Court-Martial of Billy Mitchell* tells the story of an officer who criticized higher-ups for not modernizing air power, even though he knew it would get him court-martialed.

Filmmakers also use military trials to score broader political points. *Paths of Glory* and *King and Country* are all-out attacks on war and the utter misery of the men who fight and die in the trenches. In films like *Paths of Glory, Rules of Engagement, Breaker Morant, Man in the Middle,* and *Prisoners of the Sun,* the military justice system scapegoats unfortunate defendants in order to solve the political problems of the higher-ups. A military trial even served as an anticommunist exercise in *The Rack*.

Modern military justice is professionalized, at least on paper. The system provides for ample procedural protections for defendants and for specialized and independent lawyers to represent both sides. *Rules of Engagement, High Crimes,* and *A Few Good Men* depict contemporary military trials, but even today, as those films suggest, the system is far from ideal and various forms of command influence can still exist.

Breaker Morant

Synopsis: Injustice goes global when the British scapegoat Australian soldiers during the Boer War in South Africa.

South Australian Film Corp., 1980. Color. Running time: 107 minutes.

Screenplay: Jonathan Hardy, Bruce Beresford, and David Stevens. Original play: Kenneth Ross. Director: Bruce Beresford.

Starring: Edward Woodward (Lieutenant Morant), Jack Thompson (Major Thomas), Bryan Brown (Lieutenant Handcock).

Academy Award nomination: Best Screenplay.

Rating: ──▄█ ──▄█ ──▄█ ──▄█

The Story

The Boer War (1899–1902) was a brutal struggle between the British, who wanted to maintain colonial control over South Africa, and the Boers (Dutch settlers now called Afrikaaners), who sought independence. To combat the Boers' guerrilla tactics ("A new kind of war for a new century," one character says), the British organized an elite unit made up mostly of Australians called the Bushveldt Carbineers.

In retaliation for the brutal killing of his close friend and commanding officer, Breaker Morant orders the execution of captured Boer fighters, even though they surrender to the Carbineers under white flags. Morant also authorizes Lieutenant Handcock to kill a German missionary named Hesse who talked to the prisoners against Morant's orders. Another soldier, Lieutenant Witton, killed a captured Boer who attacked him while trying to escape from a firing squad.

British commander Lord Kitchener orders a court-martial of Morant, Handcock, and Witton on murder charges. Kitchener wants to placate Germany, which is temporarily at peace and is thinking of joining the Boers. As "colonials with bad habits," Australians are convenient instruments of appeasement. Even the Australian government supports

Breaker Morant: Breaker Morant (Edward Woodward) knows that the fix is in and he doesn't have a chance.

Kitchener's decision. Kitchener asks Major Charles Bolton to prosecute, telling him, "The Germans couldn't give a damn about the Boers. It's the diamonds and gold of South Africa that they're interested in." "They lack our altruism, sir," quips a cynical Bolton.

Captain Robertson testifies for the prosecution that Aussie Carbineers were an unruly lot who operated stills and failed to salute superior officers, especially him. Moreover, Handcock violated rules by placing Boer captives in open freight cars, where they could be easily killed when the Boers attacked the trains. Defense counsel Major J. F. Thomas forces Robertson to concede that Handcock's policy ended attacks on the trains and that Robertson followed the same practice.

Thomas contends that the killing of Boer captives was necessary because the Carbineers had no means of feeding or locking up captives. Moreover, the Carbineers often couldn't distinguish soldiers from civilians. Morant testifies, "We didn't have time for the niceties in military procedure manuals. We were out there on the veldt, fighting the Boer the way he fought us." Morant says that the captives were shot "under Rule 303," referring to his British Enfield 303-caliber rifle. Thomas' defense that Kitchener had ordered the killing of captives goes nowhere. Kitchener refuses to testify, an aide denies that Kitchener issued such an order, and the judges are outraged that Thomas suggests otherwise.

The three defendants are all convicted of murder, and Morant and Handcock are sentenced to die. Witton gets a life sentence because he killed in self-defense. Thomas rushes to Kitchener's office to seek a stay of execution, but in modern computer parlance he receives an "out of the office" response. At sunrise the next morning, a firing squad executes Morant and Handcock. Witton served three years, returned to Australia, and wrote a book, *Scapegoats of the Empire*.

Legal Analysis

In *Breaker Morant*, the trial is a vehicle for exposing a specific historical example of injustice while suggesting that war and justice are incompatible. In the service of political expediency, Morant and his co-Carbineers are punished for doing what they were trained to do. Command influence reduces the trial to a formalistic ritual that provides only an illusion of fairness. Kitchener tells an aide, "The war leaders must see this trial as a demonstration of our impartial justice. If these three Australians have to be sacrificed to help bring about a peace conference, it's a small price to pay." For Kitchener, at least.

Defenses against war crimes. The rules of war state that POWs must be sent to secure areas for imprisonment and that the lives and property of civilians must be safeguarded. The tribunal correctly rejected Thomas' argument that these rules shouldn't apply in view of the Boers' unconventional tactics. Killing prisoners and civilians is wrong, no matter what the circumstances. Still, the judges might have taken the novelty and harshness of guerrilla warfare into account in determining the severity of punishment.

Under military law in effect at the time of the Boer War, the following-orders defense was generally accepted. The Nuremberg trials (which occurred about fifty years after the Boer War) established that soldiers cannot rely on a following-orders defense unless they honestly and reasonably believe that the orders are lawful. Even under this modern standard, if the tribunal believed that Kitchener ordered prisoners killed, Morant and his co-defendants might have had a valid defense for killing the prisoners (although not for killing the missionary). Given the unconventional warfare they were conducting, they could have reasonably believed that Kitchener's orders were lawful.

Selective prosecution. Even in the absence of a valid defense, the convictions seem unjust because they resulted from selective prosecution.

The court-martial panel refused to admit evidence that other British officers had executed prisoners. Morant and Handcock were selected to die simply because, like the Goldilocks story, the Australians were "just right." Kitchener is too powerful to punish, and the British soldiers who were equally guilty were politically protected. Morant and Handcock were thus Kitchener's victims as much as the Boers were theirs.

Military injustice. The film illustrates the dangers of leaving justice in the hands of the military. Kitchener holds a trial to legitimate the deaths of Morant and Handcock to the outside world. He authorized a "take no prisoners" response but created plausible deniability by not putting the orders in writing. Kitchener exerted command influence over the judges, Thomas was given inadequate time to prepare, and his right to produce evidence was restricted.

An inspiring defense attorney. Thomas was a small-time property lawyer from Australia who had never tried a case before he was assigned to defend at the court-martial. Insulated from reality by his own naïveté, Thomas provides great representation. He demands additional time to prepare, infuriates the judges by asking that Kitchener testify personally, cross-examines effectively, and stands up for his clients at every opportunity. Thomas also tries to humanize his clients by arguing, "The barbarities of war are seldom committed by abnormal men. The tragedy of war is that these horrors are committed by normal men in abnormal situations." Like so many heroic cine-lawyers (such as Atticus Finch in *To Kill a Mockingbird*), Thomas' efforts seem the nobler for being employed in a cause that was hopeless from the beginning.

Picturing justice. A number of characters, including Morant, perform melodic and often patriotic songs throughout the film. Moreover, a British band plays in a nearby gazebo while Morant and Handcock are sentenced to death. The beauty of the music magnifies the ugliness of the trial process.

Trial Brief

The Bushveldt Carbineers were formed in 1901 to combat the Boers' last-gasp guerrilla-style tactics. The unit was disbanded seven months later. In October 1901, Lieutenants Morant and Handcock were two of seven officers charged with killing Boer prisoners. They were the only two who were executed.

As in the film, defense attorney Thomas was an inexperienced solicitor and had only two days to prepare his defense. However, the prosecutor, Major Bolton, had no formal legal training at all and had never participated in a felony trial. All copies of the trial transcript have been lost or destroyed, so none of the surviving evidence establishes whether the outcome was fixed by higher-ups. As the film depicts, Morant, Handcock, and Witton were all temporarily released during the court-martial to help hold off a Boer raid, and they fought valiantly.

Morant ordered the shooting of at least eight Boers who had surrendered to his patrol. Fearing that the German missionary Hesse had witnessed the shootings and would turn him in, Morant ordered Handcock to kill Hesse. Morant later had three other Boer prisoners executed, one of them a fourteen-year-old boy. Numerous members of the Carbineers wrote letters to British authorities complaining of Morant's shooting of prisoners. Thus, the actual circumstances inspire less sympathy for Morant than does the account given in the film.

Kitchener's unwritten orders to "take no prisoners" were widely circulated in the Transvaal area of South Africa, where the fighting depicted in the film took place. Some justify the punishment of Morant and Handcock because Kitchener's orders were to shoot prisoners only if they "wore khaki," meaning either that they were disguised as British soldiers or that possibly they were badly dressed. Others claim that Morant and Handcock were punished because they shot Boers after and not before they had formally surrendered. In any event, the bottom line is that many British soldiers shot Boer captives yet only Morant and Handcock were executed.

Morant remains a folk hero to many Australians. As depicted in the film, he was a Renaissance man, as adept at poetry as at breaking in horses. Luckily he drew his nickname from the latter rather than the former. "Wordsworth" Morant wouldn't have instilled much fear in an enemy.

The Caine Mutiny

Synopsis: A naval officer faces a court-martial for seizing command of a ship from its paranoid captain.

Columbia Pictures, 1954. Color. Running time: 124 minutes.

Screenplay: Stanley Roberts. Book: Herman Wouk. Director: Edward Dmytryk.

Starring: Humphrey Bogart (Lieutenant Commander Queeg), Jose Ferrer (Lieutenant Barney Greenwald), Van Johnson (Lieutenant Steve Maryk), Fred MacMurray (Lieutenant Tom Keefer).

Academy Award nominations: Best Picture, Best Actor (Humphrey Bogart), Best Supporting Actor (Tom Tully), Best Screenplay, Best Editing, Best Music, Best Sound.

Rating:

The Story

The *Caine* is a grubby minesweeper that has made it through World War II without ever having swept a mine. Lieutenant Keefer tells the newly minted Ensign Keith that the *Caine* "is an outcast ship, manned by outcasts, and named after the greatest outcast of all time." (Keefer has apparently discovered that the ship's true name is the *Pete Rose*.)

Captain Queeg takes over command of the *Caine* and immediately establishes that on board ship it's his way or the waterway. But the war has been no kinder to Queeg's mentality than to the *Caine*'s rusted hull. Queeg berates officers and swabbies for petty violations, like having their shirttails out, while not noticing that his orders have caused the *Caine* to circle and sever its own tow rope. When the *Caine* participates in a major landing assault, Queeg panics under fire and orders the *Caine* out to sea, abandoning the marines the *Caine* was supposed to be protecting. Queeg also turns the ship upside down in a fruitless quest to find out who took a missing quart of strawberries.

Keefer tries to convince Lieutenant Maryk, the ship's executive officer, that Queeg has a serious mental illness. Keefer refers Maryk to Rule 184 of navy regulations, which authorizes taking over a ship's command in extraordinary circumstances. Maryk initially supports Queeg, but when Queeg's orders put the *Caine* in danger of capsizing during a typhoon, Maryk contradicts Queeg's orders, takes command, and saves the ship.

When the *Caine* returns to port, Lieutenant Maryk and Ensign Keith, who supported the takeover, are court-martialed for mutiny and face possible execution. Their attorney, Lieutenant Barney Greenwald, probably doesn't bolster their confidence by telling them, "I'd much rather prosecute." Prosecutor Challee presents psychiatric testimony that Queeg is sane and offers evidence suggesting that Maryk and not Queeg panicked during the typhoon. Keefer protects his own rear by

The Caine Mutiny: Captain Queeg (Humphrey Bogart) rolls the steel balls.

claiming that he wasn't present when Maryk seized command and that it was Maryk rather than himself who talked about Queeg being paranoid. Maryk testifies to Queeg's instability, but Challee effectively belittles his familiarity with the symptoms of mental illness.

Queeg's testimony turns the tide in favor of the defense. Greenwald confronts him with the tow-line incident and accuses him of leaving the scene of battle. When the court-martial judges caution him about the seriousness of accusing Queeg of cowardice, Greenwald explains that they misunderstand him: "It is not the defense's contention that Captain Queeg is a coward. Quite the contrary. The defense assumes that no man who rises to command a U.S. Navy ship can possibly be a coward. Therefore, if he commits questionable acts under fire, the explanation must be elsewhere." When Greenwald brings up the strawberry inquiry, Queeg goes bananas. He brings out the small steel balls that he twirls in his hand whenever he's under pressure and accuses everyone of disloyalty and incompetence. His rant shocks Challee and the hearing officers, and the charges against Maryk and Keith are dismissed. Greenwald, however, is in no mood to celebrate. He takes no pride in getting the mentally ill Queeg to crack and criticizes Maryk, Keefer, and the other officers for waiting for Queeg to fall apart rather than helping him.

Legal Analysis

Even among a group of sailors who risked their lives in battle, defense attorney Greenwald seems to be a good candidate for the film's hero because he violated the taboo about challenging the near-absolute authority of a commanding officer. Indeed, he may have jeopardized his own naval career by doing so. His aggressive cross-examination of Queeg saved his clients' lives. But Greenwald downplays his rhetorical skills, telling the celebrating officers that destroying Queeg was "like shooting fish in a barrel."

Greenwald delivers the film's ironic message that Queeg is the true hero, because "Who was standing guard over this fat, dumb country of ours? Who did the dirty work for us? Queeg did." Greenwald won because he didn't let the court-martial judges in on one important detail. Queeg had appealed to the officers for help. Instead they turned him down and made up songs about him. At the end of the day, perhaps it was the officers, and not Queeg, "a sick man who couldn't help himself," who endangered the ship's safety.

Mutiny. As defined by the Uniform Code of Military Justice, mutiny consists of a refusal to obey orders by two or more people acting together with the intent to usurp lawful military authority. Mutiny is a grave crime, punishable by death. Determining what someone "intended" by refusing to obey an order can sometimes be difficult to determine, but there was no doubt about Maryk's intent.

Vague standards. Article 184 (now Section 1088) of naval regulations allows a subordinate to relieve a commanding officer when it is "obvious and clear . . . that the retention of command will seriously and irretrievably prejudice the public interest." A subordinate who relieves a commanding officer "must bear the legitimate responsibility for, and must be prepared to justify, such action." Normally, the prosecution must prove all the elements of a crime beyond a reasonable doubt, but the effect of Article 184 was to force mutineers to justify their actions.

How to apply the vague terms of a law such as Article 184 to the messy circumstances of a particular case can never be a mechanical process. Deciding whether a commanding officer's disability is "obvious and clear" and whether his retention of command "will seriously and irretrievably prejudice the public interest" requires judges and jurors to make difficult value judgments. To Maryk, Keefer, and others aboard the *Caine,* Queeg's irrational behavior endangered their lives. Yet because that behavior could not be fully reproduced in the courtroom, Challee was able to characterize Queeg's behavior as rational and the mutineers' behavior as motivated by anger over Queeg's harsh enforcement of naval regulations. If Queeg had not come unglued during Greenwald's cross-examination, the hearing officers would probably have condemned Maryk and Keith to death, and that decision might have been justifiable under Article 184.

Picturing justice. Queeg's rolling of the steel balls in his hand during Greenwald's cross-examination is an obvious sign that he is not to be believed. In real life, witnesses are seldom so transparent.

Trial Briefs

1. The U.S. Navy endorsed the film and agreed to cooperate in filming only after producer Stanley Kramer responded to the Navy's concern that viewers would believe that the film depicted a true story. Kramer included a notice at the outset that no mutiny has ever occurred in the Navy. However, the notice is inaccurate. In 1842, an officer and several crew members (including the son of the secretary of war) of the vessel *Somers* were hanged as mutineers after a hasty court-martial concluded that they tried to seize the ship to launch a new career as pirates.

2. *The Caine Mutiny* was Humphrey Bogart's last film.

3. Running downwind is generally the most prudent manner to ride out a major storm. Thus, Queeg's orders to steer the *Caine* in the same direction as the typhoon may have been correct, because the ship had neither taken on water nor sustained structural damage. As Greenwald suggested, "the wrong guy was on trial," because Maryk and Keith were not justified in seizing command based on Queeg's orders during the typhoon.

A Few Good Men

Synopsis: A flippant lawyer confronts an authoritarian marine base commander.

Columbia Pictures, 1992. Color. Running time: 138 minutes.

Screenplay: Aaron Sorkin. Play: Aaron Sorkin. Director: Rob Reiner.

Starring: Tom Cruise (Lieutenant Kaffee), Jack Nicholson (Colonel Jessep), Demi Moore (Lieutenant Commander Galloway), Kevin Bacon (Captain Ross), Kiefer Sutherland (Lieutenant Kendrick).

Academy Award nominations: Best Picture, Best Supporting Actor (Jack Nicholson), Best Editing.

Rating:

The Story

Private First Class Santiago, an unhappy marine anxious to transfer off Guantanamo, Cuba, sees Corporal Dawson unlawfully fire a shot into Cuban territory. Ignoring the chain of command, Santiago offers to rat out Dawson to anybody who might transfer him. Soon thereafter, Dawson and Private First Class Downey subject Santiago to a "Code Red" hazing and accidentally kill him. Dawson and Downey are charged with murder. Their defense is that Lieutenant Kendrick had ordered them to administer the Code Red.

Lieutenant Kaffee is a brash neophyte in the Navy Judge Advocate General (JAG) Corps whose father was a famous trial lawyer. He has plea-bargained forty-four straight cases and cares more about softball than about his clients. The brass appoint him to represent Dawson and Downey, hoping that he will quietly make two more deals. Kaffee tries to, but his clients refuse.

Kaffee and his team travel to Cuba to meet with Kendrick and Colonel Jessep, the hard-as-nails base commander. Jessep claims that he ordered that no harm come to Santiago, and Kendrick states that he dutifully passed the order on to his men. Jessep also declares that he ordered that Santiago be transferred on the first available military flight, which unfortunately wasn't scheduled to depart until the morning after the hazing.

Prosecutor Captain Ross offers evidence suggesting that Dawson and Downey intended to kill Santiago. They tied him up and forced a poisoned rag down his throat. Santiago's threat to report Dawson provided a motive to kill, and the two men ignored Kendrick's order not to harm Santiago.

Lieutenant Colonel Markinson, Jessep's assistant, secretly provides Kaffee with a bombshell: Jessep ordered a Code Red on Santiago, and he never ordered Santiago to be transferred off the base. If Jessep had

A Few Good Men: Colonel Nathan Jessep (Jack Nicholson) lacks a few good answers.

really wanted to protect Santiago, he could have put him on a red-eye flight from Guantanamo to Andrews Air Force Base that left before Santiago was killed. Unfortunately for Kaffee, Markinson is Code Very Blue over his role in the coverup, and he commits suicide before Kaffee can call him to testify. Moreover, Kaffee can find no record of a red-eye flight from Guantanamo to Andrews for the night Santiago was killed. It might be the military's way of cheating marines out of a few good frequent flyer miles, but Kaffee is convinced that Jessep doctored the records.

* * *

SPOILER ALERT: You may not want to read further if you plan to see the film.

* * *

Kaffee's only hope is to put Jessep on the stand and induce him to admit that he ordered a Code Red. Jessep is arrogant and insulting, but he loses his cool when Kaffee confronts him with inconsistencies in his story. Kaffee directly accuses Jessep of ordering the Code Red and destroying the records of the red-eye flight. When Kaffee demands the truth, Jessep turns Code Deep Purple and snarls, "You can't handle the truth. . . . Santiago's death, while tragic, probably saved lives. And my existence . . . saves lives. . . . You want me on that wall, you need me on that wall. . . . I have neither the time nor the inclination to explain myself to a man who rises and sleeps under the blanket of the very freedom that I provide and then questions the manner in which I provide it." Kaffee: "Did you order the Code Red?" Jessep: "You're goddamn right I did." This startling admission causes Ross to order that Jessep be arrested. Kendrick is next.

Dawson and Downey are found not guilty of murder. However, they are convicted of engaging in conduct unbecoming a marine and dishonorably discharged. Kaffee is a star in his first trial, following in the footsteps of his famous father. Nothing like a few good genes.

Legal Analysis

The murder trial in *A Few Good Men* is a springboard for questions about when a soldier should be held responsible for following an illegal order issued by his superior. Soldiers can properly claim a following-orders defense if they honestly and reasonably believe the orders are legal. Dawson and Downey might well have met this standard. They may not have known that the marines had banned Code Reds, because these were commonly administered at Guantanamo. Moreover, Kendrick ordered Dawson and Downey to "teach Santiago a lesson," not slaughter civilians or violate human rights. As a result, the following-orders defense probably should have been accepted by the tribunal. In any event, the dishonorable-discharge sanction seems unduly harsh.

Kaffee's "J'Accuse." A number of people warn Kaffee that he will be court-martialed for unethical conduct if he accuses Jessep in court of giving an illegal order and falsifying records and can't back it up. However, this advice is not correct. As a JAG officer, Kaffee is independent of the chain of command. He would not be subject to discipline simply because he contested the word of a superior officer. Still, if Jessep had not broken down, Kaffee might have hurt his chances for advancement within JAG and limited his opportunities to wear dress whites at fancy military balls.

Of course, like any civilian lawyer, Kaffee has an ethical obligation not to hurl unfounded charges around the courtroom. In *A Few Good Men*, Markinson's information provides Kaffee with a good-faith basis for accusing Jessep of wrongdoing.

Female cine-lawyers. Lieutenant Commander Galloway is an experienced female JAG lawyer who outranks Kaffee. She schemes her way onto the defense team as co-counsel for Downey but does a miserable job. She's emotional rather than logical and makes foolish objections during the trial. Thus, the film provides another in a long line of unflattering images of female lawyers.

Picturing justice. (1) There's a sharp contrast between the military's unbending moral code and a lawyer's pragmatic approach. Dawson's first loyalty is to the chain of command, and he refuses to plead guilty because he believes that he was right to carry out Kendrick's order. Kaffee thinks Dawson should take the deal, because if he loses at trial the punishment will be much more severe. (2) Kaffee's dramatic cross-examination of Jessep fuels the false impression given by many movies that cross-examination is the key to victory or defeat. Skillful cross-examinations can undermine the credibility of witnesses, but they almost never determine the outcome of trials.

Trial Brief

A Few Good Men is based loosely on an incident that took place at Guantanamo in 1986 involving Private First Class Willie A an unhappy marine who sought to transfer and threatened to report a colleague who fired his weapon over the fence line. About ten marines then conducted a Code Red blanket party. They woke Willie A, shoved a pillowcase down his throat, and gave him a severe haircut. Willie A lapsed into a coma but survived. Guantanamo brass allegedly refused to transfer Willie A and authorized the hazing.

The character of Kaffee may be based on Don Marcari, who tried his first case as the lawyer for one of the ten marines. His client was one of three marines who were found guilty of assault and sentenced to time served. They were allowed to remain in the Corps. The other seven alleged assailants entered pleas and received less-than-honorable discharges. Deborah Sorkin, whose brother Aaron wrote the original play and the film's screenplay, also represented one of the ten marines who were charged with assaulting Willie A.

Five of the ten marines who allegedly hazed Willie A sued the producer of *A Few Good Men* for libel, invasion of privacy, and invasion of the right of publicity. The court dismissed most of their claims before trial and threatened sanctions against the plaintiffs for filing a frivolous lawsuit. At that point, the parties agreed to settle the case for a small sum.

Paths of Glory

Synopsis: A French court-martial serves up a generous helping of "le scapegoat."

United Artists, 1957. Black and white. Running time: 86 minutes.

Screenplay: Stanley Kubrick, Calder Willingham, and Jim Thompson. Novel: Humphrey Cobb. Director: Stanley Kubrick.

Starring: Kirk Douglas (Colonel Dax), Adolphe Menjou (General Broulard), George Macready (General Mireau).

Rating: ——■ ——■ ——■

The Story

The French and German armies are bogged down in deadly trench warfare during World War I. The cynical General Broulard dangles a promotion before General Mireau if he'll take "the anthill," an impregnable German position. Mireau orders Colonel Dax to lead the ragged 701st regiment in the hopeless assault. Mireau estimates that only half the troops will die, and you know which half he'll be in.

The assault is a catastrophe even by French military standards. Most of the men are slaughtered, others retreat, and some never leave the trenches. Mireau furiously calls for an artillery bombardment on his own troops, and when nobody will carry out his order he orders the court-martial of three soldiers for cowardice in the face of the enemy. "If those little sweethearts won't face German bullets, they'll face French ones," he declares. One soldier is picked at random, another because he's a social misfit, and the third because he knows too much. Colonel Dax, in civilian days one of the best criminal lawyers in France, represents the soldiers.

Responding to prosecutor Saint-Auban's questions, each of the soldiers explains the impossibility of completing the attack, but the court is not interested in explanations. Dax criticizes the entire process, concluding: "The attack yesterday morning was no stain on the honor of France, but this court-martial is such a stain. . . . Gentlemen of the court, to find these men guilty will be a crime to haunt each of you to the day you die." Dax asks for mercy, but there is no *merci* from the judges and the soldiers are condemned to die. The next morning, amid stirring pageantry, the three scapegoats are led to their death. General Broulard assures Dax that the executions will enhance discipline and thus serve as "a perfect tonic for the entire division."

Paths of Glory: Colonel Dax (Kirk Douglas) defends his scapegoated clients.

Dax ends Mireau's career by giving Broulard evidence that Mireau ordered artillery fire on his own men. Broulard, assuming that Dax turned in Mireau in order to get his job, offers Dax a promotion, but Dax contemptuously turns him down.

Meanwhile, the surviving soldiers of the 701st regiment are packed into a barroom. They hum along with a German woman as she sings a sad old military tune "The Faithful Soldier." A few weep as they contemplate the hideous tragedy in which all are engulfed. Then they are ordered back to the front.

Legal Analysis

Considered by many one of the greatest antiwar movies, the ironically titled *Paths of Glory* is black and white in more than its cinematography. There's little nuance, just an all-out attack on the incompetence and corruption at the top of the military hierarchy and the utter misery of the men in the trenches. The troops are considered little more than cannon fodder, while the generals focus on their own careers (the "paths of glory") and on living pleasurably.

Military injustice. Virtually everything that could be wrong with a trial occurs in this film. Procedural niceties like an indictment and a transcript are dispensed with. The judges hurry the testimony along to please General Mireau, whose constant presence at the proceedings ensures that the judges won't exercise independent judgment.

It is obvious that the soldiers were not guilty of cowardice. They tried to advance, but the suicidal attack had no chance of success and they had to retreat (indeed, many were ordered to do so). The judges prevent Dax from introducing evidence that one of the soldiers had been decorated for bravery in earlier battles. This evidence should have been relevant to the issue of whether he was a coward.

That a trial takes place at all demonstrates that trials are important cultural rituals. The process might be a sham, but it must occur to legitimate the outcome. At the same time, the trial format offers the filmmakers an opportunity to drive home the antiwar message by having the characters testify directly to the film's viewers.

One for all and all for one. Underlying the soldiers' convictions is the theory of collective guilt. The regiment as a whole is guilty of cowardice because it didn't take the anthill or die trying. Three sacrificial lambs must bear the guilt of all. This idea of collective guilt is repellent, similar to the Nazis shooting a hundred civilians because an unknown person attacked a German officer. Such reprisals are now prohibited by the Geneva Conventions. Even in conditions of deathly combat, there is no room for a theory of collective guilt in a civilized justice system.

Picturing justice. The injustice of the sham trial is heightened by the opulent ballroom of the spacious and lavishly furnished chateau in which it takes place.

Trial Briefs

1. Because of its harsh attack on the honor of the French military, the film was banned in France for eighteen years.

2. The events pictured in the movie appear to be inspired by a 1917 battle along a road called the *Chemin des Dames*. The French army attacked a well-defended German position and was repulsed with heavy losses. Around 40,000 soldiers mutinied in protest against the horrible conditions of trench warfare. The commanders arrested the leaders of the mutiny and condemned 412 of them to death, although

only a few (estimated at between 27 and 49) were actually executed. In 1998, leftist politicians in France called for the rehabilitation of the soldiers who had been executed, but President Jacques Chirac refused. His office wrote: "The moment just wasn't right. To put those who refused to fight and those who fought and died on the same level—it just wasn't the right time to do that, and we have had an enormous negative reaction."

3. Two of director Stanley Kubrick's other notable antiwar films are *Dr. Strangelove: Or How I Learned to Stop Worrying and Love the Bomb* (1964) and *Full Metal Jacket* (1987). The title of the film *Paths of Glory* probably comes from a Thomas Gray poem, "Elegy Written in a Country Churchyard": "The paths of glory lead but to the grave."

Rules of Engagement

Synopsis: A marine colonel goes on trial for murdering unarmed civilians—or were they?

Paramount Pictures, 2000. Color. Running time: 128 minutes.

Screenplay: James Webb and Stephen Gaghan. Director: William Friedkin.

Starring: Tommy Lee Jones (Colonel Hays Hodges), Samuel L. Jackson (Colonel Terry Childers).

Rating: ——◼ ——◼

The Story

The U.S. embassy in Yemen is under siege by a mob. Terry Childers, a highly decorated marine officer, and his squad rescue the terrified Ambassador Mourain by helicopter while taking heavy fire from snipers. When three marines are killed and Childers sees more gunfire coming from the crowd below, he orders his men to open fire. They kill eighty-three people and wound hundreds more.

To try to defuse the international uproar created by the "slaughter," the higher-ups decide that Childers should take the fall and charge him with murder and conduct unbecoming an officer. Major Biggs presents a strong case at the court-martial. Ordered to toe the line, Mourain testifies falsely that everything was calm and that Childers forced him to evacuate against his will. Another marine testifies that he saw no firing

Rules of Engagement: Colonel Hays Hodges (Tommy Lee Jones) has the difficult task of defending Colonel Terry Childers (Samuel L. Jackson).

coming from the crowd and that he was reluctant to carry out the open-fire order. Yemeni doctor Ahmar found no weapons on the bodies of the dead, though on cross he admits that audiotapes they carried call for all loyal Muslims to kill Americans. National Security Advisor Sokal, who had destroyed a videotape that depicted what really happened, condemns the slaughter.

Childers persuades his old Vietnam War buddy Hayes Hodges, a washed-up marine lawyer, to defend him. Childers doesn't want to be represented by "a Starbucks drinker who's never seen combat." (Childers has apparently never been in a line of sharp-elbowed coffee drinkers anxious for a caffeine fix.) Childers testifies that he gave the open-fire order because people in the crowd were still shooting at them, not in retaliation for the death of the three marines. On cross, Biggs gets Childers to admit that he didn't follow the rules of engagement for ground combat in urban areas, which require the firing of warning shots and requests for surrender before firing on civilians. Childers also admits that he ordered his men to "waste the motherfuckers." He loses his temper and shouts that he wasn't going to stand by and see another marine die.

The panel acquits Childers of murder and conduct unbecoming an officer, though it convicts him of breach of the peace. A crawl states that Ambassador Mourain was charged with perjury and removed from the diplomatic service and that Sokal was compelled to resign.

Legal Analysis

Disqualified from combat duty by his injuries in Vietnam, Hayes Hodges went to law school and had a thoroughly undistinguished career as a marine lawyer. Close to retirement, he spends his days fly-fishing. He's suffered through a divorce and has a serious drinking problem. When Childers asks him to undertake the defense, Hodges replies, "I'm a good-enough lawyer to know you need a better lawyer than me." As the trial begins, Hodges is in the head barfing because he's afraid that he's not up to the job. Like Frank Galvin in *The Verdict*, Hodges finds redemption for a wasted career in the greatest case of his life—the defense of his friend Terry Childers.

Familiar tropes. *Rules of Engagement* uses a courtroom conflict to frame much-larger issues. Rules that may sound good on paper can put soldiers in a dangerous no-win situation in combat. To defuse a major political crisis that could jeopardize U.S. relations with moderate Arab regimes, Security Advisor Sokal badly needs a scapegoat. Sokal bulldozes the army brass into casting all the blame on Childers. Scapegoating is a frequent theme of military justice movies, such as *Breaker Morant* and *Paths of Glory*.

In American popular culture (as in real life), government officials often engage in cover-ups to achieve political goals. *Rules of Engagement* follows that well-worn path. Sokal withholds, then destroys, the critical videotape that shows gunfire coming from the crowd. Of course, his decision was stupid as well as corrupt, given that he destroys the tape in front of witnesses and there's a paper trail showing that he received it. Even in the movies, corrupt government officials are usually smarter than that. Similarly, at the time of the rescue Mourain was hiding under his desk and was pathetically grateful to Childers for saving his life and that of his family. Yet he unhesitatingly betrays Childers and commits perjury to save his own career.

Arabs have often been portrayed negatively in U.S. films, and *Rules of Engagement* is no exception. The film suggests that the siege was a plot to provoke a massive military overreaction that would discredit Americans throughout the Middle East. The film even shows a little girl firing a pistol at the marines. The message is that Yemeni terrorists were more than willing to risk the death or injury of hundreds of their own women and children in order to demonize the Americans. Not a pretty picture.

Command decision. The fundamental issue raised by the movie is whether an officer can be expected to comply with the rules of engagement or the laws of war in intense combat when the lives of his men are at stake. Rather than firing warning shots and demanding surrender as required by the rules of engagement, Childers opened fire on the crowd without warning, even though his second in command told him that women and children would be caught in the crossfire. Thus Childers took innocent lives to save his own men, just as he had in Vietnam when he killed a POW in violation of the Geneva Conventions. In both situations, Childers made command decisions that can be criticized in hindsight. However, his decisions were understandable in the heat of battle. Violating the rules of engagement during the rescue should have ended his career as a marine officer, but it should not have been prosecuted as mass murder.

Picturing justice. The closing argument by the lawyer for the underdog is often the dramatic climax in courtroom movies, and *Rules of Engagement* is no exception. Knowing that the judges are all marine officers, Hodges argues that hanging Childers out to dry to solve the government's foreign policy crisis is "worse than leaving him wounded on a battlefield. That is something you do not do if you are a United States marine." The argument recognizes the values of the judges and, the filmmakers imply, those of many viewers.

Town Without Pity

Synopsis: A defense lawyer reluctantly humiliates a rape victim.

United Artists, 1961. Black and white. Running time: 105 minutes.

Screenplay: George Hurdalek. Novel: Manfred Gregor. Director: Gottfried Reinhardt.

Starring: Kirk Douglas (Major Steve Garrett), E. G. Marshall (Major Jerome Pakenham).

Academy Award nomination: Best Original Song.

Rating: ——🔨 ——🔨 ——🔨

Town Without Pity: Major Garrett (Kirk Douglas) despises his clients, but he must ruin a rape victim's reputation to save them.

The Story

Karin Steinhof, a German teenager, is necking with her boyfriend, Frank, by a river. When Frank won't go further than second base, Karin angrily swims across the river to where she'd left her clothes. She removes her bikini, perhaps to excite him. She's spotted and gang-raped by four bored and slightly drunk American GIs. They are quickly caught and court-martialed.

Defense attorney Major Garrett hopes to spare his obviously guilty clients from the death penalty, while avoiding the harm to Karin's reputation that will surely result from his discrediting her on the witness stand. He repeatedly tries to negotiate a plea bargain, but under pressure from the outraged locals and Karin's overbearing father, the army refuses.

Garrett's cross-examination of Karin is as destructive as he promised. Karin claims that the GIs ripped off her bikini. After Garrett easily tears her undamaged bikini top in half, Karin has to admit she was naked when the rapists spotted her. Indeed, Garrett's questions make it seem that she liked having men watch her nude. Overcome by the brutal cross-examination, Karin faints and is carried from the courtroom. Karin's father withdraws her from the trial. Because the cross-examination was not completed, the court cannot sentence the men to death. Instead, each receives a dishonorable discharge and a lengthy sentence of imprisonment at hard labor.

Garrett's strategy of blaming Karin has a terrible outcome. The nasty and prudish people of the town turn against her, she is taunted wherever she goes, and her father rejects her. Soon thereafter, Karin throws herself into the river and drowns.

Legal Analysis

Garrett found his duties as defense council distasteful. He despised his clients and felt genuine compassion for Karin. Nevertheless, he does his job competently and even admits to a journalist that he got a bang out of doing it. (The journalist's annoying voice-over detracts from the narrative power of the film.)

Defending rape cases. This film illustrates, perhaps better than any other, how defense lawyers in a rape case have traditionally tried to put the victim on trial An estimated two-thirds of rape victims don't report the crime or refuse to testify because the prospect is so terrifying. Indeed, rape trials are often described as a second rape.

In a rape case, the prosecution must show that the victim was compelled to submit by force or the threat of force. The typical defense tactic (especially in date-rape cases) is that the victim consented. Indeed, women were once deemed to have consented to sexual intercourse unless they physically resisted (or were prevented from resisting by threats to their safety), although this rule is no longer followed in most states. At one time, defense lawyers were able to introduce evidence about the victim's sexual history to show that she was promiscuous and likely to have consented. In nearly all states, rape shield laws (discussed below) preclude the defense lawyer from using this tactic. Another approach, also a theme in *The Accused,* is to argue that the victim provoked the assault by her seductive behavior. Jurors are less likely to convict a defendant of rape when they think the victim "asked for it."

Rape shield laws. Rape shield laws did not exist at the time of the events depicted in the film. The federal version of the rule prohibits introduction of evidence offered to prove that a victim engaged in sexual behavior that is unrelated to the charged rape. It also bars evidence offered to prove the victim's "sexual predisposition." The rape shield law is followed in military justice proceedings.

Garrett elicited testimony from Karin's neighbor that he had seen her exercising in the nude in front of her window. Garrett also offered evidence that Karin and Frank made out with each other on the river-bank before the rape and that they had spent a weekend together at a ski cabin. From this evidence, the jurors might infer that Karin had a propensity to engage in sexual behavior and thus consented to have sex with the soldiers. This is exactly the type of "sexual-predisposition" inference that the rape shield laws make inadmissible. In short, a rape shield law would have knocked out most of Garrett's defense.

Picturing justice. The haunting lyrics of the title song blare constantly from jukeboxes and car radios. "How can we keep love alive, how can anything survive, when these little minds tear you in two? . . . No, it isn't very pretty, what a town without pity can do." The tune suggests that a community's beliefs and attitudes can spill over into trials and distort their outcomes.

Trial Briefs

1. In 1977, the U.S. Supreme Court ruled that it was unconstitutional to impose the death penalty for rape in the case of *Coker v. Georgia.* Before *Coker,* there was a huge racial disparity in the application of the death penalty in rape cases. The vast majority of men executed for rape were black men who had raped white women.

2. Under the Status of Forces Agreement (SOFA) in effect between other NATO countries and the United States, the rapists could have been tried either by a local court under German law or by an American court-martial. The locals had the primary right to try the men but allowed the military to try them because the officials wanted to see the men executed and Germany does not have the death penalty. However, the officials were probably wrong. SOFA prohibited the court-martial from sentencing the defendants to death as punishment for a crime against a German civilian if the local courts are barred from using the death penalty.

Cases involving crimes by U.S. service personnel against local people often produce great controversy. In 1995, three servicemen from a local base on Okinawa raped a twelve-year-old Japanese girl. Although the Japanese SOFA gave the local courts the primary right to try the soldiers, it also allowed the United States to hold the soldiers in custody until the local courts formally charged them. This hindered the local prosecutors from properly investigating the crime, because American law gives crime suspects much greater protections from interrogation than does Japanese law. Passions boiled over, and a mass protest resulted. The 1995 incident jeopardized the agreement basing U.S. troops on the island. It led to changes in practice that now allow Japanese investigators to interrogate U.S. servicemen before charging them.

Short Subjects

Billy Budd, 1962. Terence Stamp, Peter Ustinov, Robert Ryan. Book: Herman Melville. ——▋ ——▋

In 1797, the British and the French are as usual at war. Billy Budd is impressed into duty on a British naval warship. In front of Captain Vere, Master-at-Arms John Claggart falsely accuses Budd of plotting a mutiny. Budd strikes Claggart, and the single blow is fatal. Though Vere and the judges agree that Budd acted morally, Vere insists that the Articles of War require them to hold a court-martial, convict Budd, and sentence him to death. *Picturing justice*: (1) No sooner is Budd hanged than the crew mutinies, the French attack, and the British ship is destroyed, equating the court-martial and war as equally unjust ways of killing. (2) Vere admits to an aide, "Battle makes a mockery of justice." (3) A voice-over at the end provides the highly ironic message that "men are perishable things, but justice will live as long as the human soul, and the law as long as the human mind." *Trial brief*. Under British law, the trial should have been held by the Admiralty after the ship returned to port. Budd would have had legal assistance, and a death sentence would have been unlikely because the Articles of War were often not carried out strictly.

Carrington V.C., 1955. David Niven, Margaret Leighton. ——▋ ——▋ ——▋

Major Carrington has desperate financial problems because his commanding officer, Colonel Henniker, refused to approve an expense reimbursement. He helps himself to £125 from the regimental safe and is court-martialed for fraudulent misappropriation.

Carrington's defense is that Henniker knew in advance of his plans. However, Henniker is jealous of Carrington's war record and popularity, so he falsely swears that Carrington had said nothing to him. Carrington hopes that his wife, Val, will confirm that he told her on the phone that he'd notified Henniker before removing the money. Though the judge is willing to admit this hearsay evidence, Val has just learned that Carrington has been unfaithful to her, and she refuses to back up his story. The jurors convict Carrington, but because of a nosy switchboard operator, justice may yet prevail.

The Court-Martial of Billy Mitchell, 1955. Gary Cooper, Rod Steiger, Ralph Bellamy. ——■ ——■

The 1925 court-martial of Colonel (formerly General) Billy Mitchell is the backdrop for lauding a farsighted hero and attacking the military command structure. Mitchell, a World War I flying ace, complains to reporters that the deaths of flyers in his squadron "are the direct result of incompetence, criminal negligence, and the almost treasonable administration of our national defense." A court-martial convicts Mitchell of engaging in conduct prejudicial to the good of the service, but the attendant publicity produces his desired results. *Courtroom highlight*: Ridiculed by the prosecutor for his predictions about the future of air power (all of which came true), Mitchell testifies: "If being a good soldier is submitting dumbly and passively to injustice, indecision, and complacency, then I'm glad I'm a bad one." *Picturing justice*: (1) Mitchell and his attorney argue over both trial and settlement strategy, and in each case the attorney properly accedes to Mitchell's wishes. (2) The harsh chief judge initially forbids the defense from explaining why Mitchell spoke out, but he relents when a colleague argues, "The whole foundation of our legal system, of our country for that matter, rests on the right of a man to defend himself."

High Crimes, 2002. Ashley Judd, Morgan Freeman. ——■

You can just imagine the meeting where they pitched *High Crimes*—it's *A Few Good Men* meets *Jagged Edge*! All right! Green light! Unfortunately, the film has few good scenes and is ragged around the edges. The marines charge Tom Kubik with having slaughtered nine civilians while serving in El Salvador. Kubik's lawyer is his wife, big-firm lawyer Claire Kubik. Teaming up with burned-out and alcoholic military lawyer Charley Grimes and awkward JAG lawyer Terrence Embry, Claire does a competent job of defending her husband. Of course, her investigation reveals that the military is covering up its own blunders and that the "high crimes" go all the way to the top. *Picturing justice*: The film serves up the usual biased court-martial judge and a rushed and unfair procedure.

King and Country, 1964. Dirk Bogarde, Tom Courtenay.

This grim portrait of war and injustice focuses on the court-martial of Private Hamp, who volunteered to serve in the British army in World War I. After three horrible years in the trenches, Hamp leaves his post and begins walking toward England. He is convicted of desertion and executed, despite defense attorney Captain Hargreaves' creative and eloquent defense. The troops are soon to undertake a dangerous mission, and the brass needs to discourage deserters. *Courtroom highlight*: Hargreaves attacks army doctor O'Sullivan's testimony that Hamp fully understood what he was doing. *Picturing justice*: After Hamp thanks Hargreaves for his efforts, a frustrated Hargreaves replies, "I was only doing my duty. If you had done your duty, I wouldn't have had to do mine."

Man in the Middle, 1964. Robert Mitchum, Keenan Wynn, Trevor Howard.

Stationed in India during World War II, U.S. officer Charles Winton kills a British soldier in front of numerous eyewitnesses. Winton is viciously racist and clearly insane; he murdered the soldier because the man was consorting with native women. The U.S. brass needs to convict and hang Winton to promote a united war effort. Though the trial is supposed to be a formality, Colonel Adams risks his career in a courageous effort to defend Winton by establishing his insanity. When the U.S. medical staff puts one obstacle after another in his way, Adams turns to a plucky British psychiatrist for help. Unusual for a military justice movie, the film leaves the panel's verdict in doubt. *Courtroom highlight*: The expert's testimony that Winton was insane goads Winton into a wild outburst in front of the judges. *Picturing justice*: Adams tries to convince a witness to testify by saying, "It's easy to fight for the innocent, but when you fight for the sick, for the warped, for the lost, then you've got justice."

Prisoners of the Sun, 1990. Bryan Brown. ──▪ ──▪ ──▪

The Australian military prosecutes Japanese officers for murdering Australian captives on Ambon Island during World War II. Vice-Admiral Takahashi ordered the killings, but he is too important to convict because the Allied War Command needs him to help pacify and rebuild Japan. By contrast, Tanaka, a menial signals officer, is convicted and executed for carrying out an order to kill a captured Australian airman. Heightening the sense of injustice, Tanaka's guilt is based on a technicality: He failed to demand a written order from a court-martial that authorized the airman's execution. *Picturing justice:* The Aussies execute Tanaka in much the same way that Tanaka killed the airman, suggesting the immorality of both events. *Trial brief:* Academy Award winner Russell Crowe made his film debut in this movie.

The Rack, 1956. Paul Newman, Walter Pidgeon. Original tele-play: Rod Serling. ──▪ ──▪ ──▪

A court-martial of a brainwashed soldier who collaborates with his North Korean captors warns viewers that young Americans are ill-prepared to ward off communism. Decorated hero Captain Ed Hall admits that he publicly praised North Korea, signed written leaflets asking U.S. soldiers to surrender, and turned in fellow prisoners who were attempting to escape, but only after he was subjected to extreme physical and psychological torture. Hall is convicted, but the film leaves it to viewers to decide what, if any, punishment is warranted. *Picturing justice:* The prosecutor and defense attorney are admirable and effective, and the trial is entirely fair.

Family Law

About half of all marriages in the United States end in divorce. As a result, more people probably encounter the legal system in the context of family law than any other area of law. Often, the parties are bitter and the stakes are high. The disputes can involve divorce, property division, support, and child custody. The stories often feature betrayal, greed, and clashing values. Lawyers are necessary but may make a bad situation even worse. Because of the universality of these themes in our culture, divorce is the setting for countless movies, and many of them focus on family law and trials.

Divorce in the movies has had a tangled history. Numerous candid divorce stories were made in the silent movie era (such as Alfred Hitchcock's *Easy Virtue*) and in the early 1930s. However, Hollywood's system of self-censorship—the Production Code, which became binding in 1934—prohibited candid treatment of divorce. As "Sidebar: The Production Code" explains in Chapter 3, the code stifled serious treatment of divorce from 1934 until the 1960s. By the 1970s, filmmakers had returned to the subject of divorce. Ingmar Bergman led the way with *Scenes from a Marriage.* By the late 1970s, filmmakers created numerous fine movies centering on divorce, including *Kramer vs. Kramer, An Unmarried Woman,* and *Manhattan.* Contemporary cine-divorce sometimes turns into all-out war, as in *The War of the Roses,* where the spouses literally battle to the death over the family house.

Today, no-fault divorce exists everywhere in the United States so that couples cannot litigate about which of them committed adultery (that was a staple of earlier films from the pre-code fault era, such as *One More River* and *No Other Woman*). Today, the battleground is division of marital property, as in *It Could Happen to You* and *Laws of Attraction,* or child custody. In numerous custody films, including

Kramer vs. Kramer, Losing Isaiah, Evelyn, I Am Sam, The Good Mother, and *Man on Fire,* the judge always seems to get it wrong, suggesting that there must be a better way to resolve custody disputes than through nasty and adversarial trials.

Evelyn

Synopsis: A single father's crusade to regain custody of his children from an orphanage leads to a dramatic change in Irish law.

MGM, 2002. Color. Running time: 94 minutes.

Screenplay: Paul Pender. Director: Bruce Beresford.

Starring: Pierce Brosnan (Desmond Doyle).

Rating: ——■ ——■ ——■

The Story

In Dublin in 1953, Desmond and Charlotte Doyle are raising three children: Evelyn, who is seven, and two younger boys. When Charlotte runs off with another man and vanishes, the children are committed to Catholic orphanages because Desmond is unemployed and addicted to "the drink." Although some of the nuns are kindly, Evelyn is abused by Sister Brigid, who seems addicted to "the whipping."

Desmond gets his life back together and seeks to regain custody of his children. The minister of education refuses, pointing to a provision in the Children's Act that requires the consent of both living parents to withdraw children from a state facility. Desmond rounds up three terrific lawyers, who agree to work for free. The four toast justice and Saint Jude, the patron saint of hopeless cases.

Desmond's suit in the High Court (that is, the trial court) hits a dead end. The flinty Judge Ferris reads the law literally, ruling that both living parents must consent even if one of them has vanished. Thus, the children must remain in custody until they're sixteen. Desmond's lawyers file a writ of *habeas corpus* in the Irish Supreme Court and persuade the court to hold an evidentiary hearing. Although Judge Ferris is one of the three judges on the Supreme Court panel, the other two vote to invalidate the statute under the Irish constitution of 1937. Desmond is reunited with his children, and all the other orphans fantasize that they'll soon be going home too.

Evelyn: Desmond Doyle's lawyers, Tom Connolly (Alan Bates), Michael Beattie (Stephen Rea), and Nick Barron (Aidan Quinn), contemplate courtroom developments in the custody case of little Evelyn.

Legal Analysis

Michael Beattie, one of Desmond's lawyers, warns him that Irish family law is a cozy conspiracy between the Catholic Church and the state and that all the precedents are against them. Desmond says, "We'll make the bloody precedent. I want justice." Echoing a frequent message in courtroom films, Beattie replies, "The law and justice are two entirely different things." But in this uplifting film, the law delivers justice because the Irish constitution trumps the statute.

Statutory interpretation and judicial review. All courts are required to interpret statutes, because actual cases present situations that the legislature (here, the Irish parliament) never anticipated. Judges often debate whether they are allowed to depart from a law's literal language when it seems to produce an absurd result. Most modern judges would say that the word "parents" means only one "parent" when the other abandoned the children and cannot be found. Judges would try to understand the intent of the parliament that enacted the law, rather than give the law a literal but nonsensical interpretation. This approach would have avoided the need to apply the constitution.

Forced to resort to a constitutional attack, Desmond's lawyers focused on two provisions of the Irish constitution. Article 41 stated that parents and children have a fundamental and God-given right to the enjoyment of each other's mutual society. Article 42 stated that a blameless parent should not be deprived of his right to direct his child's education.

Declaring a statute unconstitutional was a daring step for the Irish Supreme Court in the 1950s. Irish law is derived from Britain, which has no written constitution and for centuries has maintained a tradition of parliamentary supremacy. Although Ireland had a constitution (adopted only nineteen years before the *Doyle* case), the judges were educated in the British tradition and were reluctant to invalidate a statute. Nevertheless, they did so, and their decision in the *Doyle* case became a landmark that established the supremacy of the Irish constitution over laws enacted by the parliament.

Striking a chord. Evelyn's whippings by the cruel Sister Brigid surely resonated with viewers in light of contemporaneous revelations of physical and sexual abuse of children by Catholic priests. These feelings were intensified by the way the abuse issue was treated during the Supreme Court hearing. Sister Brigid falsely testifies that Evelyn's bruises came from falling down the stairs. Wolfe, the government barrister, calls the dazzling Evelyn to the stand and tries to discredit her. Evelyn denies that she's lying, because that would violate the rule in the Ninth Commandment about bearing false witness. "I'm surprised you don't know that, as you're a lawyer," she tells Wolfe.

Picturing justice. As Evelyn concludes her testimony, the camera pulls back, isolating the tiny girl in the witness box, dwarfed by the huge and crowded courtroom. She repeats the prayer she'd said before coming to court: "Lord God, you guide the universe with wisdom and love. . . . Hear the prayer we make to you for our country, the beautiful country of Ireland. . . . May lasting peace be delivered, and truth and justice flourish. Amen." Truly the judges (and weeping viewers) would have to be made of iron not to be swayed by such eloquence.

Trial Briefs

1. The film's account of the *Doyle* case is basically correct, although a few departures from historical fact simplify the story and add to its dramatic appeal. For example, there was no harsh Judge Ferris; the

three trial judges were sympathetic to Desmond but felt that they had to interpret the statute literally. None of the Supreme Court justices had been previously involved in the case. The Supreme Court's decision was unanimous, not split. There had been a few previous cases in which the Supreme Court had applied the Irish constitution to invalidate a statute, but *Doyle* was the most conspicuous, and it is a true leading case in Irish law.

2. The personal story of *Evelyn* is more blarney than actual fact. In her memoir, *Tea and Green Ribbons,* Evelyn Doyle says she was never mistreated by the nuns. Her time in the orphanage (referred to as an industrial school) was quite happy. None of the reported judicial opinions in the *Doyle* case make any reference to physical abuse. Evelyn felt ambivalent about going home, because she disliked Desmond's new live-in girlfriend. Desmond couldn't marry the girlfriend because Ireland did not then permit divorce and Charlotte Doyle was apparently still alive.

3. The film leaves viewers wondering why the minister of education would oppose Desmond's request to take custody of the children. After all, the statute gave the minister discretion to release the children. It's costly to maintain children at state expense, and surely there were plenty of other orphans or needy kids who could have filled the beds.

The apparent reason for the minister's position emerges from Evelyn's memoir. It centers on Desmond's girlfriend, who was a member of the Church of England rather than Roman Catholic. The real back story of *Evelyn* is the collaboration of the Irish government in the Church's determination to keep the children away from a non-Catholic mother. If this theme had been introduced into the story, it would have deepened the political impact of the film and helped viewers understand what the minister of education was really up to. But perhaps the filmmakers figured they had gone quite far enough in attacking the Irish Church.

I Am Sam

Synopsis: A mentally retarded man fights to keep his parental rights.

New Line Cinema, 2001. Color. Running time: 132 minutes.

Screenplay: Kristine Johnson and Jessie Nelson. Director: Jessie Nelson.

Starring: Sean Penn (Sam Dawson), Dakota Fanning (Lucy Dawson), Michelle Pfeiffer (Rita Harrison).

Academy Award nomination: Best Actor (Sean Penn).

Rating: ⎯⎯▪ ⎯⎯▪

The Story

Sam Dawson is a mentally retarded single parent with the emotional and intellectual development of a seven-year-old. Sam works at Starbucks and is obsessed with the Beatles. His seven-year-old daughter, Lucy, holds herself back in school so she won't outstrip him. Without warning, social workers crash Lucy's birthday party, and their "present" is to place her into foster care and start proceedings to strip Sam of his parental rights.

Impressed by her firm's ad in the telephone book, Sam asks Rita Harrison to represent him. Harrison is a high-powered lawyer with no time for a nonpaying client or her son Willy, who like Lucy is seven. Harrison tries to get rid of Sam, but she reluctantly takes his case *pro bono* to save face with her friends.

In the juvenile-court hearing, county attorney Turner elicits Dr. Davis' opinion that a person with Sam's intellectual and emotional development cannot be a fit parent. Sam told her during their consultation that he had made huge mistakes in raising Lucy. Harrison gets Davis to admit that all parents make mistakes and sometimes find the task of parenting overwhelming. Of course, Harrison is really talking about herself and her own inability to handle Willy.

Lucy tries to stay with Sam by testifying to a few fibs, like denying that she told school friends that she was adopted. When Turner asks her whether deep down inside she knows that she needs more than her daddy, she quotes the Beatles song "All You Need Is Love." Luckily she didn't sing "We all live in a yellow submarine" or the judge would have been even more concerned about Sam's fitness.

Sam testifies that Lucy is better off living with him, but many of the questions confuse him. When Turner asks him how he can raise Lucy when she becomes older, Sam replies: "It's about constancy and it's about patience and it's about listening and it's about pretending to listen even when you can't listen anymore." Unfortunately, he refers to "Billy" rather than "Lucy" in his testimony, and Turner catches on that he's parroting lines from the film *Kramer vs. Kramer*. The judge orders that Lucy remain in foster care.

Lucy's foster parents, the Carpenters, love her and want to adopt her. But after Lucy repeatedly sneaks out at night to be with her dad, they return Lucy to Sam. The film ends happily but ambiguously at Lucy's soccer game. Sam is joyously coaching the team while Harrison, her son Willy, and the Carpenters cheer Lucy from the sidelines.

Legal Analysis

Reasonable people can disagree about whether Lucy would be better off staying with Sam or being raised by the Carpenters. However, the law does not permit the juvenile court to play God by yanking custody from parents just because richer and smarter alternatives are available. The court can remove a child from a parent's custody only if a serious risk of physical or emotional harm exists. Lucy is not at risk of any such damage. Thus, the county should be providing services to Sam and Lucy, not trying to break up a warm and loving family relationship.

Dependency proceedings. When a child must be removed from the custody of a parent, the juvenile court often places the child in foster care while ordering reunification services aimed at reuniting parent and child. In an extreme case, the court will terminate parental rights in order to free the child for adoption.

Parents who are threatened with the loss of parental rights are entitled to legal representation. In California, where the film is set, most parents involved in dependency cases are indigent and are represented by public defenders. A judge may appoint a separate lawyer to represent the child because a child's and a parent's best interests may conflict

In theory, dependency proceedings are informal and cooperative. But the film depicts just the opposite—a highly adversarial courtroom battle between two hard-charging lawyers. The question of who should raise Lucy should have been resolved in a nonadversarial manner that promotes compromise and creativity. For example, a disabled adult like Sam should be allowed to respond to gentle questions from a judge or other decision-maker, rather than being coached by his lawyer and verbally assaulted by the opposing lawyer.

Harrison and Turner. Like many female cine-lawyers, Rita Harrison cannot seem to manage either her professional life or her personal life. She frantically juggles clients, making false excuses to everybody for being late or for not finishing work on time. She lies to Sam and every one else. She throws tantrums at the office, drives insanely, and is abusive to her staff and to other lawyers. She's so materialistic that her friends burst out laughing at the very idea of her taking a *pro bono* case. On the personal level, Harrison's marriage is breaking up. She is completely incompetent at parenting, never finding any time for Willy and trying to bribe him with expensive gifts. She is, in short, a personal and professional disaster.

However exaggerated, the character of Rita Harrison will resonate especially with women lawyers who have to juggle parenthood with a high-powered law practice. Few human beings can successfully practice law sixty or eighty hours a week and also succeed as the primary caretaker of a young child. Some law firms have instituted "mommy tracks" so that parents can continue to practice law but work fewer hours; however, jumping onto the mommy track isn't generally considered a good career move. Other women have left law firms for government jobs or for working in-house for a corporation because these jobs have more predictable work demands (even if they pay less money).

County lawyer Turner, by contrast, is devoted to his thankless job of taking abused children away from their parents. He has to confront sexual abuse of children, and drug-addicted parents, on a daily basis. He's contemptuous of Harrison, who has never before come within miles of the dependency court. Turner tells her, "This is an award for you at some luncheon, but I'm here every day. You win, you're out the door. But you know who I see come back? The child. Only this time it's too late." Turner is rough and tough, but he's just doing his job.

***Pro bono* practice.** The film encourages lawyers to take cases for free by showing how Harrison's work for Sam redeems her and makes her more appreciative of her own son. Yet the film also sends a warning that *pro bono* work can be frustrating and time-consuming.

Picturing justice. Turner pounds away at Sam, asking him complex questions that he cannot possibly understand. Finally, Sam just gives up, uttering words that many victims of withering cross-examination have probably longed to say. "Okay, so no more now, okay? . . . I want to stop right now. This is the end of this for me, okay?"

It Could Happen to You

Synopsis: A promise to share a lottery ticket turns into history's largest tip.

TriStar Pictures, 1994. Color. Running time: 101 minutes.

Screenplay: Jane Anderson. Director: Andrew Bergman.

Starring: Nicolas Cage (Officer Charlie Lang), Bridget Fonda (Yvonne Biasi).

Rating: ——🔨 ——🔨

It Could Happen to You: Charlie Lang (Nicolas Cage, right) finds out that courts can be meaner than the streets.

The Story

Charlie Lang is a softhearted New York City cop who's married to Muriel, a shrill and materialistic hairdresser. When the Langs win four million dollars in the New York lottery, Muriel envisions a future of furs, jewels, and (viewers can hope) voice lessons. However, short of change for a tip, Charlie promised waitress Yvonne Biasi that she could have either a double tip the next day or a half share in his lottery ticket. Biasi chose the ticket, and Charlie believes that he has a moral obligation to keep his promise. Muriel has a different plan: "Stiff her and smell the flowers." Muriel agrees to the split only after Charlie assures her that her kindheartedness will bring her fame and even more fortune.

Charlie and Biasi fall in love while using their money to do good deeds all over town. Because Muriel has become even greedier—no mean feat—it's time for the divorce lawyers. Hale, Muriel's lawyer, is a shark who insists that Muriel is entitled to the entire four million dollars. Charlie's lawyer, Zakuto, is an ineffectual boob who is intimidated by the view from Hale's skyscraper law office. Muriel falsely testifies that she selected the winning numbers for the lottery ticket. Hale accuses Charlie of being a wife-beater and Biasi of being a bankrupt harlot. The jury awards Muriel the four million dollars, thrilling both her and local jewelers.

The verdict leaves Charlie and Biasi broke but happy. Soon they are rich and happy, as contributions pour in from strangers who appreciated all the good they had done. Meanwhile, Muriel is scammed out of all her money.

Legal Analysis

Like most fairy tales, the film has an ogre: the legal system. The law rewards Muriel's greed, and one lawyer is an unethical tyrant while the other lawyer is an ineffective whiner. The portrayal of law and lawyers makes the film's title seem more of a threat than a promise.

Was Charlie's promise to Biasi legally enforceable? Charlie acted nobly, but he was not legally required to split the lottery winnings with Biasi. To protect people who unthinkingly make rash promises, promises are legally enforceable only if "consideration" exists, meaning that an exchange of value has to occur. As Biasi gave up nothing of value in exchange for Charlie's promise (she had finished serving him), his promise was not legally binding. Nevertheless, once Charlie actually transfers the money to Biasi, he's made a binding gift and neither he, Muriel, nor the divorce court can revoke it.

Muriel vs. Charlie. New York is an "equitable distribution" state. This means that divorced couples usually split their property straight down the middle no matter which spouse earned it or which one "caused" the marriage to fall apart. However, judges can in the interests of justice award one spouse a larger share of a couple's marital property. For example, if a judge decided that Charlie squandered a share of the lottery winnings without Muriel's knowledge and without producing any tangible benefits, the judge might decide to award Muriel the lion's share of the remaining two million dollars. Here's where Charlie's hack lawyer, Zakuto, neglected a critical fact. At the media event at which Charlie and Muriel received the lottery check, they both told the world that they would share their winnings with Biasi. Because they jointly gave away the two million, Muriel is not entitled to any more of the remaining two million dollars than Charlie. The court should have awarded each of them one million.

Trial Briefs

1. New York did not allow winners of big lottery payouts to collect a lump sum in lieu of payments over a period of years until two years after the film was released.

2. As in most states, New York divorce cases are decided by a judge, not by a jury.

3. It not only could happen, but something very much like the film's story did happen to Bob Cunningham in 1984. Bob, a New York City detective, had no money for a tip. He asked his waitress, Phyllis Penza, to choose three numbers of his lottery ticket, promising to split the proceeds with her if the ticket was a winner. Bob won four million dollars and with the full support of his wife split the amount with Phyllis. At the time of the film, both Bob and Phyllis were retired and happily married to their respective spouses.

Kramer vs. Kramer

Synopsis: Mom runs off and seeks custody of her son when she returns.

Columbia Pictures, 1979. Color. Running time: 105 minutes.

Screenplay: Robert Benton. Novel: Avery Corman. Director: Robert Benton.

Starring: Dustin Hoffman (Ted Kramer), Meryl Streep (Joanna Kramer).

Academy Awards: Best Picture, Best Actor (Dustin Hoffman), Best Supporting Actress (Meryl Streep), Best Director, Best Adapted Screenplay.

Academy Award nominations: Best Supporting Actor (Justin Henry), Best Supporting Actress (Jane Alexander), Best Cinematography, Best Editing.

Rating:

The Story

As workaholic Ted Kramer moves up the ladder of success, his frustrated wife, Joanna, moves out. Ted ignores his boss' unsympathetic advice to send the couple's six-year-old son, Billy, to live with relatives

Kramer vs. Kramer: Joanna Kramer (Meryl Streep) fights for custody of her son.

and instead devotes himself to Billy. Ted's parenting skills improve from zero to sixty in a hurry, but all the time he spends on Billy forces him to neglect work. He's fired and ends up with a job that pays a lot less.

As unexpectedly as she left, Joanna reappears eighteen months later and seeks custody of Billy. Maybe she's upset that Ted allowed Billy to become seven and a half in her absence. Ted is determined to fight, but the trial bears out his lawyer's warning that courts tend to award custody of young children to mothers. Joanna testifies that she ran off because she was too depressed to care for Billy, but having gone through therapy and secured a good job, she is ready to raise him. Joanna readily admits that Ted was a good provider who was never abusive and who never drank or cheated. Ted's lawyer, Shaunessy, sarcastically comments, "I can certainly see why you left him." He then nastily attacks Joanna's character, forcing her to admit that she's had a series of boyfriends.

Ted's testimony challenges the idea that "a woman is a better parent simply by virtue of her sex." He and Billy have built a life together, and they love each other. Not to be out-nastied by Ted's lawyer, Joanna's lawyer tears into Ted for taking a lower-paying job and for failing to prevent Billy from injuring his eye.

The judge awards custody of Billy to Joanna. Ted prepares Billy to move, in a scene that must have quadrupled tissue sales. But Billy stays put because Joanna decides that he is better off with Ted.

Legal Analysis

Released during the first decade of what many called the women's liberation movement, *Kramer vs. Kramer* promoted both the idea that women should be freed from cultural shackles and the corollary idea that the legal system should not provide women with special advantages. It is all well and good for Joanna to find herself and embark on a satisfying career, but she shouldn't at the same time argue that she's entitled to custody of Billy simply because she's his mother. On the other hand, many so-called "difference feminists" would respond that the law should recognize differences between men and women and that the judge was right to award custody of Billy to Joanna because women are generally better parents to small children than men.

"Tender years" vs. "best interests." The New York judge hews to the traditional "tender years doctrine," which favors awarding custody of young children to mothers. However, New York had already rejected this doctrine by the time of the film, and it has since been discarded nearly everyplace else. Moreover, the judge misapplied the tender years doctrine, because it should apply only to an initial custody decision, not to a change in custody.

Today the laws of nearly all the states provide that the "best interests of the child" dictate custody decisions. Had the judge followed this principle, he would have awarded custody to Ted, because Ted was a perfectly fit custodian and a change in custodial arrangements could only be deeply disruptive to Billy. Perhaps an even more satisfactory outcome would have been for the judge to award Ted and Joanna joint physical and legal custody of Billy. Joanna and Ted would then have been expected to share responsibility for making the critical decisions in Billy's life, and Billy could have alternated living with each of them on a schedule that minimized disruption.

Hamlet without the ghost? Just as no production of *Hamlet* is complete without the ghost, the custody hearing should not be complete without input from Billy. Billy needn't testify, nor would the judge be bound to accede to Billy's wishes as to where he prefers to live. However, Billy's thoughts and experiences are certainly pertinent to custody, and the judge should have at least sought a report from a psychologist or a social worker who had talked to Billy and analyzed the family dynamics.

Boy-oh-boy friends. Shaunessy's questions about Joanna's lovers hearken back to an earlier time when society tended to condemn women who had sexual relations outside of marriage. However, Joanna's behavior is not immoral, and Shaunessy's questions are irrelevant and invasive of her privacy. In the absence of evidence suggesting that Joanna exposed Billy improperly to her sexual relationships, the judge should have protected Joanna from Shaunessy's attack.

Picturing justice. An enduring image of *Kramer vs. Kramer* is that of two snarling attorneys trying to demolish the opposing parent while ignoring what's best for little Billy. Viewers are left with the impression that the system of adversarial trials is just about the worst possible way to decide the sensitive question of which parent should get custody.

Trial Briefs

1. As explained in "Sidebar: The Production Code" in Chapter 3, Hollywood's system of self-censorship banned serious treatment of divorce and family law during the middle third of the twentieth century. When the code finally fizzled out, *Kramer vs. Kramer* was among the first movies to treat the subject of divorce seriously. It also effectively portrays a single father as a great parent, ranking with *To Kill a Mockingbird* in this respect.

2. Ted's testimony in the custody hearing was so memorable that it was memorized by Sam Dawson, the retarded father in *I Am Sam* who tried to hang on to custody of his little girl Lucy. Sam repeated it line for line on the stand, but he forgot to change the word "Billy" to "Lucy" and was caught by opposing counsel.

Losing Isaiah

Synopsis: A black drug user abandons her baby, then seeks to regain custody from his white adoptive parents.

Paramount Pictures, 1995. Color. Running time: 111 minutes.

Screenplay: Naomi Foner. Book: Seth Margolis. Director: Stephen Gyllenhaal.

Starring: Jessica Lange (Margaret Lewin), Halle Berry (Khaila Richards), Samuel L. Jackson (Kadar Lewis).

Rating: ——◾ ——◾

Losing Isaiah: Kadar Lewis (Samuel L. Jackson) and Khaila Richards (Halle Berry) fight for custody of Isaiah.

The Story

Khaila Richards, a black, crack-addicted mother, abandons her infant son, Isaiah, in a Dumpster. When Isaiah miraculously survives, Margaret and Charles Lewin, a well-to-do white couple, raise Isaiah and eventually adopt him

Four years later, Richards is through with jail and drugs. She has a job in child care, though her looks suggest that she ought to be in infomercials touting illegal drugs as beauty aids. Kadar Lewis, a black civil rights attorney, petitions to restore Richards' parental rights in an effort to "set legal precedent." Lewis helps Richards move into her own apartment and instructs her to abandon her boyfriend (though not in a Dumpster). Richards accuses Lewis of jealousy, but his motives are purely legal: "Don't flatter yourself. This goes way beyond you. Black babies belong with black mothers. I'm not going to let you do anything to mess it up."

At the hearing, Lewis' expert testifies that children should be raised by parents of the same race, even at the cost of stability. Lewis asks Margaret whether she wonders how "Isaiah must feel living in a world where he never sees anyone who looks like himself." Charles admits that he and Margaret haven't invited black friends to dinner. Finally, Richards testifies that she's drug-free and that a higher power has given her a second chance to raise Isaiah.

Caroline Jones, the Lewins' black lawyer, attacks Richards' parenting abilities: She doesn't know who Isaiah's father is, and most of her friends are former drug addicts. Jones' expert testifies that Isaiah needs the stability of the Lewins' household because he will probably always be emotionally disturbed.

Judge Silbowitz orders Isaiah returned to Richards. But Richards can't handle him, and weeks later Isaiah still screams for his mommy. Richards returns Isaiah to the Lewins for the time being, but she plans to remain involved in his life.

Legal Analysis

As in *Kramer vs. Kramer,* the judge's narrowly legalistic ruling sets up the film's emotional climax. Nevertheless, the film implicitly criticizes the judge and both lawyers. For them, the issue is black and white, so to speak; one party must win and the other must lose. The adversarial legal system seems incapable of responding to Isaiah's more nuanced emotional needs. By contrast, Margaret's and Richards' love for Isaiah enables them to find a solution to which the legal system is blind. However, the unrealistic conclusion sidesteps the important issues the film raises.

Fostering adoption. U.S. law regards raising children as a fundamental right of parenthood. As a result, social-welfare agencies that remove children from abusive or neglectful parents typically try to reunite families even if children languish for years in foster care while the efforts continue. The current perspective, however, emphasizes children's need for stability and permanence. If parents who abandon or severely harm their children can't demonstrate that they are likely to become fit parents in the near future, judges can terminate parental rights at once and free children for adoption. Under the new rules, Isaiah's adoption would probably have become final before he was a year old.

Déjà vu all over again. Even though the prospect of a hearing is gut-wrenching for the Lewins, Judge Silbowitz correctly gave Richards a chance to overturn the adoption decision. The only notice of the hearing on Isaiah's adoption was buried in a newspaper, meaning that even dedicated searchers for a good deal on a used exercycle would have had a hard time finding it. The county should have made some effort to find out who Isaiah's mother was and given her a chance to prove that she was going to turn her life around. Because no such effort was made and Richards filed a petition as soon as she realized that Isaiah was alive, she was entitled to her day in court. Ironically, the passage of four years probably improved Richards' chances of regaining custody of Isaiah, for by that time she had become a fit parent.

Interracial adoption. The film exposes important arguments about the role of race in adoptions. Some people argue passionately that any consideration of race in making adoption decisions should be a prohibited form of racial discrimination. Others believe that race should be a factor in making a determination about the "best interests" of a child, particularly in the case of white families seeking to adopt black children, because of the problems a black child may encounter when raised in a mostly white environment. The debate rages on in part because little satisfactory empirical evidence exists on either side of the question.

At the time of the film, racial factors were often considered in making the "best interests" determination. Indeed, in many states, placement of a child of color with a Caucasian family was possible only as a last resort. The result was that black children often languished for years in institutions or in foster care while waiting for black adoptive parents to come forward. However, federal laws passed in the mid-1990s forbid state child-welfare agencies to consider race or ethnicity when making "best interests" determinations. Only in exceptional cases involving the special needs of a child can these factors be lawfully taken into account, and in such cases the use of racial factors is subject to strict scrutiny by reviewing courts. However, these statutes apply only to state child-welfare agencies, not to private adoption agencies or to courts that are called on to resolve custody disputes as in the movie.

Losing tactics. Lewis makes a tactical error by introducing evidence that Charles once cheated on his wife. An isolated act of infidelity hardly undermines the Lewins' claim that their home is a safe and stable environment for Isaiah. Even worse, it deflects the judge's attention from the broader position that led Lewis to take the case in the first place, which is that a black child should be raised by a black parent.

Picturing justice. During a recess in the hearing, Margaret's white hand and Lewis' black hand are together as he helps her light a cigarette while they protect themselves from the rain. The image foreshadows the conclusion by suggesting that interracial cooperation is more likely to produce justice than the parties' adversarial courtroom arguments. But couldn't they cooperate by holding an umbrella instead of a cigarette?

Short Subjects

Big Daddy, 1999. Adam Sandler. ——■ ——■

Sonny Koufax, a clueless and boorish law school graduate, gains temporary custody of five-year-old Julian by pretending to be his father. When a child-welfare worker takes Julian away, a redeemed Koufax tries to convince a judge that he can raise Julian. *Courtroom highlights*: (1) Koufax asks his father, a respected lawyer, to conduct his direct examination because "nobody in this world thinks I shouldn't have a child more than this man. . . . If I can make a believer out of him, I can make a believer out of everyone in this court." The welfare agency's lawyer withdraws his objection after the father calls Koufax a moron. (2) Koufax's testimony about his love for Julian causes everyone in the courtroom to pull out cell phones and call their parents. *Picturing justice*: The female judge is harsh and unmoved by Koufax's emotional testimony and awards custody to the real father, who has never met Julian.

The Good Mother, 1988. Diane Keaton, Liam Neeson, Jason Robards. ——■ ——■

Anna Dunlap fights to retain custody of her daughter, Molly. Anna's ex-husband Brian, an uptight, prudish lawyer, seeks custody based on a claim that seemingly trivial and ambiguous sexual conduct occurred between Molly and Anna's live-in boyfriend, Leo Cutter. Anna's lawyer, Muth, advises her not to defend her uninhibited lifestyle and to instead blame Cutter for behaving inappropriately. Muth's strategy fails miserably. Anna ruins her relationship with Cutter, and the judge transfers custody to Brian despite a psychologist's contrary recommendation. As in other family-law films, such as *Losing Isaiah* and *Kramer vs. Kramer*, the judge abuses his discretion to decide what's in the "best interests of a child." *Picturing justice*: Muth imposes his values on Anna, and he doesn't even allow Cutter to explain his side of the story.

Intolerable Cruelty, 2003. George Clooney, Catherine Zeta-Jones.
——▪

Divorce lawyer Miles Massey engages in a battle of half-wits with an opposing client, Marylin Rexroth. *Picturing justice:* The lawyers are greedy, foolish, and wildly unethical. Some of them are repulsive, particularly the senior partner of Massey's firm, who lives on a feeding tube and croaks on about billable hours. *Legal analysis:* Underlying the film is the false premise that fault matters in California divorces. In fact, testimony about adultery or any other type of fault is strictly barred by California's no-fault divorce law. Rarely has a film's misrepresentation of applicable law been so intolerable.

Laws of Attraction, 2004. Pierce Brosnan, Julianne Moore. ——▪
Daniel Rafferty and Audrey Woods are vicious pit-bull divorce lawyers who regularly oppose each other in high-stakes cases while struggling unsuccessfully with their strong mutual attraction. As Rafferty and Woods battle over which nasty spouse gets to keep a castle in Ireland, their stale blarney is even less amusing than the occasional court sequences. This failed romantic comedy is a takeoff on *Adam's Rib* that doesn't even reach the kneecap.

Man on Fire, 1957. Bing Crosby, E. G. Marshall. ——▪ ——▪
Two years after agreeing that her ex-husband, Earl Carleton, could have sole custody of their seven-year-old son, Ted, Gwen sues for custody. After tactfully questioning Ted, Judge Randolph determines that Ted wants to stay with his dad and doesn't like Gwen or her husband. Perversely, Judge Randolph awards sole custody to Gwen so that Ted can bond with her. Thereafter, Ted ping-pongs back and forth between his parents, and Earl nearly steals him off to Europe. *Picturing justice:* (1) The camera's focus on the scales of justice outside the courtroom magnifies the seeming irrationality of the judge's decision. (2) Earl is represented by the highly professional Sam Dunstock and his associate Nina Wylie. A competent female attorney is rare in 1950s films. Of course, she falls in love with Earl.

A Map of the World, 1999. Sigourney Weaver, Julianne Moore.
——▪ ——▪

Robbie Mackessy, a troubled young student, accuses Alice Goodwin, a school nurse, of abuse. Halfway into a nervous breakdown anyway, Goodwin makes incriminating statements to the police. Defense lawyer Paul Reverdy's excellent fact investigation and cross-examination skills demolish the prosecution's case. Reverdy shows that Robbie charged Goodwin with committing sexual acts that he'd seen his own mother perform. *Courtroom highlight*: Goodwin surprises Reverdy during direct examination by revealing for the first time that she had slapped Robbie after he'd spat in her face. *Picturing justice*: Child abuse is a difficult crime both to prove or disprove in court, but the consequences of being charged with this crime can be catastrophic.

No Other Woman, 1933. Irene Dunne, Charles Bickford.

Made during the Great Depression, when many viewers were dirt poor, this film glorifies laborers and warned audiences that wealth corrupts the soul. Jim Stanley, a rugged steelworker, becomes a wealthy captain of industry. To allow Stanley to divorce Anna, the mill girl he married, Stanley's lawyer presents perjured testimony that Anna committed adultery and viciously cross-examines Anna when she denies it. The judge issues a divorce decree and awards Stanley sole custody of their son. *Courtroom highlight*: A rueful Stanley admits to the judge that he'd paid the witnesses to lie and that Anna is blameless. *Picturing justice*: Stanley goes to jail for perjury and a year later is back in the steel mill, happy and married to Anna. *Trial brief*: This picture was made before Hollywood's self-censorship system prohibited virtually all serious treatment of divorce and adultery. See "Sidebar: The Production Code" in Chapter 3.

One More River, 1934. Diana Wynyard. Novel: James Galsworthy.

The film condemns the now largely abandoned system of fault-based divorce. Claire Corven's husband, Sir Gerald, is publicly respectable but privately a sadist and a rapist. Claire cannot divorce him because she can't prove he committed adultery—the only ground for divorce in England in the 1930s. Yet when Sir Gerald seeks a divorce based on false claims that Claire committed adultery, she fights the divorce to protect her personal honor. Ironically, only by losing the case can Claire rid herself of Sir Gerald. *Courtroom highlight*: Mercilessly cross-examining Claire, Sir Gerald's attorney pounds away at her testimony that her postseparation friendship with Tony Croom was platonic. *Trial brief*: The film was directed by James Whale, who directed the original *Frankenstein* (1931) and whose life was the subject of the film *Gods and Monsters* (1998).

The Unfaithful, 1947. Lew Ayres, Ann Sheridan. ⎯⎯■ ⎯⎯■

Chris Hunter has an affair while her husband, Bob, serves in the military during World War II, then kills her paramour. The D.A. claims that Chris' motive was to prevent Bob from learning about the affair, while Chris claims that she killed in self-defense. The film is loosely based on the more atmospheric *The Letter* (1940), though if this later version had also been named after the incriminating evidence it would have been called *The Sculpture*. *Courtroom highlight*: The D.A. belligerently cross-examines Chris. *Picturing justice*: Larry Hannaford, Chris' defense attorney and Bob's good friend, forgoes a hefty fee by convincing the couple that they are better off together than divorced.

Why Do Fools Fall in Love?, 1998. Halle Berry, Larenz Tate. ⎯⎯■

Three women claim to be the surviving spouse of early rock-and-roller Frankie Lymon. Judge Lambrey patiently endures a paucity of written records and the women's *Rashomon*-like accounts of life with Lymon to pick a winner, but by then the film seems longer than Lymon's heroin-shortened life.

Notes

Introduction

Books on law in the movies: Asimow & Mader 2004; Black 2002; Chase 2002; Denvir 1996; Freeman 2005; Greenfield, Osborn & Robson 2001; Machura & Robson 2001; Sarat, Douglas & Umphrey 2005; Sherwin 2000.

Symposia in law journals on law and film: *New York Law School Law Review* 1999; *Nova Law Review* 2000; *Syracuse Law Review* 2003; *UCLA Law Review* 2001; *University of San Francisco Law Review* 1996; *Vermont Law Review* 2004; *Yale Law Review* 1989.

Articles on courtroom movie genre: Mezey & Niles 2005; Silbey 2001, 2002; Papke 2001.

Movies since 1980 portray most lawyers negatively. Asimow 2000b. Movies both reflect and influence public opinions about lawyers. Asimow 2000b.

Chapter 1. Courtroom Heroes

Chapter introduction: Lawyers as heroes. See Clark 1993; Rosenberg 1991; Greenfield 2001.

The Accused. Projansky 2001; Corcos 2003; Friendly 1984; Rangel 1984. *Brady v. Maryland,* 373 U.S. 83 (1963).

Ghosts of Mississippi. We thank Stephanie Hosea for her seminar paper on closing arguments. Vollers 1995; Lief, Caldwell & Bycel 1998 at 289; Russell 2003 at 1236-39, 1263-67. *Beckwith v. State,* 615 So.2d 1134 (1992); *Beckwith v. State,* 707 So.2d 547 (1998). Speedy trial cases: *Barker v. Wingo,* 407 U.S. 514 (1972); *Doggett v. United States,* 505 U.S. 647 (1992); *United States v. Lovasco,* 431 U.S. 783 (1977).

Judgment in Berlin. Stern 1984. Judge Stern"s opinion is reported in *United States v. Tiede & Ruske,* 86 Federal Rules Decisions 227 (U.S. Court for Berlin 1979).

The People vs. Larry Flynt. Smolla 1988. *Hustler Magazine v. Falwell,* 485 U.S. 46 (1988); *Leis v. Flynt,* 439 U.S. 438 (1979); *State v.*

Hustler Magazine, 1979 Ohio App. LEXIS 10141 (1979). Some of the information in the "trial briefs" came from Alan Isaacman.

To Kill a Mockingbird. Shaffer 1981a; Asimow & Mader 2004, ch. 3. *Strauder v. West Virginia,* 100 U.S. 303 (1879); *Batson v. Kentucky,* 476 U.S. 79 (1986). On the Scottsboro Boys, see *Powell v. Alabama,* 287 U.S. 45 (1932); *Norris v. Alabama,* 294 U.S. 587 (1935); Goodman 1994.

12 Angry Men. Clover 1998; Papke 2001; Asimow & Mader 2004, ch. 9. The survey about Americans' views of the jury system is published in American Bar Association 1999.

Young Mr. Lincoln. Ford 1998, at 137–39 (story of how Ford persuaded Fonda to play Lincoln); Steiner 1997 (information about Lincoln's law practice).

Chapter 2. Injustice for All

A Dry White Season. Abel 1995.

In the Name of the Father. Rasul v. Bush, 542 U.S. 466 (2004). Victory 2002; Greenfield, Osborn & Robson 2001 at 62 64; Bennett 1994; Travis 1994.

Let Him Have It. The 1998 decision pardoning Derek Bentley is available on the Internet at http://www.innocent.org.uk/cases/derek-bentley/judgement.htm. Bentley 1995; Pook 1993.

A Man for All Seasons. Herbruggen 1983, Marius 1995, Kinsella 1985; Morant 2004.

10 Rillington Place. Kennedy 1961. *Atkins v. Virginia,* 536 U.S. 304 (2002).

The Wrong Man. "All Around Town with 'The Wrong Man,'" *New York Times,* April 29, 1956; "Court Is Turned into a Movie Set," *New York Times,* April 9, 1956.

Chapter 3. Experts or Charlatans?

Chapter introduction: *Daubert v. Merrell Dow Pharmaceuticals,* 501 U.S. 579 (1993).

Anatomy of a Murder. Asimow 2005.

Sidebar: The Production Code. *Mutual Film Corp. v. Ohio Industrial Commission,* 236 U.S. 230 (1915); *Joseph Burstyn, Inc. v. Wilson,* 343 U.S. 495 (1952). Sklar 1994; Asimow 2000a; Doherty 1999.

A Cry in the Dark. Special thanks to Penny Pether, Ian Barker QC, Damien Considine, Ysaiah Ross, Rick Mohr, Gary Edmond, and Cassandra Sharp. Chamberlain 1991; Crispin 1987; Cockburn 1992; *Daubert v. Merrell Dow Pharmaceuticals,* 501 U.S. 579 (1993). The

Federal Court opinion is reported at (1983) 72 FLR 1. The High Court case is reported at (1983) 153 CLR 521. After Lindy's release, the Royal Commission issued a report. The citation is 22/5/1987, report of Morling J, printed by the Legislative Assembly of N.T., Government Printer no. ISBN 0-7245-1298-5. An extensive website of materials on the Chamberlain case is http://www.law.umkc.edu/faculty/projects/ftrials/chamberlain/chamberlainlinks.html.

Inherit the Wind. Larson 1997; Ginger 1958; Lee 2004. *Epperson v. Arkansas,* 393 U.S. 97 (1968); *Edwards v. Aguillard,* 482 U.S. 578 (1987); *Scopes v. State,* 154 Tenn. 105 (1927).

Presumed Innocent. Corcos 1997.

Primal Fear. Palmer 1982; Saks 2001; Orr 1999. Illinois Supreme Court Rule 413(d); *People v. Houser,* 712 N.E.2d 355 (1999). Thanks to Steven Lubet, Tom Geraghty, and Lawrence Marshall of Northwestern University Law School for help with Illinois criminal procedure.

Chapter 4. Courtroom Comedies

Adam's Rib. Buchanan 1998; Freeman 1991; Hartog 1997; Ireland 1989.

The Castle. Kelo v. City of New London, 125 S.Ct. 2655 (2005); *Mabo v. State of Queensland (No. 2)* (1992) 175 CLR 1.

Chapter 5. Corruption of Justice

Chicago. Evans 1998; Fowler 1931; Schulte-Sasse 2004. On William J. Fallon, Nevins 2005, pp. 113–22.

Judgment at Nuremberg. Müller 1991 (describing Katzenberger case at pp. 113–15); Papke 2001; Shale 1996; DeLage 2005; "War Crimes" (*Newsweek*) 1949; Taylor 1949; "Finis" (*Time*) 1949. *Buck v. Bell,* 274 U.S. 200 (1927) (the case cited by Rolfe in which the U.S. Supreme Court once upheld a law sterilizing the feeble-minded).

The Life of Emile Zola. Bredin 1986; Snyder 1973. *New York Times v. Sullivan,* 376 U.S. 254 (1964). Thanks to Bill McGovern for help with the French law of criminal libel.

Murder in the First. Farber 1995; *New York Times,* 1995; Lunes 1995; Stack 1995.

The Star Chamber. Special thanks to Judge Robert Altman (whom Michael Douglas used as a model for this film).

Chapter 6.
It's Just a Bunch of Circumstantial Evidence

Chapter introduction: Bergman 1996b.
Fury. Nash & Ross 1987; Mnookin & West 2001.

Chapter 7. Uncivil Actions

Chapter introduction: Asimow & Mader 2004, ch. 11; Weisberg 2000.
A Civil Action. Harr 1996; Schlichtmann 1999; Facher 1999; Chase 2002, pp. 113–16. *Anderson v. Cryovac,* 862 F. 2d 910 (1st Cir. 1988) (finding that Facher violated discovery rules).
Class Action. Asimow & Mader 2004, ch. 12; Schwartz 1991.
Mr. Deeds Goes to Town. Schickel 1999, pp. 61–78; Sklar 1994, pp. 205–14.
The Rainmaker. Asimow 2001; Pendo 2004. Limitation of punitive damage awards: *State Farm Mutual Auto Insurance Co. v. Campbell,* 538 U.S. 408 (2003). Ambulance-chasing: *Ohralik v. Ohio State Bar Assoc.,* 436 U.S. 447 (1978) (upholding Bar rule banning face-to-face solicitation of accident victims); *Florida Bar v. Went for It, Inc.,* 515 U.S. 618 (1995).
Sidebar: John Grisham's Lawyers. Owens 2001; Simon 2001; Scheinberg 1998
Runaway Jury. Current information on gun litigation: www .gunlawsuits.org.
The Verdict. Reed 1980; Weisberg 2000; Mezey & Niles 2005, pp. 153–61; Bergman 2001; Chase 2002, pp. 105–7; Denvir 2005; Greenfield, Osborn & Robson 2001, ch. 4.
North Country. Jenson v. Eveleth Taconite Co., 130 F.3d 1287 (8th Cir. 1997).

Chapter 8. Familiarity Breeds Contempt (of Court)

Music Box. Chutkow 1989.
The Paradine Case. Perry 2004; Sinyard 1986.
Sidebar: Memorable Courtroom Demonstrations. Bergman 1996a.

Chapter 9. Prejudice on Trial

Amistad. Cable 1971; Tripp 2003; LeBel 2002. http://mysticseaport .org (website consisting of documents in *Amistad* case). The *Amistad* decision is reported in 40 U.S. 518 (1841).

Philadelphia. On sociology of legal profession, Heinz & Laumann 1982; Asimow & Mader 2004, ch. 13. *Cain v. Hyatt,* 734 F. Supp. 671 (E.D. Pa. 1990).

Pinky. Cimeno 1974, pp. 59–62; Kazan 1988, pp. 374–78.

Snow Falling on Cedars. Aoki 2001; Aoki 1998. *Korematsu v. United States,* 323 U.S. 214 (1944); *Ex Parte Endo,* 323 U.S. 283 (1944); *Korematsu v. United States,* 584 F. Supp. 1406 (N.D. Calif. 1984). Another film about the internment camps: *Come See the Paradise* (1990).

Sommersby. Binder 2004 at p. 120; Smith 1993.

They Won't Forget. Oney 2003. *The Murder of Mary Phagan* (1988) is a docudrama about the Leo Frank case. Jack Lemmon starred as Governor Slaton. *Frank v. Mangum,* 237 U.S. 309 (1915), upheld the Leo Frank conviction. The Georgia Supreme Court considered the case three times in 1914, in each case upholding the trial court's decision. 141 Ga. 243, 142 Ga. 617, 142 Ga. 741.

A Time to Kill. Batson v. Kentucky, 476 U.S. 79 (1986) (bans racial peremptory challenges). Mississippi Rules of Professional Conduct, Rule 1.6 (disclosure of confidential client information); Mississippi Code §99-15-35 (change of venue).

Chapter 10. The Death Penalty

Chapter introduction: Asimow & Mader 2004, ch. 11; Sarat 1999; Harding 2005.

Beyond a Reasonable Doubt. Bergman 1996b.

Compulsion. McKernan 1924; Levin 1956.

I Want to Live! Howard 2004; Asimow & Mader 2004, ch. 11; Sarat 1999; Foster 1997. *People v. Santo,* 43 Cal.2d 319, 273 P.2d 294 (Calif. Supr. Court 1954); *Graham v. Teats,* 223 F.2d 680 (9th Cir. 1955).

Knock on Any Door. Sperber & Lax 1997.

Sidebar: Character Evidence. See Federal Rules of Evidence 404–5 and 412–15.

Chapter 11. Military Justice

Breaker Morant. Bleszynski 2005; Fox 1902; Denton 1973; Pakenham 1979; Kershen 1997; Kirschke 2004; *Washington Post* 1981.

A Few Good Men. Weaver 1992; Weinraub 1992; Phelps 1993; Glauber 1994. Our thanks to Major Jeff Hagler, Colonel James Gerstenlauer, Robinson Everett, David A. Brahms, Chief Judge Gene

Sullivan (U.S. Court of Appeals for the Armed Forces), Major Nancy LaLuntas, and Christopher J. Steritt.

Paths of Glory. Whitney 1998; Robert Barr Smith 1997; Leonard V. Smith 1991; Oram 2003, pp. 11–14. Special thanks to Major Jeff Hagler and to Leonard V. Smith.

Town Without Pity. Estrich 1986; Norman 1996; Gher 2002. *Coker v. Georgia,* 433 U.S. 584 (1977).

Chapter 12. Family Law

Chapter introduction: Asimow 2000a.

Evelyn: Doyle 2002. The original High Court decision is reported in *In re Doyle* [1956] Irish Reports 217. The decision of the Irish Supreme Court was not reported until more than thirty years after it was rendered. *In re Doyle* [1989] Irish Law Rep. Monthly 277. The original High Court decision is reported in *In re Doyle* [1956] Irish Reports 217.

I Am Sam. Thanks to Rob Waring and LeAnn Bischoff. Thanks also to Carrie Menkel-Meadow, Lev Ginsberg, and Leesa Sylyski, whose reviews of this film are posted on the Picturing Justice website (www.picturingjustice.com). The applicable dependency statute is California Welfare & Institutions Code section 300.

Kramer vs. Kramer. Asimow 2000a.

Losing Isaiah. Bartholet 1991; O'Keefe 1991. *In the Interest of Ashley K.,* 571 N.E.2d 905 (Ill. Ct. App. 1991). Thanks to Joan Hollinger.

Bibliography

Abel, Richard L. 1995. *Politics by Other Means: Law in the Struggle Against Apartheid.* New York: Routledge.

American Bar Association. 1999. *Perceptions of the U.S. Justice System.* Chicago: American Bar Association.

Aoki, Keith. 1998. "No Right to Own? The Early Twentieth-Century 'Alien Land Laws' as a Prelude to Internment." *Boston College Law Review* 40:37.

———. 2001. "Is Chan Still Missing? An Essay About the Film *Snow Falling on Cedars* and Representations of Asian Americans in U.S. Films." *UCLA Asian Pacific American Law Journal* 7:30.

Asimow, Michael. 2000a. "Divorce in the Movies: From the Hays Code to *Kramer vs. Kramer.*" *Legal Studies Forum* 24:221.

———. 2000b. "Bad Lawyers in the Movies." *Nova Law Review* 24:533.

———. 2001. "Embodiment of Evil: Law Firms in the Movies." *UCLA Law Review* 48:1339.

———. 2005. "Popular Culture and the American Adversarial Ideology." In *Law and Popular Culture*, ed. Michael Freeman. Oxford: Oxford University Press.

Asimow, Michael, and Shannon Mader. 2004. *Law and Popular Culture: A Course Book.* New York: Peter Lang.

Bartholet, Elizabeth. 1991. "Where Do Black Children Belong? The Politics of Race Matching in Adoption." *University of Pennsylvania Law Review* 139:1163.

Bennett, Ronan. 1994. "The Big Screen Trial of the Guildford Four." *The Observer,* February 6, p. 2.

Bentley, Iris. 1995. *Let Him Have Justice.* London: Sidgwick & Jackson.

Bergman, Paul. 2001. "The Movie Lawyer's Guide to Redemptive Legal Practice." *UCLA Law Review* 48:1393.

———. 1996a. "Pranks for the Memory." *University of San Francisco Law Review* 30:1235.

———. 1996b. "A Bunch of Circumstantial Evidence." *University of San Francisco Law Review* 30:985.

Binder, Guyora. 2004. "The Origins of American Felony Murder Rules." *Stanford Law Review* 57:59.

Black, David A. 2002. *Law in Film: Resonance and Representation*. Urbana: University of Illinois Press.

Bleszynski, Nick. 2005. *Shoot Straight You Bastards*. http://www.lighthorse.org.au/military/bushveldt.htm (last visited in February 2005).

Bredin, Jean-Denis. 1986. *The Affair: The Case of Alfred Dreyfus*. New York: G. Braziller.

Buchanan, Deena. 1998. "Strange Bedfellows? Married Lawyers and Conflicts of Interest." *Georgetown Journal of Legal Ethics* 11:753.

Cable, Mary. 1971. *Black Odyssey: The Case of the Slave Ship "Amistad."* New York: Viking Press.

Chamberlain, Lindy. 1991. *Through My Eyes: An Autobiography*. London: Heinemann.

Chase, Anthony. 2002. *Movies on Trial*. New York: New Press.

Chutkow, Paul. 1989. "From the 'Music Box' Emerges the Nazi Demon." *New York Times*, December 24, sec. 2, p. 11, col. 1.

Cimeno, Michael. 1974. *Kazan on Kazan*. New York: Viking Press.

Clark, Gerald J. 1993. "The Lawyer as Hero." In *The Lawyer and Popular Culture: Proceedings of a Conference,* ed. David Gunn. Littleton, Colo.: F. B. Rothman.

Clover, Carol J. 1998. "God Bless Juries." In *Refiguring American Film Genres*. Edited by Nick Browne. Berkeley and Los Angeles: University of California Press.

Cockburn, Robert. 1992. "Dingo Baby Couple Wins 540,000 Pounds." *The Times* (London), May 26.

Corcos, Christine Alice. 1997. "Presuming Innocence: Alan Pakula and Scott Turow Take on the Great American Legal Fiction." *Oklahoma City University Law Review* 22:129.

———. 2003. "'We Don't *Want* Advantages': The Woman Lawyer Hero and Her Quest for Power in Popular Culture." *Syracuse Law Review* 53:1225, 1263–67.

"Corrections." 1994. *New York Times*, April 6, sec. A, p. 2.

Crispin, Ken. 1987. *Lindy Chamberlain: The Full Story*. Sydney: Pacific Press Publishing Association.

DeLage, Christian. 2005. "Image as Evidence and Mediation: The Experience of the Nuremberg Trials." In *Law and Popular Culture,* ed. Michael Freeman. Oxford: Oxford University Press.

Denton, Kit. 1973. *The Breaker*. New York: Washington Square Press.

Denvir, John, ed. 1996. *Legal Reelism: Movies as Legal Texts*. Urbana: University of Illinois Press.

———. 2005. "What Movies Can Teach Law Students." In *Law and Popular Culture*. ed. Michael Freeman. Oxford: Oxford University Press.

Doherty, Thomas. 1999. *Pre-Code Hollywood: Sex, Immorality, and Insurrection in American Cinema, 1930–34.* New York: Columbia University Press.

Doyle, Evelyn. 2002. *Tea and Green Ribbons.* New York: Free Press.

Estrich, Susan. 1986. "Rape." *Yale Law Journal* 95:1087.

Evans, Colin. 1998. *Super Lawyers: 40 Top Lawyers and the Cases That Made Them Famous.* Detroit: Visible Ink Press.

Facher, Jerome P. 1999. "The View from the Bottomless Pit: Truth, Myth, and Irony in *A Civil Action.*" *Seattle University Law Review* 23:243.

Farber, J. Stephen. 1995. "A Drama That Puts Alcatraz on Trial." *New York Times,* January 15, sec. 2, p. 12.

"Finis." 1949. *Time,* April 25.

Ford, Dan. 1998. *Pappy: The Life of John Ford.* New York: De Capo Press.

Foster, Teree. 1997. "*I Want to Live!* Federal Judicial Values in Death Penalty Cases." *Oklahoma City University Law Review* 22:63.

Fowler, Gene. 1931. *The Great Mouthpiece: A Life Story of William J. Fallon.* New York: Grosset.

Fox, Sir Frank. 1902. *Bushman and Buccaneer.* Sydney: H.T. Dunn.

Freeman, Kathleen. 1991. "On the Killing of Eratosthenes the Seducer." In *The Murder of Herodes and Other Trials from the Athenian Law Courts.* New York: Legal Classics Library.

Freeman, Michael, ed. 2005. *Law and Popular Culture.* Oxford: Oxford University Press.

Friendly, Jonathan. 1984. "The New Bedford Rape Case: Confusion over Accounts of Cheering at Bar." *New York Times,* April 11, sec. 1, p. 19.

Gher, Jaime. 2002. "Status of Forces Agreements: Tools to Further Effective Foreign Policy and Lessons to Be Learned from the U.S.-Japan Agreement." *University of San Francisco Law Review* 37:227.

Ginger, Ray. 1958. *Six Days or Forever? Tennessee v. John Thomas Scopes.* Oxford: Oxford University Press.

Glauber, Bill. 1994. "Ex-Marine Who Felt 'A Few Good Men' Maligned Him Is Mysteriously Murdered." *Baltimore Sun,* April 10, p. 1.

Goodman, James. 1994. *Stories of Scottsboro.* New York: Vintage Books.

Greenfield, Steven. 2001. "Hero or Villain? Cinematic Lawyers and the Delivery of Justice." In *Law and Film,* ed. Stefan Machura and Peter Robson. Oxford: Blackwell.

Greenfield, Steven, Guy Osborn, and Peter Robson. 2001. *Film and the Law.* London: Cavendish.

Harding, Roberta. 2005. "Reel Violence: Popular Culture and Concerns About Capital Punishment in Contemporary American Society." In *Law and Popular Culture,* ed. Michael Freeman. Oxford: Oxford University Press.

Harr, Jonathan. 1996. *A Civil Action.* New York: Vintage Books.

Hartog, Hendrik. 1997. "Lawyering, Husbands' Rights, and the 'Unwritten Law' in Nineteenth-Century America." *Journal of American History* 84:67.

Heinz, John P., and Edward O. Laumann. 1982. *Chicago Lawyers: The Social Structure of the Bar.* Chicago: Northwestern University Press.

Herbruggen, Hubertus Schulte. 1983. "The Process Against Sir Thomas More." *Law Quarterly Review* 99:113.

Hoff, Timothy, ed. 1994. "Symposium: *To Kill a Mockingbird.*" *Alabama Law Review* 45:389-594.

Howard, Clark. 2004. *Barbara Graham*, electronically published by Court TV's Crime Library, http://www.crimelibrary.com/classics/graham1 (last visited in January 2005).

Ireland, Robert M. 1989. "The Libertine Must Die: Sexual Dishonor and the Unwritten Law in the Nineteenth-Century United States." *Journal of Social History* 23:27.

Kazan, Elia. 1988. *Elia Kazan: A Life.* London: Andrew Deutsch.

Kennedy, Ludovic. 1961. *Ten Rillington Place.* New York: Simon & Schuster.

Kershen, Drew L. 1997. "Breaker Morant." *Oklahoma City University Law Review* 22:107.

Kinsella, William. 1985. "Thomas More: A Man for Our Time." *Catholic Lawyer* 29:323.

Kirschke, James. 2004. "Breaker Morant: Guilty or Not Guilty? The Film and the Historical Record." *Rocky Mountain Review of Language and Literature.*

Larson, Edward J. 1997. *Summer for the Gods: The Scopes Trial and America's Continuing Debate over Science and Religion.* New York: Basic Books.

"Law and Humanities: Symposium on the Image of Law(yers) in Popular Culture." 2003. *Syracuse Law Review* 53:1161.

"Law and Popular Culture." 2000. *Nova Law Review* 24:527.

LeBel, Paul A. 2002. "Misdirecting Myths: The Legal and Cultural Significance of Distorted History in Popular Media." *Wake Forest Law Review* 37:1035.

Lee, Kevin P. 2004. "Inherit the Myth: How William Jennings Bryan's Struggle with Social Darwinism and Legal Formalism Demythologize the Scopes Monkey Trial." *Capital University Law Review* 33:347.

Levin, Meyer. 1956. *Compulsion*. New York: Simon & Schuster.

Lief, Michael S., H. Mitchell Caldwell, and Ben Bycel. 1998. *Ladies and Gentlemen of the Jury: Greatest Closing Arguments in Modern Law*. New York: Scribner.

Lunes, Gregory. 1995. "Truth Comes Last in Murder in the First." *Dallas Morning News,* March 10.

Machura, Stefan, and Peter Robson. 2001. *Law and Film*. Oxford: Blackwell.

Marius, Richard. 1995. "A Man for All Seasons." In *Past Imperfect: History According to the Movies,* ed. Mark C. Carnes. New York: Henry Holt.

McKernan, Maureen. 1924. *The Amazing Crime and Trial of Leopold and Loeb*. Chicago: Plymouth Court Press. Reprinted 1996 by Gaunt, Inc.

Mezey, Naomi, and Mark C. Niles, 2005. "Screening the Law: Ideology and Law in American Popular Culture." *Columbia Journal of Law and the Arts* 28:91.

Mnookin, Jennifer L., and Nancy West. 2001. "Theaters of Proof: Visual Evidence and the Law in *Call Northside 777*." *Yale Journal of Law and the Humanities* 13:329.

Morant, Blake. 2004. "Lessons from Thomas More's Dilemma of Conscience: Reconciling The Clash Between a Lawyer's Beliefs and Professional Expectations." *St. John's Law Review* 78:965.

Müller, Ingo. 1991. *Hitler's Justice: The Courts of the Third Reich*. Cambridge: Harvard University Press.

Nash, Jay Robert, and Stanley Ralph Ross. 1987. *The Motion Picture Guide, 1927–1983*. Chicago: Cinebooks.

Nevins, Francis M. 2005. "When Celluloid Lawyers Started to Speak: Exploring Juriscinema's First Golden Age." In *Law and Popular Culture,* ed. Michael Freeman. Oxford: Oxford University Press.

Norman, Adam. 1996. "The Rape Controversy: Is a Revision of the Status of Forces Agreement with Japan Necessary?" *Indiana International and Comparative Law Review* 6:717.

O'Keefe, James G. 1991. "The Need to Consider Children's Rights in Biological Parent v. Third-Party Custody Disputes." *Chicago-Kent Law Review* 67:1077.

Oney, Steve. 2003. *And the Dead Shall Rise: The Murder of Mary Phagan and the Lynching of Leo Frank*. New York: Pantheon Books.

Oram, Gerald Christopher. 2003. *Military Executions During World War I*. New York: Palgrave.

Orr, Juliette K. 1999. "Multiple-Personality Disorder and the Criminal Court." *Southwestern University Law Review* 28:651.

Owens, John B. 2001. "Grisham's Legal Tales: A Moral Compass for the Young Lawyer." *UCLA Law Review* 48:1431.

Pakenham, Thomas. 1979. *The Boer War.* New York: Random House.

Palmer, Richard. 1982. "Disposition of the Mentally-Ill Offender in Illinois—'Guilty But Mentally Ill.'" *DePaul Law Review* 31:869.

Papke, David Ray. 2001. "Law, Cinema, and Ideology: Hollywood Legal Films of the 1950s." *UCLA Law Review* 48:1473.

Pendo, Elizabeth A. 2004. "Images of Health Insurance in Popular Film: The Dissolving Critique." *Journal of Health Law* 37:267.

Perry, Dennis R. 2004. "Hitchcock's Archetypes in *The Paradine Case.*" Unpublished paper.

Phelps, Dan. 1993. "A Few Good Men." *Needham Times*, February.

Pook, Sally. 1993. "Bentley Given Part Pardon 40 Years After Being Hanged." *Daily Telegraph,* July 31, p. 7.

Projansky, Sarah. 2001. *Watching Rape: Film and Television in Postfeminist Culture.* New York: New York University Press.

Rangel, Jesus. 1984. "Two Are Convicted in New England Rape Case." *New York Times,* March 18, sec. 1, p. 1.

Reed, Barry. 1980. *The Verdict.* New York: Simon & Schuster.

Rosenberg, Norman L. 1991. "Young Mr. Lincoln: The Lawyer as Super-Hero." *Legal Studies Forum* 15:215.

Russell, Margaret M. 2003. "Cleansing Moments and Retrospective Justice." *Michigan Law Review* 101:1225.

Saks, Elyn. 2001. "Multiple-Personality Disorder and Criminal Responsibility." *Southern California Interdisciplinary Law Journal* 10:186.

Sarat, Austin. 1999. "The Cultural Life of Capital Punishment. Responsibility and Representation in *Dead Man Walking* and *Last Dance.*" *Yale Journal of Law and the Humanities* 11:153.

Sarat, Austin, Lawrence Douglas, and Martha Merrill Umphrey. 2005. *Law on the Screen.* Stanford, Calif.: Stanford University Press.

Scheinberg, Pauline. 1998. *Grisham's Law.* UCLA law student paper on file with the authors.

Schickel, Richard. 1999. *Matinee Idylls.* Chicago: Ivan R. Dee.

Schlichtmann, Jan Richard. 1999. "To Tell the Truth." *American Bar Association Journal,* March, 85:100.

Schulte-Sasse, Linn. 2004. "All That Jazz: *Chicago*'s Indictment of Our Legal System." UCLA Law Student paper on file with authors.

Schwartz, Gary T. 1991. "The Myth of the Ford Pinto Case." *Rutgers Law Review* 44:1013.

Shaffer, Thomas L. 1981a. "The Moral Theology of Atticus Finch." *University of Pittsburgh Law Review* 42:181.

———. 1981b. *On Being a Christian and a Lawyer.* Provo, Utah: Brigham Young University Press.

Shale, Suzanne. 1996. "The Conflicts of Law and the Character of Men: Writing *Reversal of Fortune* and *Judgment at Nuremberg."* *University of San Francisco Law Review* 30:991.

Sherwin, Richard K. 2000. *When Law Goes Pop.* Chicago: University of Chicago Press.

Silbey, Jessica. 2001. "Patterns of Courtroom Justice." *Journal of Law and Society* 28:97.

———. 2002. "What Do We Do When We Do Law and Popular Culture?" *Law and Social Inquiry* 27:139.

Simon, William. 2001. "Moral Pluck: Legal Ethics in Popular Culture." *Columbia Law Review* 101:421.

Sinyard, Neil. 1986. *The Films of Alfred Hitchcock.* New York: Gallery Books.

Sklar, Robert. 1994. *Movie-Made America.* New York: Vintage Books.

Smith, J. Clay. 1993. *Emancipation: The Making of the Black Lawyer, 1844-1944.* Philadelphia: University of Pennsylvania Press.

Smith, Leonard V. 1991. "The Disciplinary Dilemma of French Military Justice, September 1914-April 1917." *Journal of Military History* 55:47.

Smith, Robert Barr. 1997. "What Price Propaganda? When the *Paths of Glory* Led But to the Pulpit." *Oklahoma City Law Review* 22:89.

Smolla, Rodney. 1988. *Jerry Falwell v. Larry Flynt: The First Amendment on Trial.* New York: St. Martin's Press.

Snyder, Louis L. 1973. *The Dreyfus Case: A Documentary History.* New Brunswick, N.J.: Rutgers University Press.

Sperber, A. M., and Eric Lax. 1997. *Bogart.* New York: William Morrow.

Stack, Peter. 1995. "Ex Con Disputes Film's Tale of the Rock." *San Francisco Chronicle,* January 21.

Steiner, Mark E. 1997. "Lawyers and Legal Change in Antebellum America: Learning from Lincoln." *University of Detroit Mercy Law Review* 74:427.

Stern, Herbert J. 1984. *Judgment in Berlin.* New York: Universe Books.

"Symposium: Film and the Law." 1997. *Oklahoma City University Law Review* 22:1.

"Symposium: Law and Popular Culture." 2001. *UCLA Law Review* 48:1293.

"Symposium: Law in Film/Film in Law." 2004. *Vermont Law Review* 28:797.

"Symposium: Law/Media/Culture." 1999. *New York Law School Law Review* 43:653.

"Symposium: Picturing Justice." 1996. *University of San Francisco Law Review* 30:891.

"Symposium: Popular Legal Culture." 1989. *Yale Law Journal* 98:1545.

Taylor, Telford. 1949. "Nuremberg Trials: War Crimes and International Law." *International Conciliation,* April, p. 286.

Travis, Alan. 1994. "The Report: Process Attacked from Beginning to End." *The Guardian,* July 1, p. 2.

Tripp, Bernell E. 2003. "The Case of the Amistad Mutiny." In *Illusive Shadows: Justice, Media, and Socially Significant American Trials,* ed. L. Chiasson. Westport, Conn.: Praeger.

Victory, Patrick. 2002. *Justice and Truth: The Guildford Four and Maguire Seven.* London: Sinclair-Stevenson.

Vollers, Maryanne. 1995. *Ghosts of Mississippi.* Boston: Little Brown & Co.

"War Crimes: The Last Judgments." 1949. *Newsweek.* April 25, p. 36.

Washington Post. 1981. August 9, Style sec. p. 1.

Weaver, Jacqueline. 1992. "Stage to Screen: Branford Lawyer's Story Told." *New York Times,* Connecticut ed., November 8, sec. 13 CN, p. 12, col. 3.

Weinraub, Bernard. 1992. "Film: Reiner's March to a Few Good Men." *New York Times,* December 6, sec. 2, p. 1, col. 1.

Weisberg, Richard. 2000. "*The Verdict* Is In: The Civic Implications of Civil Trials." *DePaul Law Review* 50:535.

Whitney, Craig R. 1998. "World War I Sets Off a New Battle in France." *New York Times,* November 7, p. A3.

Indexes

Index by Movie Title

(Page numbers of principal treatments
are in *italics*.)

Index by Number of Gavels

■ ■

—◼

Index by Topics

54182562R00211

Made in the USA
Charleston, SC
27 March 2016